KV-645-421

WHICH? WAY TO SAVE AND INVEST

WHICH? WAY TO
SAVE AND INVEST

CONSUMERS' ASSOCIATION

Which? Books are commissioned and researched
by Consumers' Association and published by Which? Ltd,
2 Marylebone Road, London NW1 4DF
Email address: books@which.net

Distributed by the Penguin Group:
Penguin Books Ltd, 27 Wrights Lane, London W8 5TZ

Editor: Eve Bignell
Acknowledgement to: Jonquil Lowe for Chapters 7, 8, 13, 14 and 15

First edition 1982
Second edition 1983
Third edition 1988
Fourth edition August 1989
Fifth edition January 1991
Sixth edition January 1993
Seventh edition April 1994
Eighth edition April 1995
Ninth edition April 1997, Reprinted October 1997
Tenth edition September 1998

Copyright © 1982, 1983, 1988, 1989, 1991, 1993, 1994, 1995, 1997, 1998
Which? Ltd

British Library Cataloguing-in-Publication Data
A catalogue record for this book is available from the British Library

ISBN 0 85202 741 9

For a full list of Which? books, please write to Which? Books,
Castlemead, Gascoyne Way, Hertford X, SG14 1LH
or access our web site at www.which.net

Typographic design by Paul Saunders
Cover design by Paul Wootton Associates
Typeset by Business ColorPrint, Welshpool, Powys, Wales
Printed in England by Clays Ltd, St Ives plc

CONTENTS

Section III Other Ways of Investing

* An asterisk next to the name of an organisation or a publication in the text indicates that the address can be found in this section.

INTRODUCTION

Some things change . . .
Nineteen ninety-seven and 1998 have been busy years in terms of changes in government, taxation and financial regulation. In 1997 the financial industry experienced the start of the biggest shake-up in its regulatory system since Big Bang in the mid-1980s, with the introduction of a new super-regulator, the Financial Services Authority (FSA). This new regulatory body has already adopted the role of the Securities and Investments Board and will, within the next few years, replace all the existing financial regulators.

As financial organisations diversify their businesses it can be hard for consumers to differentiate between them. Banks, building societies and insurance companies each offer similar investment products or packages. At least with a single regulator the fact that you will be dealing with, say, an insurance company as opposed to the investment division of a bank, will not matter – each organisation will be abiding by the same rules and will be subject to the same process of redress if investors complain. Thus, the FSA will be more approachable, with a single point of contact, and this should reduce the current confusion faced by investors who encounter problems.

Tax-free products such as TESSAs and PEPs have played a prominent part in financial planning for many people during the 1990s. In the March 1998 Budget it was announced that both these products will be gradually phased out and replaced by the new tax-free Individual Savings Account (ISA). Investors will be able to include within their ISAs savings products similar to TESSAs, stocks and shares like PEPs, as well as life insurance. The March Budget also proposed a reduction of tax for shares and other similar investments from 20 per cent to 10 per cent for lower- and basic-rate taxpayers. These changes will affect the way investors manage their savings and investments.

Changes in government policy can also have a strong impact on how we manage our finances; whether we need to build up our personal pensions or whether the views on future inflation rates encourage investors to buy (or sell) more index-linked investments such as index-linked gilts or National Savings certificates.

. . . some changes take a while
One change that has been awaited for some time is an overhaul of the insurance industry. The government has issued a consultative paper on the issues surrounding selling insurance-based products, but despite receiving comments from the industry and other interested parties (including Consumers' Association), no changes have been made. And so

the wait goes on while investors still need to plough through a variety of regulations and tax treatments for different types of insurance-based products

And some things stay the same . . .
This is the tenth edition of *Which? Way to Save and Invest*. Since the first edition in 1982, the world of finance has become a very different place. However, despite the vast amount of revision and updating which the book has undergone, reflecting the changes in taxation, legislation and products, for consumers the underlying principles of sensible investment do not change:

- *assess* your financial priorities
- *plan* your financial package
- *monitor* your finances
- *check* for changes in tax and products offered by financial organisations
- *adjust* your financial management to reflect any changes in your circumstances.

The first section of the book, 'Choosing a home for your money', explains how to work out an investment strategy and assess your priorities. It examines the investment choices open to you, explains why tax must be a major consideration in your planning and how it can affect your choices, and what protection you have if things go wrong.

The second section of the book, 'Where to put your money first', looks at your home as an investment, your bank account, your pension and safe savings products like National Savings.

Having devised your basic investment strategy and reviewed your circumstances, you may wish to explore a wider variety of investments and perhaps take a greater risk with your money in the hope of a better return. The last section of the book, 'Other ways of investing', considers a number of different individual investments including shares, unit trusts, British Government stocks, life insurance and annuities. It also offers an introduction to some less conventional areas such as commodities, overseas investments and 'alternative' investments, including diamonds, memorabilia and wine.

It is important today, perhaps more than ever, that individuals take responsibility for their own financial security and future. It is never too early to start to prepare yourself for increased commitments such as having children (school fees), caring for elderly dependants or even just ensuring a comfortable old age. Whether you have thousands of pounds to invest or just a few left over at the end of the month to save, *Which? Way to Save and Invest* can help you make the decisions which are right for you.

Choosing a Home for Your Money

1

INVESTMENT
STRATEGY

Whether you're a small-scale investor, or looking for a home for many thousands of pounds, your problem will not be lack of choice. The difficulty arises in making sensible choices from all the investments available, and, in some cases, finding out all the details needed to come to these decisions. Your aim should be to end up with a number of different investments, covering your differing needs. So before getting down to the nitty gritty of the various investments, we've set out a plan for working out your overall investment strategy.

In the next chapter we give examples of different people putting their individual strategies into effect. The two chapters after that look in detail at the particular questions to be answered when investing for retirement and for children. We then look at where to go for advice and what to do if things go wrong. Chapters 7 and 8 explain how tax affects your investments and in Chapter 9 we give a bird's-eye view of the different investments open to you – you'll find more details on each in the rest of the book.

Of course, deciding now on a particular set of investments isn't the end of the story. It's important to keep a close eye on your investments and to review them periodically – see 'Review your investments regularly', on page 23, for a list of things to bear in mind.

Investment priorities checklist

Your personal circumstances are bound to affect your choice of investments, but no matter what your situation is, some things are worth considering *before* you start thinking about investments in detail.

Are your dependants protected?
What would happen if you died tomorrow? Would your mortgage be paid off? Would your spouse have to go back to

work earlier than planned? Would he or she have a big enough income to pay someone to look after the children?

For most people, the solution to this protection problem is life insurance, not saving and investing. A cheap type of life insurance is *term insurance* – see Chapter 21.

Have you put some money aside for emergencies?
Could you cope with an unexpected disaster (major car repairs or damage to your home, say)? If not, concentrate on building up an emergency fund from where you'll be able to withdraw the money at short notice (within a week, say). See 'Investing your emergency fund', on page 17, and Chapter 2 for investments to consider.

Are you buying your own home?
Although owning property has been less attractive following the boom years of the late 1980s, as the graph in Chapter 10 shows, over the long term investing in property tends to produce a real return over inflation.

Your home, if you buy it, is probably the biggest investment you will ever make and managing your mortgage to your best advantage must be one of your first considerations.

If you've got money to invest, you might want to use some to repay part of your mortgage, depending on how big your mortgage is, how interest rates on borrowing and investing compare, and how much flexibility you have if your financial circumstances change.

Are you planning for your retirement?
Preparing for retirement is no longer only for those in the latter years of employment. The limitations of the state pension mean that everyone must take some responsibility for their financial future. In Chapters 13 and 14, we give details of pension schemes, both from the state and from employers. Try to work out how well off the state pension together with any employer's pension and income from your savings will leave you – see Chapter 3. If you're self-employed, or not in an employer's pension scheme, consider taking out a personal pension plan – see Chapter 15 for details.

Investment strategy checklist

Once you have covered the priorities set out above, your next step is to choose the investments that are best for you, taking your own personal circumstances and aims into account.

Some investments make sense only for people of a certain age (annuities for the over-70s, say); others (e.g. school fees policies) are obviously suited only to those with children to educate. These are extreme cases of the ways in which your personal circumstances can shape your investment strategy, but there may also be less dramatic repercussions. Most people will be saving and investing for a number of purposes. Are you saving for something in particular – a new car or holiday, for example – or simply to accumulate cash?

Different investments may be suitable for each purpose, so most people ought to end up putting their money into a variety of investments. It's worth thinking about the points below, and reading the sections on keeping up with inflation and on risk, before you decide on a particular investment, and when comparing interest rates on different investments (see 'Keep an eye on interest rates', on page 24).

Your age
If you are 50, for example, you are more likely to be concerned with saving up for retirement and thinking about how to invest any lump sum you get than with building up a deposit for your first home. Your children may be off your hands too, and you have more spare cash to save than you had in your 30s.

Your health
If you have a weak heart, for example, you may find it difficult (or expensive) to get the right kind or amount of life insurance. You may want to supplement your life cover with additional savings. Investing through a life insurance policy is likely to be less worthwhile for you than for someone in good health.

Your family
You may want to save up (or invest a lump sum) for your children's education. And you need to think about how your assets will be passed on when you die. You may want to build up a capital sum for your heirs to inherit.

Your expectations
If you expect your income to drop at some point (when you start a family, perhaps, or when you retire), you may want to build up savings to draw on when you're hard up. On the other hand, if you expect a big rise in salary (when you get an additional qualification, say, or finish training) you may feel you can run down your savings a bit since you expect

to be better off later. Alternatively, you may be coming into a large inheritance and need to find a suitable home for it.

Your tax position

Some investments are particularly suitable for non-taxpayers, while others may be particularly good for higher-rate taxpayers. You should always consider the effect of your tax position before making an investment decision. We cover tax in Chapters 7 and 8. People aged over 64 should look out for the effect of losing age-related allowances – see page 51.

What you want from your investments

If you want to build up a fund for next year's holiday, you probably need to consider a different range of investments from those of someone saving up for retirement or passing on a capital sum to his or her heirs. Similarly, if you are looking for a high income from your investments, the ones you select will differ from those chosen by someone prepared to accept a mixture of income and capital growth. For more details, see Chapter 2.

How much you can invest

How much money can you afford to invest? Some investments are open to you only if you have a sufficiently large lump sum, whereas other investments are open only to those who can save a regular sum each month. Others are more flexible and can take your savings as and when they arise.

How long you can invest for

Think carefully before you commit yourself to saving a definite amount each month for a long time (25 years, for example), or locking up a lump sum for a lengthy period. All sorts of changes could happen over the period of the investment that might make it hard to continue, and most long-term savings plans penalise you if you cash in early.

The range of investments you're prepared to consider

When you save or invest your money, it will be put to work – for example, a unit trust company may well use your money to buy shares in a company that the unit trust managers think will provide them with a good return. You may want to restrict the uses to which your money might be put; for example, you may not want it to be invested in companies making weapons. Alternatively you might want to see your money going to help causes you support. These days, there is a range of *ethical investments* designed to make this easier – see page 22.

Keeping up with inflation

With some savings the amount of the capital you invest stays the same; but, of course, this doesn't allow for the effects of inflation. If you invest £1,000 now, spend the income (i.e. any interest) from the investment and get your £1,000 back in five years' time, it will be worth only £884 or so in terms of today's buying power if inflation averages 2.5 per cent a year; (with the same rate of inflation) if you got your money back in 20 years' time, it would be worth only £610 in terms of today's buying power.

Looked at another way, an inflation rate of 5 per cent means that you have to see the total value of your investments (after allowing for tax) rise by at least 5 per cent a year on average just to be able to spend that money in the future in the same way as you can today. That's before you draw an income from your investment.

The diagram below shows the devastating effect of long-term inflation, even at the current low levels. Bear this in mind when considering how much your investments (or the income from them) will be worth in the future.

One strategy you could consider for long-term investing is to go for index-linked investments which keep pace with

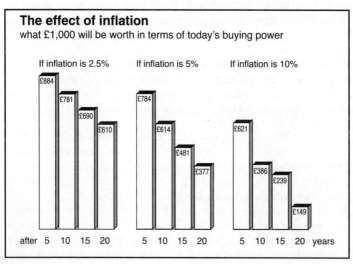

The effect of inflation
what £1,000 will be worth in terms of today's buying power

If inflation is 2.5%   If inflation is 5%   If inflation is 10%

£884
£781
£690
£610

£784
£614
£481
£377

£621
£386
£239
£149

after 5   10   15   20   5   10   15   20   5   10   15   20   years inflation (and perhaps give a little extra interest too). Alternatively, you could go for riskier investments like unit trusts, shares or alternative investments which might do a lot better than keep up with inflation (but could do a lot worse, or even end up worth less than at the start).

In the diagram on page 18, we compare the rates of return you might have got over different periods of time for various lump sum investments. You can see that over the longer period the riskier investments such as shares have made a better job of keeping up with inflation than have safer ones such as building societies. On the other hand, some of the more conservative homes for your money, such as building society ordinary shares, have produced a more constant and reliable return. (Note that over different periods the results have been very different, so don't use this diagram in isolation to draw conclusions about where to invest your money.)

Of course, you may be prepared to put up with a drop in purchasing power for some of your money because, for example, you're looking for a particularly 'safe' investment or you want to be able to withdraw your money at short notice (e.g. for your emergency fund).

Risk

One of the major risks you face is seeing the purchasing power of your investments drop over time as a result of inflation. This applies to practically any investment or savings scheme. However, there are two additional risks you may face:
- **risk to capital** – the value of what you've invested in shares, unit trusts, property and so on is likely to fluctuate. You may find that when you need to cash in your investment, the value of, say, your shares or unit trusts is particularly low. Alternative investments (e.g. antiques, jewellery, Persian carpets) are at risk in this way too – when you want to sell, you may not be able to find a buyer at a price which gives you a reasonable return. It is only savings accounts, such as building society or National Savings accounts, where your capital does not fluctuate.
- **risk to income** – the size of the interest (or dividend) you get may vary considerably, depending on the performance of the company, fund, investment or whatever. At worst, you might get no income at all from the investments.

To minimise the impact of these risks on your investments, the golden rule is to spread your money around. Decide first what proportion of your capital (if any) you are prepared to put into risky investments and what proportion you want in safe ones. Accepting a degree of risk is, in the main, a price you have to pay to stand at least some chance of increasing the buying power of your investments.

Aim to spread your money among different types of investments, e.g. a pension, unit trusts and building societies. With riskier investments in particular, try to put your money with a number of different investments; if some prove disastrous, others will, it is hoped, be successful. Also, try to stagger investing over a long period (at least a year, preferably longer). By spreading your investments in these ways you'll reduce the risk of doing very badly. Bear in mind though that you'll also reduce your chances of doing extraordinarily well.

If you decide to go for a high-risk investment (like shares or alternative investments), don't be tempted to withdraw your emergency fund from its safe home and invest it in the same way. This should cut down the risk of having to sell your investments (to pay for a new cooker, for example) when prices are low. You should also steer clear of direct investment in shares unless you've got a substantial amount to invest.

If you know you will need your money on a particular future date, be prepared to cash in investments beforehand (a few years in advance, if need be), ideally at a time when their value is high. If you wait until you need the money, you may find you have to cash your investments when prices are low.

Investing your emergency fund

When deciding on a home for this part of your capital, you need to look for three things:
- safety – no risk that when you cash in you'll get fewer pounds back than you put in
- instant accessibility – you don't usually get even two weeks' notice of an emergency, so you want to be able to get the money back on the spot or in a couple of days at most
- highest possible return – but you'll have to be prepared to take less than you'd get for an investment that ties your money up for longer.

See the route maps in Chapter 2 for some suggestions. Remember to update regularly the amount of money you

Investments compared: What you'd get back in the last quarter of 1997 on £1,000 invested 5, 10, 15 and 20 years before in various investments

Investment	Made in: Last quarter 1977	Last quarter 1982	Last quarter 1987	Last quarter 1992
Building society ordinary shares [1]	£3,717	£2,414	£1,654	£1,146
Shares [2]	£22,646	£10,378	£3,899	£2,078
Houses [3]	£4,702	£2,417	£1,394	£1,232
Gold bullion [4]	£2,011	£761	£680	£860
Antique furniture [5]	£4,334	£2,671	£1,243	£1,156
What you'd need to keep pace with inflation [6]	£3,350	£1,939	£1,549	£1,149

[1] Based on the Building Society Investment Index, assuming net income reinvested; source Micropal
[2] Based on the FT Actuaries All-Share Index, assuming income reinvested on an offer to bid basis (but no allowance for Capital Gains Tax); source Micropal
[3] Based on Nationwide Index of Average House Prices
[4] Source: Gold Investments Ltd
[5] Based on Antique Collectors' Club Antique Furniture Price Index, with allowances for costs of buying and selling at auction, for VAT and differences between buying and selling price – 1997 figures
[6] Based on Retail Prices Index, no income available; source Micropal

keep in reserve for emergencies. Inflation will erode its buying power unless you reinvest the interest you get.

Your aims in investing

Many people want their investments to produce an income now. Others invest for capital growth, either to provide an income later (on retirement, say) or to pass on to their heirs, or to build up a fund to buy something (a house or car, for example). Below, we outline some factors to consider in each of these cases.

You might in fact want a combination of income and growth, although of course you can always cash in some investments from time to time to give you income, and if you reinvest income from your investments, the value of your capital should go up over time. However, there can be considerable tax differences between receiving income or capital gain (see the box on 'Building capital by reinvesting income' on page 22).

Investing for income now

You need to consider how long you're likely to go on needing the income from your investments. If it's for more than a couple of years, you can't afford to ignore the effect of inflation on the purchasing power of any income your investments produce. You'll need a rising income. To achieve this, you are likely to have to put some of your capital at risk, or buy an index-linked investment. It may be sensible to invest some of your money for capital growth, with a view to cashing part of it in on a regular basis to provide income.

You have to make your own choice about how much of your capital to risk. Put the remainder in a place where the income from it will be assured – see the route maps in Chapter 2 for suggestions.

If you don't anticipate having to rely on your extra investment income for longer than a year or two, you may well decide there is no point taking risks to get an income that will keep up with inflation.

If you don't pay tax, some investments may be particularly attractive if the interest is paid without deduction of tax. These investments are marked with • in the route maps. On the other hand, some investments, where the return is tax-free, look more attractive the higher your rate of tax. These investments are marked with * in the route maps. Check in the route maps (and with current rates of return) that your investments are giving you the best possible return, after tax.

Investing to provide income later

If you're going to need your capital to give you an income later, you can't afford to risk all of it. But you do need to try to make up for the effects of inflation on its buying power over the years between now and the time you plan to draw the income.

You could consider investing part of your money in index-linked National Savings Certificates. With this investment, the value of what you've invested is adjusted each month in line with inflation (provided you've held the certificate for at least a year). You can invest up to £10,000 per person, or jointly as a married couple. You could also consider index-linked British Government stocks – see Chapter 19.

If you have capital left over, it makes sense to put some of your money into investments which may give a return high enough to make up for inflation. To minimise the chances of all your risky investments doing a nose-dive at once, follow the advice given in Risk, on page 16.

Investing to pass on more for your heirs

You may feel you can take risks with more of your capital for longer if the main aim is to pass money on to your heirs.

What you need to be particularly aware of is the impact of inheritance tax on what your heirs will get when you die, though it won't strike unless what you leave (together with taxable gifts made in the seven years before your death) tops £223,000 (in the 1998–9 tax year). This may seem like a very high tax-free limit and many people will not need to worry about potential inheritance tax. But if you have life insurance or a mortgage that is covered by a life insurance policy, then your total assets may include these. It is worth checking the value of all your finances from time to time. To minimise the effect of inheritance tax, consider:
- giving away each year as much as is allowed without incurring any liability to inheritance tax
- taking out life insurance, with the proceeds going straight to your children

■ leaving your possessions directly to the youngest generation (your grandchildren rather than your children) if you want the possessions to go to them eventually.

For more details on inheritance tax, see Chapter 7. *The Which? Guide to Giving and Inheriting* covers this in detail.

Investing to build up a fund to buy something

If you are investing in order to buy something in the future, bear in mind that the value of some investments (e.g. shares, property or alternative investments) tends to fluctuate, so you may find that when you want to cash in your investments the return is not very good. It makes sense to steer clear of these investments if you are likely to want to use the money in the very near future.

If, on the other hand, you'll need the money in, say, ten years' time, you could still go for investments that fluctuate in value, but be prepared to cash the investments in *before* you need the money (preferably when they're doing well) or transfer the cash to a safer place such as a building society account. Try to avoid being forced into cashing in your investment when its value is depressed – by a slump in the share or property markets, for example.

Cashing in investments to give income

With certain lump sum investments (e.g. single-premium bonds), it's possible to cash in part of the investment each year to give yourself an income. However, you should note that with, for example, single-premium bonds or unit trusts which run a withdrawal scheme, because the value of your investment fluctuates, you may have to cash in a higher proportion of your investment from time to time, or else face a drop in income. And if you cash in more than the growth of your bond, you'll be eating into your capital. This will make it even harder for your capital to meet your income requirements the following year and so you risk reducing your capital even more in future years.

With other investments (e.g. shares, alternative investments and so on) there are no special schemes. You may get a poor price at the time you want to cash part of the investment and the cost of selling may be high if you want to sell small parts of your investments to provide an income.

Building capital by reinvesting income

As the tax system stands, if you invest for income with a view to reinvesting it to build up capital, you may pay more tax than if you had got an equivalent rise in value through a straight capital gain. Most investment income is taxed at either 20 per cent or 40 per cent for the 1998–9 tax year, depending on your taxable income. Capital gains are taxed at the same rate, but the first £6,800 of capital gains you make by disposing of assets in the 1998–9 tax year is tax-free. If you haven't used up all of this tax-free allowance it may be sensible to invest for capital gains rather than income.

Ethical investment

The investment policies of institutions such as banks may be shrouded in secrecy for legitimate commercial reasons. This means that finding out how the money in your savings account is being used is difficult and it can be equally difficult to be sure that the company you're investing in is using your money in a way you would approve of. However, you can take positive steps to screen for companies you would be happy to invest in or save your money with. Some companies offer off-the-peg ethical investments.

While there is no exact definition, ethical investment generally means that money is invested by you or on your behalf so that certain areas are either avoided or promoted: for example, you might want to avoid investing in companies involved with tobacco, or to promote environmental causes by helping companies developing alternative sources of energy. There are now ethical unit trusts, investment trusts, life insurance funds, personal pension plans and even a building society (the Ecology Building Society). The Co-operative Bank has publicly stated what sort of businesses it will and will not do business with and also offers an Ethical Savings Account.

Most ethical investment goes on through unit trusts. With these, your money goes into a pool or fund that is invested in a range of shares or other assets. The fund is managed on a day-to-day basis by a fund manager but the assets are held by trustees (usually a bank). It is the trustees who have to authorise the issuing and reclaiming of units and make sure that the management of the fund is in accordance with the trust deed. In the case of ethical unit trusts there may also be a research committee and/or a vetting committee involved in the decisions over which shares to buy and sell.

However, it is difficult to be entirely sure that your money is being used as you would wish. As there is no agreed definition of what constitutes an ethical investment, this is reflected in the diversity of areas that different funds seek to avoid. Some keep it very simple, such as one scheme which avoids only those companies materially involved in the tobacco industry. Others have policies on everything from advertising complaints to repressive regimes. The ethical criteria used may be inexact and open to interpretation: advisory boards might be presented with too little information to make a proper judgement; you can't assume that the fund managers have the same perception of a company as you do. Investors should look out for the following in a managed fund:

■ whether there is an advisory committee and who is on it
■ the way in which any advisory committee is consulted – either before or after shares are purchased – and whether it is given sufficient information in enough time to make informed decisions
■ how investors are involved – whether they are invited to regular unit-holder meetings
■ whether investors are kept in touch with how the fund is managed beyond the six-monthly reports required by regulation.

If the off-the-peg options of ethical investment are not to your taste, it's possible to have a portfolio tailored to your own individual requirements but there could be problems:

■ you need a lot of money – to get the same spread of risk that a unit trust provides you need to invest in a wide range of shares
■ you need access to information to keep up-to-date with changes in company policies.

If you want research done on your behalf, the Ethical Investment Research Service (EIRIS)* will screen shares according to your own ethical concerns. It will charge £54 for screening up to 20 companies and holds files on all FTSE All-share companies. EIRIS also publishes a newsletter (£12 for six issues a year), and will provide a free list of financial advisers and fund managers specialising in ethical investments.

Finally, remember that it may prove impossible to meet all of your aims in investment. You may have to compromise if, for example, the sort of investment that would really suit your financial needs doesn't tie in with your ethical aims.

Review your investments regularly

You can't assume that the best investments for you today will still be the best in a few months' time. For example, the rates of return offered by different investments will change. New types of investment may come on the market. Tax laws may change too. Inflation will mean that your investments need topping up. And changes in your circumstances, not to mention the effect of external factors (like political pressures throughout the world), could make a nonsense of your original choice. So it's vital to keep an eye on what's happening at least monthly and for more risky investments weekly, and alter your investments when necessary.

Keep an eye on interest rates

One difficulty in comparing the return you can get with different types of investment is that the rates of interest quoted with some investments aren't strictly comparable. This is because they don't make any allowance for how frequently interest is paid out. To make comparison easier, banks, building societies and finance companies should follow a Code of Practice which lays down rules about how rates of interest should be advertised. The only problem with this is that the Code allows them to quote *several* different rates in an advertisement, and sorting out which rate to use for comparison can be a bit difficult. See the box on 'The different rates – what they mean', on page 27.

Interest rates aren't always what they seem

When interest is paid out to you, you can spend it or reinvest it: if you reinvest it, you earn interest on the interest. The more frequently interest is paid to you, the sooner you can reinvest it and the higher will be the overall return.

Suppose, for example, that you invest £1,000 for a year at 10 per cent interest a year. If the interest is paid out once a year, £100 is all you can get. But if the interest is paid out at six-monthly intervals and you reinvest it, you will end up with more. This is because after six months, £50 (5 per cent of £1,000) will be added to the £1,000, giving £1,050;

in the second six months, another 5 per cent interest will be earned on this £1,050, i.e. £52.50. The £50 plus £52.50 gives interest of £102.50 for the year – the same as you'd get if you put your money in an investment paying 10.25 per cent only once a year.

If the interest is paid quarterly, the return is even higher, at £1,103.81. Monthly interest would bring the return up to £1,104.67. And these differences would build up over the years, as Table 1 below shows. So the true rate of return, opposite, depends not just on the amount of interest paid out, but also the frequency with which it is paid out.

Table 1: How £1,000 grows if interest at 10% is added

	yearly	half-yearly	quarterly	monthly
after 1 year	£1,100	£1,103	£1,104	£1,105
after 2 years	£1,210	£1,216	£1,218	£1,220
after 5 years	£1,611	£1,629	£1,639	£1,645
after 10 years	£2,594	£2,653	£2,685	£2,707
true return	10%	10.25%	10.38%	10.47%

Find the true rate of return

The rates quoted on investments where interest is added once a year are true rates of return – this applies to the National Savings Investment account, for example. The returns quoted on National Savings Certificates are true returns which can be directly compared one with another.

However, many other investments add interest more often than once a year: with most building society accounts (other than regular savings accounts), bank deposit and savings accounts and finance company deposits, interest is added twice a year (sometimes quarterly). National Savings Income Bonds pay out income monthly, and you can ask for monthly interest with some other savings accounts. In all these cases, you need to know the true rate of return to compare them with investments paying out interest less frequently.

Table 2, below, sets out the true rates of return for a variety of quoted rates, when the interest is paid out half-yearly, quarterly or monthly. Banks, building societies and finance companies should quote true rates in their advertising – they call them the *compounded annual rates*, or CAR.

Note that with the National Savings Ordinary account, interest is paid once a year, but only for complete calendar months. So if you pay in or withdraw money during a month, the true return may be *lower* than the quoted rate.

Gross rates of return

Interest on most types of savings account is now usually paid after deduction of tax at 20 per cent. There is no more basic-rate tax to be paid on the interest. If you expect to be a non-taxpayer, even after taking into account interest from your savings, you may be able to have the interest paid out before tax by filling in form R85 (from your bank or building society).

Advertisements for savings accounts often quote a *gross* rate of return to compare with the return from investments which pay interest without deduction of tax (mainly National Savings schemes). Be careful to avoid comparing gross interest rates with tax-free interest rates unless you are a non-taxpayer. (For how to work out the gross rate from the after-tax rate, see Example on page 97). As a general rule, you should compare gross rates of return on the same compounding basis wherever possible.

Suppose, for example, that you get 5 per cent net interest from a building society account. With a tax rate of 20 per cent, you'd have to earn a before-tax rate of interest of 6.25 per cent to have 5 per cent left after tax (6.25% less 20% of 6.25% = 6.25% less 1.25% = 5%). So the gross rate would be 6.25 per cent.

Table 2: True rates of return

| quoted rate | true rate if interest is paid out or added | | |
	half-yearly	quarterly	monthly
3%	3.02%	3.03%	3.04%
4%	4.04%	4.06%	4.07%
5%	5.06%	5.10%	5.12%
6%	6.09%	6.14%	6.17%
7%	7.12%	7.19%	7.23%
8%	8.16%	8.24%	8.30%
9%	9.20%	9.31%	9.38%
10%	10.25%	10.38%	10.47%
11%	11.30%	11.46%	11.57%
12%	12.36%	12.55%	12.68%

The different rates – what they mean

Various different rates of return may be quoted in savings advertisements by banks, building societies and finance companies that follow the voluntary Code of Practice:

■ **tax-free** – if interest from the account is not liable to income tax

■ **net** – if you draw out the income and don't reinvest it, the rate you'll get with no more basic-rate tax to pay

■ **gross** – the rate you'd have to get before deduction of tax to end up with the net rate after basic-rate tax had been deducted

■ **net compounded annual rate (CAR)** – if you reinvest the income, the rate you'll get with no more basic-rate tax to pay

■ **gross compounded annual rate (CAR)** – the rate you'd have to get before deduction of tax to end up with the net compounded annual rate after tax had been deducted at the basic rate.

If you're choosing between different investments, some paying interest after deduction of tax and some before tax, make sure you compare like with like to see which gives the better return. Suppose, for example, you want to compare the National Savings Investment account (interest paid before tax) with a building society account (interest paid after tax). The National Savings Investment account pays out interest once a year, so the quoted interest rate is the true rate of return. Compare this with the gross CAR for the building society.

2

INVESTMENT CHOICES

Now that you have worked out your investment strategy, you can start to think about the investments themselves. To help narrow down the choice of investments to those which would be most suitable for you, use the route maps later in this chapter. One is for lump sums, the other for savings (either on a regular basis or piecemeal).

Follow the route maps for each sum of money you want to invest, e.g. your emergency fund, money you're willing to see fluctuate in value and money you can invest for ten years. You'll end up with a different shortlist for each sum.

For any investments you think might suit you, read the relevant chapter in the book and then find out what is happening to that investment at the moment. You should also check in the newspapers for the up-to-date rates of return being offered by the investments you have in mind. There's a bird's-eye view of different types of investment in Chapter 9.

Armed with these facts, narrow down the investments on your shortlists to those which suit you best. Do not forget that work on your investments does not end there – you'll need to keep them under review to make sure that they continue to suit you.

To show you how this can be done, we look at the choices facing a number of investors. For example, Roger and Rose Steele want to find homes for both a lump sum and for their savings. Their strategy and decisions are followed through from start to finish. The other six examples look at only one of the problems each investor faces. Three investors have lump sums of varying sizes to invest; with the other three investors, it's savings of various amounts that are presenting difficulties.

Of course, your own final choice out of the shortlist that each investor ends up with might be different from that in our examples, because of your particular preferences.

Planning your investments

Roger and Rose Steele have one child, Alex. Roger earns around £24,000 a year as a teacher; Rose does not go out to work. They want to save for quite a few things: a holiday next year, and then a new car, furniture and so on. They don't want to lock their money away for too long. They have already got some money saved up in a building society instant access account and wonder whether that's the best place for it.

How Roger and Rose decide what to do with their money

First of all, they look at the investment priorities checklist in Chapter 1.

Both Roger and Rose have life insurance cover. They have policies that will pay out lump sums and a regular income if either partner dies. At present they have £5,000 put aside in a building society instant access account, but they feel that £2,000 is as much as they need in an emergency fund.

Roger and Rose are buying their own home and don't intend to move in the next few years; their £40,000 mortgage is quite low compared to the value of their house. Roger is in the teachers' pension scheme, which offers good benefits.

Roger and Rose would like to save something each month, so they've got to decide how to invest:
- their £2,000 emergency fund
- the additional £3,000 lump sum
- the money they manage to save in future.

They use the investment strategy checklist (see Chapter 1) to help sort out their investment plan:

Age: Roger is 30 and Rose 28. Rose is hoping to go back to work when Alex, their three-year-old, goes to school, but they're not going to rely on this

Health: both are in good health

Family: apart from Alex, there are no immediate dependants. But they feel that if any of their parents were widowed or became ill, they'd like to help out. At the moment, this prospect seems unlikely, but it means they don't feel like committing themselves to very long-term savings, which they might not be able to keep up if they do have to help out. They don't intend giving Alex a private education. If they did, they would consider saving in a school-fees scheme

Expectations: if Rose cannot go back to her old job, she might need some sort of retraining. This could involve some expense. There are no large inheritances coming their way, though eventually they will share in the proceeds from the sale of their parents' houses

Tax: Roger is a basic-rate taxpayer, and any investment income won't put him into the higher-rate tax bracket. However, Rose doesn't pay tax, and any investment income is unlikely to put her into the lower- or basic-rate tax bracket. It would make sense to put all their investments in her name only, so that she can make use of her personal allowance

What they want from their investments: their main aims are: to pay for a holiday next year and later for a new car; to pay for any retraining that Rose may need in a couple of years or so; and to be able to help out their parents, if necessary. They aren't looking for income from their investments

How much they can invest: apart from the £5,000 in the building society, they can save about £100 a month, but most of this is earmarked for their holiday next year

How long they can invest for: the Steeles have decided to keep £2,000 as an emergency fund, and they need £70 a month of their regular savings available for their planned holiday. The other lump sum of £3,000 and £30-a-month regular savings can be invested for somewhat longer. But long-term investment clearly doesn't suit their needs

The range of investment they're prepared to consider: although their main aim is to find a suitable type of investment, they're interested in ethical investments, particularly those that might benefit the environment.

Once Roger and Rose have chosen their investments they'll keep an eye on what's happening and may move their money around from time to time. However, first they follow the route maps below to see what choices they have.

How Roger and Rose choose their investments

Lump sum
First of all they try to sort out what to do with the £5,000 they have. They intend keeping £2,000 of this as an emergency fund, and following the route map find three types of investment where they can put this money and get it out at short notice: a bank or finance company deposit account, building society instant access account including postal or telephone accounts or National Savings Ordinary account. They read about these and check on the rates of

return currently offered. They choose a building society tiered interest postal account that pays a higher than normal rate of interest on £2,000 or more. They'll keep a close watch on rates of return in the future in case other investments offer a better return.

Now they follow the route map again to see what they could do with the £3,000. They skip the next few steps – they have a moderate mortgage compared to the value of their home, are in a pension scheme, not close to retirement and can leave their money invested for at least a year. At the next step they have to decide whether to consider an index-linked investment. They'd like to put about £2,000 somewhere it won't lose its buying power so that it can pay for a new car. They plump for index-linked National Savings Certificates.

They go through the route map again for the last part of their lump sum, which they are prepared to risk in the hope of a windfall. After answering *No* to the question *Looking for income now?* they come to investments they should consider if they're prepared to see the value of their investments go down rather than up in the hope of a better return. They see that these include Personal Equity Plans (PEPs) or from April 1999, the new Individual Savings Accounts (ISAs), shares, unit trusts, investment trusts, corporate bonds and single-premium investment bonds. Despite the uncertainties of the stock market, they look to the long term and pick a PEP with low charges; £1,000 can go into unit trusts within a PEP to spread the risk (see Chapter 17). Their PEP manager offers a range of funds, including an ethical fund which they choose.

Regular saving

They follow the route map on the next pages to see what to do with the £100 they reckon they'll be able to save each month. They come to the question *Prepared to save a regular amount for a year or more?* for the £70 a month they're saving for their next year's holiday. As the answer is *No*, they have a choice of building society and bank savings schemes. After checking on current interest rates, they decide that a building society account with a high interest rate will offer them the best overall return and the opportunity to withdraw their money at short notice without being penalised. For the remaining £30 a month they are prepared to consider saving for more than a year, but not as long as ten years. They could choose a unit trust or investment trust savings scheme but they choose the safer option of a Tax-Exempt Special Savings Account (TESSA).

Route map for lump sums

Start here for each chunk
of your money

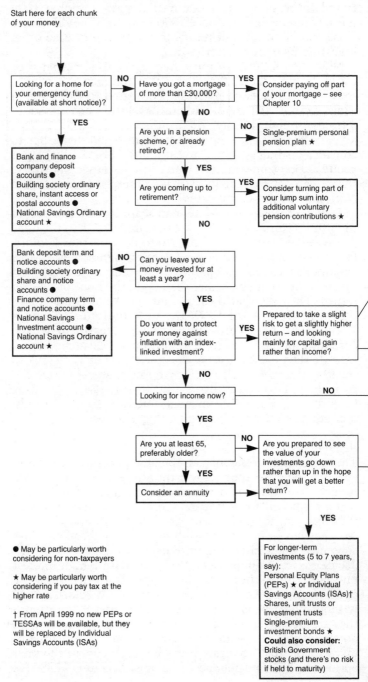

● May be particularly worth
considering for non-taxpayers

★ May be particularly worth
considering if you pay tax at the
higher rate

† From April 1999 no new PEPs or
TESSAs will be available, but they
will be replaced by Individual
Savings Accounts (ISAs)

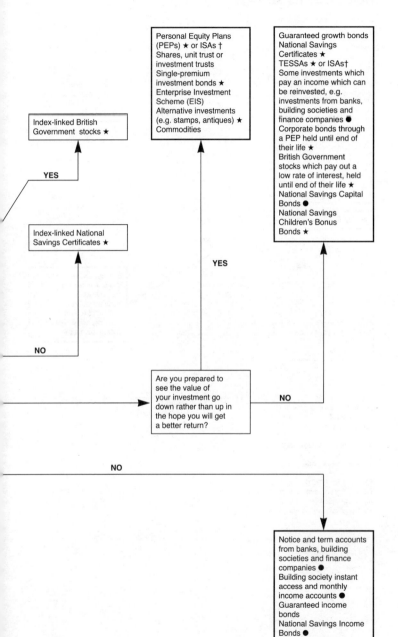

Index-linked British Government stocks ★

Index-linked National Savings Certificates ★

Personal Equity Plans (PEPs) ★ or ISAs †
Shares, unit trust or investment trusts
Single-premium investment bonds ★
Enterprise Investment Scheme (EIS)
Alternative investments (e.g. stamps, antiques) ★
Commodities

Guaranteed growth bonds
National Savings Certificates ★
TESSAs ★ or ISAs†
Some investments which pay an income which can be reinvested, e.g. investments from banks, building societies and finance companies ●
Corporate bonds through a PEP held until end of their life ★
British Government stocks which pay out a low rate of interest, held until end of their life ★
National Savings Capital Bonds ●
National Savings Children's Bonus Bonds ★

YES

YES

NO

NO

Are you prepared to see the value of your investment go down rather than up in the hope you will get a better return?

NO

Notice and term accounts from banks, building societies and finance companies ●
Building society instant access and monthly income accounts ●
Guaranteed income bonds
National Savings Income Bonds ●
National Savings Investment account ●
FIRST Option Bonds

Route map for savings

Start here for each chunk of your money

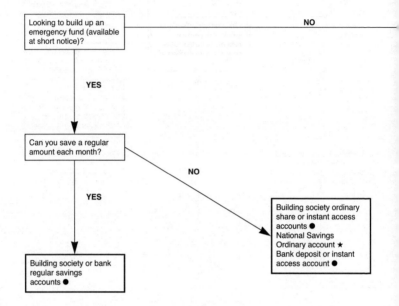

● May be particularly worth
considering for
non-taxpayers

★ May be particularly worth
considering if you pay
tax at the higher rate

† From April 1999 no new PEPs or
TESSAs will be available, but they
will be replaced by Individual
Savings Accounts (ISAs)

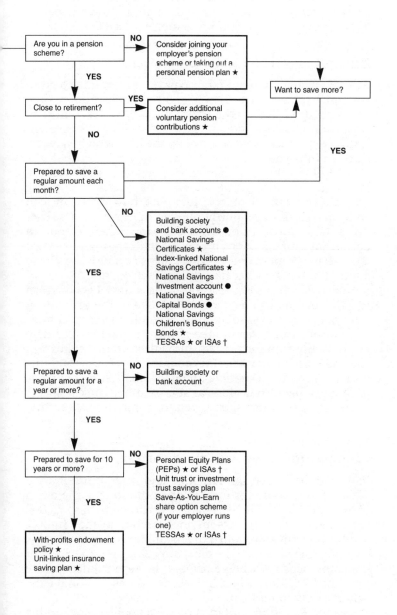

Are you in a pension scheme?

NO → Consider joining your employer's pension scheme or taking out a personal pension plan ★

YES ↓

Close to retirement?

YES → Consider additional voluntary pension contributions ★

NO ↓

Want to save more?

YES

Prepared to save a regular amount each month?

NO → Building society and bank accounts ● National Savings Certificates ★ Index-linked National Savings Certificates ★ National Savings Investment account ● National Savings Capital Bonds ● National Savings Children's Bonus Bonds ★ TESSAs ★ or ISAs †

YES ↓

Prepared to save a regular amount for a year or more?

NO → Building society or bank account

YES ↓

Prepared to save for 10 years or more?

NO → Personal Equity Plans (PEPs) ★ or ISAs † Unit trust or investment trust savings plan Save-As-You-Earn share option scheme (if your employer runs one) TESSAs ★ or ISAs †

YES ↓

With-profits endowment policy ★ Unit-linked insurance saving plan ★

Summary
They're going to invest £2,000 in a building society account, £2,000 in index-linked National Savings Certificates and £1,000 in unit trusts through a PEP. They're going to save £70 a month in a building society high-interest account and £30 a month in a TESSA.

Example: Saving for something special

Anne Stevens is a basic-rate taxpayer. She wants to go to Australia to see her daughter and her grandchildren, and needs about £1,000 for the return air fare. She can afford to save around £25 a month, so will need an investment lasting four or five years to save up the fare (which may rise through inflation).

She follows the route map until she gets to the question, *Prepared to save a regular amount each month?* Answering *Yes*, she moves on to consider just how long she can commit herself – over one but not as long as ten years. That presents various options: share option schemes (not an option for Anne as her employer isn't offering one); unit trust or investment trust savings plans or a PEP, which are a mite too risky for her liking; TESSA accounts.

She considers a TESSA account that offers a good return and the income will be tax-free if she holds the account for five years. She can save into this account on a regular basis to help her to be disciplined about her savings. To help build up the sum for her trip Anne decides that whenever she has spare money she'll try to put it in another building society account – a suitable home for small, irregular sums of money. She also decides to approach her bank manager to see whether, once she's saved for some time, she could get a loan.

Example: Investing with an eye on tax

Paul Mitchell is in his late 40s, and finds himself with £50,000 from a life insurance pay-out following the death of his wife, Sheila. He lives in his own home with a £75,000 repayment mortgage, has an adequate emergency fund, a TESSA account and enough life insurance to take care of his children's needs should he die. Paul belongs to an excellent company pension scheme (though he won't quite qualify for a full pension when he reaches 65 as he joined the scheme only in his 30s).

Despite Paul's high salary, private school fees make a big dent in his income, and will continue to do so for some time.

Therefore, he'd like to invest some of his lump sum to increase his income while these fees continue, but is worried about extra income tax he might have to pay (he pays tax at the higher rate of 40 per cent). He also wants to invest a little with as minimal risk as possible (he's hoping to buy a boat in five years' time when the children are older).

Following the route map, he sees that it suggests paying off part of the mortgage if it's more than £30,000 (above which you get no tax relief on the mortgage interest). This makes a lot of sense for Paul – his mortgage is his second biggest outgoing after the school fees, and since April 1998 tax relief has been limited to 10 per cent. Each £10,000 of his mortgage above the £30,000 limit that he repays will save him around £850 a year in interest and capital repayments, whereas if he were to invest the £10,000 he'd be lucky to get that much in income from his investment unless he were to choose a risky investment. He therefore decides to repay £24,000 of his mortgage, which will give his income an immediate boost. He does not want to pay off more because having some money in investments he can cash in gives him some flexibility.

He goes on through the route map for the safe investment. He checks investments with a * next to them carefully (these are particularly worth considering if you pay tax at the higher rate). Early on he comes to index-linked National Savings Certificates, which guarantee to maintain the buying power of his money. After a year, he can withdraw some money (tax-free) if he needs it and still get index-linking. He sees he should also consider index-linked British Government stocks if he's prepared to take a slight risk. He checks on the current prices for the stocks and finds that, for his rate of tax, the return should just beat inflation. He decides to put £2,500 into each of these index-linked investments.

Next he follows the route map for his longer-term investment until he comes to the question about whether he is looking for income now. Yes, he is. He passes over the next question about age and is then asked if he is prepared to see the value of his money go down rather than up in the hope of a better return. Once again the answer is *Yes*. He sees he can choose between PEPs, ISAs, shares, unit trusts, investment trusts, corporate bonds or convertibles and single-premium investment bonds plus even riskier investments like antiques and commodities. Deciding to give the riskier options a miss, he invests the maximum £6,000 in a PEP to benefit from the tax advantages. By investing in corporate bonds through a PEP he can increase his income without increasing his tax bill; furthermore, he is not taking as much risk with a bond as he would with shares as long as he is prepared to hold it until redemption. The remaining £15,000 is invested in unit trusts – ones that aim for capital growth rather than income. He plans to cash in some of his units each year to help with the school fees if he needs to, but will make sure that he doesn't make net capital gains of more than the £6,800 limit free of capital gains tax. As he approaches retirement and the school fees come to an end, he'll consider making additional voluntary contributions to his pension scheme to make up for the missing years.

Example: Saving for a rainy day

Mike and Sue English are in their late 20s, with one baby and another due soon. Mike is a basic-rate taxpayer, Sue pays no tax at all. They've got little cash left over at the end of each month. They are worried because they have no savings or life insurance.

For people in their position, with dependants, life insurance should come before any attempt to save money. If Mike died, Sue would have to rely on social security to make ends meet, and if Sue were to die, Mike would have a hard time looking after the babies *and* going to work. They realise that investment-type life insurance is not really for them. With this firmly sorted out, they decide to go to an insurance adviser to arrange protection-type life insurance to cover them should one or other partner die.

Next they think about their emergency fund, follow the route map and see that they are advised to consider a building society instant access account, a bank deposit account or a National Savings Ordinary account. They go for a building society instant access account. One advantage of this is that they get a cash card giving them access to their money round the clock from the machines outside hundreds of building society branches – useful in a real emergency.

Once they've built up a large enough emergency fund, they'll go through the route map again and look for a somewhat longer-term investment for their additional savings. They will probably transfer money to a savings account that pays a higher rate for higher minimum levels of investment, even if they have to give notice before withdrawing money. This account will be opened in Sue's name only as she doesn't pay tax. (They decide to open the instant access account in joint names so that both can have access to it in an emergency.)

Example: Investing a windfall

Marianne Fortune, 21, has just inherited £9,000 from her grandmother. She's single, lives with her parents, has a large enough emergency fund and is a basic-rate taxpayer. She reckons that some time in the future she'll want to buy a home and decides to put £7,500 towards this. She decides to try to turn the remaining £1,500 into something bigger; she's prepared to take risks with it.

Marianne follows the route map for lump sums and sees that investing the £7,500 earmarked for a future home might not be easy now that house prices have started to rise again, particularly if they continue to rise faster than prices in general, so Marianne wants an investment that offers the chance of outstripping inflation in the future. Index-linked investments do that, but only just, so she rules them out. Accepting that she is going to have to take some risk, Marianne plumps for a couple of unit trusts – both growth funds with any income reinvested.

She goes back to the route map, to see how she should invest the £1,500 with which she's going to gamble. She looks up the short-listed investments in the table and in the chapters later in the book. She toys with putting her money into shares, but could really only afford to invest in one company – a very risky idea. She decides instead to allocate the £1,500 towards improving the eighteenth-century glass collection she started a couple of years ago; even if the bottom drops out of antique glass, she'll get a bit of pleasure out of the collecting.

Example: Investing for extra income

Amy Simmons is aged 80, and lives alone. She lives on her state pension and a small pension from her ex-employer and wonders what to do with the £7,000 she has to invest, which is at present in a bank deposit account. She's alarmed at the way inflation has made inroads into the buying power of the interest she receives. She'd like to get a bit of extra income to allow herself a few more treats.

She realises that she can leave some of her money in the bank deposit account to act as an emergency fund, but she reckons she will not need more than £500 for this. Thinking about it, though, she decides to leave twice this amount in her account – so that she can draw on it if she wants extra income.

Amy already owns her home, so does not need to worry about getting a mortgage. She has no index-linked investments, and reckons that index-linked National Savings Certificates will suit her very well. Although this investment does not pay out a regular income, she sees she could cash certificates to get an income. She realises that the value of what she invests will go up in line with the Retail Prices Index (though not if she cashes the certificates before a year is up). This index-linking seems to offer a big advantage to Amy, so she decides to put £2,500 into these certificates, and, after the first year, to cash some of her investment if she feels particularly hard-pressed.

She decides not to put any money into index-linked British Government stocks – she does not want to take any risks and, besides, they do not provide a worthwhile income (nor can they be cashed cheaply in bits and pieces).

As Amy is over 70, she could consider an annuity or cashing in on her home through a home income scheme. She's not really tempted by a home income scheme as she may want to move home later, so she decides to put the remaining £3,500 into an annuity. She realises that the income from this is set the day she buys the annuity and will not be protected against inflation so she decides to give more thought to moving to a smaller house and investing any money from the sale to give her more income. She realises also that there are heavy expenses involved in buying and selling property and that she'll have to allow for these before going ahead.

Example: Saving for retirement

Bob Mason, self-employed, earning around £25,000 a year, and his wife, Cathy, are in their late 40s. Their three children have all left home and Cathy thinks it's time they started saving for their retirement. They don't want to rely on their business for their retirement funds.

The Masons already have an adequate emergency fund, permanent health insurance in case either of them is too ill to work and are buying their home with a mortgage. They follow the route map for savings to the question *Are you in a pension scheme?* Bob is self-employed, and already contributes £50 a month (£600 a year) towards a personal pension plan. He asks the insurance company that runs the pension plan what he might get in the way of a pension at 65 if he kept up this level of saving. They say about £750 a month, but this could look rather feeble by the time Bob retires if inflation eats into it, so Bob and Cathy decide to step up the amount they save.

Bob can get tax relief on up to 25 per cent of his £25,000 a year, i.e. £6,250 a year or around £520 a month. The

Masons reckon that they can afford another £70 a month without too much trouble, so take out a second personal pension plan for this amount (having plans with two companies means that they haven't got all their eggs in one company basket).

Like many self-employed people, Bob has earnings that fluctuate from month to month, and even with these higher pension contributions he and his wife would have something extra to save in good months. The Masons therefore decide to add occasional savings to their emergency fund in a building society instant access account. Their emergency fund is over £500, so they switch it to a tiered interest rate account where they get a higher than normal rate of interest. If the account drops below £500, they won't lose out: the interest rate falls back to the lower rate. Once their emergency fund is up to £1,000, Bob and Cathy plan to look again at their pension provision. They should also be careful to check that their pension provider offers a plan that has a 'waiver of premium' option. If times are hard and they cannot meet the monthly contribution, they will not be penalised for missing payments occasionally. They'll need to put away much more than £120 (the existing £50 plus the additional £70 a month) a month if they're not to suffer a hefty drop in income on retirement, and the tax relief on any increased contributions eases the burden.

3

INVESTING FOR RETIREMENT

For many people, ensuring an adequate income in retirement is a major motive behind saving and investing. This chapter will help you formulate a strategy to achieve this, whether you're still working, close to retirement or have already retired.

The first step in sorting out your retirement finances is to look at how your income measures up to your expenditure when you retire. Of course, inflation makes budgeting for retirement difficult if you're looking a good many years ahead. Currently the state retirement pension is increased each year in line with rising prices, and the amount you can expect from an employer's pension should go up too, at least in the period up to retirement. However, the buying power of the income you can expect from any savings could be drastically reduced by inflation. The best you can probably do is to work out what you'll get (and what'll you need) in terms of today's prices and pensions; then make regular checks – once a year, say – that you aren't going too far off course.

If your retirement income is not going to meet your needs, even after taking into account any likely shifts in spending when you stop work, then you will need to consider the options for boosting your retirement income. There are two main routes: building up your pension, and building up other savings, which you can use to provide an income when you retire. Chapters 13, 14 and 15 of this book look in detail at the various types of pension scheme – use these to work out how much you can expect from pensions.

Investing through a pension

The three main types of pension are:
- your state retirement pension – covered in Chapter 13
- an employer pension scheme – covered in Chapter 14
- a personal pension plan – covered in Chapter 15.

Everyone who has worked for long enough (and paid enough National Insurance contributions of the right type) is entitled to a basic pension – £64.70 a week for a single person, £103.40 for a married man from April 1998. Although you may get an additional state pension related to your earnings while you were working, state pensions on their own are unlikely to provide an adequate income in retirement. The state pension age for women is also being put back from age 60 to 65 from the year 2020, with the age being moved back gradually from the year 2010. Until 2010, the state pension age for women remains at 60.

If you are eligible to join an employer pension scheme, you should certainly consider joining it: if you are not eligible for such a scheme, or have any earnings that are not covered by one, e.g. because you are self-employed, look at a personal pension plan instead. However, you can take out a personal pension plan instead of or (in certain circumstances, as well as) an employer scheme – see Chapter 14 for guidance on which sort of scheme to choose.

Unless you belong to an employer scheme where the pension is fully index-linked (e.g. some public-sector schemes) you should allow for inflation in working out how well off you'll be after you retire. Even if a pension from an employer scheme or personal pension plan seems handsome when you first retire, it's likely to seem less appealing after ten years or so if it hasn't increased in line with inflation. Many employer schemes have some increases built in, or have, in the past, given special increases to help cope with inflation; and in future, pensions linked to your 'final pay' will have to be increased by 5 per cent (or the actual inflation rate if lower) once they start being paid. But this will apply only to pension rights built up after April 1997. It's likely that most schemes will apply the increase to the whole pension rather than splitting it into pre-1997 and post-1997 segments. A survey published in *Occupational Pensions* (December 1997) found, of 179 schemes surveyed all but two of them made pre-1997 increases and 151 said they would guarantee the increases to pensions in payments in respect of service before 6 April 1997.

Personal pension plans have no built-in way of coping with inflation before you retire: your pension fund on retirement depends on how well your contributions have been invested, though when you retire you can choose to settle for a lower pension to start with in return for a pension which is guaranteed to increase by a certain amount each year.

Another pension choice you are likely to be faced with at some stage before you finally retire is what to do if you change jobs. Changing jobs may mean you end up with less pension than if you'd stayed with one employer. You will have several options:

- a *preserved pension* from the job you leave (based on the number of years you were in the scheme)
- a *transfer payment* from your old pension scheme into the new one you're joining, to increase the benefits you'll get from it
- a *transfer payment* into a personal pension scheme.

See Chapter 14 for guidance on which option to choose.

If your pension will not be enough

If you are a member of an employer scheme, you can make Additional Voluntary Contributions (AVCs) either to your existing scheme or to a Free-Standing AVC scheme with a different pension provider, such as an insurance company. See Chapter 14 for the pros and cons of each type. However, there are limits to what proportion of your income you can put into your pension.

If you have a personal pension plan, you can either increase your contributions to your existing scheme or make a lump sum payment to a different plan. As with employer schemes, there are limits on contributions to personal pension plans. However, you can increase considerably the amount you can invest by making use of the 'carry-back' and 'carry-forward' provisions explained in Chapter 15.

A major benefit of saving via an employer scheme or personal pension plan is that your contributions get tax relief at your highest rate of tax, grow tax-free and that on retirement you can often draw a limited lump sum free of tax. However, the downside is that you cannot get your money back until you retire. Rather than invest all your spare income this way, you may be prepared to sacrifice some of the tax advantages a pension offers: you may, for example, want to help a child through college, or be worried about possible redundancy.

Other ways of investing for retirement

If you have some spare money that you've decided not to tie up in a pension scheme, you can either commit yourself to regular saving, or put something away when you can spare it, say in a building society, and then transfer it into a lump sum investment. The first two chapters of this book will help you in making your choices. However, depending on how long there is until you retire, some investments do offer tax advantages (though none is as generous as pensions).

If you can tie savings up for five years

From 6 April 1999 you will be able to invest up to £5,000 a year into an Individual Savings Account (ISA) which will be completely free of tax – see Chapter 8. In the meantime, invest the maximum you can in a Tax-Exempt Special Savings Account (TESSA) from banks and building societies. You can start a new TESSA up to 5 April 1999 and pay into it under the existing rules for its full five-year life. Other tax-free schemes are Personal Equity Plans (PEPs). You can continue to buy shares or unit trusts through a PEP until 5 April 1999, and the 10% tax credit will be the same as the new ISAs until 5 April 2004.

If you can tie savings up for five to ten years

An investment which gives the possibility of a capital gain, e.g. one based on shares, probably offers the best chance of beating inflation, and five to ten years at least gives time for your investment to recover from periods when values fall. You have the option of investing lump sum or regular savings. From 6 April 1999, investment through the new ISA will be a good option for tax-free savings, particularly if you want to continue to add to your investments year after year. If you have already made investments through a PEP they will continue to attract the same tax advantages as the ISAs. British Government stocks (gilts – see Chapter 19) are also worth considering: any capital gains made on these are free of capital gains tax, and taxpayers who do not need income now can choose ones that pay out only a very small income.

If you can tie savings up for at least ten years

Look at investments where your capital can grow (or shrink). Life insurance savings plans are worth considering if you're the sort of person who needs a disciplined way of saving! However, steer clear of life insurance unless you are sure you can keep the policy up, because there are steep penalties on early withdrawal. They offer tax advantages for higher-rate taxpayers who have used up their capital gains tax allowance, although if you're getting age-related allowances there could be snags (see 'Losing age-related allowance', on page 51). Friendly society tax-exempt savings plans are completely tax-free, but the maximum contribution is small.

Widows, widowers and dependants

While planning your retirement finances, it's vital to check that your family wouldn't be left short should you die. Many employers' pension schemes provide a pension for widows and dependants (and sometimes for widowers) on the death of the employee, whether before or after retirement. If your family couldn't manage on this (together with any income from their jobs, savings and state benefits) you need life insurance. See Chapter 21 for the different types of policy, and for how to work out how much life insurance you need, see *Time to get life insurance*, in *Which?*, August 1996, page 46, or see *Be Your Own Financial Adviser* and *The Which? Guide to Insurance*, both published by Which? Books.*

There is no automatic package of benefits when you take out a personal pension plan (except where the plan has been used to 'contract-out' of the State Earnings-Related Pension Scheme), but you can choose to pay extra for:
■ a pension for your widow, widower, children or dependants
■ life cover from a special type of life insurance policy (you can get tax relief at your highest rate of tax on premiums for this sort of policy).

When you retire, you can sacrifice some of your own pension from a personal pension plan in order to provide a pension for any dependants.

Investing after retirement

For income later

When you first retire, your pension income may be enough for you not to need much extra income from your investments, in which case you will be looking to make your savings grow as much as you can against the day when you need the capital, either to turn it into an income or to replace expensive durables such as a car. However, you need to balance the risk of losing your capital against the other risk, of having it reduced by inflation. Assuming that you have enough money to spread over several types of investment, consider putting some in each of the following categories:

- index-linked investments, such as index-linked National Savings Certificates or index-linked British Government stocks
- secure savings schemes, such as building society and bank accounts or National Savings schemes
- investments where you have the chance of making a capital gain (but the risk of making a capital loss), such as shares, investment trusts or unit trusts. Over the long term these give you at least a chance of beating inflation, and you can reduce the risk by spreading your money across a range of companies – either by buying shares in lots of companies (if you have enough to invest at least £1,500 to £2,000 in each of say, five to ten companies), or by pooling your money with other investors in a unit or investment trust.

Don't forget that British Government stocks are a very versatile investment, depending on which particular stock you choose, and don't assume that lump sum investments are the only ones to consider. If a particularly attractive savings scheme is on offer you can always set up your own 'feeder' account in a bank or building society account, and transfer the money across by standing order. Alternatively, buying, say, National Savings Certificates regularly will produce a stream of income as they start to mature in five years' time.

When you retire, you could also consider 'investing' some of your money in a way that will cut down expenses in the future. You may want to change your car, washing machine or other equipment for a model that costs less to run, and you should certainly check whether you could improve your home's insulation: for example, draught-proofing single-paned windows and external doors yourself will cost you around £50 for an average-sized house, but could save you over £40 a year.

For income now

There are a few investments whose main purpose is to produce income:

■ building society monthly income accounts (many societies also give the option to have interest paid out monthly on other accounts, in return for a slightly lower rate of interest)

■ National Savings Income Bonds

■ National Savings Pensioners' Guaranteed Income Bonds

■ guaranteed income bonds sold by insurance companies (not to be confused with the National Savings Bonds above, which work in a completely different way – see Chapter 21)

■ annuities, also sold by insurance companies. Note that annuities you buy yourself (rather than ones which are bought on your behalf with the proceeds of a personal pension plan) are favourably taxed – only part of the regular income is taxable, the rest is regarded as a return of your original capital

■ split-capital investment trusts – broadly, these are investment companies that split their shares into two basic types, income shares and capital shares. However, these may involve special risks (see Chapter 18).

Note that minimum investments have to be fairly high (i.e. thousands, rather than hundreds, of pounds) in order to pay out a worthwhile monthly income. However, do not confine yourself to specialist income-producing investments. For the advantage of regular income, you may have to accept other risks, such as tying up your capital.

When interest rates are low you will have to be particularly inventive to get a decent income. Some ideas are:

■ using unit trust and investment trust companies marketing 'income' funds: they invest in companies that tend to pay high dividends

■ investing in unit trusts which offer income schemes that will pay out a set income, although to achieve this when prices are falling they may have to cash in some of your units

■ designing your own income-producing portfolio, by choosing categories of investments that achieve a sensible balance between risk, security and growth, but then buying specific investments paying income at different times throughout the year. For example, shares pay their dividends at different times, so do British Government

stocks and when a building society credits interest to your
account varies from society to society
- buying single-premium insurance bonds (see Chapter
22), which are useful for higher-rate taxpayers needing
income
- using what has probably been one of the single biggest
investments you've ever made – your home. Selling it and
moving to a cheaper one may give you a lump sum to
invest: you could also consider mortgaging it and using the
proceeds to buy an annuity (known as a home income plan
– covered in Chapter 23). Letting out part of your home or
taking in a lodger is another option, but it is sensible to find
out about your rights and obligations, from a solicitor or
Citizens Advice Bureau, before doing this.

Traps to avoid

Using up capital too fast

You cannot tell for certain how long you (and your partner)
are going to need an income. You have to take into account
how much your investments will earn, how fast inflation
will erode your income's purchasing power, and how long
you are likely to live. For how inflation can affect your
income, see Chapter 1.

Failing to monitor your investments

Jumping on to the latest investment bandwagon might not
be for you – and in any case, switching from one scheme to
another could incur extra costs, such as unit trust initial
charges or early redemption penalties. Be especially wary of
an adviser who recommends particularly frequent or
unjustified changes in your existing investments – known
as 'churning'; this earns commission for them, but incurs
costs for you, and is in breach of investor protection rules.
    Even so, you should still check regularly that your
investments are working as well as they can for you, taking
into account the way you are taxed and any changes, either
in the financial world or in your own circumstances.

Forgetting that things may change

If one partner dies, pension income may drop sharply,
forcing the surviving partner to depend more upon

investments (unless life insurance will fill the gap). What happens to any jointly held investments and savings accounts depends on whether they are held by 'joint tenants' or 'tenants in common'. In England and Wales it is assumed, in the absence of any other arrangement, that jointly owned property is owned by joint tenants. This means that when one owner dies the whole account or investment automatically passes to the other, irrespective of any will, and whether there is a will or not. In Scotland, this may not be the case, although there may be a special wording in the account terms to ensure that the property passes automatically to the partner.

The surviving partner's investment priorities are almost bound to change. He or she may be particularly at the mercy of inflation and should beware of putting too much in an investment which is secure in that its value can't go down, such as a building society account, but where inflation will erode its value over time. Instead, the surviving partner should consider index-linked investments such as index-linked British Government stocks and index-linked National Savings Certificates, or, if there is enough capital to risk losing some of it, investments such as shares which have a chance of beating inflation.

Selling at the wrong time

When a long-term investment matures, for example a pension or some types of life insurance policy, you might lose out badly if the stock market happens to be low at the time. Clearly, you cannot foresee this at the time you invest. One way to avoid this is to ask the company if you can transfer your money to a safer (probably more pedestrian) fund, a little before maturity. Things like shares or unit trusts you can, of course, sell at any time. But if at all possible, avoid being forced to sell them when their value is very low, by making sure that you always have a safer investment to fall back on until prices improve.

Buying at the wrong time

You would need a crystal ball to avoid this trap completely but you should be particularly careful about when you invest in schemes that provide a fixed return, such as a fixed-interest savings account or an annuity. These usually have penalties if you close the account early; so if you buy a long-term scheme at a time when interest rates are low, you could lose out badly should interest rates then rise.

This is a particular problem with annuities. Once you have bought an annuity, you cannot usually get any of your money back. Annuities usually involve very large sums of money (for example, when your personal pension plan investment fund is converted into a pension on your retirement, you are technically buying an annuity). The annuity marketplace is also highly competitive, with some companies offering very much better rates than others. Therefore, it is vitally important that you shop around as many companies as possible or, if you can, consider waiting or even deferring your pension until rates improve.

Losing age-related allowance

If you are aged 65 or over at any point in the tax year, you can claim a higher tax-free personal allowance, and it's higher still if you reach 75 or over: you can claim up to £5,410 (£5,600 if you're over 75) in the 1998–9 tax year. Likewise, you can claim a higher married couple's allowance if either you or your husband or wife is 65 or over during the tax year. The figures for 1998–9 are £3,305 or £3,345 if either of you is aged 75 or over. All married couple's allowances including the higher married couple's allowance are restricted to 15 per cent tax relief in 1998–9.

But you start to lose your age-related allowance once your 'total income' (see page 93) rises above a certain limit – £16,200 in the 1998–9 tax year. The extra allowance is reduced by half the amount by which your 'total income' exceeds the limit, but will never be reduced below the level of the basic personal and married couple's allowance. Note that even if a married man gets a higher married couple's allowance based on his wife's age (because she is older than him) it is *his* total income figure that determines the amount of allowance received.

If your 'total income' is above the limit, and you are at risk of your age-related allowances being reduced, consider tax-free or favourably taxed investments that won't swell your income, or investments where the return comes mainly in the form of capital gain.

Cashing in part of some life insurance policies

If you've invested in a single-premium life insurance policy (e.g. an insurance bond), and you're getting age-related allowances, be careful. Although any taxable gain you make when you cash in this type of life insurance policy is free of basic-rate income tax, it is counted as part of your investment income for the year; and increasing your income can mean you get less age-related allowance and so pay more tax.

Cashing in part of your policy *won't* affect your tax position in this way if you cash in no more than 5 per cent of the premiums you've paid so far: if you cash in less than 5 per cent in any one year you can carry the unused portion forward indefinitely to add to the amount you can withdraw in future years. However, if you cash in more than your accumulated allowance, the excess is counted as a 'gain' in the year you make it, regardless of how much of it (if any) is in fact gain and how much is return of premiums. The 'gain' would be added to your 'total income' and could reduce your age-related allowances dramatically. Therefore it's wise not to cash in more than the allowances you've built up, unless you cash in the whole of your policy (in which case only the actual gain is added to your income).

See Chapter 22 for more on the taxation of single-premium life insurance policies.

4

INVESTING FOR CHILDREN

Choosing an investment for a child under 18 involves much the same principles as for an adult: you have to take account of how much there is to invest, how long you want to invest it for, what rate of tax will be paid on the income and so on. But the range of investments to choose from is not quite the same as for adults:

■ not all investments allow children to invest in their own name. There are age limits for some (7 or 16 are common ages), while others are not open at all to children under 18. However, even for a child below the age limit, you may still be able to invest on the child's behalf

■ there are investments open only to children, usually offering perks and free gifts to win the custom of the next generation of money magnates.

When investing for a child, follow the guidance in Chapters 1 and 2 on sorting out an investment strategy and finding a shortlist of likely investments. Then use the table on pages 56–7 to eliminate any investments that require too high a minimum investment. You can find more details of particular investments in Chapters 10 to 26.

How tax affects your choices

Which investment to choose will depend very much on the child's (or, in some cases, the parents') tax position.

The first point to note is that income above a certain amount which comes from investing money given by a child's parent is taxed as the parent's income. The income limit is £100 a year from each parent. Note that a child under 18 ceases to be taxed as a child if married.

Any other income the child gets is taxed as the child's, whether from investments handed on by doting grand-parents, earnings from a paper round or appearance fees from advertisements. It will not be taxed at all unless it exceeds the personal allowance (£4,195 for the 1998–9 tax year). If a child is a non-taxpayer it is worth considering investments that pay interest out before tax, such as most National Savings products, or where you can arrange to have interest paid out gross, such as bank or building society accounts. This will save the bother of having to reclaim tax later. If there is any likelihood of tax being payable it might be sensible to invest gifts from parents separately from other gifts, and keep a record of gifts made. More details about children and tax are covered later in the chapter.

Special children's investments

On the high street

Banks and building societies know that today's young savers are the next generation of investors and aim to catch them young. Some offer higher rates of interest to young savers; others tempt the nation's youth with perks such as books, badges, magazines, school gear and the like. A few offer both though, not surprisingly, the higher the rate of interest, the fewer the goodies. A few also now offer cash cards to children aged around 13 or over (although children cannot use them to overdraw).

Some of the gifts are designed to help children learn about money and draw up budgets – you might find them worthwhile even if the rate of interest is not top of the league. If money boxes, record tokens or real china piggy banks help children to learn thrift, you might not be too concerned at the loss of a pound or two in interest. However, if it's interest you want, don't let the goodies distract your attention from the best rates going. Accounts are usually instant access but some do not allow for withdrawals before a given age.

Building society and bank interest is normally credited after deduction of tax at 20 per cent, unless you are registered as a non-taxpayer. Since many children are likely to be non-taxpayers, don't forget to register to get the account interest paid before tax, by completing *form R85* (available from the society or bank).

From the post office

National Savings Children's Bonus Bonds can be bought by anyone over the age of 16 for anyone under 16, and can be held until the child reaches age 21. If children under 16 want to invest their own money in the bonds, they must enlist the help of an adult. For full details of how these bonds work, see Chapter 12, but to give the best return they must be held for five years. The return is tax-free, so they are particularly worth considering if the child is a taxpayer, or if he or she is likely to breach the £100 limit above which income from parental gifts is taxed as the parent's.

From friendly societies

Friendly societies offer similar products to life insurance companies, but are also allowed to offer tax-free savings plans. In particular they can offer children's savings plans, often called 'baby bonds', aimed at people under the age of 18. Either children can invest in the plan themselves, or an adult can make investments on the child's behalf. Baby bonds work in the same way as savings-type insurance policies (see Chapters 21 and 22) and usually last for ten years, but the maximum investment is fairly small, at £25 a month or £270 a year.

EXAMPLE

Samantha (who is 16) is saving up for a CD player costing £120. She has a £20 birthday present from her parents to start her off and reckons on saving £2 a week out of her pocket money. She earns the occasional few pounds from baby-sitting and any cash gifts at Christmas could also be added. She doesn't pay tax, and the interest from her savings isn't going to add up to enough for her parents to worry about paying tax on her interest.

Using the route map in Chapter 2, she whittles her choice down to a National Savings Investment account or some sort of bank or building society account. She thinks she'll find a suitable savings account from a bank or building society in her local high street, and doesn't mind going for an account where she has to give one month's notice. But she'll also find out how a National Savings Investment account compares.

Investing on a child's behalf

Although children cannot open many types of investment themselves before they reach a certain age, you can often buy the investment on the child's behalf before that age. Banks, building societies and National Savings will usually open some types of account in a child's name, but check

Which investment suits your child?

Type of investment	Age child can operate account in own name [1]	Minimum investment
British Government stocks bought through post office	7	none [2]
British Government stocks bought through stockbroker	18	none – but £1,000 a sensible minimum [2]
National Savings Certificates	7	£100
National Savings Ordinary account	7	£10
National Savings Investment account	7	£20
National Savings FIRST Option Bonds	7	£1,000
National Savings Income Bonds	7	£2,000
National Savings Capital Bonds	7	£100

National Savings Children's Bonus Bonds	16: bonds for a child aged under 16 must be bought by a person aged 16 or over	£25
Premium Bonds	16: bonds for a child under 16 must be bought by a parent, guardian or (great) grandparent	£100
Building society or bank instant access account	varies – often 7	Normally £1 to £10
Building society notice or term shares	varies – often 7	£500 upwards
Friendly Society 'Baby Bonds'	16	usually £25 a month
Life insurance policies	varies widely – often 16 to 18, can be younger	often £15 to £20 a month; lump sum usually £250 to £1 000
Shares	18	none – but £1,500 a sensible minimum [2]
Unit trusts	varies – usually 18	usually £250 to £500, but can be less

[1] See 'Investing on a child's behalf', if the child is too young to invest in his or her own name
[2] You have to pay commission each time you buy or sell, so investing or withdrawing small amounts may not be worthwhile

how withdrawals or other transactions can be made before
the child reaches the age at which the building society,
bank or other institution will act on the child's own
signature (often seven). Usually, a parent or other guardian
living with the child will be allowed to make the withdrawal on his or her behalf.

Most unit trust companies will not register units in the
name of a child aged under 18, though a few will do this
from the age of 14. However, they will usually allow units
to be bought in the name of an adult with the account
'designated' for a particular child – the adult runs the
account, but it will be treated for tax purposes as the child's.
On the child's eighteenth (or fourteenth) birthday the trust
can be transferred to the child's name.

Note that if you want to invest a lump sum, for a
grandchild, say, you're not confined to lump sum investments. For example, friendly society baby bond premiums
have to be paid regularly over at least ten years, but many
friendly societies allow you to pay with a lump sum, which
is invested in a 'temporary annuity' (see Chapter 23). This
produces a regular amount to pay the premiums.
Alternatively, you can simply put a lump sum in a building
society or bank account and make regular payments by
standing order.

If you're planning on giving substantial amounts of
money to a child, you may be worried that he or she might
squander it. You could, of course, keep the money in your
own name and hand it over when the child reaches 18, say.
But doing this has disadvantages. For example, *you* may be
tempted to squander the money, or it might mean more
inheritance tax to pay if you were to die within seven years
of making the gift, and so on.

A way out of this problem is to set up a trust for the child.
A trust is managed by *trustees* for the benefit of those for
whom it was set up (the *beneficiaries* of the trust). The
people setting up the trust (the parents, say) can act as
trustees, or they can appoint friends or relatives, or a
professional adviser (such as a solicitor or accountant) as
trustees. Below we give brief details of how a trust is set up,
and look at some short-cuts you can take.

A trust can have more than one beneficiary, so you can,
for example, set up a trust for the benefit of all your ten
grandchildren (plus any more that come along). In this
chapter we assume a trust has only one beneficiary, but
what we say holds equally well for more than one.

When a trust is set up, the trustees may be given the
power to invest in specified investments, or to invest *as*

they think fit. If they are not given these powers, there are special rules about how they can invest the money.

However, putting money into a trust could mean an inheritance tax bill – see below.

Setting up a trust

The rules concerning trusts are extremely complicated, so we recommend you ask a solicitor with experience of setting up trusts to draw up a *trust deed* for you. This will specify who the trustees are, who is entitled to benefits from the trust, when income and capital are to be paid out, ways in which the trustees can invest the money, and so on.

Even a fairly straightforward trust might cost several hundred pounds to set up, and there could be a charge each year from any professional trustees for running the trust (as much as £100 or more, say). So it's probably not worth setting up a trust unless you plan to give a lot of money to your children (at least £10,000, say) and feel the cost of setting up and running the trust is worthwhile or that it would be outweighed by tax savings.

There are two basic types of trust:

■ **interest in possession trusts** (also known as 'fixed interest' or 'life interest' trusts) where a particular person (or people) has the right to the income from the trust (or the equivalent of income, e.g. the right to live in a rent-free home). The trustees have no choice but to hand over the income to the beneficiaries at the times stated in the trust

■ **discretionary trusts** where it is left to the discretion of the trustees which of the possible beneficiaries should be paid income. They may also be free to decide which beneficiary should get capital. If the trustees have the power to accumulate income, i.e. not to pay it out at all (until the trust ends), the trust is called an *accumulation* trust. An *accumulation and maintenance* trust is a type of accumulation trust from which income can be paid out only for the maintenance, education or benefit of the beneficiaries (until the beneficiaries get an interest in possession, that is).

The distinction between interest in possession and discretionary trusts is important because there are special tax rules for the different types of trust – see 'Children and tax', on page 67.

Broadly speaking, the current tax rules mean that:

■ setting up an interest in possession trust for your own child won't normally save you income tax – the income from the trust will be taxed as yours

■ setting up an accumulation trust means that income which is accumulated will be taxed at 34 per cent (in the 1998–9 tax year) and there will be no further income tax to pay as long as it is not paid out before your child reaches 18. So this could be worthwhile if you pay tax at more than 34 per cent (i.e. 40 per cent).

Note that once you've set up a trust, you cannot normally change your mind and take the money back. Also, while you can indicate your preferences to the trustees about how they should manage the trust's affairs, the trustees do not have to follow them.

If you think you or your family could benefit from a trust, you should discuss it with a solicitor or other professional adviser.

Short-cut trusts

There are ways of making sure that money you invest for your children is held in trust for them without going to the expense of setting up a tailor-made trust.

Life insurance policies
You can take out a life insurance policy (on your, or your husband's or wife's life) with the proceeds made payable to your child. The insurance company should be able to advise you of the options available and will have standard forms for setting up various types of trust.

The policy can be a single-premium one (e.g. a managed bond) or a regular-premium one (e.g. a unit-linked savings plan or an endowment policy).

The premiums you pay count as gifts for tax purposes (but will probably come into one of the tax-free categories – see page 115). There's no inheritance tax to pay on money paid out by the policy, and if the policy is handed over to the child after the age of 18, any taxable gain on the policy is taxed as the child's, not the parent's. However, if the policy ends before it is handed over, the gain is taxed as the parent's, though the trust pays the tax.

EXAMPLE

John and Susan Lime both pay tax on the top slice of their income at 40 per cent. They've got £5,000 from a with-profits endowment policy, and want to invest it for their ten-year-old daughter, Sally. They don't want her to have the money until she's 18.

They consider whether to set up an *accumulation and maintenance* trust (which could save them income tax), but they decide that the amount they're investing does not justify the expense of setting up a tailor-made trust. So they put £3,000 into a single-premium life insurance bond, taken out on John's life, but with the proceeds payable to Sally and the policy being handed over to her when she is 18, so that any gain on it will count as hers for tax purposes. They invest the remaining £2,000 in unit trusts on behalf of Sally – the income from this will count as the Limes' for tax purposes (though any gains will be taxed as Sally's).

The £5,000 will count as a gift for inheritance tax purposes. However, Mr and Mrs Lime have not used their tax-free quota of £3,000 each for this year (i.e. they have £6,000 tax-free in hand). So they can invest the money for Sally without fear of inheritance tax. And there will be no inheritance tax to pay when the investments are handed over to Sally.

Planning for education

If you've decided to send your child (or children) to a private school, you're going to be faced with substantial bills. School fees range from around £3,000 a year for the cheapest day preparatory school to around £13,500 for an expensive senior boarding school. Even if your child is educated in the state system, university or further education could place a heavy burden on a parent.

You may well find paying for your child's education out of your current income hard going, so if there's time in hand, it's worth looking into ways of saving now for the future. When working out how much you might need, do not forget that school fees (along with prices in general, and your earnings) are likely to rise over the years. In recent years, school fee increases have outstripped the rise in the cost of living.

Various insurance companies and investment advisers specialise in arranging schemes to provide the money that's needed for school fees or further education at the time it's needed. These schemes are often based on investment-type life insurance policies and annuities.

Below, we give details of the main types of scheme. Broadly speaking, they fall into two groups:
- **capital** schemes where you invest a lump sum now to provide fees in the future
- **income** schemes where you save on a regular basis to build up the money needed to pay fees.

Depending on your circumstances, a mixture of the different types may suit you best.

It's worth bearing in mind that there's nothing magical about such schemes. They are simply a way of investing money in order to make a set of payments some time in the future (which may turn out to be less than, or more than, enough to pay the fees). They use the sorts of investment that you might well choose to invest in yourself if you were arranging to save up for school fees independently. However, there has to be careful timing of the investments to make sure there's money around when the fees are due, and there are tax complications that have to be taken into account. So although you can go it alone, you may decide it's best to make your investments through a special scheme.

Where to go for education funding schemes

A reputable independent financial adviser should be able to help you, or put you in touch with an insurance company or adviser specialising in such schemes. Alternatively, you could try the Independent Schools Information Service (ISIS)* for help. But get quotes from more than one source – different schemes suit different people – and ask how any adviser will be paid: they may get commission for selling particular products, or give you the option of paying a fee, reduced by any commission received.

How capital schemes work

Educational trusts

You pay a lump sum to an educational trust either direct or via an insurance company or adviser. Your lump sum is invested to provide guaranteed amounts each term for an agreed number of years, at a level decided by you at the outset. Your money can be used only for paying school fees (the trust will make out cheques for the fees only to the school) though you are not tied to a particular school. If the fees have risen above the amounts guaranteed to be paid out, you will have to meet the shortfall.

If, when the time comes, you do not need to pay school fees, you may be able to transfer the plan to a different child. Alternatively, you may be able to get back the amount of your original investment (though it may then be worth much less because of inflation).

Lump sum investments

If you don't want your lump sum to be tied to paying school fees, you can simply invest it in a way that suits your circumstances. For example, investment advisers may first suggest you make full use of the tax-free investments open to you, such as Tax-Exempt Special Savings Accounts (TESSAs) and Personal Equity Plans (PEPs) or, from 6 April 1999, Individual Savings Accounts (ISAs): then, depending on how much risk you are prepared to take, building society, bank or National Savings accounts, with-profit endowment policies, through to investments that can go up and down in value such as unit trusts, unit-linked life insurance policies and single-premium life insurance bonds (for more about unit-linked life insurance and bonds, see Chapter 22). With this latter category, remember the risk that their value may be low when you need to sell them to pay the fees.

How much do you need to invest?

With most schemes there's a minimum investment, usually £1,000. Beyond this, the amount you need to invest will depend on how long there is until the fees start and what the fees are expected to be. If you have a newly born child, you should think about investing a lump sum of at least £60,000 to £70,000 to pay for private boarding secondary education (assuming fees went up from current levels by 7 to 10 per cent a year).

Cutting the cost

Many schools offer scholarships to academically, musically or artistically gifted children, subject to entrance exam results. These can help pay part or all of the fees. A leaflet on grants and scholarships is available from ISIS. If you've already chosen a school, ask the bursar.

Some employers may help with fees, especially for staff posted overseas (there are schemes, for example, for parents working for the Diplomatic Service or serving in the armed forces). Financial help from an employer can count as a taxable fringe benefit in some cases – check with the Inland Revenue.

Tax

An educational trust has charitable status and does not have to pay tax on its investments, as long as the money is used for educational purposes. And you do not have to pay tax on the money that goes to pay fees. A future government might choose to remove an educational trust's charitable status; you would then have to meet the shortfall in fees created by the loss of the tax benefits.

With other schemes, the tax you pay will of course depend on the investments on which the scheme is based, and your own circumstances. See the relevant chapter for more details.

How much inheritance tax has to be paid and when depends on who gives the money:

- **if the parents give the money** Payments made by the parents solely for the *maintenance, education or training* of their children are free of inheritance tax. So there's no inheritance tax to pay when the money is first invested, nor when the fees are paid. However, if the money is not held in trust, or if it is held in trust and the parents keep the right to cash in the scheme, there may be inheritance tax to pay if the parent who gives the money dies. The cash-in value of the investment will form part of his or her estate, and will be taxed in the normal way. If the parent gives up the right to cash in a trust scheme, the money will remain in trust for the child and will be used for his or her maintenance, education or training – the money will not form part of the parent's estate

- **if someone else (e.g. grandparents) gives the money** If the grandparents (or whoever) do not set up a trust scheme, the money they eventually pay over for school fees may count as gifts for inheritance tax. If they do set up a trust scheme – and they give away the right to cash in the scheme – the money they invest in the first place may count as a gift for inheritance tax purposes. If they keep the right to cash in the scheme, what counts as a gift is the cash-in value of the scheme when fees start being paid (which will almost certainly be higher than the value of the original investment).

Note that even if there is a potential liability to inheritance tax, gifts of money can still be tax-free. For example, gifts made out of normal income are free of inheritance tax, as are gifts totalling up to £3,000 a year – for more details see page 115.

Composition fees

You can, with many private schools, pay school fees in advance by what's known as a *composition fee*. In this case, the school then invests the money, often in an annuity which starts paying out when the child goes to school. The amount you have to pay could be either fees frozen at current levels, or reduced fees, but check what happens if you decide to send your child to a different school.

How income schemes work

There are a number of different ways in which these schemes can be set up, but most involve saving regularly by taking out a series of investment-type life insurance policies, which mature year by year as the fees become due.

For example, suppose you plan to send your child to private school in ten years' time for five years. You could take out five with-profits endowment policies which end after 10, 11, 12, 13 and 14 years respectively. For the first ten years you'd pay a flat amount (the premiums for all the policies). From the eleventh year onwards, the premiums would start to tail off, as each policy ended.

If you expect your income to go up over the years you might prefer to pay premiums which increase rather than decrease. In this case, it may be best to take out five ten-year policies in successive years. Your premiums will increase each year up to the fifth year, stay level for the next five years, then tail off as policies end.

Some companies use unit-linked policies (see Chapter 22), unit trusts, investment trusts to provide part or all of the fees. With all of these, there is the risk that the value of your investment will fluctuate, depending on how well the units, shares or whatever have performed. If their value was low when you wanted to cash in your investment, you might get less than you'd hoped for.

If you change your mind about sending your child to private school, what happens depends on whether or not the policies are being held in trust for the child. If they *are* being held in trust (which gives a possible inheritance tax advantage – see above) the money from the policies must be used for the benefit of the child. If they *are not* being held in trust you can either cash in the policies or keep them as a form of saving.

How much do you need to invest?

As with capital schemes, the amount you need to invest will depend on how much time there is before your child goes to private school and what the fees are expected to be. If you were hoping to provide private boarding secondary education for a child who's a baby now, you would have to think about investing around £5,000 to £8,000 a year (assuming fees went up from current levels at 7 to 10 per cent a year).

Tax

There's normally no income tax to pay on the money paid out by schemes based on life insurance (except, in certain circumstances, when a life insurance policy has to be cashed in early). The proceeds from a PEP are free of income and capital gains tax, but you may have to pay these taxes on the return from unit or investment trusts.

If it's the parents who pay for the scheme there's no inheritance tax to pay on the premiums or on the money paid out by the schemes. If people other than the parents pay for the scheme, there's no inheritance tax to pay as long as the scheme contributions are paid out of their normal income or count as tax-free for some other reason. If there are life insurance policies being held in trust for the child, there's no inheritance tax to pay if the person who set up the scheme dies. However, if the policies are not being held in trust, the proceeds on death count as part of the person's estate.

Failed to plan?

If you've left it too late, or the fees are more than you anticipated, you may be able to borrow the money for the fees. But first compare the monthly cost of any loan with the outlay if you pay as you go, to see whether you could not meet the cost out of your income. The occasional overdraft may be cheaper and you will not be committed to paying off loans for years to come.

Banks and insurance companies offer special loan packages for school fees, which usually involve a second mortgage on your home (and some sort of arrangement fee). The money is lent to you as the fees fall due, and you repay it after, say, 25 years (or when you retire) with the proceeds of an investment-type insurance policy. The monthly cost (insurance premiums plus interest) rises as you draw more of the money to pay the fees.

If you manage most of the cost out of day-to-day income but need to top it up with more than an overdraft, you could ask your bank or building society for a straightforward loan. If you have an investment-type life insurance policy, you may be able to borrow from the insurance company on the strength of it.

Children and tax

Tax-saving tips

We gave details about tax as far as children are concerned at the beginning of this chapter, and there's yet more on tax in Chapters 7 and 8. Here we point out the main things to bear in mind, and some ways you can take advantage of the income tax, inheritance tax and capital gains tax rules to keep tax bills to a minimum when investing for children.

■ **There's a limit to the tax you can save by giving money to your own children** Income of more than £100 a year, resulting from gifts each parent makes to his or her own children, counts as the parent's income for tax purposes; and, if it's taxable, it's taxed at the parent's highest rate of tax.

■ **Giving money to your grandchildren (or any other children who are not your own) could mean less tax to pay on the income it produces** Income which comes from gifts made to a child by anyone other than his or her parents counts as the child's own income for tax purposes. A child can have income of at least as much as the personal allowance (£4,195 a year in the 1998–9 tax year) before starting to pay tax.

■ **Giving money to your children during your lifetime could save inheritance tax** In general, you have to pay inheritance tax on anything over a set amount (£223,000 in the 1998–9 tax year) that you give away during the seven years before you die or on your death. However, some types of gift are tax-free and don't count towards the £223,000 limit. It makes sense to take advantage of these tax-free ways of handing money to your children during your lifetime. For a list of the main tax-free gifts you can make, see pages 115–16.

In general, gifts which are taxable are taxed at a lower rate if you live for at least three years after making them, rather than leaving them in your will. If you live more than seven years after making a gift, there will be no inheritance tax to be paid on it.

■ **You can, if you want, invest money for your children without their being able to get their hands on it for the time being** You can do this by taking out an insurance policy where the proceeds are made payable to your children – see 'Short-cut trusts' on page 60.

■ **Consider setting up an accumulation trust** if you pay income tax at 40 per cent, want to give your children large amounts of money and do not want to put the money into investment-type life insurance. Income which is accumulated is taxed at a flat rate: 34 per cent for 1998–9.

Tax on income from interest in possession trusts

An interest in possession trust pays tax at the basic rate on its income. Any income paid out of the trust comes with a tax credit of the amount of tax deducted (23 per cent of the before-tax income for the 1998–9 tax year).

If the trust was set up by the parents, the income counts as theirs (see above), and they get the 23 per cent tax credit. If the trust was set up by anyone other than the parents, the income counts as the child's and the child gets the tax credit.

If the parents (or child, as the case may be) do not pay tax, or pay less than the tax deducted, they can claim tax back. If the highest rate of tax the parents (or the child) pay is 23 per cent, the tax liability on income from the trust is automatically met by the tax credit. If the parents (or child) pay tax at a rate of more than 23 per cent, they will have to pay extra tax, calculated on the income paid out plus the tax credit.

Tax on income from discretionary trusts

These pay tax on their income at a special rate: 34 per cent for the 1998–9 tax year.

As with an interest in possession trust, any income paid out is taxed as either the parents' income (if the trust was set up by the parents) or the child's income (in any other case). But with a discretionary trust, the income comes with a tax credit of 34 per cent of the before-tax amount of income. Whether or not there's more tax to pay (or whether a rebate can be claimed) depends on whether the parents' (or child's) top rate of tax is more or less than 34 per cent. If the top rate is *less* than 34 per cent, it would be worth asking the trustees to pay as much income out as possible, as tax could then be claimed back from the Inland Revenue. With an accumulation trust, if the income is accumulated and not paid out until your children are 18 or over, there'll be no further income tax to pay; but neither you nor your children will be able to claim tax back.

Inheritance tax

If you make a gift to your child (or set up a trust under which he or she benefits) it normally counts as a gift for inheritance tax purposes. But some gifts you make are free of inheritance tax. For brief details of how inheritance tax works, see Chapter 7.

Below, we tell you some of the special inheritance tax rules that apply to trusts. However, the taxation of trust funds and settlements can be very complicated – one reason for getting professional advice if you're setting up a tailor-made trust.

Gifts to trusts

In general, the value of the money, property or whatever you put into the trust counts as a gift. With gifts to the following types of trust, there may be an inheritance tax bill only if you die within seven years of making the gift (in the same way as for any other gift):

- an accumulation and maintenance trust
- a trust for disabled people
- an interest in possession trust.

With gifts to all other trusts, you may have to pay inheritance tax at the time you make the gift, even though you live for more than seven years after the gift is made. The gift is added to the value of other such gifts made within the previous seven years; if the total comes to more than £223,000 (for gifts in the 1998–9 tax year) then inheritance tax is charged on the excess at 20 per cent (which is half the rate payable for gifts on death). If you survive for seven years after the gift, no further inheritance tax will be due on it, but if you die within seven years, then the gift is included in the reckoning for inheritance tax on your death (with credit for the tax already paid).

Note that gifts to trusts count as tax-free if they would be tax-free when made to an individual (e.g. if made out of normal spending).

Inheritance tax on trusts

With an *interest in possession trust*, anyone with the right to income or the equivalent of income (e.g. the right to live in a rent-free home) from the trust is considered to own the trust's capital, or part of the trust's capital, if the rights to the benefits are shared among several people. When a person's right to the trust's benefit goes to someone else, this is considered to be making a gift, e.g. your son may have the right to income from a trust once he reaches 18. If this right passes to his younger sister when he reaches 21, he is considered to make a gift at that time. The gift is valued as the share of the trust's capital, which he's considered to own, at the time the right to the income is transferred. Inheritance tax will be due if the son dies within seven years of the gift; but this tax is paid by the trust.

When the trust finally comes to an end, and the capital is handed over to beneficiaries who until that time had the right to the income, there's no more inheritance tax to pay.

Discretionary trusts (other than accumulation and maintenance trusts – see below) may be charged inheritance tax even if payments are not made out of the trust. Inheritance tax is automatically charged on everything in the trust every ten years – the *periodic charge*. The rules for calculating the periodic charge are complex, but the overall aim is to collect the same amount of tax as would be paid if the trust's property were owned by an individual and passed on at death every 33 years.

When payments are actually made from a discretionary trust's capital (or if fixed interests are created) the trust is also charged inheritance tax. The value of what's paid out (or turned into a fixed interest) is charged at the rate of tax which applied at the last periodic charge; but this rate is scaled down in proportion to the time since the last ten-yearly charge, e.g. if it's one year since the ten-yearly charge the rate is one-tenth of the rate at the last ten-yearly charge. If the payment from the trust is made within three months after a ten-yearly charge, there's no tax to be paid.

Payments of capital from certain *accumulation and maintenance* trusts are free of inheritance tax and these trusts are also free of the ten-yearly tax bills. To qualify, a trust must be for the benefit of one or more people under the age of 25, who must get the capital of the trust (or at least the right to the income, or use of the trust property) on or before their twenty-fifth birthday. If any income is paid out from the trust before this, it must be used only for the maintenance, education or training of the beneficiaries. In addition, payments from the trust will be free of inheritance tax only if the children who benefit have a grandparent in common or the trust is less than 25 years old.

Capital gains tax

If you hand over assets (such as shares or your second home) to your children, or put them into a trust, you *dispose* of what you've given, and there may be some capital gains tax to pay (as well as inheritance tax). The asset is valued at its market value at the time you make the gift. For the rules about capital gains tax, see Chapter 7.

Bear in mind that the first £6,800 (for the 1998–9 tax year) of net capital gains you make from disposing of assets during a tax year is tax-free.

Once a gift has been made, how much capital gains tax has to be paid on any further gains depends on whether the child controls the investment, or whether the gift is in trust.

Gains made by a child

Capital gains made by a child are taxed as the child's own gains, not as those of the parents. The normal rules for working out capital gains tax apply; so, for example, the child can make £6,800 of gains in the 1998–9 tax year without paying tax.

Gains made by a trust

Trusts pay capital gains tax at a flat rate of 23 per cent for a fixed trust, 34 per cent for a discretionary trust (including an accumulation and maintenance trust). But the first £3,400 (for the 1998–9 tax year) of net capital gains is free of capital gains tax. This lower tax-free limit for trusts means that trusts are often liable for more capital gains tax than is an individual.

If a beneficiary becomes entitled to some or all of the assets of the trust, e.g. on reaching the age of 18, this counts as the trust disposing of the assets. If there are gains, capital gains tax may have to be paid by the trust. However, there is no capital gains tax for the beneficiary to pay, and he or she cannot reclaim any capital gains tax paid by the trust.

5

SAFETY
FIRST

'Remember that the value of investments and the income from them can go down as well as up and you may not get back the amount you invest.' This is a statement which by now should be familiar to all of us as it, or something similar, should be included in any advertisement offering investment products. It outlines succinctly the risk you take that the shares, bonds or fund you choose may do badly. There's no law to protect you against such risks, but there are some risks against which you can guard. The world of investment has its share of rogues who will not think twice before disappearing with your hard-earned cash. In this chapter we look at what legal protection there is to stop things going wrong, and where to look for possible compensation if they do. We also outline some actions you can take to protect yourself from the rogues.

The Financial Services Act 1986

Before this Act, regulation of investment businesses used to consist of a piecemeal collection of Acts of Parliament plus the self-regulation of such bodies as the Stock Exchange. For example, bank deposits were, and still are, protected by the Banking Act (which, among other things, guarantees 90 per cent of the first £20,000 of your deposit if the bank goes bust) and life insurance policyholders by the Policyholders' Protection Act (which guarantees 90 per cent of your entitlement in a long-term policy).

However, there used to be many loopholes and areas where there was no protection at all for the investor. For example, anybody could set themselves up as an 'investment consultant'. In 1986, Parliament passed the

Financial Services Act (the Act), a mammoth piece of legislation designed both to fill the gaps in investor protection and to boost confidence in financial services. And although regulation under the Act has evolved over the years it is limited to investments.

This means some areas of finance are still not covered by the Act, including savings, or deposit accounts, tangible assets such as gold coins or antiques, mortgages (although the Act will cover any investment element – endowment insurance – linked to a mortgage) and some areas of insurance such as term insurance or health insurance.

The Act was never intended to encompass all areas of finance and at the time it was a logical step to address the regulation of investments in isolation. But even from the start there was criticism from within the industry that to comply with the regulations was both costly and cumbersome. Consumers equally had problems, both with finding their way around the different regulators and with the time it took to sort out complaints (including the well-publicised scandals such as the mis-selling of pensions).

To compound problems and expose further limitations, the financial industry has changed dramatically over the last decade. The distinction between banks, building societies, insurance companies, investment advisers and other financial organisations has become blurred, as have the products available to consumers. Financial conglomerates have grown out of the industry, offering one-stop shops for all your financial needs. Furthermore, many new products available can no longer be slotted into easily definable categories, for example investment-linked mortgages or life insurance policies linked to your pension. Some aspects of these products will be regulated by the Act while others may not.

A new Financial Services Act in 1999

In 1997 the limitations of the 1986 Act were acknowledged and at the time of writing a transformation of the whole regulatory system is underway. This will involve creating a new 'super-regulator', the Financial Services Authority (FSA).* Initially, this new regulator is simply the Securities and Investments Board (SIB) renamed. However, over the next two years the role of the FSA will encompass the powers of the nine existing regulators.

These are:
- The Building Society Commission*
- Friendly Societies Commission*

- Insurance Directorate of the Department of Trade and Industry*
- SIB and the three Self-Regulating Organisations (SROs)
  – Personal Investment Authority (PIA)*
  – Investment Managers Regulatory Organisation (IMRO)*
  – The Securities and Futures Authority (SFA)*
- Registrar of Friendly Societies*
- The Supervision and Surveillance Division of the Bank of England.*

The FSA will also take over the regulatory responsibilities for investment business currently delegated to the nine Recognised Professional Bodies (RPBs). These are: The Association of Chartered Certified Accountants;* the Institute of Actuaries;* the Institute of Chartered Accountants in England and Wales;* Ireland;* and Scotland;* the Insurance Brokers' Registration Council;* and the Law Society of England and Wales;* Scotland;* and Northern Ireland.*

The timetable for change

The handover of power is taking place in several stages:
- The first was in **October 1997** when the FSA replaced SIB (in practice, SIB was simply renamed). This has been followed up by the appointment of FSA officials, a re-organisation of staff and consultation on the key issues
- **Spring 1998 to Autumn 1999** As we went to press the first steps of co-ordinating supervision of firms across all SROs had started. While regulation continues to be the responsibility of the individual SROs, working teams are being set up to co-ordinate the regulators. For example, there is a cross-regulator team addressing the issue of pension mis-selling headed by an FSA official
- **'N1' (June or July 1998)** This is the date on which the FSA takes over the regulation of banks from the Bank of England. The exact timing cannot be set as this change will require a separate Act of Parliament.
- **'N2' (late 1999)** The date on which the new regime becomes fully operational. The FSA will have its full complement of powers, and new complaints-handling and compensation arrangements will come into force.

Although the FSA will be fully operational only from 'N2' the co-operation of the existing SROs means that you, the customer, can contact the FSA over all issues of regulation or compensation today. You will be directed to the relevant SRO but at least there is now a central point of contact.

The role of the FSA

Broadly speaking the functions of the new regulator will be the same as those of the regulators it will replace. However, emphasis will be on the different *regulatory functions* rather than on different *areas of investment business*. This is expected to provide a clear and unified approach to all aspects of the regulations of the financial industry.

What are the regulations?

Although the changes outlined above are still to a greater extent in a consultation phase and many months of drafting will take place before the new rules are finalised, it seems likely that the bulk of the existing rules and regulations will continue largely unchanged. The noticeable changes expected will be as a result of the improved efficiency with which the regulation is carried out. The remainder of this chapter explains the current investment regulations and how they can protect you.

Authorisation

All businesses dealing in or giving advice on investments, with certain very limited exceptions, must be *authorised* to carry out their business. To become authorised, businesses have to meet certain standards, for example, they need to show they are properly run, have sound financial backing and keep adequate records. Furthermore, all staff who advise on and sell investments must pass examinations showing they have reached a minimum level of competence.

Keeping the rules

Once authorised, investment firms that fail to abide by the rules of their regulating organisation can be disciplined, fined or, at worst, have their authorisation removed and be banned from the industry. Each of the SROs or RPBs have their own rule books and so the specific rules will vary depending on which regulator is protecting you, for example, if you are buying shares you will be covered by the SFA, whereas for most other investments such as life insurance, personal pension plans or unit trusts you will be

protected by the PIA (or occasionally IMRO or the FSA).
The main points of the rules are:
- investment businesses have to take into account *your*
best interests when giving you advice. This means that
they are to recommend only products which are suitable for
you
- in most cases an adviser has to *know the customer*, i.e.
be fully aware of your personal and financial situation. This
is often done by filling in a systematic questionnaire called
a 'fact-find'
- independent advisers must take into account the range of
products on the market and your particular needs.
Company representatives (or *tied agents*) have the same
responsibilities as far as the range of products and services
the company they're tied to provides. In either case, if
nothing they can offer suits your needs, they must tell you
so
- at the start of the selling process, both independent
advisers and company representatives must give you a
leaflet making their status clear
- when you pick a pension or investment-type life
insurance policy, you must be given a *key features
document* before you make your investment. See pages
332–3 for more details on key features documents
- in most cases (but not when buying only life insurance or
unit trusts), written *customer agreements* – also known as
terms of business letters – are required, which give details
of the services being provided and their cost, set out your
investment objectives and the responsibilities of your
adviser and warn of the risks of certain investments
- if an adviser 'cold calls' you, he or she must make it clear
that he or she is hoping to sell you something and make
sure you are happy to discuss it. Formerly the adviser may
have pretended to be doing market research
- after you have invested in life insurance, pensions or unit
trusts, you normally have a 14-day *cooling-off period*
during which you can change your mind by cancelling the
investment and getting your money back. But this doesn't
apply to unit trusts or single-premium life insurance bonds
if you received no advice, or bought either through an
advertisement or in line with your customer agreement
- *best execution* rules apply for most transactions. This
means that the firm must carry out the deal on the best
terms available
- advertisements and illustrations of benefits have to
comply with rules about comparisons, references to past
performance and give risk warnings if necessary.

Illustrations must be based on standard assumptions about investment growth, but must reflect the company's own charges for life insurance, pensions products, unit and investment trusts and PEPs

■ proper arrangements must be made for keeping your money (e.g. money awaiting investment) separate from an adviser's money. A really determined fraudster could still run off with your money, but at least the FSA should make it easier for you to get compensation – see below

■ some of this protection isn't available to you if you're classed as a professional or business investor, or if you're classed as an *experienced* investor in your customer agreement (i.e. one with plenty of recent experience in a particular field of investment). Watch out if this applies to you – read your customer agreement carefully and query it if you think your investor status should be different.

Independence

Advisers selling life insurance and unit trusts must either give completely independent advice, selecting products for you from all those on the market, or act as representatives selling and advising on one single company's or group's products. (Although you can ask a company representative to sell you another company's product, the rep can't actually give you advice on it.) This has become known as *polarisation*. Unless you are already sure that you want to invest with a specific company, or you are yourself collecting quotations from a handful of preferred companies, your best course is to seek independent advice.

The status of banks and building societies can be particularly confusing. A few use their branch networks as outlets for independent advice. But, with most you can buy only the investments of a single insurance company through the branch networks: many banks and societies operate their own insurance company (the so-called *bancassurers*); others have an agreement with a separate insurance company to sell their products (i.e. they act as tied agents for the company). However, some banks and societies also run a separate independent advice service – you'll usually be put in touch with this only if you ask and if you have a considerable sum to invest.

Compensation

A compensation scheme is available if you lose money because your adviser goes bust or turns out to be a fraud (but see Chapter 11 for the protection you get with deposit accounts at banks and building societies). The scheme is financed by a levy on all investment businesses. You should be covered if your investments were made after 28 August 1988, when the scheme started. If you invested before then you might still be covered in some circumstances.

If you find yourself in the unfortunate position of having lost money in a bankrupt investment company, you should be contacted by the Investors' Compensation Scheme.* If you're not contacted, contact the scheme with any proof you have of the amounts involved. The scheme can pay up to £48,000 – full protection for the first £30,000 invested, then protection for 90 per cent of the next £20,000. So, it's worth bearing in mind that, in most cases, you'll be assured of getting all your money back only if you've invested £30,000 or less. If you've invested through a member of a Recognised Professional Body (RPB) you should also get compensation, but from a different scheme.

When the new FSA fully integrates the regulation, the compensation schemes for both savings accounts and investments will be unified.

Suing a company

You also have the right to sue a company for damages if you believe that:
- the company has broken the rules of its regulating organisation, and
- as a result of this you have lost money.

How to complain

There are three stages that you can go through if you have a complaint about an authorised investment business. First, all authorised businesses must have a complaints procedure set up to deal with problems. You should approach the company in writing, providing evidence of your complaint. If you are not happy with the response you get from your first complaint or from the branch with which you were dealing, take your complaint higher up to the managing director or head office.

Second, if your complaint isn't resolved satisfactorily, you can approach the appropriate regulating body – the letterhead or other stationery of all authorised businesses should tell you which this is. If you are unsure who to contact, the FSA Enquires Unit* can point you in the right direction. The regulating body involved will have a system set up to deal with investor complaints (in some cases, one of the Ombudsman schemes, e.g. the Pensions Ombudsman,* the Insurance Ombudsman Bureau*). If they think that the rules may have been broken, they will investigate. Complaints procedures vary between the SROs and the RPBs, but all have a number of ways of dealing with a justified complaint, such as giving a private or public reprimand or withdrawing authorisation (so that the firm will have to stop business). You may receive payment to compensate for any loss or suffering caused to you.

Finally, if you're unhappy about the way the SRO or RPB has handled your complaint, you can go to the FSA, which will be able to look at any *procedural* problems you've had with the complaints system of the SRO or RPB (e.g. they're taking too long to deal with the complaint). It won't be able to give an opinion on the actual outcome of your complaint. If you're not happy with the outcome, you can go to the regulating body's independent complaints investigator. Simplification of the complaints procedure will be one of the major benefits of the new integrated FSA.

Self-protection

Even though the regulations give you a safety net, it's still a good idea to take precautions before deciding where and with whom to put your money. You should weigh up both the potential risks and benefits of your planned investments. Chapter 6 outlines a number of points to consider when choosing someone to advise you on what to do with your money. Other things to watch out for are:

■ particularly good deals – don't allow greed to overcome your commonsense. Investing money is a business like any other and a competitive one at that. If you come across an adviser who promises you returns way beyond the norm, the chances are that either he or she's not planning to return your money or there's a lot of risk involved – either way you could end up with nothing

■ 'guaranteed' returns – if the sales pitch refers to a 'guaranteed return', find out exactly who or what is giving this guarantee. Words alone are not enough (especially if the company is based abroad)

■ writing cheques – make cheques out to the company you're going to invest in rather than to the adviser you're dealing with, wherever possible

■ high-pressure selling – no deal is so urgent that you have to decide immediately whether to invest; it's your money, so don't allow yourself to be pushed into deciding what to do. Give yourself time to find out more

■ commission – commission rates do vary, making some investments more attractive for advisers to sell. Despite the *conduct of business rules* of the FSA, it's still a good idea to look at how much commission your adviser is getting on each proposed investment

■ unauthorised advisers – never deal with anyone who doesn't have authorisation; report him or her to the FSA (you can check with the FSA as to who is authorised) and, if you find out that an authorised business is breaking the rules of its regulating body, report it also

■ being classed as an *experienced* investor (see 'Keeping the rules' on page 75) – if you are, some of the protection outlined earlier in this chapter will not apply, e.g. the obligation on an adviser to find out your needs before giving advice.

One final warning: remember that the FSA is there to protect you against rogues and the negligence of others, not the unavoidable perils of investment. Investment will never be totally risk-free.

6

GETTING ADVICE

Lots of people offer investment advice, but how good is the advice? In this chapter we look at the various sources of professional advice, what they might offer, and what they might cost.

Who's offering advice?

Various groups of people give investment advice of one sort or another. For example:
- banks
- building societies
- independent financial advisers
- insurance brokers
- insurance company representatives
- stockbrokers.

Accountants and solicitors may also offer investment advice; details of these services are at the end of this chapter.

In order to offer investment advice, a person must be authorised to do so. However, that does not guarantee that advisers from each of the categories outlined above will be suitable to advise you on all aspects of your financial affairs. You need to be sure you are dealing with an adviser who specialises in your area of needs. If in doubt check with more than one adviser before acting on any advice.

What types of advice can you get?

Investment advice falls broadly into two categories:
- general advice – such as how your money should be split between different types of investment
- specialist advice – such as which shares to invest in or which kind of investment-type life insurance to buy.

It is unlikely that any adviser will offer general advice without then going on to offer specific investment recommendations. You may find, however, that your adviser cannot offer more general advice but can simply offer a specific type of investment such as insurance or pensions advice. If you are sure that you only need specific pensions advice, say, then you probably will find a pensions expert will be more useful than a general investment adviser.

You may also simply want a dealing service, known as an *execution only* service, without any advice, e.g. buying or selling shares under specific instructions. This is the only occasion whereby you can deal with someone who is not authorised to offer investment advice.

If your adviser manages all, or a large portion of, your investments for you (called *portfolio management*), you can often ask for the management to be *advisory*, where the adviser needs your prior approval to act, or *discretionary*, where he or she doesn't. Most advisers prefer discretionary management for larger sums of money (say, £50,000 or more), so that they can act quickly when necessary. If you decide on discretionary management it is normal to agree certain criteria. Your adviser should, for example, agree a general investment strategy which suits your needs and is aware of your attitude to risk and your investment time frame. More detailed considerations such as broad limits to your adviser's discretion (for example, investing not more than 5 per cent of your money in the shares of any one company) and, whether or not your money should be invested in traded options or foreign investments, should also be decided.

Choosing an adviser

It's not hard to find an investment adviser – finding one that's right for you is the problem. Some general advisers, such as solicitors and accountants, normally give such advice as a sideline to their main business. Other advisers will not be interested in your business unless you have a lot of money to invest – say £100,000, or even more.

So it's best to do a bit of homework before you go out to look for an adviser. Opposite is a checklist of points that you should consider to help you decide what your investment needs and aims are. In going through this checklist you will have to put a bit of thought into exactly what you want from your investments: whether you are willing to risk losing money in hope of a capital gain, whether you want your money available at short notice and so on. See Chapters 1 and 2 for help in sorting out your priorities.

You should also expect to be asked about all these points by an adviser (unless your needs are very specific, e.g. you're just asking him or her to sell some shares). It's likely that your adviser will use a fact-finding questionnaire to establish what your circumstances and needs are. Be wary of advisers who don't ask the right questions. Not only will they be contravening the rules of the FSA, they will not be in a position to give you suitable advice.

Checklist of points to consider

- your age
- your health
- your marital status
- number and ages of children and other dependants
- size and make-up of family income
- your tax position
- possible changes in your financial circumstances
- your regular financial commitments
- your investments
- your home and mortgage
- your pension
- existing insurance policies
- how long you want to invest for
- your reasons for investing, e.g. how important it is to you to get a high income or make a capital gain
- whether you want to be able to get your money back quickly
- what degree of risk you're prepared to take with your money
- whether there are any sorts of investments you're not prepared to consider – e.g. investing in weapons manufacturers.

Once you've decided on your investment aims, it should be a little easier to choose a suitable type of adviser – see our guide to advisers for what each type offers. When you've found the adviser you want, check that he or she is authorised. You can do this either by asking the adviser or checking either directly with the FSA* or the appropriate regulating body – see Chapter 5. Make sure you see more than one authorised adviser so that you can compare what they're offering.

It's not only the adviser who should ask questions – *you* should too. It's important you're clear about exactly what kind of adviser you're dealing with. You should find out:

- whether the adviser is independent or tied to selling the products of only one company
- which Self-Regulating Organisation (SRO) or Recognised Professional Body (RPB) he or she is regulated by (see Chapter 5)
- what compensation scheme he or she is covered by
- whether he or she has professional indemnity insurance which will pay out if he or she loses your money through fraud or negligence.

Another important question you should ask is how the adviser will be paid. Some advisers charge fees, usually a percentage of your investment. Others will get commission from the companies with which you invest money. Of this latter group, it's important to bear in mind that while the advice may seem free, there *is* a cost involved. The commission will be deducted from your funds. If you do pay a fee, the adviser may undertake to pass on to you any commission he or she receives. See the following pages for how each type of adviser is paid.

Don't make your final decision until you're satisfied on all these points. Steer clear of advisers who make fantastic claims for what they can do for your money. Investment that supposedly brings high returns is usually fraught with risk or, worse, fraudulent.

Once you've decided on your adviser, make sure you specify exactly what you want him or her to do and get this in writing. Your adviser will, in most cases, have to draw up a *customer agreement* which sets out your investment objectives, the services to be provided, the responsibilities undertaken and the charges being made. Avoid making cheques out in your adviser's name if at all possible – make out your cheque to the company providing the investment. If a firm has *got* to handle your money, check that it's held in a separate client account. And, if an adviser is going to be looking after your money over a long period, make sure that he or she sticks to your customer agreement. Ask how he or she will keep in touch, who will be dealing with you and how often. Expect your investment to be reviewed at least every three months and a report at least once a year.

Guide to advisers

Banks

All the high-street banks offer investment advice. Most advise about their own investment products only, but a few advise about all products on the market. Banks that sell their own products at branch level generally also offer independent advice through a connected company, e.g. a trust company.

■ **What they offer** – varies from bank to bank and within banks themselves, but includes advice on the bank's own products (e.g. insurance and unit trusts), on buying and selling stocks and shares, on tax, on pensions and on portfolio management.

■ **What they charge** – usually nothing if you buy life insurance or unit trusts, as the bank gets commission; normal stockbrokers' commission for buying and selling shares (maybe with an *administration fee* on top); for managing a portfolio, either a flat fee or 0.5 to 1.5 per cent a year of the portfolio's value. There could be an extra fee for tax help.

■ **What to watch out for** – most banks' branches sell only their own products.

■ **Who to complain to** – if you can't get the head office of your bank to deal satisfactorily with your complaint, try the Office of the Banking Ombudsman.* Alternatively contact the FSA for the appropriate SRO – see Chapter 5 for details.

Verdict
Useful if you want advice on or management of smaller sums of money – under £10,000, say. For management of larger amounts you may have to approach a bank's investment company. Alternatively, you could go to a merchant bank, which can offer a more personalised service and usually advises only customers with large sums of money.

Building societies

Building societies can provide a wide range of financial services and products, e.g. share-dealing services in conjunction with stockbrokers.

■ **What they offer** – not all societies offer the full range of financial services the law allows them to provide, but you may be able to get share-dealing or unit trust services (through links with other financial bodies). Some also offer independent advice through a connected company.

■ **What they charge** – normally nothing, because the society gets commission from the company whose product you buy. If you are referred to another adviser, e.g. a stockbroker, you will pay that adviser's charges.

■ **What to watch out for** – at branch level many building societies offer advice only on the products of one company.

They have a vested interest in selling insurance products, e.g. endowment mortgages, because of the commission.
■ **Who to complain to** – if you can't get the society's head office to deal satisfactorily with your complaint, try the Building Societies Ombudsman.* Alternatively, ask the FSA for the relevant regulator.

Verdict
An obvious (though rarely independent) choice for advice on ways of investing to pay off a mortgage. They are worth contacting if you want advice on their own products, e.g. instant access accounts, or if you want to find out about any of the other services or products they may offer.

Independent financial advisers (IFAs)

This term covers a range of advisers, from those who mainly sell life and pensions products, through to those who deal in a wide variety of schemes, but strictly speaking, they should all look at all types of investment when advising you. IFA Promotions* will send a list of six of its members in your area.
■ **What they offer** – includes: general investment advice, advisory or discretionary portfolio management, advice on tax and pensions, life insurance products, shares and unit trusts, and alternative types of investment.
■ **What they charge** – usually nothing if they're just selling a life insurance policy or unit trust, as they get commission. For managing a lump sum, charges can range from 0.5 to 1 per cent a year of the value of your portfolio. Charges may be less for very large amounts. Instead, advisers may charge a flat fee, such as £100 a year or a slice of your profits, or even both. Services like tax help may cost extra. If you'd prefer to pay a fee for advice, the Money Management National Register of Independent Fee-Based Advisers* can provide you with a list of IFAs in your area who charge fees. See 'Addresses' at back of this book.
■ **What to watch out for** – charges for advice can vary widely. If your adviser charges a fee, ask if it will be reduced if commission is paid on any of the investments purchased.
■ **Who to complain to** – if you have problems, get in touch with the appropriate regulating organisation, which is likely to be the PIA or the Investment Management Regulatory Organisation (IMRO)*; if in doubt, check with the FSA. Advisers should have professional indemnity insurance which will pay out if you can prove your money was lost through their negligence or fraud.

Verdict
Worth trying if you want general advice or someone to manage a lump sum for you (say, £10,000 plus). They should be able to advise you on all aspects of your investments.

Insurance brokers

Anyone can call himself or herself an independent insurance *adviser*, but to be a *broker* a person must meet set conditions and register with the Insurance Brokers' Registration Council (IBRC).* Any advisers and brokers dealing with investment-type life insurance must be authorised by an SRO or by the IBRC.

■ **What they offer** – advice on life insurance and pensions, plus general insurance advice (for home, car, etc.) and sometimes tax advice and unit trust advice.

■ **What they charge** – usually nothing, as they earn commission on what they sell.

■ **What to watch out for** – commission rates can vary from product to product and company to company. So ask your adviser what commission he or she will get on each investment recommended and then probe the recommendation. Research done for *Which?* in the past has found that advice from registered brokers was not any better than that from other independent insurance advisers.

■ **Who to complain to** – if more than 49 per cent of a broker's business is involved with investments, the broker must be authorised by an SRO – usually the PIA; for other brokers contact the IBRC; if in doubt, check with the FSA. This has a fund which may pay out if you lose money through a broker's negligence or fraud. Brokers must also have professional indemnity insurance.

Verdict
Worth trying, particularly if you've already decided that you want investment-type life insurance, pensions or unit trusts. Don't always expect general advice on all investments.

Insurance company representatives

Life insurance companies often employ representatives to deal with you in person. Some companies sell their products through their representatives, press advertisements and direct mailing, others sell them only through independent advisers, while some use both methods. Some companies have a policy of passing direct enquiries on to independent financial advisers.

■ **What they offer** – includes: advice on which of their products best suits your needs, advice on tax implications of their products, retirement planning, their company's own unit trusts and general information on the financial markets (e.g. through talks and seminars).

■ **What they charge** – nothing, since most representatives get commission from their company on the products that they sell.

■ **What to watch out for** – in the past, it was not unknown for company representatives to pass themselves off as independent; this is no longer allowed. Do not be pressurised into buying their products if you're not convinced they're right for you. Also, get quotations from more than one company. You're unlikely to save any money dealing directly with a company (rather than through an adviser); commission costs are built into the price of an investment.

■ **Who to complain to** – If an insurance company head office does not deal satisfactorily with a complaint, see if the company belongs to the Insurance Ombudsman Bureau* or the PIA Ombudsman,* if you are in any doubt as to who to go to check with the FSA.

Verdict
Obviously, you will get advice on only one company's products, though their knowledge of these products may be more specialised than other advisers'. But if you know you want to invest with that particular company, and you are sure you cannot get a better deal elsewhere, it's worth trying.

Stockbrokers

These specialise in shares and British Government stocks, but many have widened their services in recent years.

■ **What they offer** – mainly advice on buying and selling shares and British Government stocks, usually unit trusts too; also advisory and discretionary portfolio management (for sums starting at around £15,000, but often much more), unit-trust portfolio management, their own unit trusts and Personal Equity Plans (PEPs), investment research, general investment advice (sometimes through a subsidiary company). A *Private Investors' Directory* is available from the Association of Private Client Investment Managers and Stockbrokers.*

■ **What they charge** – commission for buying and selling shares on your behalf ranges from 1 to 2 per cent of the price of the shares, plus VAT. Most stockbrokers have minimum commissions of around £20 or £25. For portfolio management, there's an annual fee of, say, 1 per cent of the value of the portfolio. You may also be charged a small fee (around £5) to cover the cost of complying with Financial Services Act rules. Others may have increased commission rates to reflect this.

■ **What to watch out for** – charges both for buying and selling shares and for general management of a portfolio vary a lot, so it's worth shopping around. But don't expect a stockbroker to be able to choose shares that consistently do better than average; investing in shares is a risky business – see Chapter 16. Not all stockbrokers are prepared to deal with individuals.

■ **Who to complain to** – the Securities and Futures Authority (SFA).* Some may also belong to the PIA. If you're having problems with an individual unit trust company, you can go to the Insurance Ombudsman Bureau (if the trust company is a member).

Verdict

If you want advice on shares, British Government stocks or unit trusts, a stockbroker may be your best bet. They are worth considering for management of a lump sum, say £10,000 plus, though some stockbrokers manage only very large sums.

Accountants

Generally, these are not investment specialists, but they may offer independent advice, or refer you to a specialist.

■ **What they offer** – varies considerably, but includes general investment advice, tax planning, advice on wills and trusts, sometimes advisory or discretionary portfolio management, contact with specialist advisers, e.g. stockbrokers.

■ **What they charge** – their normal fees, which depend on the time spent and can vary greatly. *Which?* suggests you will typically pay £60–£100 for each hour the adviser works on your case, so shop around. They may get commission if you buy life insurance, unit trusts or shares through them. *Chartered accountants* are supposed to tell you in writing about any commission they expect to receive as a result of your investment. *Certified accountants* are supposed to tell you about any commission and deduct it from their fee.

■ **What to watch out for** – although some accountants may be well qualified to advise you about investments, others may not.

■ **Who to complain to** – the RPB to which the accountant belongs. Check to see if your accountant has professional indemnity insurance; almost all should have this. If a large part of the practice's business comes from advising on or managing investments, it may belong to the PIA or IMRO; if in doubt check with the FSA.

Verdict
Worth trying if you want advice on an overall investment strategy, or you have complex tax affairs and can afford the fees.

Solicitors

Solicitors are not generally investment specialists, but nearly all will give existing clients advice; most will give it to anyone who comes to see them. All solicitors have to give independent advice.

■ **What they offer** – varies considerably, but includes general advice, contacts with specialist advisers (such as stockbrokers), sometimes advisory or discretionary portfolio management, tax planning, advice on wills and trusts.

■ **What they charge** – a fee based on the time spent (rates can vary, so shop around). If commission is received it can be kept only with your permission. In practice, fees are often reduced by the amount of the commission.

■ **What to watch out for** – some may be well qualified to tell you where to put your money, others may not.

■ **Who to complain to** – The RPB, e.g. the Law Society.*
They all have professional indemnity insurance. They may also belong to the PIA if a large part of their business comes from advising on or managing investments.

Verdict
Worth considering for general discussion of investments.

7

TAX

Why bother about tax? Because whatever investment you choose, it is the after-tax return that counts. The impact of different tax rules can play a major part in the return you can expect from different investments. If you are a lower- or basic-rate taxpayer, the tax treatment of many investments these days is effectively the same. But non-taxpayers and higher-rate taxpayers should be especially careful to keep a weather eye on the tax position. And all taxpayers should consider using special schemes, such as TESSAs, PEPs and the new ISAs, which are designed to encourage investment by offering tax incentives – for details of these, see Chapter 8.

EXAMPLE

Dave Comfort pays income tax at the higher rate of 40 per cent. He has a choice between two investments:
- investment A will pay him an income of 10 per cent a year
- investment B will not pay any income, but will, he hopes, show a capital gain of 8 per cent a year.

Both these figures are before tax, and, at first sight, investment A looks more attractive. But let's assume that investment A pays an income of £10,000. The effect of income tax at 40 per cent will be to reduce this sum to £6,000. Investment B on the other hand, producing a gain of £8,000, is liable for capital gains tax (CGT). This tax is also at 40 per cent, but the first slice of total yearly gains (£6,800 in the 1998–9 tax year) is tax-free. So Dave would pay tax at 40 per cent on only £1,200, ending up with an overall return of £7,520 – higher than that from investment A.

Tax can also affect the cost of an investment, particularly where pensions and mortgages are concerned. With personal pension schemes, tax relief can save up to 40 per cent of the cost – see Chapter 15, and most people qualify for tax relief at only 10 per cent on the interest they pay on the first £30,000 of their mortgages – see page 153.

Which taxes?

The most common tax you'll have to pay is income tax on investment income. The other main tax to watch out for is capital gains tax. Inheritance tax does not directly affect the return you get on your investments, but we give the basic rules at the end of this chapter.

Which tax will hurt you most depends very much on your investment choice. You have an annual slice of tax-free capital gains: provided your returns do not exceed this, you will not pay tax at all if you go for investments that produce a capital gain rather than income. If, however, you've used all your tax-free slice for capital gains tax, you'll have to pay tax at the same rate as your top rate of income tax. So you should look for investments offering you the highest rate of return *after* tax, either as income or as capital gain.

Income tax

There are three ways in which investment income can be treated. It can be:
- tax-free
- taxable, but not taxed before you get it
- paid with some tax already deducted.

Income tax is charged on your income for a tax year. Tax years run from 6 April in one year to 5 April the following year. Your tax bill for 1998–9, say, will be based on your income from 6 April 1998 to 5 April 1999. All income whether taxed at source or paid gross is now taxed on a current-year basis, i.e. your tax bill for 1998–9 is based on the income paid (or credited) to you in that year.

From April 1994 all new sources of investment income have been taxed on a current-year basis. Previously, if the income was paid gross (without the deduction of tax) you were taxed on a preceding-year basis, e.g. your tax bill for the 1994–5 tax year was based on the income paid (or credited) to you in the 1993–4 tax year. The 1996–7 tax year was a transitional year where the tax bill was assessed on half the income from 1995–6 and half the income from 1996–7.

How much income tax?

All your income is added together, to arrive at your *gross income*   say £25,000
From this you deduct your *outgoings* (certain payments you make, e.g. expenses paid in connection with your work)
                                                    say £2,000
This leaves what the Inland Revenue calls your *total income*
                                                    £23,000
From this you deduct your *personal allowance* (and blind person's allowance if appropriate)
                                                  say £4,195
This leaves your *taxable income*   £18,805
Tax is charged on your *taxable income.*
Tax bill (say £4,300 at 20% and £14,505 at 23%)   £4,196
From this you deduct your other allowances at 15% (e.g. married person's allowance) say £1,900 at 15%   £285
This leaves a *final tax bill*   £3,911

Rates of income tax for the 1998–9 tax year
The first £4,300 of your taxable income is taxed at the lower rate of 20 per cent: income between £4,301 and £27,100 is taxed at the basic rate of 23 per cent. Anything more is taxed at the higher rate of 40 per cent.

Independent taxation

In the past, a married woman's investment income counted as her husband's for tax purposes, and so was added to his income to work out their joint bill. From 6 April 1990, a married woman's income has been taxed as her own and she has been responsible for paying the tax on it: both husband and wife have their own personal allowance and they also get a married couple's allowance.

Married couples
If you are married and own investments in the joint names of you and your partner, income will automatically be treated as if it is paid to you both in equal shares, with each of you paying tax on half the income.

If you own the investment in unequal shares, the income can be taxed accordingly. You *both* have to make a joint declaration to one of your tax offices setting out how the capital and income are shared between you. To do this you need *Form 17* – you can use one form for more than one investment. The different tax treatment applies from the date that the declaration is made. You cannot *choose* the proportions in which the income from joint investments will be taxed. You can make a declaration to be taxed only according to your real shares in the capital and income.

As married men and women now have the same personal allowance and lower- and basic-rate tax bands, it may be worth transferring some investments currently from one to the other so that the income is more evenly distributed. Bear in mind that, to be effective for tax purposes, such gifts have to be outright, i.e. without strings attached. Note that there is no capital gains tax on any gifts or sales of assets between husband and wife.

From April 1995 the married couple's allowance is restricted to relief at 15 per cent. From 6 April 1993, married couples have been able to choose how to split the married couple's allowance, by completing *Form 18* (from their tax office) and returning it before the start of the tax year. This means that if a wife has a lot of income-producing investments in her name, say, and her husband has little or no taxable income of his own, the couple's overall tax bill can be reduced if the wife takes advantage of the rules which allow her to claim half or all of the married couple's allowance. Before 1993, to achieve the same effect they would have had to transfer ownership of some of her investments to the husband.

Tax-free investment income

■ proceeds from Save-As-You-Earn linked to an approved employee share option scheme
■ proceeds from National Savings Certificates (and, in most cases, Ulster Savings Certificates if you live in Northern Ireland)
■ proceeds from a National Savings Yearly Plan
■ proceeds from National Savings Children's Bonus Bonds
■ some friendly society savings plans
■ proceeds from a qualifying life insurance policy – see 'Income tax and life insurance', on page 100
■ premium bond and lottery prizes
■ interest on tax rebates
■ first £70 interest each year from a National Savings Ordinary account
■ interest on Tax-Exempt Special Savings Accounts (TESSAs) – see Chapter 8
■ interest received in connection with delayed settlement of damages for personal injury or death

- part of the income from many annuities
- income from a family income benefit life insurance policy
- income from share dividends or unit trust distributions in a qualifying Personal Equity Plan (PEP) – see Chapter 8
- from 6 April 1999, income from investments held in an Individual Savings Account (ISA) – see Chapter 8

Investment income taxable but not taxed before you get it

Interest from the investments listed below comes into this category:

- National Savings accounts and National Savings Income and Capital Bonds
- British Government stocks unless you choose to be paid with tax deducted – see page 99
- interest on loans you make to private individuals
- deposits at non-UK branches of building societies and UK or overseas banks
- deposits made by people not ordinarily resident in the UK
- co-operative society deposits
- credit union dividends.

How it is taxed
The interest is paid gross, and you have to account to the Inland Revenue separately for any tax you owe.

Any income received on or after 6 April 1994 will be taxed on a current-year basis, i.e. your tax bill for the 1998–9 year is based on the income paid (or credited) to you in that year.

Where the tax you owe is no more than £1,000 and you pay tax on other income – either earnings or a pension – through Pay-As-You-Earn (PAYE), tax on your investment income can also be collected through PAYE. In other cases, tax will be collected through the self-assessment system: you make two equal payments on account on 31 January during the tax year and 31 July following the tax year – these are based on your tax bill for the previous year – plus a balancing payment or refund on 31 January following the tax year to clear the account. For example, suppose your tax bill for 1997–8 was £5,000 and, in 1998–9 tax due on your income – including investment income – turns out to be £4,500. For 1998–9, you make two payments on account each of £2,500 (i.e. half your tax bill for the previous year) on 31 January 1999 and 31 July 1999. This means that you have paid £5,000 in total which is more than the eventual bill of £4,500, so on 31 January 2000 you get a refund of £500.

Investment income paid with tax deducted

Examples of income with some tax already deducted are:
- proceeds from National Savings FIRST Option Bonds
- most interest from banks, building societies and other authorised institutions, e.g. finance companies
- interest from foreign-currency deposits made at UK banks
- interest on most local authority loans issued after 18 November 1984
- interest on certain loans, e.g. loans to foreign governments
- interest on certain British Government stocks – see page 99
- interest on company fixed-income investments (loan stocks or debentures)
- part of the income from annuities
- income from certain income and growth bonds
- income from certain trusts and settlements
- income from a will, paid out to you during the administration period (i.e. while the details of who gets what under the will are being worked out)
- dividends from shares, distributions from unit trusts and similar investments.

How it is taxed
This type of income is taxed on a current-year basis, i.e. your tax bill for the 1998–9 tax year is based on the income paid (or credited) to you in that tax year.

With most of these investments, tax has already been deducted at the savings rate (20 per cent in 1998–9) before you receive the income. If you are a lower- or basic-rate taxpayer, this is the total tax due and there is no more tax to pay. If you are a non-taxpayer, you can reclaim the tax already deducted or, in most cases, arrange for the income to be paid to you without tax deducted – see below. Higher-rate taxpayers have extra tax to pay – see Example opposite. Extra tax due is collected either through PAYE or the self-assessment system as described on page 95.

You get a statement or tax voucher from the investment provider showing the amount of tax which has been deducted. Do not send these to your tax office, but keep them safely in case the tax office asks to see them.

If you are certain that you will be a non-taxpayer for the year, you can arrange to have interest from bank and building society accounts and some other investments paid to you without any tax deducted. To do this, complete *Form RG85* available from banks, building societies, post offices and tax offices.

With some of the investments listed above (e.g. income from some trusts and settlements), tax will have been deducted, not at the savings rate, but at some other rate. In general, if your personal tax rate is lower, you can reclaim some or all of the tax.

From 6 April 1999, the way in which income from shares, unit trusts and other investments is taxed is being changed, see page 98.

EXAMPLE

George Streatley is a higher-rate taxpayer. He got £440 in building society interest in the 1998–9 tax year. He divides £440 by 0.80 to find the grossed-up amount, £550. He's liable for tax at 40 per cent on £550, i.e. £220. However, he's treated as having already paid tax on this interest at the 20 per cent lower-rate (i.e. £110 in tax). So he has to hand over an extra £220 – £110 = £110.

Points to watch

Annuities
If you have bought an annuity voluntarily with your own money (not, for example, as part of a personal pension), part of the income each year is treated as a return of capital, part as interest on the capital. Only the interest part is taxable; the insurance company will say how much this is. Non-taxpayers may be able to have the income paid out before tax; again, ask the insurance company.

Discretionary trusts
For the 1998–9 tax year, discretionary trusts pay tax at 34 per cent on most of their income. This applies whether the income is kept by the trust or paid out to you. If it is paid out to you, you get a credit of 34 per cent of the gross (before-tax) amount. If your income, including the income from the trust, is too low for you to pay tax, or you pay tax at a lower rate, you can claim back some or all of the tax deducted (but higher-rate taxpayers will have some more tax to pay).

Income and growth bonds

There are several different types of bond, which work (and are taxed) in different ways – see Chapter 20.

Unit trusts

With the first distribution you get from a unit trust, you're likely to get an *equalisation payment*. This is a return of part of the money you first invested, so it does not count as income and is not taxable. But see 'Capital gains tax', on page 103, for how it affects any capital gains you make.

With an accumulation unit trust (where income is automatically reinvested for you) the amount reinvested, apart from any equalisation payment, counts as income and is taxable at 20 per cent in 1998–9.

Shares, unit trusts etc

From 6 April 1999 onwards, the rate of tax already deducted from income from shares, unit trusts and similar investments will fall from 20 per cent to 10 per cent. Lower- and basic-rate taxpayers will have no further tax to pay. However, unlike the current treatment of this type of income, non-taxpayers will no longer be able to reclaim the tax deducted. Higher-rate taxpayers will have extra tax to pay but at a new rate of 32.5 per cent. This rate maintains higher-rate taxpayers' after-tax income from these types of investment at the same level as now – see Example below.

EXAMPLE

Maria Harvey is a higher-rate taxpayer. In 1998–9 she receives dividends from shares amounting to £720. Tax at 20 per cent (£180) has already been deducted from this income but she has further tax to pay. In 1999–2000, she once again received £720 income from her shares. The tax position for each year is set out below:

	1998–9	1999–2000
Dividends received	£720	£720
Tax already deducted	£180 (20%)	£80 (10%)
Before-tax dividend	£900	£800
Higher-rate tax	£360 (40%)	£260 (32.5%)
less tax already paid	£180	£80
Extra tax to pay	£180	£180
After-tax dividend	£540	£540

PEPs

Cash may be deposited in a PEP – see Chapter 8 – for the purpose of buying investments. The interest is paid gross if it is reinvested in the plan or if the total amount withdrawn in any tax year is less than £180. But interest withdrawn of more than £180 a year is taxable and you will need to declare it on your tax return.

National Savings Capital Bonds

Although interest is credited to your Capital Bond each year, you don't receive it until you have held the bond for a full five years (or you cash in early). However, you still have to declare the interest and pay tax on it each year. You will receive a notice of interest credited each year from National Savings.

National Savings Ordinary accounts

You and your spouse are each allowed £70 interest free of tax from a National Savings Ordinary account. But you are taxed on anything more.

Any one person is allowed only £70 free of tax, however many accounts he or she has. So, if you have, say, £100 interest and your spouse has £20, *you* will have to pay tax on £30 of your interest, even though the combined interest isn't more than 2 × £70 = £140. If you have a joint account, however, you can have £140 interest between you free of tax.

British Government (and some other) stocks

British Government stocks are listed on one of two separate registers. Up to 5 April 1998, when you bought stocks listed on the Bank of England Register, interest was paid to you after deduction of tax at the savings rate. Stocks bought through the National Savings Stock Register (NSSR) paid gross interest – i.e. without any tax deducted.

For stocks on both registers which are bought on or after 6 April 1998, interest is paid without tax deducted. However, for Bank of England registered stocks, you can, on request, have interest paid net of tax at the savings rate.

Where you were already holding stocks on 6 April 1998 and had been receiving interest after deduction of tax, for convenience this will continue to be the case unless you opt to receive gross interest.

If you sell British Government stocks before a date when you're due to receive an interest payment (normally twice yearly), part of the price you get is deemed to be the interest you would otherwise have received. It is calculated on a daily basis and taxed as income. This is known as the *accrued income scheme*, and also applies to building society Permanent Interest-Bearing Shares (PIBS) and to sales of local authority and company loan stocks. When you buy the stock, any accrued interest included in the price can be offset against the dividend that will be paid, so you won't have to pay tax twice on the same income. Provided your holdings of all stocks covered by the scheme remain below £5,000 *nominal* or face value in total, the above rule will not apply. In this case, any accrued income included in the price of stock you sell will be considered to be part of the capital value and will not be taxable as income. See Chapter 19 for how to work out your accrued income.

Income tax and life insurance

There are two main types of life insurance policy for tax purposes. These are:
- qualifying policies – including most regular-premium policies, e.g. most endowment policies and low-cost endowment policies linked to mortgages
- non-qualifying policies – e.g. single-premium policies.

The insurance companies' investment funds are taxed, but you don't have to pay basic-rate income tax on policy proceeds yourself (and as the proceeds always count as income, there's no capital gains tax to pay). From 6 April 1999 onwards, you will be able to invest in life insurance through an ISA, in which case there will be no tax on the insurance companies' investment funds and no tax for you to pay – see page 123.

When you do have to pay tax
You have to pay tax only if you're a higher-rate taxpayer (or would be once the gain from the policy is added to your income) and:
- *either* the policy is a non-qualifying policy
- *or* the policy is a qualifying policy but you cashed it in or made it paid up in its first ten years (or the first three-quarters of its term, if less).

So you may need to work out your *taxable gain*. This is the amount you get when a policy comes to an end (plus any amounts you've had from the policy in the past), less the total premiums paid (including any subsidy you got on the premiums).

If you cash in only part of a policy before it matures, you get an allowance for each 12-month period since you first took out the policy. If you've received more from the policy than the amount of your allowances, the excess counts as your gain. For the first 20 years of the policy, the allowance is 5 per cent of the total premiums paid so far. For each year after that, the allowance is 5 per cent of the total premiums paid in that year and in the previous 19 years.

This means that you can take a yearly income from non-qualifying policies up to the yearly allowance without paying any tax until you finally cash in the policy. Any income above the yearly allowance is free of basic-rate tax, but if you are a higher-rate taxpayer you will have to pay tax at the higher rate for the year in which you take the income. If you don't use the full 5 per cent allowed in any tax year, you can use it in future years.

Should a taxable gain arise because the person insured dies, you work out the gain by taking the cash-in value of the policy just before death, and deducting the total of premiums paid.

How the gain is taxed

Any gain is added to your income for the tax year in which the policy matures or is cashed in. There's no basic-rate tax to pay on the gain, only any higher-rate tax. So if you are liable to tax at the higher rate of 40 per cent, you'll pay tax at $40 - 23 = 17$ per cent.

If adding the gain to your income means that part of your income is pushed from the basic to the higher tax bracket,

---

EXAMPLE: HOW TOP-SLICING RELIEF CAN SAVE TAX

Arnold Archer bought a £25,000 single-premium bond in December 1992, and cashed it in for £37,000 in July 1998, making a gain of £12,000. He already has taxable income for 1998–9 (after deducting his allowances and outgoings) of £24,300. If his taxable income exceeds £27,100 (in the 1998–9 tax year) he would become liable to higher-rate tax.

Arnold realises he can claim top-slicing relief. With this, the average yearly gain of £2,400 (the £12,000 total gain divided by the five complete years the bond ran for) is added to his other income for the year. His total tax bill on the gain is the tax on the average yearly gain multiplied by the number of complete years for which he held the bond. Top-slicing relief means that Arnold doesn't have to pay any tax on the gain and so saves £1,564 – see the table overleaf. The existence of the lower-rate tax band has no effect on the calculation. If Arnold had a higher income and the calculation showed he had higher-rate tax to pay on the gain of, say, £60, then the total tax bill would then have been £60 × 5 = £300.

Without top-slicing relief

Rate of tax %	Income on which you pay this rate £	Tax on income £	Gain on bond £	Tax on gain £
20 (first £4,300)	4,300	860		
23 (£4,301 to £27,100)	20,000	4,600	2,800	644
40	nil	nil	9,200	3,680
total gain			12,000	
basic- and higher-rate tax on gain				4,324
subtract tax at basic rate on gain (23% of £12,000)				2,760
higher-rate tax bill on gain				1,564

With top-slicing relief

Rate of tax %	Income on which you pay this rate £	Tax on income £	Gain on bond £	Tax on gain £
20 (first £4,300)	4,300	860		
23 (£4,301 to £27,100)	20,000	4,600	2,400	552
40	nil	nil	nil	nil
subtract tax at basic rate on average yearly gain (23% of £2,400)				552
so tax bill on average yearly gain is				nil
higher-rate tax bill on gain (nil x 5)				nil

you should claim *top-slicing relief*. This spreads the gain over the years that the policy has run. Your tax bill is based on the average gain for each complete year that the policy has run, multiplied by the number of years. If the average gain added to your other taxable income does not take you into the higher tax bracket, there's no further tax to pay (but see page 51 for a possible complication if you are aged 65 or over).

Tax relief on your premiums
Premiums on qualifying policies taken out before 14 March 1984 get a subsidy of 12.5 per cent from the Revenue, irrespective of whether you pay tax or not.

You'll continue to get the subsidy unless you alter the policy in a way which increases the benefits payable. That could include taking up an option attached to the policy, e.g. to increase your premiums and therefore your amount of cover, to extend the term, or to convert the policy into another kind of policy. You won't lose the subsidy if the increased benefits are due to an increase that's built in, e.g. if premiums and cover automatically increase by a fixed percentage. But there's a limit on premiums of £1,500 or one-sixth of your total income, whichever is greater, and if you pay premiums of more than this you won't get the subsidy on the excess.

Capital gains tax

You can make a capital gain (or loss) whenever you stop owning something, no matter how you came to own it. However, you won't always be taxed on gains when you dispose of an asset. Anything you own (whether in the UK or not) counts as an asset, e.g. houses, jewellery and shares.

You dispose of an asset not only if you sell it, but also if you give it away, exchange it or lose it. You also dispose of an asset if it is destroyed or becomes worthless, if you sell rights to it (e.g. grant a lease), or if you get compensation for damage to it (e.g. insurance money) and don't spend it all on restoring the damage. But a transfer of an asset between a husband and wife doesn't count as a disposal (unless they are separated), nor does the transfer of an asset you leave when you die. Some types of gain are tax-free altogether (see page 106) and the first slice of total chargeable gains made in the tax year is also tax-free. In the 1998–9 tax year, your tax-free slice is £6,800.

Working out the gain

To work out the basic gain (or loss) you make when you dispose of an asset, you have to:
■ take the *final value* of the asset when you dispose of it – its sale price (or market value at the time, if you gave it away or sold it for less than its full worth)
■ deduct its *initial value* when you got it – the price paid (or the market value at the time if you were given or inherited it). For assets acquired before 31 March 1982, you have a choice of initial value – see page 112.
■ deduct any *allowable expenses* you incurred in acquiring, improving or disposing of the asset, such as the costs of advertising, commission, legal fees and stamp duty.

If the answer is zero or a negative figure, there is no gain and no tax to pay. You may, however, be able to set losses against gains on other assets – see page 105. If the answer is a positive figure, you have made a gain, but there are various adjustments you can make before deciding whether or not the gain is taxable.

If you started to own the asset on or after 1 April 1998, you might be eligible for *taper relief* when you come to dispose of it. Your gain is reduced by a given percentage which increases the longer you hold the asset – see table below. The maximum reduction is given on assets you have held for at least ten years. (There is a higher rate of taper relief on assets – which can include shares in a family company – which have been used for business purposes.)

Where you first acquired the asset before 1 April 1998, you may be able to claim *indexation allowance*. This strips out any gain in value due simply to rising prices up to April 1998 by increasing the amount of the initial value and each allowable expense in line with changes in the Retail Prices Index. See page 108 for how to calculate this allowance.

Where, after 5 April 1998, you sell or dispose of an asset which you started to own before 1 April 1998, you can claim indexation allowance for the period up to April 1998. For the period of ownership from April 1998 up to the date

Capital gains tax taper relief

Number of complete tax years after 5 April 1998 for which asset held	Taper relief	Percentage of gain which is taxable	Example: amount of £1,000 gain which remains chargeable after taper relief
0	0%	100%	£1,000
1	0%	100%	£1,000
2	0%	100%	£1,000
3	5%	95%	£950
4	10%	90%	£900
5	15%	85%	£850
6	20%	80%	£800
7	25%	75%	£750
8	30%	70%	£700
9	35%	65%	£650
10 or more	40%	60%	£600

EXAMPLE

Maxine Miller inherited units in a unit trust when her aunt died in June 1990. At that time the units were valued at £1,500. In July 2000, she sells the units for £5,800. To see if she has any tax to pay, she does the following sum:

Final value	£5,800
less Initial value	£1,500
less Allowable expenses	£ 0
Basic gain	£4,300
less Indexation allowance for period June 1990 to April 1998	£ 425
Indexed gain	£3,875
Loss on another asset	£ 383
Gain before taper relief	£3,492
Number of complete tax years after 5 April 1998 for which units held	2
plus one year because units held on 17 March 1998	3
Taper relief (see Table)	5%
Chargeable gain (95% x £3,492)	£3,317

The chargeable gain falls well within Maxine's tax-free slice for the year and so she has no tax to pay.

of disposal you may qualify for taper relief which reduces the gain after indexation allowance has been deducted. As a concession, where you held the asset on Budget Day, 17 March 1998, you are treated as having held the asset for an extra year.

Where you have made a loss on an asset, you can set the loss against gains made on other assets in the same tax year. You do this after deducting indexation allowance but before calculating taper relief. Bear in mind that the first slice of your gains (£6,800 in 1998–9) each year is tax-free. Do not waste losses by reducing your chargeable gains below the tax-free slice. Any losses you cannot offset in the tax year can be carried forward to set against chargeable gains made in a future year. Losses brought forward from an earlier year are also subtracted after indexation allowance but before calculating taper relief.

How much tax?

Capital gains tax is charged at the same rate you'd pay if your gain was your top slice of income. So if you pay only lower-rate tax you'll pay capital gains tax at 20 per cent, if you pay basic-rate tax you'll pay capital gains tax at 23 per cent, and if you pay higher-rate tax you'll pay tax at 40 per cent (1998–9 tax rates). If you're in the 20 or 23 per cent tax bands, but your net taxable capital gains plus your taxable income come to more than the amount of that tax band, you pay tax on the excess at 23 or 40 per cent, whichever is the next rate up. Suppose you had net taxable gains of £10,000 and taxable income of £20,000, i.e. £30,000. You would pay lower-rate tax of 20 per cent on the first £4,300 of your taxable income, basic rate of 23 per cent on the next £22,800 of taxable income and chargeable capital gain and 40 per cent on the remaining £2,900 of chargeable capital gain.

Declare any taxable gains on your tax return. If you do not receive a tax return you must tell the Revenue about any taxable gains you have made in the 1998–9 tax year by 5 October 1999. Any tax due has to be paid on 31 January after the end of the tax year in which the gains were made (31 January 2000).

Tax-free gains

The gains you make on some assets are tax-free, but any losses you make on them cannot be used to offset chargeable gains. The main tax-free gains are those on:
■ your own home – see Chapter 10
■ private cars
■ British money (including post-1837 gold sovereigns and Britannia gold coins)
■ foreign currency for personal and family expenditure (e.g. for a holiday abroad)
■ British Government stocks
■ National Savings Certificates, Save-As-You-Earn, National Savings Yearly Plan, Premium Bonds, Capital Bonds, Children's Bonus Bonds and FIRST Option Bonds
■ personal belongings (chattels) with a predictable life of less than 50 years when you got them (e.g. electronic

equipment, machinery, but also some investments such as racehorses)
■ personal belongings expected to last more than 50 years (e.g. antiques, jewellery and other moveable items) provided their value when you dispose of them is £6,000, or less. If their value is higher, your gain is taken to be the lower of *either* the actual gain *or* the final value, minus £6,000 multiplied by five-thirds. But if you dispose of something for less than £6,000 and make a loss, your loss is worked out as if you had actually got £6,000 for the item
■ gifts to charities
■ gifts to some *national heritage bodies* (e.g. some museums and the National Trust)
■ proceeds from life insurance policies, unless you bought the policy from a previous holder
■ *qualifying* corporate bonds – those quoted on the Stock Exchange or traded in the Unlisted Securities Market, and acquired after 13 March 1984 (including building society Permanent interest-bearing shares (PIBS)
■ shares issued after 18 March 1986 under the Business Expansion Scheme sold more than five years after you bought them (on their first disposal only)
■ shares in qualifying venture capital trusts
■ shares issued under the Enterprise Investment Scheme
■ disposals made after 1 July 1986 of futures and options in British Government stocks and qualifying corporate bonds. This does not apply to disposals of commodity futures, financial futures and traded options
■ shares, unit trusts and investment trusts held in a PEP or, from 6 April 1999, in an ISA
■ damages for any wrong or injury suffered by you in your private or professional life (e.g. damages for assault or defamation)
■ betting and Lottery winnings.

Route map: how much capital gains tax?

The route map on page 110 takes you through the steps involved in working out your capital gains tax (CGT). It's illustrated with an example, showing how much tax Matthew Parsons had to pay when he sold his holiday cottage (Matthew's main home is exempt from capital gains tax, so there'll be no tax to pay when he sells that).

He bought his cottage in April 1985 for £20,000, and sold it at the end of August 1998 for £55,000. He had buying costs of £700, spent £2,500 installing central heating in June 1986, and had selling costs of £1,200 – costs of £4,400 in all.

Matthew has made no other disposals for CGT purposes, except for an unlucky share investment in 1998, when he made an allowable loss of £2,870.70. His taxable income is £30,000 so he is a higher-rate taxpayer.

Indexation

Indexation allows for inflation by linking the values of your assets and expenses to changes in the RPI. It is worked out from the date you acquired the asset or incurred the expense until April 1998 or the date you dispose of it if this was earlier (but see below for assets owned on or before 31 March 1982). So if you incurred an expense in a different month from acquiring the asset, you need to work out the indexation allowance for that expense separately. For assets sold on or after 30 November 1993 the indexation allowance cannot be used to create or increase a capital loss. From April 1998 onwards, indexation allowance ceases and is replaced by taper relief – see page 104.

To work out your indexation allowance you first need to find out the RPI for:
- A – April 1998 (or the month of disposal if earlier)
- B – the month in which you acquired the asset, or incurred the expense (or March 1982 if later).

See the box opposite for a list of RPI figures since March 1982.

The calculation is as follows: take the RPI for the month of the disposal if earlier and subtract the RPI for April 1998 or the month when indexation begins. You then divide the result by the RPI for the month when indexation begins, and work out this figure (called the *indexation factor*) and round to the nearest third decimal place. Or:

$$\frac{A - B}{B} = \text{indexation factor}$$

The indexation factor, multiplied by the initial value of the asset, or your allowable expense, gives you your indexation allowance.

So before Matthew starts the route map he gathers together the RPI figures he needs:
- A – RPI for April 1998. This figure was 162.6.
- B – RPI for month of indexation; April 1985 for the house and costs of buying it (94.78), June 1986 for the cost of installing central heating (97.79).

Retail Prices Index

Use these figures for working out your capital gains tax bill. The RPI was rebased (i.e. went back to 100) in January 1987. We've reworked the figures for previous months so that they are comparable with the rebased figures.

	Jan	Feb	Mar	Apr	May	Jun	Jul	Aug	Sept	Oct	Nov	Dec
1982	[1]	[1]	79.44	81.04	81.62	81.85	81.88	81.90	81.85	82.26	82.66	82.51
1983	82.61	82.97	83.12	84.28	86.64	84.84	85.30	85.68	86.06	86.36	86.67	86.89
1984	86.84	87.20	87.48	88.64	88.97	89.20	89.10	89.94	90.11	90.67	90.95	90.87
1985	91.20	91.94	92.80	94.78	95.21	95.41	95.23	94.49	95.44	95.59	95.92	96.05
1986	96.25	96.60	96.73	97.67	97.85	97.79	97.52	92.82	96.30	98.45	99.29	99.62
1987	100.0	100.4	100.6	101.8	101.9	101.9	101.8	102.1	102.4	102.9	103.4	103.3
1988	103.3	103.7	104.1	105.8	106.2	106.6	106.7	107.9	108.4	109.5	110.0	110.3
1989	111.0	111.8	112.3	114.3	115.0	115.4	115.5	115.8	116.6	117.5	118.5	118.8
1990	119.5	120.2	121.4	125.1	126.2	126.7	126.8	128.1	129.3	130.3	130.0	129.9
1991	130.2	130.9	131.4	133.1	133.5	134.1	133.8	134.1	134.6	135.1	135.6	135.7
1992	135.6	136.3	136.7	138.8	139.3	139.3	138.8	138.9	139.4	139.9	139.7	139.2
1993	137.9	138.8	139.3	140.6	141.1	141.0	140.7	141.3	141.9	141.8	141.6	141.9
1994	141.3	142.1	142.5	144.2	144.7	144.7	144.0	144.7	145.0	145.2	145.3	146.0
1995	146.0	146.9	147.5	149.0	149.6	149.8	149.1	149.9	150.6	149.8	149.8	150.7
1996	150.2	150.9	151.5	152.6	152.9	153.0	152.4	153.1	153.8	153.8	153.9	154.4
1997	154.4	155.0	155.4	156.3	156.9	157.5	157.5	158.5	159.3	159.5	159.6	160.0
1998	159.5	160.3	160.8	162.6	[1]	[1]	[1]	[1]	[1]	[1]	[1]	[1]

[1] Indexation allowance only runs from March 1982 to April 1998

Will you have to pay capital gains tax?

Have you made a gain?   **Matthew's calculations**

Write down the final value of the asset. Then deduct from this the initial value and any allowable expenses	Final value	£55,000
	Less:	
	Initial value	20,700
	Expenses	2,500
		1,200
		£30,600

Is the answer a plus figure?

NO   **YES**

This is your loss, go to ●	This is your gain before indexation	Gain before indexation	£30,600

Work out your indexation allowance. If you incurred expenses at the same time as acquiring the asset, add them together and work out the indexation allowance as one figure. Expenses incurred after acquisition will have to be worked out separately

First find the figure to index-link (Matthew starts with the purchase price plus costs of buying the house). Find the RPI for April 1998 or the month of disposal (A) and the RPI for the month in which indexation begins (B). Subtract B from A, and divide the answer by B. Round your answer to three decimal places. This gives your indexation factor. Multiply the initial value by the indexation factor	Figure to index-link: £20,700 A = 162.6 B = 94.78 Indexation factor is: $\frac{162.6 - 94.78}{94.78} = 0.716$ (rounded) Indexation allowance is: £20,700 x 0.716 = £14,822

Did you incur any expenses in a different month from the acquisition?

NO   **YES**

Work out indexation allowance for each expense (Matthew does this for his central heating installation costs)	Figure to index-link: £2,500 A = 162.6 B = 97.79 Indexation factor is: $\frac{162.6 - 97.79}{97.79} = 0.663$ (rounded) Indexation allowance is: £2,500 x 0.663 = £1,658

Work out your gain (or loss) after indexation

Write down your gain before indexation. Subtract your total indexation allowances		£30,600
	Less:	£14,822
		£1,658
	Gain after indexation	£14,120

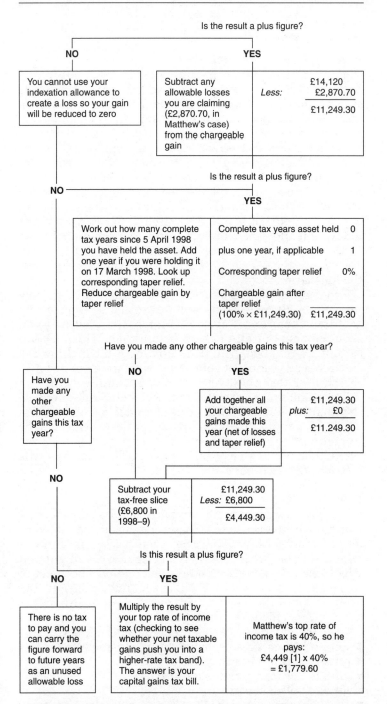

Is the result a plus figure?

NO

You cannot use your indexation allowance to create a loss so your gain will be reduced to zero

YES

Subtract any allowable losses you are claiming (£2,870.70, in Matthew's case) from the chargeable gain

Less:	£14,120
	£2,870.70
	£11,249.30

Is the result a plus figure?

NO

YES

Work out how many complete tax years since 5 April 1998 you have held the asset. Add one year if you were holding it on 17 March 1998. Look up corresponding taper relief. Reduce chargeable gain by taper relief

Complete tax years asset held	0
plus one year, if applicable	1
Corresponding taper relief	0%
Chargeable gain after taper relief (100% × £11,249.30)	£11,249.30

Have you made any other chargeable gains this tax year?

NO

YES

Have you made any other chargeable gains this tax year?

Add together all your chargeable gains made this year (net of losses and taper relief)

	£11,249.30
plus:	£0
	£11,249.30

NO

Subtract your tax-free slice (£6,800 in 1998–9)

	£11,249.30
Less: £6,800
	£4,449.30

Is this result a plus figure?

NO

There is no tax to pay and you can carry the figure forward to future years as an unused allowable loss

YES

Multiply the result by your top rate of income tax (checking to see whether your net taxable gains push you into a higher-rate tax band). The answer is your capital gains tax bill.

Matthew's top rate of income tax is 40%, so he pays:
£4,449 [1] x 40%
= £1,779.60

[1] You are taxed on the whole pounds only – Matthew would be taxed on the extra 30p only if another 'whole pound' were made when the gain is added to his taxable income.

Points to watch

Assets owned on 31 March 1982

Capital gains tax first came into force in 1965, but from 6 April 1988 the law was changed so that only gains made after 31 March 1982 are now taxable. This means that if you dispose of an asset you already owned on 31 March 1982, you can choose whether you want to be taxed under:

■ the new rules: you use the market value in March 1982 as the initial value, ignoring the asset's value when you got it. But you cannot deduct expenses incurred before 31 March 1982

■ the old rules: you generally use the market value of the asset when you got it as the initial value and you can deduct expenses incurred before 31 March 1982. However, the indexation allowance for both initial value and pre-March 1982 expenses still runs only from 31 March 1982, so you always use the March 1982 RPI figure when working out the indexation factor.

You can elect for all your assets to come under the new rules – i.e. all your assets will be treated as though you acquired them on or after 31 March 1982, even if you acquired some or all of them before then. This election cannot be revoked. You'll be no worse off making the election if all or most of your assets were worth more on 31 March 1982 than they were when you acquired them.

If you don't make the election, whichever rules produce the smaller gain or loss will be used. And if you make a gain under one set of rules, but a loss under the other, it will be treated as though you made neither a gain nor a loss. There'll be no tax to pay, but you won't be able to use the losses to reduce other gains.

Gifts

If you give an asset away, or part with it for less than its true worth, your gain is worked out as though you had sold it for its full market value. However, there's a special form of relief available when you make certain types of gifts on which the tax is due, called *hold-over relief*. The effect of this relief is to avoid a CGT bill at the time of the gift. Tax is put off until the recipient parts with the gift, although it could mean a higher tax bill then.

Gifts on which you can claim hold-over relief are:

■ gifts of business assets including certain unquoted shares
■ gifts of heritage property
■ gifts to heritage maintenance funds
■ gifts to political parties
■ lifetime gifts on which you'd have to pay inheritance tax.

As the recipient, you will be counted as acquiring the asset at its market value when the giver first acquired it. You can count as your own the giver's allowable expenses, and benefit from the indexation rules up to the time of the gift, as well as any indexation allowance due from the time you receive the gift.

Both you and the giver must apply jointly for hold-over relief by contacting the Revenue. There's no point in claiming this relief if the giver's gains for the year (including the gain on the gift) won't exceed the tax-free slice (£6,800 in 1998–9). The giver won't save tax, and the recipient might pay more.

Shares and unit trusts

If you own one lot of the same type of shares in one company (or units in a unit trust), and you acquired them all at the same time, they are treated in the same way for CGT purposes as any other asset. However, if you bought shares or units of the same type, in one company, at different times, the Revenue has special rules for deciding which ones you've sold when you come to sell them. These special rules, which were altered for disposals on or after 6 April 1998, decide which shares you've disposed of, how much they cost you, and what your indexation allowance is – see Inland Revenue leaflet *CGT13*, available from local tax offices and Tax Enquiry Centres. But the rules are very complicated and you may need to get professional advice to sort matters out.

You may get an *equalisation payment* from a unit trust. The payment is not taxable, but it must be subtracted from the purchase price of the units when working out your capital gain or loss. So if you bought some unit trusts for £1,000, and received an equalisation payment of £5, the purchase price of the units for tax purposes is £1,000 – £5 = £995.

With an *accumulation* unit trust, the income for your units is automatically reinvested for you. This affects the purchase price of your units for CGT purposes. Working out the purchase price is complicated, and depends on exactly how the income is reinvested. Check with the unit trust company.

How to reduce your CGT bill

■ Be sure to deduct from a gain, or add to a loss, all your allowable expenses.
■ If you have things which have increased in value and on which you will have to pay capital gains tax when you sell them, you'll avoid tax if you can keep the gains you make

each year below £6,800 in 1998–9. It's worth making use of this tax-free slice each year if you can – it cannot be carried forward to the next year.
■ If your losses for the year add up to more than your gains, you can carry forward the balance of the losses to set against gains you would have to pay tax on in later years. So keep a careful record of your losses.
■ Husband and wife each have their own tax-free band (£6,800 in 1998–9). You may be able to save tax by giving assets to your spouse to dispose of, so that they use their tax-free slice or previous losses – but it must be a real gift, with no strings attached.

Reinvestment relief

From November 1993 to 5 April 1998, a chargeable gain made from the sale of shares or other assets could be deferred if the gain was reinvested in a qualifying unquoted UK trading company – including companies listed on the Alternative Investment Market (AIM). For gains made from 6 April 1998 onwards, reinvestment relief in this form has been abolished. To qualify for the relief, reinvestment had to take place between one year before and up to three years after making the gain, so there is still scope to claim the relief in respect of gains made before 6 April 1998.

From 6 April 1998 onwards, reinvestment relief has been amalgamated into the EIS (see page 125). You can defer gains as before but only if reinvested in shares which qualify under the EIS rules. However, you can still get reinvestment relief even if your investment overall does not qualify for the EIS income tax relief.

A major difference between the old and new systems is that, up to 5 April 1998, the purchase of any shares in qualifying companies could be eligible for reinvestment relief. Provided the March 1998 Budget changes pass into law, from 6 April 1998, only newly issued shares will qualify.

Inheritance tax

Roughly speaking, inheritance tax is a tax on the value of what you leave when you die, and on some gifts you make during your lifetime. So it's not a tax that affects investments very much. Here we give a brief outline of the rules, and then look at life insurance policies, where a little care can keep inheritance tax at bay.

When does inheritance tax have to be paid?

There may be inheritance tax to pay:
- if you die within seven years of making certain gifts, known as *potentially exempt transfers (PETs)*. These include gifts to people other than your spouse (e.g. gifts from parents to children), and some gifts to trusts
- if you make a *chargeable* transfer. These are any gifts which are neither tax-free nor counted as PETs, and include gifts to companies and gifts to discretionary trusts
- if you die, and the value of all your possessions plus any PETs and chargeable transfers you've made in the seven years before death is more than a set amount – £223,000 in the 1998–9 tax year.

However, some gifts are tax-free (see below) and ignored by the Revenue. For example, gifts between a husband and wife are normally tax-free, no matter when they're made. So if you die worth £300,000, and leave the lot to your spouse, the value of your estate, for inheritance tax purposes, is nil. Of course, when your spouse dies, there may be tax to pay on his or her estate.

Most other gifts made by individuals will count as PETs and so will be taxable only if you die within seven years of making them. Chargeable transfers are the only type of gift on which you might have to pay tax during your lifetime.

Any gifts which aren't tax-free start to clock up on a running total. When your running total of chargeable transfers goes above a certain level – £223,000 in the 1998–9 tax year – tax is payable at half the rate of tax due on death. At present the tax rate on death is 40 per cent, so the rate would be 20 per cent.

Any gifts made more than seven years ago are knocked off your running total, so it can fall as well as rise.

Note that inheritance tax replaced capital transfer tax in March 1986.

Tax-free gifts

Some gifts are tax-free only if made during your lifetime. Others are tax-free whenever they are made. Gifts that are tax-free during your lifetime include:
- gifts which are part of your normal expenditure out of income. These must be regular, e.g. covenant payments, and not reduce your standard of living

■ gifts to people getting married, with a maximum of £5,000 from each parent of the couple, £2,500 from a grandparent and £1,000 from anybody else

■ maintenance payments to ex-husbands or wives

■ gifts of reasonable amounts needed to support a dependent relative

■ gifts for the education, maintenance or training of your children if they are still in full-time education or training, or not more than 18 years of age

■ small gifts of up to £250 to each recipient each year

■ your annual exemption – gifts of up to £3,000 a year. This exemption is in addition to all the tax-free gifts above except that you can't give £3,000 plus £250 (the 'small gifts' exemption) to the same person. If you don't use the full £3,000 in one year you can carry what's left forward for up to one year (i.e. up to £6,000 in the second year), but you must use up the current year's exemption first.

Gifts which are tax-free whenever they are made include:

■ gifts between husband and wife (provided the recipient is domiciled in the UK)

■ gifts to UK-established charities

■ gifts to political parties

■ gifts to most museums and art galleries, to universities, the National Trust, local authorities and similar bodies

■ gifts of property and possessions of outstanding national interest and where the public have reasonable access to the property or possessions, provided Treasury approval is obtained

■ gifts of land in the UK made to registered housing associations after 13 March 1989

■ broadly speaking, gifts of shares to a trust which will hold more than half of a company's ordinary shares and which was set up for the employees' benefit, provided the trustees have voting control.

Inheritance tax on life insurance

Regular premium life insurance policies are an excellent way of giving chunks of tax-free capital to your dependants, or indeed to anyone.

The premiums will count as a gift, but there should not be any inheritance tax to pay on them, since they'll normally be in one of the tax-free categories above.

What to avoid

Try to make sure that the proceeds of your policies do not count as part of your estate. If they do, they'll be added to the rest of what you leave, and your inheritance tax bill could rise.

You can avoid this by getting the policy written in trust so that the proceeds go to someone else. If a policy on your life is for the benefit of your wife (or husband) or children, the *Married Women's Property Act* provides a simple way of doing this. Otherwise, you'll need to get a declaration of trust written on the policy. Ask the insurance company what to do. Alternatively, you could give away the policy after taking it out; but this could count as a gift for inheritance tax purposes.

Types of policy
■ endowment policy
what it is: a policy that pays out a lump sum on a fixed date or when you die, if this is earlier.
useful for: people who want to give tax-free capital away in their lifetime.
■ whole life insurance
what it is: a policy that pays out on your death.
useful for: paying the inheritance tax bill when you die. A husband and wife who are going to leave everything to each other could take out a last survivor or joint life and last survivor policy, which pays out on the second death (i.e. when the inheritance tax bill will arrive). The premiums are lower than for a policy on a single life. A joint life first death policy is useful for paying any tax bill on the first death.
■ term insurance
what it is: a policy that pays out only if you die before the policy ends (within three years, or ten years, say). If you survive, it pays nothing.
useful for: someone who will be faced with a large inheritance tax bill only if death occurs within a certain time. For example, someone who has received a PET may be caught by a tax bill if the giver dies within seven years.

This subject is covered in great detail in *The Which? Guide to Giving and Inheriting.**

8

TAX-EFFICIENT SAVING AND INVESTING

Several schemes have tax breaks aimed at encouraging various types of saving and investing:

■ Tax Exempt Special Savings Accounts (TESSAs) and Individual Savings Accounts (ISAs) both primarily encourage greater saving and investment by individuals

■ Personal Equity Plans (PEPs) were introduced initially to encourage wider share ownership though the scope of the scheme has been expanded

■ the Enterprise Investment Scheme (EIS), its predecessor the Business Expansion Scheme (BES) and Venture Capital Trusts (VCTs) encourage investment in new, relatively high-risk ventures

■ pensions schemes and plans aim to encourage saving for retirement – see Chapters 13, 14 and 15 for details of these.

Tax Exempt Special Savings Account (TESSA)

Anyone aged 18 and over may hold one Tax-Exempt Special Savings Account (TESSA) with a bank or building society. They are designed as a savings scheme parallel to share-holding Personal Equity Plans (PEPs). Stick to the scheme conditions and the interest you earn will be free of both basic-rate and higher-rate tax.

The tax rules

Here are the main features of TESSAs:

■ a TESSA lasts for five years (although on maturity you can reinvest up to £9,000 for a further five years from the first TESSA, providing you open the second TESSA account within six months of the maturity of the first TESSA)

■ you can save up to £3,000 in the first year, and up to £1,800 in each of the following four years, provided you don't exceeed £9,000 over the five years in total

■ the interest earned will be tax-free *provided* you withdraw no more than the interest credited to your account at the time you want to make the withdrawal *less* the tax you would otherwise have paid. If you want to withdraw more interest than this, or some of your capital, then the account is terminated. All the interest credited to the account then becomes taxable in the tax year that the account is terminated (even though some of it may have been earned in earlier tax years)

■ provided you don't overstep the mark, you aren't taxed on any interest that you withdraw: the interest you cannot withdraw stays in your account (earning interest itself) until the TESSA matures, when it's paid out to you as a sort of bonus.

Apart from these tax rules, the other details of TESSAs are up to each building society or bank. Some schemes are for regular, equal, monthly savings (maximum £150 a month); others allow you to save as and when you like (sometimes subject to a minimum investment each time). Some may not allow any withdrawals; others do; some may automatically pay you a monthly income of as much as the Inland Revenue (and the scheme's interest rate) allows.

Some banks and building societies offer a scheme that allows you to pay a single lump sum into a 'feeder' account which is then transferred into a TESSA as fast as the rules allow. Note that the interest earned on the money while it is waiting in the feeder account *will* be taxable, and may not pay as good a rate as the TESSA itself: so the true rate of interest earned may be significantly lower than that quoted in any advertisements.

Building societies and banks can set any rate of interest on their TESSAs, and this can be fixed or variable. Although you can hold only one TESSA at any one time, the Revenue will allow you to transfer from one organisation's scheme to another, e.g. to chase best interest rates. Organisations must allow you to transfer *out* (though they can impose any penalties or charges they like), but they're not obliged to let you transfer *in* to their TESSA.

You can close a TESSA whenever you like – you don't have to wait until the five years is up. You'll have to pay tax on your interest, and the organisation might charge you a penalty. If your TESSA has no penalty for closure, it could be worthwhile considering even for short-term savings.

The capital (but not the accumulated interest) from a maturing TESSA – i.e. one which has run its full five years – can be reinvested in a 'follow-on' TESSA, provided the reinvested capital comes to more than £3,000 and the reinvestment is made within six months of the original TESSA maturing. The maximum investment for the first year of the follow-on TESSA is the amount of reinvested capital (i.e. up to £9,000). In subsequent years, further amounts can be added, provided the total over the five-year life of the TESSA does not exceed £9,000.

From 6 April 1999 onwards, TESSAs are being superseded by the new Individual Savings Accounts (ISAs) – see page 123. From that date, you will not be able to take out a new TESSA or follow-on TESSA. Any TESSA you already have at that date will be allowed to run its full five-year course, at the end of which the capital (but not the interest) from the maturing TESSA can be invested in an ISA. The amount transferred from a TESSA will not count against the annual limit for ISA investment.

Verdict
Most people should hold a spread of investments, with some in relatively safe bank and building society accounts. It makes sense for part of these safe investments to be invested in a TESSA so that you can make full use of the tax benefits. The ability to transfer from an existing TESSA into a new ISA without eating into the ISA investment limit also helps you to get the most out of the ISA tax benefits. Therefore, if you do not have a TESSA at present, consider starting one before they are abolished from 6 April 1999.

Personal equity plan (PEP)

The attraction of PEPs is that the income from the shares, unit trusts, investment trusts or corporate bonds you buy is free of income tax; any capital gain when you sell is free of capital gains tax, and someone else takes care of the day-to-day detail of share-ownership – buying and selling and dealing with paperwork. You can have only one PEP each tax year. You no longer have to hold a PEP for a minimum period to get your tax relief, but can cash it in at any time.

Some PEPs, though not all, have high charges; you need to be careful when choosing a scheme as the charges may outweigh any tax benefits.

The tax rules

You can invest up to £6,000 a year (in the 1998–9 tax year) in shares and/or corporate bonds in UK companies or in certain EC shares. You can also invest any part of your £6,000 in qualifying unit trusts or investment trusts. These must have up to 50 per cent of their investments in UK qualifying EC shares, certain corporate bonds or convertibles. Alternatively, you can invest £1,500 in a unit or investment trust that does not qualify, and the rest of your £6,000 directly into UK or certain EC shares.

You can also invest a further £3,000 in a single-company PEP, which can hold the shares of only one company. You can transfer shares from an approved profit-sharing scheme or an SAYE share option scheme into a single-company PEP without paying any capital gains tax. You must invest through a *plan manager* – a bank, building society or other investment adviser. The plan manager deals with all the administration – buying the shares or bonds, registering your name with the company, collecting dividends and reclaiming tax. In general, your investment in a PEP must be in the form of cash, i.e. you cannot normally transfer shares you already own. But if the plan manager agrees, you can transfer new issues of shares (including privatisation and conversion shares from former building societies) if you decide to do so within a set time of the share allocation being announced or, in the case of former building society shares, receipt of the share certificate or other proof of entitlement. The value of the new issue shares at the offer price counts towards the £6,000 a year maximum you are allowed to invest. You are allowed to accumulate cash in your PEP, so you don't have to invest in shares straight away, but can choose what seems best to you at the right time.

Up to 5 April 1999, dividends from shares, distributions from unit trusts and interest from corporate bonds are paid with tax at 20 per cent already deducted. It is the job of the plan manager to reclaim this tax and add it to your plan.

From 6 April 1999 onwards, PEPs, like TESSAs, are also being superseded by the new ISAs. You can continue to hold any PEPs you already have and for five years (i.e. until 5 April 2004) these PEPs will enjoy the same tax benefits as ISAs. In other words, all income and gains will be tax-free, although the tax deducted from share dividends and unit trust distributions and reclaimed by plan managers will fall to 10 per cent, reducing the overall return on your PEP compared with earlier years.

The government has not said what will happen from 6 April 2004, but it is possible that PEPs will then cease to enjoy favourable tax treatment.

Types of PEP

PEPs come in many forms and the type you choose can have a significant impact on your expected return and the charges you will face. A PEP can take one or more of the following forms:

- **advisory PEP** You choose how your PEP is invested but have the benefit of advice from the plan manager. Only a handful of managers – mainly stockbrokers – offer this type of PEP. Charges may be high.
- **corporate bond PEP** A PEP investing only in corporate bonds and possibly preference shares too. If the PEP is invested in just one bond, you will get a fixed return. If, as is often the case, the PEP is invested in a selection of bonds (e.g. via a corporate bond unit trust) your return will be variable. A corporate bond PEP can be managed or self-select.
- **corporate PEP** A PEP investing in the shares of one company, usually managed by that company or on its behalf by, say, a building society or bank.
- **managed or discretionary PEP** Your investment is pooled with other investors' money and the plan manager decides in which companies to invest.
- **self-select or non-discretionary PEP** The plan manager acts on your instructions, investing in the shares, trusts or bonds which you choose. Charges for this type of PEP may be high.
- **unit trust (or OEIC) or investment trust PEP** A type of managed PEP. You can choose from a wide range of different trusts – e.g. investing in UK shares, investing for income, specialising in the Far East and so on – but the manager chooses the underlying shares or bonds and decides when to switch. Often no extra charges for the PEP are made over and above the normal unit or investment trust charges.

A good source of information about the different types of PEPs available is the *Chase de Vere PEP Guide*.*

Verdict
If you usually use up your capital gains tax-free slice each year (see Chapter 7), the prospect of tax-free gains via a PEP

will be attractive. If you do not normally pay capital gains tax, a PEP can still be worthwhile, provided the tax saved on income outweighs any extra charges. A taxpayer investing in unit trusts and similar investments anyway should try to use up his or her PEP allowance each year. Since no extra charges are usually made for investing this way, the taxpayer has nothing to lose and the advantage of tax-free income to gain. Charges mean that other types of PEP are sometimes suitable only for higher-rate taxpayers.

PEPs are being abolished from 6 April 1999 but tax advantages for existing PEPs are guaranteed to continue for five years. Therefore, if possible, make full use of your PEP allowances in 1998–9.

Individual savings account (ISA)

From 6 April 1999, TESSAs and PEPs will be replaced by a new type of tax-efficient scheme, the ISA. The government has said that its aim in introducing ISAs is to develop and extend the nation's savings habit and to ensure that tax relief on saving is fairly distributed.

The tax rules

ISAs will be open to UK residents aged 18 or over. Husbands and wives are treated independently and can each have their own ISAs. The main features of the scheme are:
■ through an ISA, you can invest in up to three components: cash (e.g. bank and building society accounts, supermarket 'bank' accounts, and National Savings), life insurance and stocks and shares (including unit trusts, OEICs and investment trusts)
■ in the first year of the scheme, 1999–2000, you can invest up to £7,000. Of this, no more than £3,000 can go into the cash component and a maximum £1,000 to the insurance component. If you want to, you can invest the full £7,000 in stocks and shares
■ in subsequent years, the limits are £5,000 a year overall, with a maximum £1,000 in cash and £1,000 in life insurance
■ under the tax rules, there is no minimum investment, though ISA providers might set their own limits
■ income from and gains on the savings and investments within your ISA will be completely free of tax. This

includes the life insurance component where, unlike direct holdings of most types of life insurance (see page 100), the investments underlying the insurance will build up tax-free
■ the ISA scheme is guaranteed to run for at least ten years
■ you can withdraw your money at any time without a tax penalty. If you make a withdrawal during the year, this does not increase the amount you can newly invest in the ISA above the normal annual limit for that year
■ like PEPs, ISAs will be run by plan managers
■ each year you have a choice. You can opt for one manager to run your whole ISA. This manager must offer the stocks and shares component but does not have to offer cash and life insurance components. Alternatively, you can choose separate managers for each component of your ISA. In this case, to ensure that the £5,000 (£7,000 in the first year) annual limit is not breached, the maximum you will be able to invest in stocks and shares will be £3,000.

If you have a TESSA which was started before 6 April 1999, you can continue to contribute to it at the same time as paying into an ISA. When the TESSA matures, you can transfer the capital (but not the accumulated interest) from the TESSA to your ISA. Neither the continuing contributions to the TESSA nor the transfer of capital from it will reduce your annual ISA investment limit.

If you have a PEP which was started before 6 April 1999, you can continue to hold it and this will not reduce your scope to invest in an ISA.

Once ISAs are up and running, if you receive shares through an approved profit-sharing scheme or savings-related share option scheme at work, you can transfer these shares into your ISA. The market value of the shares at the date of transfer will count against your annual ISA investment limit.

Shares you receive through a privatisation issue, other public offers of new shares or as a result of a building society or insurer converting into a company cannot be transferred into your ISA.

Verdict
The replacement of TESSAs and PEPs by ISAs reduces the amount you can invest tax-efficiently each year. However, it makes sense to take the fullest advantage of the tax reliefs which will remain. Taxpayers should aim to use up their full ISA limit each year and, if they do not already have a TESSA, should start one before 6 April 1999 so that the capital can be added to their ISA when the TESSA matures.

Enterprise Investment Scheme (EIS)

The Enterprise Investment Scheme was introduced in January 1994 to replace the Business Expansion Scheme (BES). No new investments qualified for the BES after 31 December 1993, although if you still hold shares through a BES you continue to qualify for the tax advantages.

Like the BES, the EIS aims to encourage investment in new ventures which are typically at a risky stage in their development.

The tax rules

The EIS offers tax advantages when you invest in the newly issued shares of a qualifying company. You get tax relief at 20 per cent on investments up to £150,000 a year from 1998–9 onwards (£100,000 in earlier tax years). Any gain when you eventually sell the shares is free of capital gains tax and a loss can be set against gains on other assets or, in some circumstances, against taxable income. To get these tax breaks, you must invest for at least five years. If you sell before then, or if the company ceases within three years to qualify for the EIS, some or all of the income tax relief may be lost and any gain could be taxed.

From 1998–9, up to £25,000 (£15,000 in earlier tax years) invested in the first half of a tax year (i.e. up to 5 October) can be carried back to the previous tax year, provided enough of the previous year's investment limit remains.

If you have made a taxable capital gain on the sale or disposal of something, you can defer paying tax on the gain if you reinvest it in qualifying shares in unquoted companies. From 6 April 1998, this means newly issued shares which qualify under the EIS rules. You can claim this reinvestment relief (see page 114) even if you do not qualify for EIS income tax relief.

Under the EIS rules, a qualifying company is an unquoted company trading in the UK. This can include a company listed on the Alternative Investment Market (AIM) and companies which are incorporated outside the UK but trading here. Companies which cannot qualify include:

■ companies quoted on the main market of the UK Stock Exchange
■ companies which deal in shares, provide financial or legal services or hold collectable goods (e.g. antiques, wines) for investment
■ a company owned by you or one in which you (or your

family or business partners) own more than 30 per cent of the business
■ a company of which you are already a paid director or employee. You may, however, become a paid director provided you were unconnected with the company before you made the EIS investment
■ for shares issued on or after 2 July 1997, a company engaged in property-backed activities, such as farming, market gardening, forestry, property development, hotel management or running retirement homes
■ for shares issued on or after 2 July 1997, a company where there is a scheme or guarantee ensuring that investors can get some or all of their money back.

Types of EIS

You have a choice. You can invest either directly in companies or through a fund. If you opt for the direct route, the minimum investment is £500 per company. You should take advice before investing directly, from a stockbroker or accountant for example.

A novice investor would probably do better to invest through a fund. Your money is pooled with that of other investors and spread around several EIS companies, which helps to reduce the risk. The minimum investment through a fund is usually £2,000 and there's likely to be an initial fee of, say, 7 per cent of your investment.

Verdict
Because EIS companies tend to be new and small, they are likely to be risky. Do not invest in an EIS unless you are happy with this level of risk and prepared for the chance that you might lose the lot.

Venture Capital Trust (VCT)

VCTs are companies – basically investment trusts – which invest in a range of unlisted trading companies. They were introduced as a way of encouraging investment in new ventures and developing companies, but addressing some of the problems investors face by:
■ spreading risk across of a range of qualifying companies
■ increasing the chance of selling the shares by allowing the VCT itself to be quoted on the Stock Exchange.

The tax rules

You get tax relief at 20 per cent on up to £100,000 a year invested in the newly issued shares of a VCT. The shares must not carry any preferential rights to receive future dividends or to receive any payment on winding up of the VCT, but any dividends which are paid will be tax-free. If you sell the VCT shares within five years, the tax reliefs are withdrawn.

Any capital gain when the VCT shares are sold is also tax-free. But, if you make a loss, it does not count as 'allowable' and cannot be set against gains on other assets.

Up to 5 April 1998, you could claim reinvestment relief (see page 114) when you invested a taxable gain made on another asset into VCT shares. From 6 April 1998, this relief is no longer available.

From 6 April 1998 onwards, the qualifying companies in which a VCT can invest are the same as those companies which qualify for the EIS, see page 125.

Verdict

By spreading your investment over a range of companies, VCTs may be a little less risky than some EIS investments, but you should still be prepared to lose some or all of your capital. Even though the VCT itself is quoted on the Stock Exchange, there may be little or no demand for its shares, so there is no guarantee that you will be able to sell when you want to.

9

A BIRD'S-EYE VIEW

Before you can put your investment strategy into effect you'll have to get to grips with the nitty-gritty of what different investments offer and what their particular advantages and disadvantages are.

In this chapter we give you a summary of the main types of investment open to you. The most important points about each investment are picked out in the table (see below for why each row is important).

In the later chapters of the book you'll find much fuller details of each type of investment.

The table explained

Regular saving or lump sum?
Some investments are very flexible. The minimum amount you can invest is fairly low, so they can be used as homes for lump sums, regular savings and odd bits of spare cash.

But some investments are open only to people who have a fair-sized lump sum of money to invest, and others only to people who want to save a regular amount each month or year, say. Of course, if you have a lump sum, you can invest it bit by bit on a regular basis, if you like.

Minimum investment recommended
This row tells you the minimum sensible amount you can invest. This isn't necessarily the same thing as the minimum amount you're _allowed_ to invest. For example, you can invest as little as you like in shares, but the commission you have to pay means that an investment of less than £1,500 to £2,000 or so may not be worthwhile.

Does it pay a regular income?
Some investments pay income direct to you at regular

intervals. With others, the income is added to the value of what you first invested.

Of course, with some investments that don't pay an income out to you, such as single-premium bonds and National Savings Certificates, you may still be able to give yourself a regular income by cashing in part of your investment at regular intervals. Indeed, with some investments (such as single-premium bonds) there are often standard schemes to allow you to do this.

With some investments that pay out a regular income, the income is fixed when you take out the investment, e.g. guaranteed income bonds. With other investments, such as deposit accounts offered by banks and building societies, the income can vary after you've invested your money.

If you need to be sure of getting a regular return on your investment each year, go for one that pays out a fixed income, but bear in mind the effects of inflation.

Note that if you go for a fixed income, you may regret your decision if interest rates in general rise; investments with interest rates that vary may turn out to have been better bets. On the other hand, if interest rates in general fall, you will feel pleased with yourself for putting your money in a fixed-income investment.

How long is the investment meant to be for?
This row tells you how long you should expect to have to leave your money invested in order to get the best return.

Can you get your money back quickly?
In some cases, you can't. So don't put your money in one of these investments unless you're certain you'll be able to leave it there for the agreed period.

With other investments, you may be able to cash in early but not get back (or not be sure of getting back) what you paid in. So, if you want a certain amount of money at a certain time, e.g. to go on holiday in two years' time, you'd be wise to steer clear of these investments.

Does the value of your capital fluctuate?
Investments can be divided into two types:
■ the value of the capital you invest stays the same (but, again, bear in mind that inflation could affect it)
■ the value may fluctuate. Unit trusts, single-premium bonds and property are examples of investments in which the value of the capital invested will fluctuate. With investments like these, you stand a chance of making a capital gain, but also run the risk of losing some of your

money. Because the value of the capital fluctuates, the success of your investment depends very much on *when* you invest and *when* you cash in your investment. For more about how to reduce the risk of doing very badly, see page 239.

Points about tax
This row picks out particular tax points for the various investments. More details on tax are given in Chapters 7 and 8, and in the chapters dealing with each investment.

For example, some investments which offer a tax-free return look more attractive if you're a higher-rate taxpayer while others may offer a good rate of return before tax but may be less competitive after tax. This also applies to investments where you get tax relief on the payments you make, e.g. contributions to an employer's pension scheme or payments to a personal pension plan.

Where can you get the investment?
This row tells you where to go to put your money in these investments.

Other comments
This gives snippets of information about how some of the investments work, who might find it worthwhile to consider or to avoid a particular investment, and so on.

Type of investment (and where to find more details)	Alternative investments (e.g. stamps, antique furniture, diamonds, gold) Chapter 26	Annuities Chapter 23
regular saving or lump sum?	lump sum	lump sum
minimum investment recommended	varies	depends on age, and income required
does it pay a regular income?	no – in fact you have to pay for insurance etc.	yes, normally arranged at time you buy the annuity. The older you are at that time, the higher the income
how long is investment meant to be for?	in the main, long-term investment	until you die
can you get your money back quickly?	as quickly as you can find a buyer. But you may get back less than you invested	you can't – once you've made an investment you can't cash it in
does value of capital fluctuate?	yes	not applicable – can't get capital back
points about tax	no capital gains tax unless value of item at time of disposal more than £6,000 (post-1837 UK gold sovereigns and Britannia coins are free of CGT). See page 106. If you count as a trader, you may have to pay income tax	you get interest and return of part of capital. Only interest taxable – normally paid after deduction of 20 per cent tax. With annuities you *have* to buy, e.g. as part of a personal pension – it's *all* taxed as income at your top rate of tax
where can you get investment?	auctions, dealers, other collectors, sometimes investment companies too	life insurance company or adviser
other comments	needs expert knowledge. Watch out for dealer's mark-up	worth considering only for older people (around 70, say). Men get higher income than women of same age because life expectancy is shorter

Type of investment (and where to find more details)	Banks and building societies Chapter 11 – instant access accounts	Banks and building societies Chapter 11 – term and notice accounts
regular saving or lump sum?	either	either
minimum investment recommended	often £1	varies – £500 to £10,000 (or more)
does it pay a regular income?	no – but interest is reinvested and can be withdrawn. Interest varies	yes – if you choose. Interest varies on notice and some term accounts
how long is investment meant to be for?	any period: suitable for emergency funds and a temporary home for other funds (unless interest rate is high)	varies from a few days to a few years
can you get your money back quickly?	in practice you can cash in at any time (but sometimes only balance over a set amount) and you may lose some interest	not until end of agreed term or notice period, or after a period (e.g. one or three months' notice) or immediately, but you'll lose some interest
does value of capital fluctuate?	no	no
points about tax	20 per cent tax normally deducted from interest before you get it. Non-taxpayers can get interest paid gross, higher-rate taxpayers will have extra tax to pay	see *instant access accounts*
where can you get investment?	banks, building societies	see *instant access accounts*
other comments	often tiered accounts, etc., the more you invest, the higher the interest rate	normally pays higher interest rate than instant access accounts. May get higher interest the more you invest. Some pay a monthly income

Type of investment (and where to find more details)	Banks and building societies Chapter 11 – savings accounts	Banks and building societies Chapter 8 – Tax-Exempt Special Savings Accounts (TESSAs)
regular saving or lump sum?	regular saving	either
minimum investment recommended	varies – could be as low as £1 a month (there may be a maximum amount too)	varies (maximum £9,000 over 5 years) 2nd TESSA accounts often have minimum £3,001 or more
does it pay a regular income?	no – interest is reinvested	no, but interest is reinvested and can be withdrawn (although withdrawals over a certain amount will lose you the tax concessions)
how long is investment meant to be for?	normally at least one year to get higher interest	5 years, though maturing TESSAs can be reinvested for a further 5 years
can you get your money back quickly?	you may be able to cash small amounts once or twice a year	an account must last for 5 years to get the tax concessions and if a TESSA is reinvested into a second TESSA on maturity it must last a further 5 years
does value of capital fluctuate?	no	no
points about tax	see *instant access accounts*	return tax-free
where can you get investment?	see *instant access accounts*	see *instant access accounts*
other comments	not common nowadays	no new TESSA will be allowable after 5 April 1999 (replaced by new Individual Savings Accounts (ISAs))

Type of investment (and where to find more details)	Building societies Chapter 11 – Permanent Interest-Bearing Shares (PIBS)	British Government stocks Chapter 19 – conventional stocks
regular saving or lump sum?	lump sum	lump sum
minimum investment recommended	varies from £1,000 to £50,000	none if bought on National Savings Stock Register; otherwise £1,000 sensible minimum
does it pay a regular income?	yes – interest fixed at the time you buy	yes – income fixed at the time you buy the stock (except with a few stocks)
how long is investment meant to be for?	no set period	until stock due to be redeemed (paid back) by government – but some stocks can also be short-term speculation
can you get your money back quickly?	in theory, yes, but you may get back less than you invested	can sell stock at any time. Can take a day or two to get money if sold through stockbroker, a week or so through National Savings Stock Register
does value of capital fluctuate?	yes	yes – but if you hold stock until redemption, you know for certain what you'll get back
points about tax	paid after deduction – tax at 20% –*accrued income* scheme applies. Free of CGT	interest is taxable – paid without deduction of tax. Free of CGT
where can you get investment?	via a stockbroker, not from the building society	stockbroker, post office, high-street bank or other agent, e.g. accountant
other comments	available from only the largest societies	best stock for you depends to large extent on rate of tax you pay. Get advice on which stock to choose, e.g. from stockbroker or bank. Buying and selling costs less for small investments if made through National Savings Stock Register

Type of investment (and where to find more details)	British Government stocks Chapter 19 **– Index-linked stocks**	Commodities Chapter 24
regular saving or lump sum?	see *conventional stocks*	lump sum
minimum investment recommended	see *conventional stocks*	several thousand pounds for direct investment; £3,000 say, for commodity fund or trust
does it pay a regular income?	yes – and income increases in line with Retail Prices Index	no, with direct investment. Some funds and trusts pay an income – with others you can get income by cashing units
how long is investment meant to be for?	see *conventional stocks*	long-term investment or short-term speculation
can you get your money back quickly?	see *conventional stocks*	if direct investment, you can sell at any time. With fund or trust, as few days or a month
does value of capital fluctuate?	yes – but at redemption, government pays back *nominal value* increased in line with Retail Prices Index since time of issue	yes
points about tax	see *conventional stocks*	gain may be taxed as income or as capital gain, depending on circumstances – see Chapter 24
where can you get investment?	see *conventional stocks*	commodity broker; direct from fund or trust or through intermediary
other comments	see *conventional stocks*	investing directly in commodities not sensible for most people. Very risky – consider commodity fund or unit trust instead. For legal and tax reasons, funds may be based offshore – Isle of Man or Channel Islands, say

Type of investment (and where to find more details)	Endowment policies (with-profits) Chapter 21	Guaranteed income and growth bonds Chapter 21
regular saving or lump sum?	regular saving (may be monthly or annually)	lump sum
minimum investment recommended	£10 a month, say	£1,000 to £10,000 but more for income bonds
does it pay a regular income?	no	income bonds – yes growth bonds – no
how long is investment meant to be for?	10 years or more – period usually agreed at outset	fixed period, varying from 1 to 10 years
can you get your money back quickly?	you can surrender policy at any time but what you get back is often at discretion of company (and in first year or two you may get little or nothing)	with some companies, at the end of agreed period only. With others, you can cash in early, but return up to company
does value of capital fluctuate?	you get at least a guaranteed amount at end of policy (or if you die), usually bonuses too	no (unless you cash early)
points about tax	because insurance fund pays tax, return is tax-free as long as you pay tax at no more than the basic rate – always tax-free if you keep policy going for at least 10 years or three-quarters of its term, whichever is less	tax treatment depends on how bonds work – can work in one of several ways. Check with company before investing
where can you get investment?	life insurance company or insurance adviser	life insurance company or insurance adviser
other comments	can be used as a way of repaying a mortgage, in which case the policy is normally taken out at the time the mortgage is arranged	return may be lower if you or your spouse is over 65 when you cash bond in because tax bill could rise

Type of investment (and where to find more details)	Home income schemes Chapter 23	Investment trusts Chapter 18
regular saving or lump sum?	lump sum (raised from mortgaging your home)	either
minimum investment recommended	normally £15,000	£1,000 to £1,500, say as a lump sum, £25 to £50 with a saving scheme
does it pay a regular income?	yes – income (from an annuity) arranged at the time you take out the scheme (amount depends on age and sex)	yes – most companies pay dividends. These can vary
how long is investment meant to be for?	until you die	long-term investment or short-term speculation
can you get your money back quickly?	you can't get your money back at all	you can sell and get money back in 2 weeks, but you may get less than you invested
does value of capital fluctuate?	with schemes based on loans, you benefit from increase in value of home. With schemes where you sell part or all of your home to the company ('reversions'), you don't	yes
points about tax	you get tax relief at 23 per cent on interest up to £30,000 to buy a scheme. Part of income tax-free	dividends are taxable, paid after deduction of tax at 10 per cent (from April 1999); higher-rate tax-payers will need to pay 32.5 per cent more. Liable for capital gains tax on gain
where can you get investment?	life insurance company, insurance adviser, building society	stockbroker, bank or other agent, e.g. accountant; savings schemes from investment trust management company
other comments	worth considering only if you are over 70. Consider companies which are members of SHIP (Safe Home Income Plans)*	you buy shares in an investment trust company – a company whose sole business is investing in other companies' shares

Type of investment (and where to find more details)	National Savings investments Chapter 12 – Ordinary accounts	National Savings investments Chapter 12 – Investment accounts
regular saving or lump sum?	either	either
minimum investment recommended	£10 (maximum £10,000), though you get a higher rate of interest if you invest £500 or more	£20 (maximum £100,00)
does it pay a regular income?	no – but interest can be withdrawn. Interest can vary	no – but interest can be withdrawn. Interest can vary
how long is investment meant to be for?	for emergency funds and a temporary home for other funds	any period over a month
can you get your money back quickly?	£100 at once (about a week to withdraw all money)	1 month's notice is required (you can withdraw money without notice – penalty of 1 month's interest charge on amount withdrawn)
does value of capital fluctuate?	no	no
points about tax	first £70 interest each year is tax-free – all interest paid without deduction of tax	all interest is taxable – paid without deduction of tax
where can you get investment?	post office	post office
other comments	interest paid only for complete calendar months money is invested	worth considering if you don't pay tax

Type of investment (and where to find more details)	National Savings investments Chapter 12 – National Savings Certificates (46th issue)	National Savings Investments Chapter 12 – index-linked National Savings Certificates (13th issue)
regular saving or lump sum?	either	either
minimum investment recommended	£100 (maximum £10,000) not including any reinvestment of mature certificates	£100 (maximum £10,000) not including any reinvestment of mature certificates
does it pay a regular income?	no – but can be cashed in to provide income	no – but you can cash certificates to get an income
how long is investment meant to be for?	for best return, 5 years (get overall return of 4.8% if held for 5 years)	initially for 5 years (overall return of at least 2.25 per cent plus inflation at end of 5 years)
can you get your money back quickly?	within 8 working days but return lower if cashed in within first 5 years	within 8 working days (but certificates not index-linked if cashed in within first 12 months)
does value of capital fluctuate?	no	yes – but you won't get back less than invested
points about tax	return is tax-free	return is tax-free
where can you get investment?	post office, high-street bank	post office, high-street bank
other comments	can also reinvest 'matured' certificates (i.e. over 5 years old), not included in the maximum investment	value goes up in line with Retail Prices Index

Type of investment (and where to find more details)	National Savings Investment Chapter 12 – National Savings Pensioners' Guaranteed Income Bond	National Savings Investments Chapter 12 – Capital Bond (Series L)
regular saving or lump sum?	either	lump sum
minimum investment recommended	£500 (maximum £50,000)	£100 (maximum £250,000)
does it pay a regular income?	yes – each month – interest rate is fixed for 5 years – (currently 6.1 per cent gross)	no
how long is investment meant to be for?	5 years	5 years
can you get your money back quickly?	60 days' notice (unless you apply within 2 weeks of the fifth anniversary of your purchase). You can withdraw money immediately but will be penalised 90 days' interest	allow 8 working days. But you lose interest if you cash in before 5 years are up (no interest at all if you cash in during year 1) You get overall return of 6 per cent if held for 5 years
does value of capital fluctuate?	no	no
points about tax	all interest is taxable – paid without deduction of tax	no tax deducted for non-taxpayers. Interest added yearly, but you can't get it until bond is repaid. If you're a taxpayer, you'll pay tax each year on the interest
where can you get investment?	post office, high-street bank	post office
other comments	currently offering a good rate of return – worth considering especially if you don't pay tax	rate of interest rises on yearly scale. Good for non-taxpayers

Type of investment (and where to find more details)	National Savings Investments Chapter 12 – Children's Bonus Bonds (series J)	National Savings Investments Chapter 12 – National Savings Income Bonds
regular saving or lump sum?	lump sum	lump sum
minimum investment recommended	£25 (maximum £1,000 in any series)	£2,000 (maximum £250,000). Each additional purchase must be for a minimum of £1,000
does it pay a regular income?	no	yes – each month
how long is investment meant to be for?	5 years	no set period
can you get your money back quickly?	1 month, but for best return need to keep for 5 years (you get overall return of 6.0 per cent if held for 5 years)	3 months' notice is required (or 90-day interest penalty if you want your money immediately)
does value of capital fluctuate?	no	no
points about tax	return is tax-free	all interest is taxable – paid without deduction of tax
where can you get investment?	post office	post office, high-street bank
other comments	can be bought for any child under 16 by anybody aged 16 or over. Can be held until child is 21	

Type of investment (and where to find more details)	National Savings Investments Chapter 12 – National FIRST Option Bond	Pension schemes – employers' schemes Chapter 14
regular saving or lump sum?	lump sum	regular saving
minimum investment recommended	£1,000 (maximum £250,000)	some schemes are non-contributory (i.e. employee pays nothing); with others you pay a fixed % of your earnings
does it pay a regular income?	no	yes – from time you retire. Often pays a lump sum on retirement instead of part of pension
how long is investment meant to be for?	1 year at a time	from time you join scheme until you retire or leave the scheme (income carries on for life)
can you get your money back quickly?	around a couple of weeks (but no interest on withdrawals before end of first year, and low interest on withdrawals part-way through a year after that)	contributions must normally stay invested until the scheme's pension age (unless you leave job within 2 years of joining scheme)
does value of capital fluctuate?	no	depends on scheme
points about tax	interest is credited to the bond after the deduction of tax at 20 per cent	you get tax relief on payments. Investment builds up free of capital gains tax and may be partly or wholly free of income tax. Lump sum taken instead of part pension is tax-free. Actual pension is taxable.
where can you get investment?	post office	employer
other comments	though they were withdrawn in November 1992, they were re-introduced in March 1993	you can choose to make *additional voluntary contributions*

Type of investment (and where to find more details)	Pension schemes – personal pension plans Chapter 15	Pension schemes – state schemes Chapter 13
regular saving or lump sum?	either	regular saving (through National Insurance contributions)
minimum investment recommended	say £25 a month or £500 to £1,000 for lump sum plans	compulsory contributions depend on what you earn and whether you are employed or self-employed
does it pay a regular income?	yes – normally from any age between 50 and 75. You can choose to have lump sum on retirement instead of part of pension	yes, from state pension age (later if you choose)
how long is investment meant to be for?	from time you begin payments until income starts or you transfer to another scheme (income carries on for life)	you normally make payments until state pension age (income carries on for life)
can you get your money back quickly?	you can't cash investments in, but with some schemes you can get a loan	you can't cash investment in
does value of capital fluctuate?	with some schemes, yes	not applicable – cannot get capital back
points about tax	you can get tax relief on payments. Investment builds up free of capital gains tax and may be partly or wholly free of income tax. Lump sum taken instead of part of pension is tax-free. Actual pension is taxable	you don't get tax relief on payments unless it is contracted out through a personal pension plan. Pension taxed as earnings, currently paid without deduction of tax
where can you get investment?	bank, building society, life insurance company, unit trust company, investment adviser	payments made through employer, or through Contributions Agency if self-employed
other comments	start saving as young as possible to give investments longer to grow	if you're earning, you cannot opt out of the state scheme altogether, but you may be able to contract out of SERPS

Type of investment (and where to find more details)	Personal Equity Plans (PEPs) Chapter 8	Premium bonds Chapter 12
regular saving or lump sum?	either	either
minimum investment recommended	minimum varies; maximum £6,000 (plus £3,000 in a single company PEP)	£100 (maximum £20,000)
does it pay a regular income?	varies – it depends on the plan	no – but might win prizes
how long is investment meant to be for?	in the main, long-term investment, otherwise costs may outweigh gains	any period – but you can't win prize until bond held for one month
can you get your money back quickly?	yes, but you may make a loss	around a couple of weeks
does value of capital fluctuate?	yes usually, but corporate bonds have a fixed value at maturity	no
points about tax	no income tax or capital gains tax payable on the return from PEPs. From 6 April 1999 to 5 April 2004 a 10 per cent tax credit will be paid on dividends in line with the rules for the new ISAs	prizes are tax-free
where can you get investment?	stockbroker, bank, building society, unit trust company, investment trust company or other agent e.g. accountant	post office, high-street bank
other comments	no new PEPs allowable after 5 April 1999 (in effect replaced by new Individual Savings Accounts (ISAs)).See Chapter 8	prizes worked out to give return of 5% on all bonds held for 3 months or more.

Type of investment (and where to find more details)	Shares Chapter 16	Single-premium investment bonds Chapter 22
regular saving or lump sum?	lump sum	lump sum
minimum investment recommended	£1,500 to £2,000, say, in each company	varies – but often £1,000
does it pay a regular income?	yes – most companies pay dividends. Amounts can vary	not usually – but most companies have schemes which let you cash in part of investment (you can cash up to 5 per cent a year without paying tax at the time)
how long is investment meant to be for?	in the main, long-term investment. But can also be short-term speculation	in the main, long-term investment
can you get your money back quickly?	you can sell shares and get money in 2 weeks – but you may get less than you invested	varies – can be straight away, sometimes up to a week or month. May get back less than invested
does value of capital fluctuate?	yes	yes
points about tax	dividends are taxable – paid after deductions of 10 per cent tax, (from April 1999); higher-rate tax-payers will need to pay 32.5 per cent more. Liable for CGT (see page 98).	when you cash in bond, you may have to pay tax on the gain you've made (including any amounts you got earlier on, not taxed at the time) if you pay tax at the higher rate. Fund pays CGT on gains
where can you get investment?	stockbroker, bank or other agent, e.g. accountant	life insurance company or insurance adviser
other comments	buying shares of just one or two companies is very risky. Special tax rules apply if you invest in higher-risk shares through an Enterprise Investment Scheme or Venture Capital Trust – see Chapter 8.	value of investment depends on performance of fund of investments, e.g. property fund. Limited appeal except to higher-rate taxpayers or people who want to switch funds frequently

Type of investment (and where to find more details)	Unit-linked regular premium plans Chapter 22	Unit trusts Chapter 17
regular saving or lump sum?	regular saving	either
minimum investment recommended	varies – £10 to £50 a month	for lump sum, often £250 to £1,500; for regular saving £10 to £100 a month
does it pay a regular income?	normally no	yes, with many trusts – amount can vary
how long is investment meant to be for?	at least 10 years	in the main, long-term investment. But can also be short-term speculation
can you get your money back quickly?	can cash in at any time but you may get back less than you invested (and in first year or two, may get little or nothing).	varies between trusts – you can normally sell each day (but may take a week or so to get paid)
does value of capital fluctuate?	yes	yes
points about tax	return tax-free as long as you pay tax at no more than the basic rate – always tax-free if you keep policy going for at least 10 years, or three-quarters of its term, whichever is less. Fund pays capital gains tax on gains	income is taxable – paid after deduction of tax at 20 per cent. From April 1999 tax deducted will fall to 10 per cent. Liable for capital gains, though basic-rate taxpayers don't need to pay any more tax but higher-rate tax payers have extra to pay
where can you get investment?	life insurance company or insurance adviser	direct from unit trust company or via insurance adviser, stockbroker, bank
other comments	money invested in unit trust or insurance company fund (as for *single-premium investment bonds*). Limited appeal except to higher-rate taxpayers or people who want to switch funds frequently	value of investment depends on performance of fund of investments selected

SECTION II

Where to Put Your Money First

10

YOUR HOME

Your home is first and foremost a place to live in, but you can look upon it as probably the largest single investment you'll ever make.

The graph on page 150 shows that house prices have, on average, increased eight times since the end of 1972. On the diagram, we've also shown the Retail Prices Index (RPI), which measures increases in prices in general. You can see that, for most of the period, house prices increased more quickly than the RPI. This means that on average the buying power of the money invested in property has gone up over this period. Of course, part of the increase in house prices is due to better standards of housing. For example, more houses now have double glazing than in 1972, and many dilapidated properties have been brought up to scratch. There have also been times, particularly after boom periods, when house price increases haven't matched inflation; this happened in 1980 and 1981. It has also happened since the end of the last boom in 1989. If you bought a home at the height of the boom, in the summer of 1988, you are likely to have seen the value of your property fall and only now (April 1998) can you expect to sell without making a loss.

Of course, not all property values have gone up by the amounts shown in the graph. The values of some types of home and in some areas will have risen more than average, others less. The map on page 152 shows how prices varied in the UK in the first quarter of 1998, and the rate at which they'd gone up over the previous 12 months. For each region, we've shown prices for three different types of property: detached, semi-detached and terraced.

Within the regions prices vary considerably, because of factors like size, number of rooms, how big the garden is and whether there's a garage, central heating and so on. However, other things, like the age of the house and its

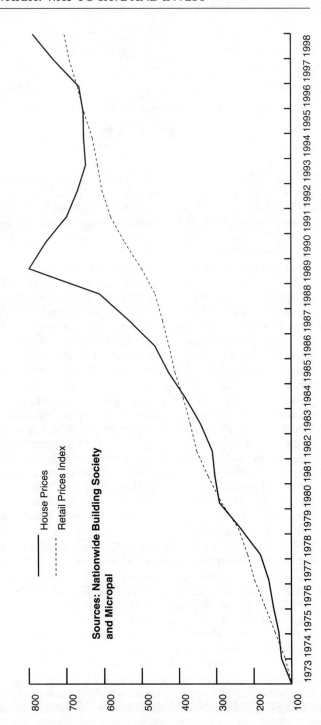

House Prices and Inflation since 1973
(first quarter 1973 = 100)

House Prices
Retail Prices Index

**Sources: Nationwide Building Society
and Micropal**

condition, architectural style and the area it's in may also affect prices and the rate at which they change.

For example, in rural areas houses in a pretty village may become expensive because people increasingly want to buy them as second homes, or as first homes if, say, they are near an improved railway service making commuting easier. However, property in a less attractive village a few miles away may be cheaper than average for the region because there are few jobs for local residents and people want to move away.

Local redevelopment or major transport schemes such as the Channel Tunnel can have a significant impact on prices. Also, if you have to sell your home quickly (because your job moves, say) you may also have to accept a cut in price.

A house as an investment

For how investing in a house has compared with other investments, see the chart on 'Investments compared' on page 18. This shows that, over the long term, houses have on average proved a worthwhile investment when compared with conventional investments, but over the past five and ten years have failed to match inflation. Bear in mind that, over the periods we've looked at, houses have improved in quality, which artificially increases the return; and, of course, the gain on a house is not easily accessible. You may have to sell and rent, or trade down, to see your money.

With a house, you have to pay various running costs, e.g. decorating, repairs, council tax and so on. If you weren't buying your own home, but renting one instead, you would be paying some of these costs anyway (perhaps indirectly in your rent). However, with a second home, these running costs are additional ones unless you can rent the home out to cover them. See page 158–9 for more on renting out a property as an investment.

A hedge against inflation?

There is a traditional belief that investing in property offers protection against the ravages of inflation, as property tends to hold its value in real terms. The graph on page 150 supports this belief over the long term. Of course, when you

House prices in the UK

Average house prices in first quarter 1998 and
average regional yearly rates of change since first quarter
1987 [1]

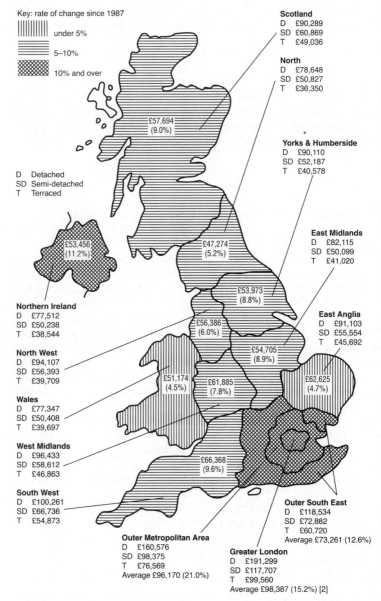

Key: rate of change since 1987

under 5%

5–10%

10% and over

D Detached
SD Semi-detached
T Terraced

Scotland
D £90,289
SD £60,869
T £49,036

North
D £78,648
SD £50,827
T £36,350

Yorks & Humberside
D £90,110
SD £52,187
T £40,578

East Midlands
D £82,115
SD £50,099
T £41,020

East Anglia
D £91,103
SD £55,554
T £45,692

Northern Ireland
D £77,512
SD £50,238
T £38,544

North West
D £94,107
SD £56,393
T £39,709

Wales
D £77,347
SD £50,408
T £39,697

West Midlands
D £96,433
SD £58,612
T £46,863

South West
D £100,261
SD £66,736
T £54,873

Outer South East
D £118,534
SD £72,882
T £60,720
Average £73,261 (12.6%)

Outer Metropolitan Area
D £160,576
SD £98,375
T £76,569
Average £96,170 (21.0%)

Greater London
D £191,299
SD £117,707
T £99,560
Average £98,387 (15.2%) [2]

£57,694 (9.0%)

£47,274 (5.2%)

£53,456 (11.2%)

£53,973 (8.8%)

£56,386 (6.0%)

£54,705 (8.9%)

£51,174 (4.5%)

£61,885 (7.8%)

£62,625 (4.7%)

£66,368 (9.6%)

[1] Based on information from Nationwide Building Society for houses on which mortgages have been approved.
[2] The average is low because of the large number of flats in London.

invest, where you invest and when you sell are crucially important. If, for example, you'd bought a house in the South-East in 1988 (when prices were booming) and sold again in 1990 or later, you could probably have *lost* money – even before allowing for inflation, or even the costs of buying and selling.

What makes property prices change?

House prices are influenced by several factors, both in the long term and the short term.

Long-term factors include:
■ people's earnings, particularly in terms of buying-power
■ the availability of homes to buy
■ trading-up (i.e. the tendency for owner-occupiers to move on to more expensive homes).

In the short term, relatively sudden increases in earnings (compared with prices in general) and in the numbers of first-time buyers, temporary shortages of houses to buy (e.g. not enough new houses being built), and speculation about house prices can fuel short, sharp booms of perhaps a few years' duration. On the other hand, lack of confidence in the economy as a whole – and likely employment prospects in particular – can depress house prices. Tax changes can affect property values, either directly with changes to the mortgage interest relief (see below), or indirectly – with higher taxation leaving people with less money to spend. The availability (or otherwise) of loan finance (mortgages from building societies, banks, etc.) has also played a part.

Other factors, which are looked at in detail later in this chapter, help to make housing a more attractive invest-ment. These include:
■ tax relief on mortgage interest
■ exemption from capital gains tax on your only or main home
■ the effects of *gearing*, although when house prices fall this can also be a disadvantage.

Tax relief on mortgage interest

In general, you can get tax relief at 10 per cent on the interest you pay on up to £30,000 of loans to buy your only or main home (normally the one you live in most of the time).

To get tax relief on a loan you must, in general, be buying an interest in the home, e.g. the whole of it, a half share, or buying out someone else. The home must be in the UK or Ireland. If you pay your mortgage under the MIRAS (Mortgage Interest Relief At Source) scheme, you get the tax relief even if you're a non-taxpayer.

What tax relief is worth

Tax relief reduces the amount you have to pay for your mortgage by 10p in each pound (in the 1998–9 tax year). This means that borrowing can be much cheaper than it seems at first sight. A mortgage rate of, say, 8 per cent costs in effect only 7.20 per cent.

However, the tax benefits have been reduced over and above the reduction in the rate of tax at which relief is available: the £30,000 limit is gradually being eroded by inflation. Note that there are some loans you can't get relief on even if they are used for buying your only or main home. These include overdrafts and borrowing on credit cards.

The £30,000 rule

The £30,000 limit applies to the total amount you and any other person buying with you owe on one property. If you are 65 or over, you can also get tax relief at 23 per cent on the interest on up to £30,000 of loans, provided the money is used to purchase an annuity, if the loan is secured on your only or main home – see Chapter 23.

Moving home

You may be faced with paying out on two loans at once – one on your new home, and one on your (unsold) old home. Under the normal rules, you get tax relief on £30,000 of loans on your new home. But for a year (longer in deserving cases) you carry on receiving tax relief as before on your old home also.

Capital gains tax

Unlike many other forms of investment, any profit from the sale of your only or main home is, in most cases, exempt from capital gains tax. When house prices are rising, this helps existing owner-occupiers to trade up, i.e. to move to a better house. The non-taxable profit from the first home can be ploughed back into the next home together with a bigger mortgage, in the hope of reaping a higher capital gain. For more details, see 'Gearing', opposite.

If you have two or more homes, you can choose which one should count as your main home for capital gains tax purposes (but married couples can have only one main home, regardless of who actually owns the homes). Make your choice within two years of acquiring the second home, otherwise the Inland Revenue can choose for you. You can alter the choice at any time, simply by telling the Inland Revenue (your new choice can be backdated by up to two years).

In addition, one home owned by you or your husband or wife, bought before 6 April 1988 and occupied rent-free by a dependent relative since before that date, may be exempt from capital gains tax (but, normally, not if the relative gave you the house in the first place).

You may not get full exemption from capital gains tax if any of the following apply:

- you let all or part of your home
- you use part exclusively for work
- the home wasn't your main one for capital gains tax purposes for all the time you owned it
- you were away from the home because of your work for periods totalling over four years (though you get full exemption for any period in which you were an employee working entirely abroad)
- you were away from the home for reasons unconnected with your work for periods totalling over three years
- you were away from the home for longer than the last three years you owned it
- your home is one of a series of homes you bought, or spent money on, in order to make a profit
- your garden is bigger than half a hectare.

For more details, see Inland Revenue leaflet *CGT4* – available free from your tax office. For how capital gains tax works, see Chapter 7.

Gearing

In the investment world, borrowing money to buy an asset, and putting down only a small part of the money yourself, is called *gearing*. This is a shrewd move – *if* the asset increases in value at a greater rate than the rate of interest you have to pay on your loan. If house prices go up by more than the after-tax relief interest on the mortgage, you'll get a relatively high return for your money.

Suppose, for example, that you had bought a home in December 1966 for £3,820 and sold it in December 1986 for £41,150. With an 80 per cent mortgage, your initial investment would have been 20 per cent of £3,820, i.e. £764. Your gain in 1986 (after buying and selling costs) would be £35,677 and the return on your investment (initial investment plus mortgage repayments, allowing for tax relief) works out at about 12.84 per cent a year. If you'd bought a home for cash, your investment would have been £3,820, and your rate of return 11.92 per cent a year. If you'd had a 90 per cent mortgage instead of an 80 per cent one, gearing would have been even more profitable.

If you sell your home at a profit and use that profit to buy another home, the size of your mortgage relative to the cost of your home is likely to decrease. So a first-time buyer might get a 90 per cent mortgage, then sell the home and get a 70 per cent mortgage on the new home. This lessens the effect of gearing, and means that the return on the investment will be smaller (of course, if house prices were to fall, the *loss* would also be smaller).

But, be warned, your investment may come adrift if the mortgage rate (after tax relief) exceeds the rate of increase in the price of your house. And when house prices are falling, you might end up owing more on your mortgage than your house would fetch (known as 'negative equity').

House prices in the future

If you've owned a home over the last 20 years, you will almost certainly have seen its value increase. Indeed, you may well have seen it do better than many other forms of investment. Is this likely to remain the long-term trend?

It's impossible to say for certain. Anyone who bought their first property, or 'geared up' into a larger property at the peak of the market in 1988 or 1989 is likely to feel less certain of the future state of the property market. On reflection it is easy to see how the property market overheated in the late 1980s. In 1986 there was a change to the way mortgage interest relief was given to joint-ownership of property. Notice of this change was given by the government many months before the restriction came into effect, and it helped fuel a short and very strong property boom in the late 1980s. This was quickly followed by an economic recession and a dramatic fall in the property market. A significant number of home-owners who took out large mortgages at the top of the market faced negative equity – where their mortgage was larger than the total value of their house or flat – and a number of homes were repossessed by mortgage lenders.

The market remained very weak for the first half of the 1990s but 1996 saw the beginning of a recovery. For the year from 31 March 1997 to 31 March 1998, the average increase in house prices across the UK was 12.7 per cent according to the Nationwide Building Society. The map on page 152 shows that most regions gained between 5 and 10 per cent with the notable exception of the Outer Metropolitan Area, where the gain was an average 21 per cent. The flurry of activity that generated this exceptional rise has already slowed down (by April 1998) and was, at least in part, due to a shortage of properties on the market. If there are more buyers than available properties, then the prices are forced up.

The good news is not spread evenly over home-owners. The one- or two-bedroom 'starter homes' which many people bought in the late 1980s just to get a foothold in the market, were among the worst hit when prices fell and now may be bypassed by new first-time buyers today. There is also a fundamental change in the property-buying population now which will have a long-term effect on the property market (and other areas). In the 1980s many young people ventured into the property market for the first time, but now the population has fewer 20–30-year olds to take up the 'first-time buyers' properties. And the numbers of new young buyers is falling each year. While this is a relatively small influence on house prices compared to economic booms or recessions, it is likely that future demand for one-bedroom 'starter homes' will not match that seen in the 1980s.

The prospects for 1998 look encouraging. As prices rise, the numbers of home-owners caught in the negative equity trap continues to fall. In the long run, buying your own property still looks to be the right decision in the UK. Several surveys and analyses in mid-1992 suggest that owner-occupation remains most people's goal – so it's unlikely that a large housing rental market will develop, as in some other European countries. But it is also unlikely that investing in property will give rise to the sorts of fantastic profits many enjoyed in the 1980s. Property prices will probably resume the gentle trend seen before this period.

A second property as an investment

With the relatively low property prices, low interest rates and high property rental rates, many investors will consider buying a second property to generate a rental income. Unlike most of the other investments covered in this book, letting property involves much more than deciding to put your money into this market. You need to do your research first.

What type of property should you buy?

You will need to decide which area of the letting market you want to target. In any region of the country there will be, in practice, a minimum rental rate and so a one-bedroom flat at the bottom of the price range will provide a better return on your capital than a three-bedroom house. However, your tenants will be different, depending on the size of your property. You may find that a one-bed flat tends to be sought by young single people for a short term (although for legal reasons the minimum let is usually six months), whereas a family house may be let by the same family for a few years. You will also need to decide whether you want to rent the property furnished or unfurnished.

A holiday home will be let on a weekly or monthly basis and (if fully let) will provide the highest return. But you will need to consider the additional costs (and responsibility) of cleaning and laundry before new guests arrive.

Sorting out a mortgage

There are specialist mortgage schemes available to potential landlords. But before you can decide on the size of your mortgage you need to work out the figures carefully. The higher the mortgage, the lower the net return on your capital. You need to calculate your expected rental against the property prices and allow for all the overheads involved. You will have start-up costs when buying the property, legal fees, and sorting out the tenancy arrangements as well as ongoing maintenance costs. You should consider the worst-case scenario, i.e. for how long can you afford the property to be sitting empty? How do the figures add up if interest rates rise? Have you an emergency fund to replace the central heating boiler? (When you let a property you may not have time to shop around for the cheapest plumber – tenants naturally expect problems to be resolved quickly.)

Should you use a rental agency?

Before you buy your property it is important to research the existing rental market in your chosen area. Speak to a number of rental agencies to see what they offer and check the local papers to see how easy it is to advertise your property yourself. If you decide not to use a letting agent, you need to consider how you will deal with awkward tenants or non-payment of the rent. You can use an agent merely to provide a tenant or to manage the property on your behalf and simply send you the rent (net of their charges and maintenance costs).

What rent should you charge?

A rental agent will be able to advise you on the local rates for different properties and what aspects of the property will enhance or reduce the level of rent you can expect. Rental income is one of the few types of investment income that is still taxed at your top rate of tax (rather than the lower 20 per cent).

Verdict

Buying and letting a property can be a profitable investment. Your return will obviously depend on the size of the mortgage compared to your capital investment. Moreover, property values are expected to rise, which will add to your investment (although they could go down as well as up).

You must be prepared to do your own research before buying a property and discuss your proposals with the experts (i.e. estate agents, letting agents and a solicitor). Property is a long-term investment: it may take months (even years) to sell your property and release your capital.

Given all this, buying property to rent out is a high-risk and time-consuming form of investment.

11

SAVING IN BANKS AND BUILDING SOCIETIES

Banks, and especially building societies, are very popular homes for people's savings. Both types of organisation offer a range of *deposit-based* savings schemes, and the difference between the two types is becoming smaller and smaller. Banks will use the money they borrow in this way to finance all kinds of lending activities; building societies still use most of their borrowings to lend to individuals who want to buy their own homes.

Most organisations which offer deposit-based accounts that are not building societies are properly called banks (including many 'finance companies'), and are authorised to do business under the Banking Act of 1987 and regulated by the Bank of England. A bank is a *limited company*, owned by its shareholders; a building society is a *mutual* organisation, owned by its investor members and regulated by the Building Societies Act 1997. From 1999, both banks and building societies will be registered by the Financial Services Authority (see Chapter 5).

The largest of the building societies can, if they and their members wish, 'convert' into banks: Abbey National did this first in 1989, and in 1997 alone the following building societies also converted into banks: Alliance & Leicester; Bristol & West; Halifax; Northern Rock; and the Woolwich.

A safe home for your savings?

Building societies have traditionally been very safe places to invest; they rarely run into difficulties and those that did were quietly bailed out by others.

This safety results partly from the fact that societies' traditional business has been restricted to lending on mortgage securities. But societies, particularly the large ones, are now diversifying into many different financial products, and some observers worry that this might in time shake their tradition of security. However, there are limits on what proportion of 'riskier' business societies can undertake, and your investment is protected by law to the same degree, no matter how large or small the society with which you invest.

If a society gets into difficulties, you are guaranteed to get back 90 per cent of up to the first £20,000 of your savings in that society; with a joint account each account-holder is separately protected up to £20,000. (Money saved with a bank has the same level of protection through the Bank Deposit Protection Scheme).

Offshore accounts

Money placed in most offshore locations and held in branches of UK banks or subsidiary companies of building societies is not covered by the bank and building society protection schemes. But building societies are required by law to make good any losses that a subsidiary fails to cover. The Isle of Man runs a compensation scheme for building societies and banks similar to the UK bank scheme.

There is also a problem with probate when you die: it may cost several hundred pounds and take a month or two for your savings to be released to your executors.

What's on offer

Building societies and banks offer a wide range of different investment schemes. Though many accounts have descriptive names, these can be a very misleading guide to the actual terms and conditions of the account. A single account may have a number of 'variations' that can completely change it. And account types vary from time to time.

So it is more useful to look at the features generally available on accounts: most 'new' account types are composed of different selections of these basic features. Armed with this knowledge, you can go on to see how these features are applied in practice to the account types currently available, and then decide how to go about choosing an account for your particular needs.

Basic features

Although schemes differ, they are all based on variations of three main factors:

- how you intend to *pay money in*, when and in what form
- how easily and quickly you want to be able to make *withdrawals*
- how the bank or building society pays *interest*.

Paying money in

Some schemes have no restrictions on how you pay your money in – you can open the account with a modest pound or two, and pay in what you like, when you like. But many do have restrictions:

- the minimum investment to open an account can vary from a pound up to tens of thousands of pounds
- you may not be allowed to make any additions to the account once it's opened
- you may be allowed to make additions only in certain multiples, e.g. in lumps of £100
- you may have to make regular additions, usually every month
- you may be restricted to a maximum investment level (though rarely less than around £20,000, except perhaps for children's accounts).

There are also practical aspects to making investments. Most organisations will accept money over the counter at their branches or through the post, and a few are linked to a network of cash machines that allow you to make deposits outside normal opening hours. Some building societies have agents such as solicitors, insurance brokers and estate agents through whom you can deposit money. Some building societies and banks market special 'postal-only' accounts. But apart from the fact that these societies should be geared up to dealing with quantities of postal transactions efficiently, there's no intrinsic difference between them and any other bank or society which will deal by post, though they often pay a higher rate of interest than branch-based instant access accounts.

There is no formal limit on how much you can invest in any one organisation, but some set their own limits, which may vary from account to account. Occasionally this may be as low as £30,000, but it's usually not less than £100,000.

Withdrawals

Some accounts let you get at your savings instantly, on demand; others require you to give some notice or lock your money away for a period of time (a *term*).

To make these *notice accounts* and *term shares* more attractive over and above a higher rate of interest than banks, building society accounts may offer a number of concessions:

■ easy access to the balance over a certain amount in your account. The 'balance-over' figure is often £10,000 and the access usually instant: that is, if you have £12,000 invested you can withdraw up to £2,000 on demand, whatever the normal conditions for withdrawals

■ instant access, in spite of the normal withdrawal conditions, if you pay a penalty charge (e.g. three months' interest, or so much for every £100 you withdraw)

■ instant access without a penalty, restricted, for example, to £3,000 or one-tenth of your balance once or twice a year.

■ up to, say, three withdrawals allowed per annum without penalty (provided the balance doesn't fall below the minimum savings balance if there is one)

■ a bonus of, say, 0.75 per cent if you make no withdrawals within the year. Beware of adverts that include this bonus in the rate quoted – will you really get it?

There may be other restrictions on withdrawals:

■ withdrawing only part of your savings may not be allowed; you may have to close the account if you want to take any money out

■ you may have to withdraw in fixed multiples of, say, £100, or even £1,000.

Interest

How often is interest paid?

Accounts are available which pay interest yearly (occasionally even less frequently), half-yearly, quarterly or monthly. For an explanation of how the frequency of interest affects the true rate of interest you get, see Chapter 1.

In most cases you can choose to have the interest:

■ paid out to you, or directly into another account with the same or a different organisation

■ kept in the same account to roll up (so that you get compound interest). This option is not often available where the interest is paid monthly.

Some accounts offer a choice of interest payment frequencies, e.g. half-yearly or monthly. If they do, there may be penalties such as lower interest rates or higher minimum investments if you choose to have your interest paid more frequently.

How are interest rates quoted?
Banks and building societies usually think in terms of gross (before-tax) rates – despite the fact that for most customers they have to deduct tax before adding it to the account.

Advertisements and rates cards will often quote up to four rates:

■ **gross** – the *flat rate* before taking into account how often interest is paid, and without deduction of any tax. This is the 'contractual' rate – the rate on which (subject to the account conditions) the bank or society is obliged to base its calculations for paying you

■ **net** – the *flat rate* after deduction of tax at 20 per cent. You'll usually find a phrase in the literature along the lines of 'net rates are illustrative only, and are based on the deduction of tax at 20 per cent'. So, if the rates of income tax change, the bank or society isn't obliged to pay you on the basis of the net rate shown

■ **gross compounded annual rate (CAR)**: a true rate of return taking into account how often interest is compounded within the account. The gross CAR is the rate at which a non-taxpayer will earn over a full year, provided the interest remains in the account

■ **net CAR** – the net rate compounded, and what a lower-rate or basic-rate taxpayer will earn over a full year. Higher-rate taxpayers will have to pay extra tax, so reducing their effective interest rate – see below.

If a CAR figure is not quoted, it usually implies that interest is paid once a year, and the compounded rates are the same as the flat rates.

Variable or fixed interest?
Most accounts are *variable*, which means that a building society or bank can change interest rates (up or down) on any of its accounts, whenever it likes, without giving any notice, and without making any special concessions to its existing account-holders.

An overall increase or decrease in bank rates is usually triggered by a change in the bank base rate, and banks tend to respond to such a change quite quickly, while building societies may move more slowly. A general change in their savings rate is usually signalled by one of the largest societies and often linked to a change in mortgage rates and a sustained change in bank base rates. Over the following couple of months almost all other societies will move their rates in line with the signallers.

Some accounts offer a *guaranteed premium* (or differential), guaranteeing to pay at least a set amount above the rate of one of the other accounts offered by the bank or building society, whatever happens to rates generally (though perhaps only for a year or two after you take up the offer). In practice, many accounts act as though they had a guaranteed premium, so this is not something you need look out for especially.

There are also accounts where the rate is *fixed* for a period, regardless of whatever happens to interest rates generally during that time: see overleaf.

How is interest taxed?
Building societies and banks will normally deduct tax at 20 per cent from your interest before adding it to your account.

If you're a *higher-rate* taxpayer, you'll have to pay additional tax of the difference between 20 per cent and 40 per cent. This isn't collected by the banks and building societies; the Inland Revenue will send you a tax bill later.

If you're a *non-taxpayer* you don't have to pay tax on your building society and bank interest. Get *form R85* from a building society, bank, or tax office: if you can declare that your total income from all sources (including interest) is likely to be less than your total tax allowances for the coming year, sign the form and take it to your building society or bank, which will then pay you interest gross.

If after the end of a tax year you find that you've had more tax deducted from your savings than you are liable for, you can claim a repayment from the Inland Revenue.

If all holders of a joint account are non-taxpayers, they will each need to complete a *form R85*. If not all are, the bank or building society may allow the non-taxpayers their share of interest gross; otherwise they will have to claim a repayment of tax from the Inland Revenue. Joint accounts are almost always deemed to be held by their owners in equal shares.

For more on tax, see Chapter 7.

How much interest?
As a rule of thumb, the longer your money is tied up, and the larger the investment required, the higher the interest rate.

Tiered interest accounts stick to this rule: the larger your investment, the higher the interest. Usually you get the higher interest automatically if your balance grows enough to tip you into a higher tier (the rate is cut automatically if it falls), but watch out for accounts that do not do so. You usually get the highest rate your investment level entitles you to on the *whole* of your balance, but a few accounts pay you the higher rates only on the amount of your money in each tier (which results in a lower average rate overall).

A tiered interest account can be linked to notice periods rather than investment levels.

Some accounts pay a bonus if you satisfy particular conditions, such as not making any withdrawals for a year.

Interest is usually calculated on the balance in your account each day, but in a few cases it may be worked out on a less advantageous basis, e.g. your lowest balance over a month.

Types of account

Cheque accounts

Quite a few savings accounts now include the use of a chequebook. Some of them are full current accounts that pay interest and offer a chequebook that allows you to write as many cheques as you like; a cheque guarantee card; cash machines; and access to overdrafts, standing orders and direct debits. But note that you will be able to get higher interest from an account that does not offer all these extras.

At the other end of the scale are instant access accounts that simply include a chequebook as your means of making easy withdrawals. You get none of the other facilities of a current account; there may be a minimum investment of £2,000 or more; and you may have to pay a fee for all or some (e.g. after the first half-dozen a quarter) of the cheques you write. In return for these restrictions you should get a better rate of interest than from an interest-bearing current account, but you might get a higher rate still from an account without any chequebook.

Fixed-rate accounts

Accounts that offer a fixed rate of interest for a fixed term are a gamble because you are 'locked in' for an agreed period of time. If rates fall you may do well; if they rise you might have been better off with a variable rate account. You cannot normally withdraw before the end of the term, and certainly not without suffering a penalty.

Beware of interest rates that are fixed for only part of the term of the account: such rates can fall dramatically when the fixed-rate period ends, leaving you locked into a poor-paying account.

Instant access accounts

Many instant access accounts have *tiered interest* rates, with minimum investment levels and tiers ranging anywhere from £1 to tens of thousands of pounds. Even though instant withdrawals are allowed, there may still be some restrictions with building society accounts: often you can draw no more than £250 in cash, perhaps as little as £5,000 as a cheque; larger cash sums or cheques could take up to three days to arrange.

Beware of accounts that give you instant access, but only if you pay a penalty charge. Beware, too, of accounts which give you instant access only to the balance over a certain amount (though if this amount is low, these accounts can still be useful if you have a large amount to invest).

A penalty charge trap

Watch out for accounts that *always* operate a penalty charge. Some of these are term shares, so you do not suffer the penalty if you leave your money invested for the full term. But some are not: if you have no way of escaping a penalty charge, it means you'll never get as high an interest rate as that quoted, taken over the whole period of your investment.

Money market accounts

With many bank accounts (and very occasionally a building society account) the interest is linked to the rates paid on the money markets. The rate can fluctuate quite frequently, in some cases every day; and often it is reviewed every week.

These accounts come with all sorts of minimum investment stipulations and notice periods, although instant access high-minimum investment types are perhaps the most common. Many offer the use of a chequebook.

Monthly income accounts

These are accounts that pay out interest monthly, to help you boost your income. They come with all sorts of minimum investment levels and notice periods. Though your capital is as safe as in any other building society or bank account , your monthly income will fluctuate as rates vary – unless you go for a *fixed-rate* monthly income account.

Monthly income accounts are often variations of other accounts, but with perhaps a higher minimum investment and a lower interest rate, so make sure that you are looking at the right version of the account.

Notice accounts

Accounts allowing you access to your money at three months' notice are very popular, but there are many with shorter notice periods (down to one week) and others with longer (four months to two years) notice periods. Notice accounts ought to pay a higher rate of interest because your money is tied up for an agreed amount of time. However, at times some institutions pay much higher interest on their instant access accounts in order to attract new savers.

Most notice accounts allow instant access if you pay a *penalty charge* of, usually, the same number of months' interest as the notice period. For example, on a three-month account you can give either three months' notice, or have instant access and lose the equivalent of three months' interest on the money you're withdrawing. These are useful in an emergency, but can reduce drastically the effective interest rate you get.

You may have access to the balance over a certain amount in a notice account without notice or penalty. And some accounts are *tiered interest* accounts with minimum investment levels and tiers ranging anywhere from £1 (though £500 is more common) to tens of thousands of pounds.

Regular savings accounts

Regular savings accounts have recently made a come back and are offered by many major banks and building societies. This means that rates have become more competitive against other types of accounts. They could be useful if you need to discipline yourself to save regularly.

Regular savings offer perhaps the most complicated conditions of any account type, so check carefully that what you are being offered suits your needs. Ask:
■ what are the minimum and maximum amounts I can save each month?
■ can I vary the amount I save as I wish each month, or only by agreement with the society?

- can I miss payments? How many can I miss, and how often?
- can I withdraw part of my savings? How much can I withdraw, and how often?
- are there any restrictions (such as a notice period) for closing the account?
- is there a maximum term for this account?

In general, the more restrictive the conditions you accept, the higher the interest rate.

Term accounts

These are accounts that lock your money up for a period of time, which can be anything from a few days to perhaps five years. The term is usually fixed at the time you open the account, either as a fixed amount of time (e.g. six months or two years), or as a fixed date (e.g. a term ending on 1 December 1998) and the rate of interest is usually fixed for the term.

Normally, you will not be allowed to withdraw until the account *matures* at the end of its term; if you are allowed withdrawals, then you will have to pay a *penalty charge* and perhaps give some months' notice as well, or be restricted to withdrawing only the balance over a certain amount. You may not be allowed to add to the account, though normally you can start another one.

Check what happens to your investment at the end of the term. It may be:
- automatically cashed in – you'll be sent a cheque
- automatically transferred to another account, which pays a different rate of interest
- left where it is, paying the same rate of interest, and converted into a notice account (in which case check whether you can give the required notice *before* the end of the term, otherwise the term will be longer than you originally thought, e.g. if you have to give three months' notice at the end of a one-year term share you've in effect got a 15-month term share)
- automatically reinvested for a further term (though not necessarily at the same rate). This is more likely to happen with the shorter-period bank term accounts.

TESSAs

Anyone aged 18 and over may hold one Tax-Exempt Special Savings Account (TESSA) with a bank or building society. They are designed as a savings scheme parallel to shareholding Personal Equity Plans (PEPs): stick to the scheme conditions and the interest you earn will be free of both basic-rate and higher-rate tax.

You can open a new TESSA at any time until 5 April 1999 and pay into it under existing rules for the full five years, thereafter the new Individual Savings Account (ISA), available from 6 April 1999, will be the tax-efficient replacement for TESSAs. For more details on TESSAs see Chapter 8.

Children's accounts

Many banks and building societies have an account aimed at children. This may offer little more than a colourful passbook with a cartoon character; or it may offer a wide range of extras, such as free gifts, membership to zoos and clubs, donations to charities, magazines and so on.

Interest rates vary from among the lowest of any account to some of the higher rates; usually the higher payers offer the least extras. However, high interest might not be the most important factor for a child in deciding where to save. See Chapter 4 for more on investing for children.

Flexible mortgage accounts

This account, as the name suggests, is a type of mortgage, however it also incorporates a current account and savings account. Flexible mortgage accounts have only recently been available and so far only two or three lenders operate the full mortgage, current account and credit package.

This unique type of account works in the following way: you pay your salary or other income direct into your mortgage account where it pays the interest and reduces the outstanding balance on your mortgage. You can then draw whatever you need (which will increase your outstanding mortgage balance) using the normal current account facilities i.e. cash card, debit card, cheque book, etc.

The benefit of this arrangement is that any excess savings you have from month to month are used to reduce your outstanding mortgage (and the interest payable on it) rather than left in a standard current account earning minimal interest. Because your 'current account balance' is reducing your mortgage, the savings you make in interest payments are equivalent to your receiving interest on the money at your mortgage interest rate free of tax. (There is no tax to pay because you are reducing your mortgage interest payments rather than earning interest.)

Flexible mortgage arrangements have been welcomed by the government as more suitable to modern lifestyles where income streams and expenditure may fluctuate from time to time.

Friendly society bonds

Some (very few) building society accounts are linked with friendly societies that are allowed to offer a very restricted tax-free regular savings scheme. You pay a *maximum* of £25 a month (or £270 a year) for ten years and the friendly society invests the money with the building society. Because the scheme is tax-free, you make a little more interest than you would by investing directly in the building society, but not as much as you might think (only 1 to 2 per cent or so extra) because of the friendly societies' management charges. The scheme is free of higher-rate tax, too, so is more appealing to higher-rate taxpayers (but the actual number of pounds involved is small because the savings limits are so restricted). From 5 April 1999 to 5 April 2004 savers will also get a 10 per cent tax credit on the interest, in line with the new Individual Savings Accounts (ISAs).

If you cash in within the first seven and a half years, you get back, at most, only your gross premiums; if you cash in between seven and a half and ten years you may get a little more.

A version allowing you to pay in a lump sum (maximum £1,145) is also available: the money goes into a building society account from which the regular premiums are automatically paid. Because you have to pay tax in the normal way on the interest on this pool of money, the lump sum scheme has a lower effective rate of interest. To a basic-rate taxpayer it could be little better than the best normal building society account, which would offer better access and fewer restrictions.

Permanent Interest-Bearing Shares (PIBS)

Building societies were first allowed to offer these from 1 June 1991, but only a few of the biggest societies have done so. They bear no relation to building society 'share' accounts (as the simplest instant access accounts are often called): instead, you buy a share in the building society, which then pays you a fixed rate of interest for an unlimited period.

PIBS are traded like ordinary stocks and shares – purchased through a stockbroker. The value of the share will depend on what the market will pay for it. The minimum amount that can be purchased varies from £1,000 to £50,000.

The coupons compared well with many other fixed-interest investments, at about 9 to 13.5 per cent before tax. The prices vary depending on the coupon, but gross yields in May 1998 are around 7.25 per cent. Like fixed-interest British Government stocks, they're likely to be bad value in times of high inflation.

If the building society goes bust, the last person in line for the remaining assets will be the PIBS-holder. And they're not covered by the compensation arrangements that normally apply to building society investments, nor by the Investors' Compensation Scheme (unless you bought through an investment adviser or manager who goes bust).

It may be less likely that a building society will go under than other types of institution, but it's still early days for PIBS, so proceed with caution.

Making your choice

Too little income to pay tax?
You can get your interest without deduction of tax from any bank or building society account provided you can sign a declaration stating that you're likely to be a non-taxpayer in that tax year.

Looking at a large tax bill?
Consider offshore accounts. You still have to pay tax – but you may be able to arrange things so that the tax bill falls due in a year that suits you.

Investing for the long term?
Building society and bank investments are safe, but over the long term may not make as much as more risky forms of investment. If you have a very large sum to invest for a long period, think about putting some of it into other investments – see Chapters 1 and 2.

Don't need your money for a year or so?
Term accounts look tempting, but you may get as good or better rates of interest (especially on large sums) from a *notice* or even *instant access* account, as well as easier access to your money. There's always the possibility with

variable-rate term shares that the rate may go down significantly once you're locked in.

TESSAs look inviting if you can keep one up for the full five years and collect the interest tax-free. But they're worth thinking about even over a shorter period provided you don't have to pay a penalty for early closure – the best can match or beat the best term shares.

Think interest rates will fall?
Check *fixed-rate* accounts – but compare them with the best variable rates on offer before you decide whether the gamble is likely to be worthwhile. Consider British Government stocks or guaranteed income bonds.

Prepared to wait a while for your money?
A *notice* account may give higher interest than one offering instant access – often, the longer the notice period, the higher the interest will be. But don't tie up money you think you may need to get out quickly. Consider a TESSA, provided it has no penalties for early closure.

Can't wait, won't wait?
Try an *instant access* account. If you have a large investment and need instant access to only part of your money, look at a notice account that gives you instant access to money above a certain amount. Or can you make do with a short notice account (say up to a month)?

Want a regular income?
You can draw a monthly income from any account, but it is easiest to do so from an account offering *monthly interest* – many different types offer this. If you want a fixed income, think also about other investments like British Government stocks or guaranteed income bonds.

Want to save regularly?
A *regular savings* account is a possibility, if you need to be disciplined. The rates are good compared to other instant access or notice accounts. A regular savings TESSA is worth considering if you can save for five years (especially if you are a higher-rate taxpayer). Use the route map on pages 32 to 35 to guide you to the other types of savings and investment available.

Expect your savings to fluctuate?
Think about an account with a *tiered interest rate* structure. But if you do, keep an eye on your balance and what it is earning.

Choosing a home for your savings

With over 3,000 accounts and variations on accounts on offer, from scores of banks and building societies, picking the best buy is not easy. Consider first *convenience*: if you want to withdraw *and* deposit money quickly and frequently (and especially if you want current-account facilities) then you will need a branch or a cash machine close to your home or place of work; this will restrict you to the larger high-street organisations and whichever local ones are in your area.

For larger, more infrequent transactions, you can deal by post. This gives you a wider range of organisations from which to choose. When comparing rates:

■ note that slight differences in interest rate are important only with large investments. For example, on an investment of £1,000, 1 per cent extra on a rate will make you only between £10 and £10.47 extra in a full year

■ make sure you are comparing the right rate. The CAR or 'true' rate applies strictly only to money that is invested for a full year or more. If you are investing for a period much shorter than a year, the 'flat' rate is a better comparative guide.

For more information check for regular surveys and the 'Savings Monitor' in *Which?* magazine,* personal finance magazines and the personal finances pages of daily newspapers and summaries in *Moneyfacts.**

12

NATIONAL SAVINGS INVESTMENTS

One way in which the government raises money is to borrow it from the public. It offers various forms of investment in the hope that people will put their money in them. One such investment is the wide range of British Government stocks, dealt with in Chapter 19. Here, we look at National Savings investments.

National Savings Certificates

The first National Savings Certificates – called War Savings Certificates – were issued in 1916. Since then, governments have brought out a new issue whenever the rate of interest on the old issue seemed too high, or too low, in the prevailing circumstances. Normally, you can buy only one issue – the current one – at any one time. In all, various governments have brought out 46 issues of National Savings Certificates (by March 1998). Once you've bought a certificate you can in practice hold it indefinitely. Moreover, you don't have to have been alive and investing in 1916 in order to own some of the first issue, because certificates can be inherited. So you could hold quite a wide range of certificates. Here we tell you about conventional National Savings Certificates – see page 179 for index-linked certificates.

How interest is paid

With all National Savings Certificates, no interest is paid out to you: it's added on to the value of your certificate, and you get it when you cash in the certificate. The interest is free of income tax and capital gains tax doesn't apply.

With the early issues (up to and including the 6th) interest is added *ad infinitum* to the value of your certificates at a fixed rate of five-twelfths a month (or, with some of these issues, 112p or 114p every three months). Because the amount of interest is fixed, it follows that the rate of interest – expressed as a yearly percentage return on the value of your investment – is going down, year by year. These now offer a miserly rate of return of well under 2 per cent a year.

For issues after the 6th, the interest paid used to vary depending on the issue and the year; the exact rates were fixed for a certain number of years at a time, e.g. five or seven years. But in 1982, the government announced that when a particular certificate got to the end of the period for which interest rates had been set, a common rate of interest called the *general extension rate* would be paid. The general extension rate was 3.51 per cent as we went to press.

Below, we give details of the 46th issue, the one available when this book went to press in April 1998. And then we look in detail at whether you should cash in any old certificates you have.

Investing in National Savings Certificates (46th issue)

Anyone can invest, irrespective of their age. You can invest anything between £100 and £10,000, so certificates are suitable for both lump sums and savings. A husband and wife can invest up to £10,000 each; if the certificates are in their joint names, however, they can invest only £10,000 between them.

If you have earlier issues of National Savings Certificates, which you've held for at least five years, or mature Yearly Plan savings, you can reinvest an unlimited amount in *Reinvestment Certificates* on top of the ordinary £10,000 limit. The terms are the same as for other 46th issue certificates, except that if you cash reinvestment certificates within one year of having invested you will get interest equivalent to 3.75 per cent a year for each complete three months of investment.

How to invest
Fill in an application form available from most post offices and banks or watch out for advertisements in the press. Your certificate showing how much you have bought will be sent to you later.

How much interest?

Interest is added to the value of your certificate over the period of its life (which is five years at the outset). The amount of interest added increases as time goes by, giving you an added incentive to hang on to your certificates. Table 1 below gives the details, and shows the rate of interest for each year. Within any year, it's the rate of interest in the right-hand column which you should compare with, say, the after-tax (or, for non-taxpayers, the gross) rate of interest on building society accounts. If you hold the certificate for the full five years, the overall yearly rate of return works out at 4.8 per cent.

Table 1: How a unit of the 46th issue grows

During year	£100 certificate increases by	For each complete	Value at end of year	Rate of interest for year
1	£3.60	12 months	£103.60	3.6%
2	£3.94	12 months	£107.54	3.8%
3	£4.73	12 months	£112.27	4.4%
4	£5.84	12 months	£118.11	5.2%
5	£8.31	12 months	£126.42	7.04%

How do you cash your certificates?

Get *form DNS502* from a post office. You shouldn't have to wait more than a couple of weeks for your money. You can also cash in part of your certificate – just let National Savings know how much you want repaid.

What happens to your certificates should you die?

Your heirs can either cash in the certificates or transfer them into their own names. *Form DNS904* from most post offices will get things under way.

What about your old certificates?

Because interest is not paid out, but added on to the value of your certificates, working out what return you are actually getting from your investment is not an easy matter. Moreover, besides needing to know the rate of interest you are getting now, you need to know what interest will be paid on them in the next year or two, in case the interest, though low at the time of investing, will get better later on.

First, find your Savings Certificates. Next, check which issue (or issues) your certificates are. This is printed on the certificates, e.g. *sixth issue, decimal issue*. Next, look at the date stamp on each certificate to find out when it was bought.

If you are still holding certificates from one of the very earliest issues – from the 1st to the 6th (on sale from 1916 until November 1939) – the interest rate you are getting on these is very poor at between 1.1 and 1.8 per cent a year.

For later issues you should look at Table 2. If there isn't an entry that matches the age and issue of certificates you hold, you are earning interest at the *general extension rate* – see page 176. At present, this is below the average instant access account rate for all building societies which is just below 4 per cent. However, depending on how much money you have in old certificates you may be able to increase your return by investing your money elsewhere, or by reinvesting in new certificates

If there is an entry that relates to a certificate you hold, then column 3 gives the value of the initial £100 investment in 1998 on the anniversary of the date it was bought. For example, £100 of the 41st issue (or 4 certificates of £25) bought on 16 January 1994 will be worth £120.95 on 16 January 1998. This value is that for a single unit. The certificate documents you have may in fact say they are for multiples of 2, 3, 4 or more units.

Interest
■ **Column 4** tells you the rate of interest paid for the year ending during 1998, on the anniversary of the date the certificates were bought. As the interest is tax-free, this is, in effect, the after-tax rate of return.
■ **Column 5** tells you the rate of interest due to be paid in the year ending during 1999 on the anniversary of the date the certificates were bought.
■ **Column 6** tells you the rate of interest for the year ending during 2000.

Value for money
As we have said, all the early issues from the 1st to the 6th give a very low return – it varies between 1.1 and 1.8 per cent. Other investments or new certificates can give a much better return. So if you have any of these early issues, cash them in at once or reinvest.

With certificates of the later issues, compare the return you're getting with that available on other investments (taking your rate of tax into account). (For details of current best buys see the 'Savings Monitor,' in *Which?* magazine.*) Don't forget to look at the rate of return next year, and the

Table 2: Old National Savings Certificates

1 Name of issue (and issue price)	2 Year bought £100	3 Value in 1998 at anniversary of date bought	4 Interest now	5 Interest next year	6 Interest year after next
			rate of interest for year ending at anniversary of date bought in:		
			1998	1999	2000
		£	%	%	%
41st (£25)	1993	130.08	7.55	[1]	[1]
	1994	120.95	6.40	7.55	[1]
42nd	1994	122.51	6.75	8.46	[1]
	1995	114.76	5.50	6.75	8.46
	1996	108.78	4.60	5.50	6.75
43rd	1996	108.06	4.15	5.00	6.15
	1997	103.75	3.75	4.15	5.00
44th	1997	103.75	3.75	4.15	5.00
	1998	–	–	3.75	4.15
45th	1998	–	–	3.60	3.90
46th	1998	–	–	3.60	3.80

[1] General extension rate

year after next, before coming to a decision. For example, with the 42nd issue bought in 1995, although the rate of return in 1998 is 5.5 per cent, in 1999 you'd get 6.75 per cent, and the year after 8.46 percent. So it may be worth hanging on to them.

Index-linked National Savings Certificates (13th issue)

These certificates are worth considering if you're worried about inflation. They guarantee that the buying power of the money you invest will keep pace with the rising prices. For how they compare with index-linked British Government stocks, see Chapter 19.

How much can you invest?
You can invest anything between £100 and £10,000, so they are suitable for both lump sums or savings (regular or a bit at a time). A husband and wife can each invest up to £10,000 (i.e. up to £20,000 in all). If the certificates are in

their joint names, however, they can invest only £10,000 between them.

If you have National Savings Certificates which you've held for at least five years, or mature Yearly Plan savings, you can reinvest an unlimited amount in *13th issue Reinvestment Certificates* on top of your normal £10,000 limit. The terms are the same as for other 13th issue index-linked certificates, except that if you cash in your investment within one year your investment will be increased in line with the Retail Prices Index (RPI) and you'll earn interest of 1.00% per annum for each complete month of investment.

How to invest
Go to a post office and fill in an application form. You'll get a receipt; your certificate, showing how much you've invested, will be sent on to you by post. You can also buy certificates direct from National Savings – there are frequent advertisements in the national press.

How index-linked certificates work

If you cash one in within a year of buying it, you get back only the money you invested in the first place. But after a year, its value is increased in line with the change in the RPI plus extra interest since you bought it. If you hold your certificate for the full five years, your overall return is 2.25 per cent a year on top of inflation. After five years, you should check what return you will get.

Table 3: How a £100 unit of the 13th index-linked issue grows

During year	Interest paid in each year %	Value at anniversary of date invested [1] £	Effective rate in year [2] %
1	1.0	103.50	3.5
2	1.2	107.32	3.7
3	1.6	111.72	4.1
4	2.6	117.41	5.1
5	4.9	126.09	7.4

[1] This is the sum of money you would get if you cashed in your unit having held it for exactly this number of years, assuming inflation runs at 2.25 per cent a year
[2] Assuming inflation runs at 2.25 per cent

Which month's index applies?
The level of the RPI for the previous month is announced on the second or third Friday of each month, and reported

in the newspapers the following day. When you buy a certificate or cash one in, the RPI figure that applies is the one announced in the previous month, which, in turn, refers to the cost of living in the month before that. See Chapter 7 for a list of RPI figures since March 1982.

Working out how much you'd get if you cashed in now
The easiest way to find out the present value of your holding in 13th issue index-linked certificates is to look at the chart on display at post offices. But to decide whether or not your return is worthwhile compared with other risk-free investments, you should also consider the rate of return you are getting. The effective rate you get varies, depending on the rate of inflation and on how long you hold the certificate.

Is there any tax to pay on the gain?
No, there isn't. The gain is free of both income tax and capital gains tax. This makes these certificates particularly attractive to people paying higher-rate income tax, or who may have chargeable capital gains from other investments.

What happens to your certificate if you die?
The certificate can be transferred into your heir's name, even if he or she already has the maximum holding of certificates.

How to cash in certificates
Get *form DNS502* from a post office. Fill it in and send it off together with the certificates in the pre-paid envelope provided with the form. You shouldn't have to wait longer than a couple of weeks for your money.

Can you cash in only part of your money?
Yes, you can cash in any amount you wish.

Any old National Savings Stamps?

Remember them – 10p each (or 6d and 1/– in pre-decimal days)? They were withdrawn on 31 December 1976, but you can still cash in any you've got knocking around. Send them to Remittance Section, National Savings,* and ask for their value to be refunded.

What happens if the RPI actually falls?
The value of your certificate goes down in line with the fall in the RPI though interest is still added. But it is guaranteed

that the certificate is never worth less than its value at the previous anniversary of purchase.

What happens if the rate of inflation goes down?
A fall in the *rate* of inflation usually means that the RPI is still going up, but not as fast as before; the value of your certificate will continue to increase, but at a slower rate. The value of your certificate will not fall. What's important from the point of view of your investment is how the rate of inflation, plus the interest, compares with the rate of return you could get on other comparatively safe invest-ments, e.g. bank and building society accounts.

Should you cash in old index-linked certificates?

You don't have to. You can keep your money where it is, and your investment will continue to be index-linked. Retirement, 2nd and 5th index-linked issue certificates that have matured are now earning only monthly index-linking. Mature certificates of the 3rd and 4th index-linked issues are now earning monthly index-linking plus extra interest of 0.5 per cent at the end of each period of a year. Generally you'll get a much better return if you reinvest in new certificates, and it's worth remembering that any amount you reinvest is on top of the normal limit for each issue.

Other National Savings investments

National Savings Ordinary account

Who can invest?
Anyone can open an account. For young children, the account can be opened by a relative or friend.

How much can you invest?
You must invest a minimum of £10 to open an account, while the maximum is £10,000, no matter how many Ordinary accounts you have. Each time you put money in you must deposit at least £10.

How to invest
You can open an account at most post offices – you'll be sent a bank book, in which a record is kept of all your transactions.

How much interest?
The rate of interest can vary, though it tends to be fixed for
at least one year at a time. For 1998, if your account is kept
open from 31 December 1997 to 1 January 1999, you'll
qualify for a higher rate of interest for each calendar month
in which the balance is £500 or more. Otherwise you'd get
the standard rate of interest. The current rates, unchanged
from April 1998, are 3.0 per cent for the higher rate and 2.0
per cent for the standard rate. Interest is worked out on each
complete £1 in the account for a full calendar month.
Money in your account doesn't start earning interest until
the start of the month following the one in which it is
deposited. And it stops getting interest from the start of the
month in which it is withdrawn. So you'll get most interest
if you put your money in on the last day of a month, and
take it out on the first day of a month.

Interest is added to your account on 31 December. The
first £70 interest is tax-free and a husband and wife can each
have this much interest tax-free (see Chapter 7 for more on
tax).

Getting your money out
You can withdraw up to £100 at once by taking your bank
book to most post offices. If you want more than £100, you
have to apply in writing on an application form available
from most post offices; getting your money could take
about a week (the limit is £250 if you have a *Regular
Customer Account* – check at your post office).

What happens if you die?
The money in your account can be cashed in or transferred
to your heir's account. *Form DNS904* gives all the details.

National Savings Investment account

Who can invest?
Anyone who can invest in the Ordinary account.

How much can you invest?
You must invest a minimum of £20 to open an account.
The maximum is £100,000, no matter how many Investment accounts you have. Each time you put money in, you
must deposit at least £20.

How to invest?
Follow the procedure for the Ordinary account.

Table 4: National Savings Investment account interest from April 1998

Investment (£)	Interest rate (%)
0–499	4.75
500–2,499	5.25
2,500–4,999	5.50
5,000–9,999	5.75
10,000–24,999	6.00
25,000–49,999	6.25
50,000 and over	6.50

How much interest?
The rate of interest varies (from April 1998 the rates are as shown in Table 4).

You receive the highest rate of interest on the whole amount invested – for example, if you invest £15,000 you will receive 6.00 per cent interest on the whole amount.

Interest is added to your account on 31 December. All interest is taxable, but is paid without tax having been deducted, which makes the account particularly suitable for non-taxpayers.

Getting your money out
You have to give one month's notice to withdraw your money. You can get an application form from most post offices. You'll have to send your bank book in with your application form. If you need to withdraw money without notice, a penalty of one month's interest will be charged on the amount withdrawn.

What happens if you die?
Follow the procedure for the Ordinary account.

National Savings Income Bonds

Who can invest?
Anyone, irrespective of age, can invest. Bonds can also be held jointly or in trust for a larger group of individuals. Income Bonds may be attractive to non-taxpayers who want a regular income from their savings.

How much can you invest?
The minimum for the first purchase is £2,000, and the minimum for each subsequent purchase is £1,000. Above these amounts you may buy a bond for any amount up to the maximum holding of £250,000.

How to invest

You can get an application form from a post office, which you send to National Savings, Blackpool.* A certificate showing the value of the bonds you have bought will be sent to you.

How much interest?

The rate of interest varies (from April 1998, the rate is 7 per cent for holdings less than £25,000 and 7.25 per cent for holdings £25,000 and over). Interest is paid out to you monthly (on the fifth day of each month). All interest is taxable, but is paid without tax having been deducted.

Getting your money out

You can give three calendar months' notice if you want to cash part or all of your bond. If you need your money immediately you can withdraw funds without notice but you will be charged a penalty of 90 days' interest on the amount withdrawn. If any holding of bonds remains after the repayment it must not be less than £2,000. Get *form DNS201* from a post office if you want to cash a bond.

What happens if you die?

Your heirs can cash the bonds without notice and with no loss of interest. *Form DNS904* gives details of what to do.

National Savings Deposit Bonds

Who can invest?

Deposit Bonds were withdrawn from sale in November 1988. However, if you bought bonds before that date you can continue to hold them and withdraw part or all of your savings.

How much interest?

The interest rate varies and is currently 6.5 per cent. Interest is added to the value of your bond each year on the anniversary of your investment. This interest is taxable, but it is paid without tax having been deducted.

Getting your money out

You can withdraw any amount above £50, as long as at least £100 of your original investment remains if you wish to keep the account open. You have to give three months' notice. Forms for withdrawals are available at post offices.

What happens if you die?
Your heirs can withdraw your investment without notice and with no loss of interest. *Form DNS904* gives the details of what to do.

National Savings Capital Bonds Series L

Who can invest?
Anyone aged seven and over can invest. Although children under seven can't buy Capital Bonds, anyone aged seven or over can buy bonds on their behalf. Bonds can also be held jointly by two savers of any age. Capital Bonds can be especially attractive to non-taxpayers who don't want income from their savings. But they are worth considering only if you are prepared to tie up your money for five years.

How much can you invest?
You have to invest at least £100. There is a maximum investment of £250,000. In addition, your total investment in National Savings Capital Bonds (excluding Series A) cannot be more than £250,000; National Savings Capital Bonds of a Reinvestment Series are not counted towards this limit. A husband and wife can each have £250,000 invested in Capital Bonds; if the bonds are held in joint names, they can invest only £250,000 between them. Capital Bonds would be suitable for lump sum investments or occasional savings.

How to invest
You can buy your bond at a post office or you can send your application direct to National Savings, Glasgow.* In either case your certificate will be sent to you later from the Capital Bond Office at National Savings, Glasgow. You can get a Capital Bond booklet *(DNS768)* from most post offices.

How much interest?
Interest is added to the value of your bond over its five-year life and the amount is fixed at the time of purchase. The interest added increases each year, giving you an incentive to hold on to your bond. Over the full five years your return works out as 6.0 per cent a year before tax, 4.8 per cent after tax at 20 per cent (see Table 5).

At the end of the five years you can have your bond repaid together with the full amount of interest earned. No tax will be deducted, which is good for non-taxpayers. If you are a taxpayer you have to pay tax each year on the interest even though you won't receive the interest until your bond

Table 5: How a £100 Capital Bond (Series L) grows

During year	Interest rate	After-tax return: basic-rate taxpayer	Higher-rate taxpayer
	%	%	%
1	4.40	3.52	2.64
2	4.80	3.84	2.88
3	5.60	4.48	3.36
4	6.80	5.44	4.08
5	8.46	6.77	5.08
Average:	6.01	4.81	3.61

Table 6: Interest when you cash in your bond early

Year in which you cash bond	Interest rate
1	No interest
2	Year 1 see Table 5, 4.40% for remainder
3	Years 1 and 2 see Table 5, 4.80% for remainder
4	Years 1, 2 and 3 see Table 5, 5.60% for remainder
5	Years 1, 2, 3 and 4 see Table 5, 6.80% for remainder

is repaid. You will receive a notice of interest credited to your bond each year which you can send to the Inland Revenue with your tax return. If you cash in your bond early you get a lower rate – see Table 6.

Should you cash in old Capital Bonds?
If you invested in the earlier Capital bonds (Series A, B, C, D, E, F, G, H, I, J or K) you may be wondering whether it is worth cashing them in and investing in the current bonds (or another National Savings scheme). If you hold them for the full five years your return over the whole period will be between 13 per cent gross (Series A), and 6.0 per cent gross (Series L).

Whatever bond you have invested in, if you have not yet held it for a full year, you should not cash it in as you will get back only your initial investment with no interest. In general, it's not worth cashing in your original bonds and investing in the new series as you will, over the length of your investment, receive a lower rate of return.

Getting your money out
You don't have to give notice to cash in your bond, but it will normally take eight days to get your money. You don't have to cash in your whole investment; part of a bond can be repaid as long as at least £100 remains invested if you

wish to keep the account open. You can get forms for withdrawal at a post office. On or before the fifth anniversary, National Savings will write and tell you if there are any reinvestment or extension terms.

What happens if you die?
Your heirs can either cash in your bond or transfer it to their own names using *form DNS904* (available at post offices).

National Savings FIRST Option Bonds

These bonds were first introduced in July 1992, but withdrawn later in the year. They were then reintroduced in March 1993.

Who can invest?
Anyone aged 16 or over. Bonds can be held jointly and in trust for personal beneficiaries of any age.

How much can you invest?
You have to invest at least £1,000 but can then invest any amount up to £250,000. A husband and wife can each invest £250,000 but if the investment is in joint names they can invest only £250,000 between them.

How to invest
Get a First Option Bond booklet *(DNS770)* from a post office.

How much interest?
The interest rate is fixed for 12 months at a time; at the end of the 12-month period you can either cash in your investment or leave the money invested at a fixed rate for another 12 months. This rate will be the fixed rate applying at that time. In April 1998 the fixed rate was 6.5 per cent gross for sums between £1,000 and £20,000; as interest is credited to the bond after deduction of tax the return for a basic-rate taxpayer is 5.2 per cent. If you invest £20,000 or more you get a higher rate of 6.75 per cent gross or 5.4 per cent after deduction of basic-rate tax.

If you are a non-taxpayer you can reclaim the tax deducted from your interest; if you pay higher-rate tax you will have to pay more.

Getting your money out
You can cash in your investment on the anniversary date without any penalty. If you withdraw during the first period of 12 months you will get no interest and will simply get

your initial investment back; after the first 12-month period you can withdraw at any time but will get the value at the most recent anniversary plus half the fixed rate of interest for the period since then. You don't have to cash in your whole investment and can take any amount as long as you leave in £1,000 or more.

What happens if you die?
Your heirs can cash in your bond or transfer it to their own names.

National Savings Children's Bonus Bonds

Who can invest?
These can be bought for any child under 16 by anybody aged 16 or over. The bonds can be held until the child is 21.

How much can you invest?
Bonds are sold in units of £25. You can invest a minimum of £25 and a child can have up to £1,000 of Issue J bonds in his or her name, in addition to holdings of Issues A to I.

How to invest
Get a Children's Bonus Bond booklet *(DNS769)* at your post office. The investment certificate will be sent to the child's parent or guardian, who will have control of the investment until the child is 16.

How much interest?
The rate of interest is fixed for five years. In 1998 the rate is 5 per cent a year. A bonus is added on the fifth anniversary of purchase which takes the full return over the five years to 6.0 per cent.

After the first five years another offer of five years' fixed interest and a bonus will be made. If the child is 16 or over when the first five years is complete, the next offer of interest and bonus will be for the length of time until he or she is 21, when the final bonus will be added.

The interest is free of income tax and capital gains tax. Although parents usually have to pay income tax on interest of £100 or more gained by their children as a result of their investing gifts from the parents, this does not apply to National Savings Children's Bonus Bonds.

Getting your money out
You can cash any number of units of £25 (plus interest) and need to give one month's notice. No notice need be given at

the end of the five-year period or when the holder reaches 21. Until the child is 16, the parent or guardian will have to apply for repayment and the money will be paid to him or her. Once the holder is 16, control is passed to him or her.

National Savings Pensioners' Guaranteed Income Bonds

Who can invest?
Anyone aged 60 or over. Bonds can be held jointly by two people over 60. The minimum investment is £500 and the maximum £50,000 (or £100,000 for joint holdings). These bonds were launched at the end of January 1994.

How much interest?
The interest rate is fixed for five years at a time and is currently 6.1 per cent gross. Interest is paid gross and monthly into your bank, building society or National Savings Investment account.

How to invest
You can get an application form *DNS773* from the post office.

Getting your money out
If you apply for repayment within two weeks of the fifth anniversary of your purchase, or any other fifth anniversary, there's no penalty. Otherwise you'll need to give 60 days' notice and there'll be no interest in the notice period. If you need your money immediately you can withdraw funds without notice but you will be charged a penalty of 90 days' interest on the amount withdrawn.

What happens if I die?
Your bond will be repaid to your heirs immediately with no interest penalty or can be transferred into another pensioners' bond if the person inheriting is over 60 years of age and wants payment this way.

Premium Bonds

Who can invest?
Anyone aged 16 or over can buy Premium Bonds. And they can be bought in the name of someone under 16 by parents, grandparents, great-grandparents or legal guardians.

How much can you invest?
Premium Bonds cost £1 each, but you have to buy a minimum of £100 worth. You can hold up to £20,000 of bonds in multiples of £10.

How to invest
You can get an application *form DNS765* from most post offices and banks. Your bonds will be sent to you by National Savings, Blackpool (which keeps all the records).

How do you know if you've won a prize?
You'll be contacted by post at the last address National Savings has for you. So make sure you let it know if you move. There's over £15 million in unclaimed prizes because the winners can't be traced.

You will be contacted in person if you have won the jackpot of £1 million.

How do you cash your bonds?
Get *form DNS303* from a post office. For each £1 invested you'll get £1 back (but, of course, if you've had your money invested for some time, inflation will have eaten away at its buying power).

Higher-value prizes	
10% of each month's prize fund	£1,000,000
	£100,000
	£50,000
	£25,000
	£10,000
	£5,000
Medium-value prizes	
15% of each month's prize fund	£1,000
	£500
Lower-value prizes	
75% of each month's prize fund	£100
	£50

Over 500,000 prizes are awarded each month and divided into three bands.

There is only ever one £1-million prize each month. However, the number of prizes of other amounts varies depending on the number of bonds eligible to take part each month.

What happens if you die?
Your bonds will remain eligible for prizes for 12 months after your death. To cash in the bonds, your heirs should get *form DNS904* from a post office.

How do Premium Bonds work?

You don't get interest on your money as such. Instead you get a chance of winning prizes. The total value of the prize money is equal to interest on all bonds that have been held for at least one month (nearly 10 billion of them) calculated at a rate of 5 per cent a year.

Once you've held a bond for one clear month it has a chance of winning monthly prizes, ranging from £50 to £1 million. All prizes are free of both income tax and capital gains tax.

There are rules about how the total prize money is divided into prizes of different amounts. From May 1996 the prize money for Premium Bonds is split up as shown in the box on page 191.

13

PENSIONS FROM
THE STATE

Your pension is one of the most important ways of saving for the future. Understanding how state pensions work is particularly important. Unless you know roughly what you are going to receive from the state, you'll be ill-prepared to sort out the rest of your savings and investments.

Over recent years the government has made changes to the state pension scheme, and created new choices which you must make between the state system, a pension from your employer and a personal pension plan. There are further changes on the horizon with the proposed introduction of *stakeholder pensions* (see page 219). In this chapter we explain the choices facing you concerning the state; for employers' schemes see Chapter 14 and for your personal pension plan choices see Chapter 15. For how pensions tie in to planning your savings and investments for retirement, see Chapter 3.

The state pension system

There are currently three main parts to the state system. Your state pension may be made up of:
■ a flat-rate *basic* pension
■ a very small *graduated* pension based on earnings from 1961 to 1975
■ an additional pension based on your earnings since April 1978, known as the *State Earnings Related Pension Scheme (SERPS)* pension.

The amount of these pensions is increased each April in line with changes in the Retail Prices Index (RPI) up to the previous September.

You start to get these pensions when you reach the *state pension age*. At present, this is 65 for men. For women born before 6 April 1950, state pension age is 60. It is being progressively increased for women born after that date until it reaches 65 for women born on or after 6 March 1955.

Basic pension

Anyone who has paid enough full-rate Class 1, Class 2 or Class 3 National Insurance contributions, or has been given credits, qualifies for this pension. There are complicated rules to work out whether you have paid enough in contributions, but you are pretty certain to qualify for the full basic-rate pension (£64.70 a week for a single person in the 1998–9 tax year) if you have paid full-rate contributions for nine-tenths of your *working life* (broadly, between 16 and 64 for a man and woman born after 5 April 1955, or between ages 16 and 59 for a woman born before 6 April 1950). Even if you don't qualify for the full pension, you may qualify for a reduced one if you have contributed for a quarter or more of the years in your working life. If there were periods when you were not working, but receiving a National Insurance benefit such as Jobseeker's Allowance (or the earlier Unemployment Benefit), Incapacity Benefit (or the old Sickness or Invalidity Benefit), Maternity Allowance, or Invalid Care Allowance, you would have been credited with contributions for these years.

Since April 1978, if you've stayed at home to look after children, or an elderly or sick person, the number of years needed to qualify are reduced. This is called *home responsibilities protection*.

The present Labour government has said that it is committed to retaining the basic pension and continuing to increase it in line with price inflation.

You can check on your basic pension and your graduated and SERPS pensions too by using the Department of Social Security's (DSS) Retirement Pension Forecast and Advice Service. You need to get form *BR19* from your local Benefits Agency, fill it in, and send it to the address on the form. The Service can tell you how much pension you're entitled to so far, how much you might get by the time you retire, and anything you can do now to increase your entitlement. For example, it's possible in some cases to make up gaps in your contribution record by paying voluntary Class 3 contributions.

Graduated pension

People who were employed in a job between 1961 and 1975, and had reached 18 before 1975, are likely to have a small graduated pension payable on top of the basic pension.

Between April 1961 and April 1975, there were two kinds of National Insurance (NI) contribution: a flat-rate one paid by almost everyone in employment, and a graduated one paid by people who earned more than £9 in any one week.

For each £7.50 a man contributed during those years, he gets a unit of pension, which is now worth 8.40p a week (in 1998–9). If you're a woman, it will have taken £9 of contributions to earn that 8.40p a week. The rules were set in this way because women have, up to now, had an earlier state pension age than men, and they live longer on average. The graduated pension has been increased since April 1978 with rising prices. But it's never going to be very large.

The DSS keeps records of how many *units* of pension each person has earned. You can check with it for your own position using the Retirement Pension Forecast and Advice Service (see page 194).

Many people were *contracted out* of the old graduated scheme because their employers ran their own pension schemes. But when the graduated scheme was wound up, many employers paid the money back into the state scheme in order to get rid of their liabilities. Again, you can ask the DSS about this. If it turns out that your employer did not buy you back into the state scheme, ask the employer for details of how much is owing to you.

State Earnings Related Pension Scheme (SERPS)

This is a supplement to the basic pension for employees paying the full NI contribution. It started in 1978, but the government has cut back on it for people retiring after April 1999. Many people are *contracted out* of SERPS – see page 201 – and it is likely that the Labour government will structure its new stakeholder pensions to make contracting out attractive for even more of the workforce, so it is possible that SERPS will eventually be allowed to wither away.

What you get from SERPS, and what you pay, depends on your earnings. We tell you later in this chapter how the scheme works and how to find out what you'll get. If you are contracted out of SERPS, the benefits from your contracted-out scheme replace SERPS. We explain the different methods of contracting out too.

Married women

If you pay the full-rate NI contribution, you are treated in exactly the same way as a man or a single woman. If you have had to spend time at home caring for children, or elderly relatives, you can qualify for a basic pension with a shorter contribution record, under *home responsibilities protection* (see page 194).

However, some married women and widows still pay the reduced-rate contribution, which used to be called the *small stamp*. No one has been able to *start* doing so since 1977. If you become divorced, you are no longer eligible to pay at the lower rate. Reduced-rate contributors qualify for a state pension only on their husband's record (in the same way as married women who have paid no contributions), and they have to wait until a husband starts to receive his pension. These women cannot qualify for SERPS. The pension for a dependent wife is approximately three-fifths of the rate the husband is getting (a maximum of £38.70 in the 1998–9 tax year).

If the man has retired, and his wife is under 60, he can draw a dependant's allowance for her too, provided she is not earning or drawing an occupational pension of more than £50.35 a week in 1998–9. If she is over 60, then the pension is the same amount, but it is paid direct to her. Earnings and occupational pension are not taken into account once she is over 60.

Widows

If your husband paid enough NI contributions, you qualify for a number of benefits, including state retirement pension when you reach pension age. For details, get leaflet *NP45* from your local Benefits Agency. All widows' benefits, except the state retirement pension, stop if you re-marry. They also stop if you live with a man as his wife, but re-start if you subsequently live alone again. Widows' benefits increase in the same way as the basic retirement pension.

If you're over 60 when your husband dies, you'll normally get the basic retirement pension. If you were under 60 and your husband was not getting the retirement pension, you will also get a tax-free lump sum *widow's payment* of £1,000. You will also be entitled to an additional pension based on your husband's SERPS record.

Is it worth putting off claiming?

You can earn extra state pension by putting off drawing your state retirement pension. Under current rules, you can do this for up to five years after pension age. For each week you postpone drawing the pension, your total state pension is increased by one-seventh of 1 per cent. But you have to put off drawing your pension for at least seven weeks before the pension is increased, because the minimum increase is 1 per cent. For each *year* that you postpone your retirement, the pension is increased by 7.5 per cent. You will not get any increases in the state pension for any weeks when you are drawing other state benefits such as Jobseeker's Allowance. Any graduated pension, and any SERPS benefits (see above) must be deferred along with the basic pension and will be increased in the same way.

Once you're 65 if a woman, 70 if a man (i.e. five years over state pension age), you must start taking your state pension, and it cannot be increased.

A wife cannot claim a pension on her husband's contributions until he starts drawing the state pension. If he puts it off, her part of the pension will be postponed too, and increased by the same percentage as her husband's.

If you've already started drawing your state pension, you can cancel your retirement *once*, and earn increases in your pension from then on.

Is it worth deferring your pension in this way? If you gave up the full basic pension in 1998–9, you'd lose about £3,375 over the year. In return, your pension next year would be 7.5 per cent higher – some £252 a year in terms of 1998–9 money. You'd need to carry on getting that extra £252 a year (increased each year in line with inflation) for 13⅓ years before you recouped the full £3,375. A single man aged 66 could, on average, expect to break even on the deal. But, as he got older, deferring the pension would look less attractive: by the age of 70, he could expect to live only 11 years – too few to recoup the pension given up. Deferring the pension looks a better deal for women, who have a longer average life expectancy than men, and for married men whose widows would continue to benefit from increased pensions even after their husbands had died.

How SERPS works

If you earn more than a certain amount, the *lower earnings limit* (£64 a week in the 1998–9 tax year), you pay National

Insurance on the whole of your earnings up to a given ceiling, the *upper earnings limit* (£485 a week in 1998–9). These contributions qualify you for a SERPS pension.

The DSS has a record of your earnings from employers for each year since 1978–9. Your SERPS pension is related to the earnings recorded for all those years, revalued in line with the way average earnings have increased between the date when they were earned and the date you retire. So it is protected against inflation.

Who's not in SERPS?

You can be in SERPS only if you count as an employee, so you're not in SERPS during periods when you're self-employed. Several groups of people who, though they are in SERPS, are not building up a SERPS pension. These are:

■ low-paid people earning less than the lower earnings limit (£64 a week in the 1998–9 tax year). They don't pay any National Insurance and, as a result, will get a lower, or no, pension at retirement

■ people paying only voluntary National Insurance contributions

■ people whose earnings are not taxed under the Pay-As-You-Earn (PAYE) system. If you are in the 'black economy' and not declaring your income to the Revenue, you will not build up a SERPS pension either

■ people who are unemployed. If you are unemployed, you receive credits for the *basic* state pension only. But for SERPS purposes, for a year of unemployment you would have an earnings record of zero, which will reduce your pension at retirement

■ people who are at home looking after children or dependent relatives. However, from 6 April 1999 onwards if they are covered by *home responsibilities protection* (see page 194) those years are not counted in their SERPS record at all, and so do not reduce their pension at retirement.

How much pension will SERPS give you?

Contributions on earnings up to the lower earnings limit count towards the basic pension, but not towards SERPS. Only earnings above the lower limit up to the upper earnings limit count towards SERPS. Each year's relevant earnings are revalued in line with earnings inflation up to your state pension age. The original idea was that after the scheme had been running for more than 20 years, the best 20 years would be picked out and averaged together, but this has now been dropped. Now, the pension is based on the average of your revalued earnings for *all* the years in your working life or since SERPS began. This will include years of self-employment, unemployment and part-time work, so, for many people, this new formula will significantly reduce their SERPS pension. If you are earning more than the upper earnings limit (£485 a week in 1998–9) these higher earnings are ignored.

How fast the SERPS pension builds up depends on when you are due to retire.

For anyone retiring before 6 April 2000, the SERPS pension builds up at one-eightieth (1.25 per cent) of your revalued earnings for each year since 1978. So the maximum available is twenty-eightieths, or 25 per cent. But for people retiring on or after 6 April 2000, SERPS will be gradually reduced. The pension earned before 6 April 1988 is always 'safeguarded' by being worked out on the one-eightieth basis, though as time goes on it will be a smaller and smaller fraction of your total SERPS pension.

The rate of build-up for post-April 1988 SERPS pension will be progressively reduced because it is based on a lower potential maximum SERPS pension – see table below. The precise rate will depend on the total number of years you could be in SERPS, which in turn depends on your age at the time SERPS started. People born on or after 6 April 1972 will be covered by the revised SERPS for their whole working life – i.e. 49 years. Their SERPS pension will build up at just 0.41 per cent of their revalued earnings for each year in SERPS, giving a maximum pension of 20 per cent of earnings between the lower and upper limits.

Year in which you retire	Maximum post-April 1988 SERPS as a percentage of earnings between the lower and upper earnings limits [1]
1999–2000	25%
2000–1	24.5%
2001–2	24%
2002–3	23.5%
2003–4	23%
2004–5	22.5%
2005–6	22%
2006–7	21.5%
2007–8	21%
2008–9	20.5%
2009–2010 and after	20%

[1] For 1999–2000, based on best 20 years' revalued earnings. For later years, based on earnings throughout your working life.

Working out your SERPS pension

It's not possible to work out your own SERPS pension accurately, because you don't know what your earnings pattern is going to be in the future. A few bad years, or a few good ones, would change the average over your working lifetime considerably. The safeguarding for the years between 1978 and 1988 also complicates the arithmetic.

But you can get a *rough* idea, in today's money, by assuming that your current earnings are what you will always earn, in real terms. This means you are ignoring the effects of inflation or changes in your earnings pattern. What it will give you is an idea of what *proportion* of your earnings you can expect from SERPS.

Step 1 Decide on the figure for your total weekly earnings before tax in the current tax year (1998–9). Deduct the lower earnings limit (£64). If your earnings figure is above the upper earnings limit (£485), then ignore the extra earnings as well.

Step 2 Work out in what tax year you will reach state pension age. If it will be 1998–9 or 1999–2000, go to **Step 3**. If it will be the tax year 2000–1 up to 2026–7, go to **Step 4**. If it will be 2027–8 or later, go to **Step 5**.

Step 3 Divide the earnings figure you worked out in **Step 1** by four. At 1998–9 rates, this gives a maximum SERPS pension of about £5,470 a year.

Step 4 You have the most difficult calculation. First you must calculate the SERPS you'll get from your pre-1988 protected SERPS rights. First, multiply the earnings figure you worked out in **Step 1** by ten and take a quarter of the result. Divide this by the number of years you'll be in SERPS – i.e. the full tax years from 1978–9 up to your retirement date. Now work out how much SERPS you'll get from post-April 1988 rights. Deduct ten from the number of years you'll be in SERPS and multiply this by the earnings figure from **Step 1**. Multiply the answer by the percentage shown in the table on page 199 for your year of retirement. Then divide the total by your years in SERPS. Add together your pre-1988 and post-1988 rights for an indication of your total SERPS pension. The answer you get will lie somewhere between the £5,470 and £4,380 figures worked out in **Steps** 3 and 5.

Step 5 Divide the earnings figure you worked out in **Step 1** by five. If you reach state pension age in the period 2027–8 up to 2036–7, this will underestimate your SERPS pension a little. At 1998–9 rates, this gives a maximum SERPS pension of about £4,380 a year.

Bear in mind that what you have worked out is a very rough indication of the SERPS you might expect in terms of today's money and based on some fairly crude assumptions. For a more sophisticated estimate of your SERPS entitlement, contact the Retirement Pension Forecast and Advice Service – see page 194.

EXAMPLE

Fred Hurst works out roughly what SERPS pension he will be able to expect when he retires.

Step 1 Fred earns £760 a week. He ignores the last £275 which is above the upper earnings limit of £485 a week for 1998–9. From the £485 that remains, he deducts £64, leaving earnings of £421.
Step 2 Fred will retire in May 1999, so he goes to Step 3
Step 3 Fred works out £421 ÷ 4 = £105.25. This is roughly the weekly SERPS pension Fred will get (i.e. about £5,470 a year).

If, instead, Fred was due to retire in May 2029, he would have gone to Step 5 instead of Step 3. In that case, his expected SERPS pension would be roughly £421 ÷ 5 = £84.20 (i.e. about £4,380).
Someone with a maximum SERPS entitlement retiring between the years 2000–1 and 2026–7 inclusive, would receive a pension somewhere between the £5,470 and £4,380 figures worked out for Fred in Steps 3 and 5.

Contracting out of SERPS

If you are contracted out, then a lower percentage of your National Insurance goes towards the state pension scheme. The remainder, called the *rebate*, is intended to be used for the contracted-out pension. From April 1997, the amount of rebate depends on the type of scheme through which you are contracted out:

■ **employer's final pay scheme** There is a flat rebate equal to 4.6 per cent of earnings between the lower and upper earnings limits, which breaks down into 3 per cent of the employer's contributions and 1.6 per cent of the employee's contributions

■ **employer's money-purchase scheme** The rebate is made up of 3.1 per cent flat rate plus an age-related element which varies from 0.1 per cent at the age of 16 to 5.9 per cent from the age of 47 onwards. A constant 1.6 per cent of the rebate represents a refund of the employee's contributions. The age-related element is due to be reduced slightly from 6 April 1999 onwards

■ **personal pension plan** The rebate is made up of a 3.4 per cent flat rate plus an age-related element which varies from nothing at age 16 to 5.6 per cent from 46 onwards. Again, 1.6 per cent represents a refund of the employee's contributions. The age-related element is due to be increased from 6 April 1999 onwards to compensate for the effect of pension funds being unable to reclaim tax on dividends since 2 July 1997 – see page 223. The rebates for personal plans are slightly higher than those for an employer's money purchase scheme to compensate for the fact that the rebate is paid later into a personal plan.

Contracting out with a pensions promise

If you contract out through an employer's final pay scheme, you are promised a certain amount of pension in place of the SERPS pension you are giving up.

For periods of contracting-out before 6 April 1997, you get a *guaranteed minimum pension (GMP)* which is broadly equivalent to the SERPS pension. At retirement, GMPs you have built up are deducted from the full SERPS pension you would otherwise have had and the difference is the SERPS pension you actually receive. The calculation is repeated each year to take account of increases in GMPs and SERPS. The result is that you could never lose out by contracting out in this way – your GMPs plus SERPS always equalled the full SERPS pension you would have had had you not contracted out.

From 6 April 1997 onwards, the link with SERPS is broken. Contracted-out final pay pensions you build up from then onwards must (for most scheme members) be at least equivalent to the benefits from a 'reference scheme' (a model pension scheme which the government has devised). The benefits include a retirement pension and widow's or widower's pension, together with increases to pensions (once they are being paid) in line with inflation up to a maximum of 5 per cent a year. Under this system of contracting out, you might end up with a lower pension than you would have had under SERPS, especially if inflation is higher than 5 per cent during most of your retirement years. In practice, the reference scheme benefits are fairly generous and it is probable that you will not lose out, but there is no longer any guarantee.

Another significant change as a result of switching to the new system is that, for benefits built up from April 1997 onwards, it will no longer be possible to separate the contracted-out benefits from non-contracted-out benefits. If you transfer post-April 1997 contracted-out rights out of a final pay scheme into a scheme which offers *protected rights* (see below), you'll lose the right to any non-contracted-out benefits such as a tax-free lump sum at retirement which the original scheme might have offered.

Contracting out with a Contracted-Out Money Purchase (COMP) scheme

Since April 1988, employers have been allowed to contract out their workers in an alternative way, with what's called a *Contracted-Out Money Purchase (COMP)* scheme. Here they guarantee only the amount of money going *in* as contributions: there's no guaranteed minimum pension or requirement to match the benefits from a reference scheme.

The money is used to create *protected rights*, which are basically a retirement pension from state pension age plus a widow's or widower's pension in the event of death either before or after retirement, with pensions (once they are being paid) increasing in line with inflation up to a maximum of 5 per cent a year. These are money purchase pensions (see page 209) and they will turn out to be worth whatever the pension fund can buy given *annuity rates* at the time. If only the minimum contribution is going in, no other benefits are possible. There are special restrictions on how the money is invested to cover your protected rights, and each person must have an individual account that can be identified. You give up your SERPS rights for those years, and the COMP pension could be greater than what you would have had from SERPS, or it could be less.

The employer and employee both pay less National Insurance than if the scheme were contracted in to SERPS. But at least as much as the rebate (see page 201) must go into the COMP scheme. The employer makes the payments, and can (but need not) recover part from the employee. It is the employer who chooses whether to run a COMP scheme or not, and what contributions to charge the employee. But you don't have to join (or stay in) a COMP scheme or any other employer's scheme if you don't want to.

Contracting out with a rebate-only personal pension

This was introduced in July 1988, and allows you to contract out of SERPS, outside your employer's scheme. You can take out a rebate-only plan if:

■ your employer doesn't have a contracted-out pension scheme *or*

■ your employer has a contracted-out scheme, but you don't belong to it *or*

■ your employer has a contracted-in scheme, whether or not you are a member of it – or

■ your employer has arranged a *group personal pension scheme (GPPS)* – see page 207. In this case, each employee individually decides whether or not to contract out.

If you take out a rebate-only plan, your National Insurance rebate (plus tax relief on the part which represents a refund of your own contributions) goes into the scheme and buys you *protected rights*, on a money purchase basis (see page 203). These entitle you to a pension at state pension age (no earlier) and a spouse's pension on your death. If you want extra pension or a different pattern of benefits, you must pay extra. You *give up* your SERPS rights for the years you are in a rebate-only plan. The resulting pension may be bigger than what you would have got under SERPS – if the plan you choose has done well – or it might be less.

If you have a rebate-only plan, you pay full-rate National Insurance contributions. You (and the organisation you take out the plan with) notify the DSS that you have taken out a rebate-only plan. After the end of each tax year the DSS calculates what your rebate is, and pays it over to the *provider* (i.e. the organisation running the plan for you). But if anything is wrong with the DSS records, or the provider's records, there will be a delay while it's sorted out, and the rebate will not reach your account (and so start earning interest or dividends) until then.

Is contracting out a good idea?

If you were contracted out through an employer's final pay scheme before April 1997, you could not lose out and, in fact, most such schemes aimed to provide pensions which were a good deal better than just the GMPs required by law. Although the link with SERPS and the absolute guarantee are now lost, you are still unlikely to lose by contracting out through an employer's final pay scheme.

The position is less clear cut with money purchase employer schemes and personal pension plans. The rebate has to be invested, and whether or not it produces better benefits than the SERPS given up depends on a variety of factors discussed below. However, do not leave or fail to join a contracted-out employer's money purchase scheme simply to join SERPS – in most cases, the scheme will offer you a whole package of benefits and you would lose more overall than you would gain by belonging to SERPS. Where you have the choice of contracting in or out of SERPS independently of your membership of an employer's scheme, or where you are saving through a personal pension plan, consider these factors:

■ **size of the rebate and the benefits to be provided** These may both be revised from time to time. Obviously, the larger the rebate, the more likely it is to produce a large enough fund to match or exceed SERPS benefits. From April 1997, the rebates have to 'buy' more benefits as the state has ceased to provide any of the inflation-proofing for pensions once they start to be paid. From 2 July 1997, pension funds have no longer been able to reclaim tax deducted from income from shares, unit trusts and similar investments. To compensate for this, rebates are being increased from 6 April 1999 onwards. But, for 1998–9, rebates remain at the original level and, as a result, some providers have advised their planholders not to contract out during 1998–9

■ **your view about investment returns.** Whether or not the rebate grows into a large enough fund to buy a better pension than the SERPS pension being given up depends largely on how well it grows. The more optimistic you are about investment returns, the more attractive contracting out will seem. And the more willing you are to accept a degree of risk, the greater your scope to choose investments with a higher expected return. The Government Actuary (a specialist who advises the government on pensions matters) has estimated that the loss of tax relief on share dividends and similar investment income, coupled with other changes made in the July 1997 Budget, has reduced the return from pension funds by about 0.5 per cent a year

■ **plan charges** With some money purchase employer schemes, the employer pays separately the costs of running the scheme, so charges do not eat into the pension fund. Where the employer's scheme is run by an insurance company or in the case of personal pension plans, charges will be met out of the contributions and/or investment returns. The rebates on their own are relatively small compared with the contributions which you would ideally pay into a personal pension plan, so any flat-rate charges will have a proportionately very large impact on your pension savings and reduce the likelihood of producing a better pension than the SERPS given up

■ **your age** Although, from April 1997, rebates are age-related, in order to keep down costs, the government has capped rebates at 9 per cent for people in their mid-40s and older. As you reach these ages, contracting out of SERPS for the first time looks progressively less attractive, because the rebate simply will not be adequate to produce a large enough fund to replace SERPS benefits given up. However, if you are already contracted out, it will often be better to remain contracted out, since penalties and/or other charges can eat heavily into your contracted-out plan if payments to it stop

■ **your gender** Protected rights are worked out using *unisex annuity rates* – in other words, for a given lump sum, men and women get the same amount of pension at any given age. This means that women born on or after 6 March 1955, who have a state pension age of 65, get more or less the same deal as men from contracting out. But for women born before then, contracting out is less attractive than for men of the same age. These women retire earlier and so give up more SERPS pension but receive only the same rebate.

14

PENSIONS FROM EMPLOYERS

Since April 1988, membership of employers' pension schemes has been voluntary. So if you are starting a new job, you can choose whether or not to join. Even if you are already in a pension scheme, you always have the option to leave your scheme and make your own provision. In the majority of cases, an employer's scheme will be the best choice, not least because of the contributions that your employer pays. However, an increasing number of employers – particularly those with a relatively small workforce – are offering employees *group personal pension schemes (GPPS)*. These are not employers' schemes in the true sense. Instead, the employer enters into an arrangement with a personal pension plan provider who offers a set plan to all the eligible employees. The plan may have special features designed to suit the particular employees – e.g. variable contributions, opportunity for contribution holidays, low charges, and so on – but it is still a personal pension plan and subject to the rules set out in Chapter 15. The employer can contribute to a GPPS but does not have to and often will not. The remainder of this chapter looks at *bona fide* employers' schemes. For more about the rules governing GPPS, refer to Chapter 15.

An employer's pension scheme may be *contributory*, which means you pay in a proportion of your pay to the scheme each week or month. Common contribution rates are 4 or 5 per cent (normally your employer will be paying the same, or more). Alternatively, the scheme may be *non-contributory*. In either case, the employer makes contributions into the scheme on your behalf. Provided the scheme meets certain conditions laid down by the Inland Revenue, it gets favourable tax treatment. You get tax relief on any contributions you make, you pay no tax on any contributions made by your employer, and the pension fund itself pays no tax on capital gains. Some of the income is also tax free. The eventual pension is taxable as income, but you can take part of the benefits as a tax-free lump sum See page 223 for more details.

To work out how much you will get from your pension scheme, you need to know what kind it is. The types covering most people are *final pay* schemes and *money purchase* schemes, explained below. Other kinds are summarised later in the chapter.

Final pay scheme

With a final pay scheme, the number of years you've been a member of the scheme, and the yearly amount you're earning at the time you retire or averaged over the few years before then, decide the size of your pension. Many schemes pay one-sixtieth of your final pay for each year of membership. Others pay, for example, one-eighteenth of final pay.

Under the Inland Revenue's rules, the maximum pension you can get is two-thirds of your final pay. There is no limit on the final pay that can be taken into account if the pension scheme was set up before 14 March 1989 and you joined it before 1 June 1989. Otherwise, there is a limit (the 'earnings cap') of £87,600 in the 1998–9 tax year; it is normally increased each year in line with price inflation.

Employers can set up 'top-up' schemes to cover earnings over the limit, but such schemes receive less favourable tax treatment.

Employers' pension schemes commonly set a normal retirement age at 65, but it can vary widely, between the ages of 50 and 70.

In what's known as a *fast accrual* scheme, you can get the maximum pension after only ten years' service, if you were in the scheme before 17 March 1987. But if you changed employer after that date, this maximum can be reached only after 20 years.

For most people, the benefits are assumed to build up over 40 years. So if you reach normal retirement age after 40 years' membership of a scheme that pays one-sixtieth of your final pay for each year, you can retire on two-thirds final pay. But even if you retire after 45 years in the scheme, you can still only have a two-thirds pension.

In a scheme that works on eightieths, you would only have a pension of half final pay (i.e. forty-eightieths) after 40 years of membership.

The higher your final yearly pay, the higher your pension from the scheme. There are different definitions, though, of what 'pay' is. Sometimes the rules define it as including bonus, commission and overtime, or some of these and not others. The Inland Revenue no longer allows income from *share option* schemes to be counted.

There are also differences in the way 'final' is defined. Common methods of definition are:

■ average pay in the best three consecutive years out of the last thirteen

■ basic salary in the last year before you retire (or the last but one year), plus the average of your 'fluctuating emoluments' such as bonus or commission over the last few years

■ average yearly pay over the last few years (most often three or five).

Check in your scheme booklet exactly how your employer's scheme works. You have a legal right to up-to-date details of your scheme.

People who left a final pay scheme before retirement used to get a very raw deal because their pensions could be frozen at the level they were at on leaving. The position is much better now because their pensions must be increased to protect them at least partially against inflation during the period between leaving and retiring. Even so, the treatment of early leavers is a weak spot in final pay schemes compared with money purchase schemes – see below.

Taking account of the state basic pension

Some final pay schemes make a deduction either from the final pay used to work out your pension, or from the pension itself, to allow for the fact that you'll be getting some basic pension from the state. Often the way this is done is to take away an amount equivalent to the lower earnings limit, or more or less than that level, from your pay before the pension and contributions are calculated. But schemes vary, so check what yours does. If the normal retirement age in your job is earlier than state pension age, the deduction for the state pension ought not to be applied until you reach the official retirement age for the state pension. It's particularly important that it should not apply if you're forced to retire early because of ill-health.

Money purchase schemes

This type of scheme is popular with smaller companies and becoming increasingly widespread for new employees of large employers too.

Your employer – and you, if it's a contributory scheme – pay contributions which are fixed as a percentage of your pay. (If the scheme is covered by the 'earnings cap' rules (see page 208), only pay up to £87,600 can count in the 1998–9 tax year.) The contributions are invested and, on retirement, the proceeds are used to buy a pension. How much pension you get depends on how the investments have done, and what level annuity rates are at when you retire. However, where scheme rules allow, the purchase of an annuity can be delayed and an income drawn direct from the pension fund, mirroring the *annuity deferral and income drawdown* rules that apply to personal pension schemes (see Chapter 15).

For pensions built up from 6 April 1997 onwards, the pensions (once they are being paid) must increase in line with inflation, up to a maximum of 5 per cent a year. This is called *limited price indexation*.

The Inland Revenue's restrictions on maximum pension, lump sum and other benefits apply to *all* types of employers' schemes, including money purchase schemes. But there are special rules for *simplified* money purchase schemes. For example, if a scheme limits the total contribution to 17.5 per cent of earnings (on top of any National Insurance rebate), there need be no limit on the amount of benefit. So, in theory, if a simplified scheme did exceptionally well, you might end up with a pension bigger than your earnings (not normally allowed). There are also various restrictions on other benefits, the way a scheme like this is run, and when the benefits may be taken.

With a money purchase scheme, you don't lose out on leaving your job; the fund simply continues to receive interest and dividends on the amount already in there, though no more will be paid in. You could transfer it to a new employer's scheme or a personal pension plan, if you felt that they were going to produce a better return on your investment than the current managers. But you would need to look carefully to see how much you would lose by leaving the existing scheme, especially if you have been in it for only a few years.

Though they are nothing new, *hybrid* schemes are now being introduced by more employers, either final pay schemes with a guarantee that you will not do worse than on a money purchase basis with a given level of contributions, or money purchase with a guarantee of at least a certain pension level worked out on the final pay basis. If the guarantees are at a reasonable level, these hybrid schemes can give you the best of both worlds. They protect the pensions of early leavers, and provide protection against inflation, in line with increases in earnings, for those who stay to claim their pensions.

Other sorts of employer scheme

Average pay schemes
With these, your pension is based on your pay in each year you belong to the scheme; there is usually a graded scale of earnings. For each year that your pay is in a particular earnings band, you get a fixed amount of pension. As you move up the earnings scale, the amount earned in pension will rise, as will any contributions you pay. The yearly pension you're eventually paid will be the total of all the little bits of yearly pension you've earned in each band, so there is no protection against inflation in these schemes.

Revalued average schemes
These work in a similar way to SERPS. Your earnings are revalued to take account of the rise in earnings (or sometimes only prices) between the date when you earned them and the date when you retire. Then an average is taken and a fraction given, depending on the rate at which the pension builds up, for each year you are in the scheme.

Flat-rate schemes
Flat-rate schemes provide a fixed amount of pension for each year's membership of the scheme.

Inflation proofing

Retirement can last a long time, particularly for women. On average, men retiring at 65 can expect 14 years of retirement; women retiring at 60 have an average 22 years and, at 65, 18 years. You want an adequate pension not just at the time you retire, but later in your retirement too. A pension of, for example, only half your final pay but with full inflation proofing, can soon overtake an apparently better pension of two-thirds of your final pay with no protection against rising prices.

In public-sector jobs, such as in the Civil Service, most pensions increase in line with the rise in the RPI. In the private sector, not many schemes do this. Many have in the past promised to increase pensions by a certain percentage each year. Often this was 3 or 4 per cent, or the increase in the RPI if less. When inflation is low this percentage is adequate but it provides poor protection at even modest rates of inflation. For pensions built up from 6 April 1997 onwards, schemes *have* to increase them by inflation, up to 5 per cent a year. Most larger schemes are applying the increase to the whole of a pension rather than splitting it into pre-1997 and post-1997 segments.

Some schemes, particularly those run by large companies, have in any case tended to give increases that do not fall far short of inflation. In periods when pension schemes have been flush with money, many have done a 'catching-up exercise' for older pensioners, increasing their pensions to the real level they were at when they retired. But there is no guarantee that this policy will continue indefinitely.

Tax-free lump sums

When you retire, you can normally exchange part of your pension for a tax-free lump sum. With some schemes, especially in the public sector, you automatically get a smaller pension and a lump sum. You can have up to one and a half times your earnings as a lump sum, subject (where it applies) to the £87,600 earnings limit for 1998–9. You may also be subject to a cash limit on the lump sum of £150,000 if you joined your scheme between 17 March 1987 and 1 June 1989.

If you have a choice, should you go for a tax-free lump sum or more pension? If the pension is usually increased quite generously, but this is not guaranteed, be wary of exchanging any of it for a lump sum. But if this is not the case, it may pay you to exchange as much as possible of your pension for a lump sum, and then buy an annuity – see Chapter 23. Your after-tax income from the annuity may be worth more than the pension you are giving up. It would be worth checking, close to the time you retire, what income you'd get from an annuity – this will depend on interest rates at the time. If they are high, you could do very well. If they are low, you could do badly – at such times, a with-profits annuity (see Chapter 23) could be a better choice.

Other benefits from your employer's scheme

An employer's pension scheme may provide other benefits besides a retirement pension, such as:
■ a pension if you are forced to retire early because of ill health; this is usually more generous than the pension if you retire early of your own accord. Or there may be a permanent health insurance scheme, which provides a long-term benefit for anyone who is off sick for a long spell, even right up to retirement
■ a pension for your husband or wife if you are the one who dies first

- pensions for children or other dependants you leave on death
- life insurance, which can be as much as four times your earnings (subject to the earnings cap if it applies), if you die before leaving or retiring.

In some cases, the permanent health insurance and the life insurance will be paid to all employees whether they are a member of the pension scheme or not. More often, employers provide these benefits only for those who are actually in the scheme, although they may provide a reduced rate of life insurance for everyone.

Additional voluntary contributions (AVCs)

All employers' pension schemes must allow members to make *additional voluntary contributions (AVCs)*, over and above those they have to make to belong to the scheme, in order to build up extra pension and other scheme benefits (except that AVCs started on or after 8 April 1987 cannot be taken as a lump sum). Some employers offer a range of AVC schemes, and some – but not many – will match the members' extra contributions with some of their own. The most you can put into an employer's pension scheme and AVC scheme altogether is 15 per cent of your earnings in any one tax year (or 15 per cent of £87,600 in 1998–9 if you earn more than this and the earnings cap rule applies). However much you put in, you cannot have more than the final two-thirds pension allowed by the Inland Revenue. But if you over-contribute, any excess AVCs will be returned to you at retirement after a special tax deduction of 33 per cent in 1998–9. Non-taxpayers cannot reclaim this tax and higher-rate taxpayers have extra to pay at a higher-than-usual rate.

You are entitled to make contributions to another scheme run by a commercial pension provider, such as an insurance company, outside your employer's scheme. These schemes are called *free-standing AVCs*, or *FSAVCs* for short. You are still not allowed to go over the two-thirds limit on pension, but excess FSAVCs will be returned at retirement after a tax deduction. You can also use an FSAVC for contracting out of the state scheme, if your employer's scheme is contracted in. This is an alternative to a rebate-only personal plan, but it is less tax-efficient because you do not receive tax relief on the National Insurance rebate this way.

For AVCs or FSAVCs made from 8 April 1987, *if your scheme allows it*, you can start and stop contributions as you like, reduce the amount or pay in windfall amounts in odd years (before then, once you'd started you were not allowed to stop or reduce the amount). Check whether the rules of your scheme are flexible in this way.

Should you make AVCs?

Before deciding whether to make AVCs or FSAVCs, check that you have the scope to increase your benefits (most people do). With an employer's scheme, find out how the AVCs will be invested – it may use a special deposit account or, more often, hand contributions over to an insurance company to be invested either on a with-profits or unit-linked basis – in the past, with-profits AVC schemes have tended to give the better return.

Your AVC or FSAVC scheme can be used to increase virtually any of the benefits offered by your employer's scheme. They can even be used to increase the life cover provided, but only if the scheme would otherwise give you less than the maximum of over four times salary allowed under the Inland Revenue rules. Because you get tax relief on the AVCs or FSAVCs, this is a very tax-efficient way of buying life insurance. Extra pension bought with AVCs and FSAVCs does *not* have to be increased by inflation up to 5 per cent a year – AVCs and FSAVCs were specifically excluded from the limited price indexation rule because the government did not want to deter anyone from making extra contributions.

Your extra contributions are normally treated in the same way as ordinary ones for tax purposes. That is, you get tax relief on them at your top rate of tax, and they go into a fund that pays no tax on its income or capital gains. But you cannot get them out until you draw your main pension, though in many cases you will be able to transfer them, along with your main pension, to another provider. AVCs can be a very good way of saving, particularly for higher-rate taxpayers and those close to retirement age. But they are less flexible than other forms of saving.

With an employer's AVC scheme, the employer almost always pays the setting-up and administrative costs. With an FSAVC scheme, *you* do so, and pay the commission to the plan provider. But you may still want to take this route, particularly where it gives you greater choice about how your contributions are invested.

Changing jobs

If you leave an employer's scheme (whether or not you also leave the job) within two years of joining, you have no rights to a pension from the scheme. Instead you can be offered a refund of your own (but not your employer's) contributions. If you had been contracted out of SERPS at any time before 6 April 1997, there will generally be a deduction from your refund to cover the cost of buying you back into SERPS. Tax at a special rate of 20 per cent will be deducted from whatever remains.

If you have been in an employer's scheme for more than two years, you must be given a *preserved pension*. You can choose what to do with this pension:

■ you can leave the preserved pension in your old employer's scheme. In general, pension rights built up since 1 January 1985 must be increased between the time you leave and the time you retire in line with changes in the RPI up to a maximum of 5 per cent a year. The exception is any guaranteed minimum pensions (GMPs), which are subject to different rules, with the effect that your employer and the state between them fully protect your GMPs against inflation. There is no obligation on schemes to increase pre-1985 benefits. In practice, your scheme might provide more than the legal minimum – e.g. increasing the whole of your benefits whenever they were built up, or providing protection in excess of 5 per cent inflation

■ alternatively, you can take a *transfer value* to a new employer's scheme, a personal pension plan, or a *Section 32* policy. A transfer value is the lump sum that the actuary of the scheme you're leaving calculates would be enough to provide your preserved benefits, if the lump sum were invested now. A Section 32 policy is a special type of deferred annuity (roughly speaking, another type of pension) that you buy with a single premium. Other names for it are *buy-out plan* or *transfer plan*. You have the right to contact any employer whose scheme you left after January 1986, and with which you have a preserved pension, at any date up to a year before retirement, and say that you now want a transfer. You lose the right to a transfer if the employer's scheme is wound up; instead, the administrators must buy you an annuity.

A transfer between two public-sector jobs is governed by special rules, which means you are unlikely to lose out. With a transfer to a private-sector employer, your new employer will:

■ if he or she runs a money purchase scheme, invest the transfer value in the same way as new contributions *or*

■ if he or she runs a final pay scheme, may agree to pay you extra pension in your retirement; this is normally fixed in pounds and not increased in line with future pay increases *or*

■ give you a credit of so many years' membership of the scheme. This is unlikely to be the full number of years that you had been in the old employer's scheme, because the benefit you get from it may be different and it will be based on your expected pay at retirement (rather than pay at the time of leaving the old scheme). If you are offered credited years, try to negotiate a guarantee of the minimum pension in pounds from the transfer payment. This should not be less than the preserved benefits you're giving up, but will help if you change jobs again.

If you are transferring a pension that has been contracted out of SERPS, then there are special rules. If you are transferring a preserved-guaranteed minimum pension into a Section 32 policy, it must guarantee to pay at least as much. On the other hand, if you are transferring it into a personal pension plan, then its money value is turned into *protected rights* within the personal pension plan. This means that it can be used only in certain ways, and you are giving up the guaranteed benefits the guaranteed minimum pension gave you. If you transfer post-April 1997 pension rights from a contracted-out employer's final pay scheme to a scheme or plan offering protected rights, you lose any benefits not included within protected rights – for example, any tax-free lump sum from the previous scheme.

How safe is your pension?

In late 1991, it was learned that the late Robert Maxwell had stolen over £400 million from the pension schemes of companies in his business empire. This raised serious doubts about the way in which company pension schemes are organised and regulated, and a government inquiry – the 'Goode Committee' – was set up to investigate whether the law relating to pension schemes should be changed.

In the light of its recommendations, Parliament passed the Pensions Act 1995. This introduced a new system of pension regulation based on three pillars:
■ **the Occupational Pensions Regulatory Authority (OPRA)*** This is a new regulatory body for pension schemes. Although it does not proactively monitor schemes, it does have very wide-ranging powers to investigate schemes where something is thought to be going wrong
■ **trustees** Pensions schemes (other than unapproved schemes and the public-sector statutory schemes set up by Act of Parliament) continue to be run as trusts to which trust law applies. However, trustees have been given much

more explicit duties and responsibilities and run the risk of hefty penalties if they fail in their duties. Schemes are also required to let members choose one-third of the trustees, unless the employer opts out of this rule, in which case he or she must follow an elaborate procedure to give members the chance to object to the opt-out

■ **scheme advisers (e.g. scheme actuary and lawyer)** Their duties have been tightened up and, in particular, they are required to 'blow the whistle' to OPRA if they suspect that anything about the scheme is amiss.

In addition, the way in which the assets of final pay (and similar) schemes are monitored will be altered. In the past, such schemes concentrated on having enough assets to pay pensions as they fell to be paid. Since this was generally many years ahead, the schemes tended to invest in long-term assets such as shares which, although subject to fluctuating prices in the short run, could be expected to grow handsomely over the long term. Now schemes will have to meet a new *minimum funding requirement (MFR)* under which assets must also be enough to meet all the benefits which would immediately crystallise if the pension scheme were wound up today – basically the preserved benefits or transfer values. To do this, schemes need to have a greater concentration of assets whose values do not fluctuate greatly in the short term, so they are likely to hold more investments such as British Government stocks than they did in the past. This makes your pension rights more secure in the short term. Unfortunately, though, Government stocks perform much more poorly than shares over the long term, so the introduction of the MFR has the effect of making pension schemes much more expensive for employers to run. Some employers have responded by closing their final pay schemes to new members and offering new employees membership of a money purchase scheme or a group personal pension scheme instead.

The Pensions Act also introduces a compensation scheme which will replace most of the benefits for members of pension schemes which have insufficient assets to pay their pensions because of dishonesty or fraud on the part of those running the scheme. The scheme does not pay out for losses due to negligence or incompetence.

Though their effects are undoubtedly serious for the unfortunate members involved, pension scheme frauds are in fact relatively rare. The risk of retiring having saved too little for an adequate pension is much greater, and an employer's scheme will usually be the best chance of saving enough for retirement. However, you can take steps to help ensure the safety of your pension: take an interest in your scheme, get to know who your scheme trustees are, consider becoming a trustee yourself, read all the information sent to you, ask questions about aspects of the scheme which you don't understand or agree with and make sure that you are given satisfactory answers. If your scheme fails to give you the answers or information you need, you can get help from the Occupational Pensions Advisory Service (OPAS).*

Verdict: employer's scheme or personal pension plan?

Employers' final pay schemes (contracted out)

If you are in a good employer's scheme that is based on final pay and *contracted out* of SERPS, you should think very seriously before deciding to leave and go it alone with a personal pension plan. It would mean that your pension would be less certain, because it would not be based on final pay, and it would depend instead on two other uncertainties: how well your money has been invested up to your retirement date, and interest rates at that time. A sudden change in the fortunes of the stock market, like the crash in share values in October 1987, or a drop in the interest rates which dictate *annuity rates* (i.e. the pension you can actually buy with your fund), could mean a big change in your pension. (Of course, all this applies also to employers' money purchase schemes as well as to personal pension plans.)

It's likely that if you go outside the scheme your employer will say that you must also provide death-in-service benefits and disability benefits for yourself. Find out about this before taking any decision, and shop around to compare the costs; if you are over a certain age, you may well find that replacing the benefits costs more than your contribution to the employer's scheme as a whole.

Before taking any decision, find out whether the employer will allow you to rejoin the pension scheme if you change your mind. In many cases, an employer allows you one change of mind, but says that if you leave again, you stay out. Other employers put an upper limit on the ages at which people will be allowed to join or rejoin, perhaps 45. Still others say that if you leave, you will be out for good.

Employers' final pay schemes (contracted in)

If your employer's scheme is contracted in, then you may want to contract out of SERPS. You can do this with an FSAVC or a rebate-only plan, without leaving the employer's scheme. The arguments in favour of employers' final pay schemes are much the same whether they are contracted in or out.

Personal pensions

Employers who have their own schemes are unlikely to contribute to a personal pension plan, unless you are in a sufficiently senior position to bargain for special treatment. As many employers contribute twice as much as the members to the employer's pension scheme, only the very young or very lucky are likely to have more pension from a personal pension plan than from an employer's scheme (unless the benefits from the employer's scheme are very poor).

For a personal pension plan, there will be administration and commission charges, while employers normally pay the running costs of their own schemes. In any case, the administration charges are likely to be higher for a personal pension plan than for an employer's scheme, because there will not be the same economies of scale in running the scheme. All this means that if you are in a personal pension plan for only a short time, it is likely to be poor value, because the administration charges will be deducted at the beginning of the policy.

On the other hand, the attraction of a personal pension plan is that there is no loss on changing jobs. There is also no limit on benefits, only on contributions – see Chapter 15. So full advantage can be gained from favourable investment conditions; in an employer's final pay scheme, the employer tends to reap the benefits in terms of lower contributions. You also have the freedom to choose who will provide the pension.

Partly in response to the mis-selling of personal pension plans during the late 1980s and early 1990s and to the damaging effect of high flat-rate charges on small pension funds, the present Labour government has committed itself to introducing new *stakeholder pensions* as part of a wider pensions review. At the time of writing, the government was still consulting on the plans and no details had been decided. However, the aim is that the schemes should be simple to understand, cheap to operate, secure, flexible and represent good value for money even for people with relatively small amounts to contribute.

Employers' money purchase schemes

If your employer runs a money purchase scheme, you may feel that you could do better with your own money purchase

personal pension plan. But find out how much your employer
is putting into the scheme, and what administrative charges
(if any) are being deducted. Doing your own thing is likely to
mean paying your own charges as well. And with an
employer's COMP scheme, part of the money goes straight in
each month when the payroll calculations are done. With a
personal pension, the the whole National Insurance rebate is
held back by the DSS until after the end of the tax year. It does
not start earning interest or dividends until it reaches the
personal pension plan provider. On the other hand, the
rebates to personal plans are slightly higher than those for
COMP schemes to compensate for this delay.

Verdict
Overall, unless you are under 30 or so, intend to move jobs
rapidly and have no dependants, a reasonable employer's
scheme is likely to be the best for you. If you take out a
personal pension plan in the early years of your working
life, you ought to aim to move back into an employer's
scheme in your 30s, or when you get married. You can join
an employer's scheme and still have your own visible
pension 'pot' by setting up an FSAVC scheme in addition,
thus taking out a two-way bet.

   If you run your own business as a company, you can set up
your own employer's scheme (for example, an executive
pension plan) – contact an insurance company or independent
financial adviser for advice. If you are self-employed, you'll
have no option but to use a personal pension plan.

Unapproved pension schemes
Your employer may offer you membership of an
unapproved pension scheme. This does not attract the
favourable tax treatment of an approved scheme but can be
more flexible, because there are no restrictions on the
amount and type of benefits – you can even take the whole
lot as a lump sum, if you choose. They are especially useful
as 'top up' schemes, if your earnings exceed the earnings
cap. Unapproved schemes work in one of two ways:
- *unfunded schemes* Your employer simply pays you
benefits at the time you retire. These will be taxed as
income
- *funded schemes* Your employer pays contributions
which count as a taxable fringe benefit on which you'll
have to pay tax. They are invested, usually in a trust, in
which case any income and gains are taxable, but generally
only at the basic rate of tax (whatever your own tax rate).
When the benefits are paid, they are tax-free.

15

PERSONAL PENSION PLANS

Personal pension plans are a type of pension scheme for individuals; they are provided mainly by insurance companies but can also be provided by banks, building societies, friendly societies and unit trusts for anyone (employed or self-employed) who is not in an employer's pension scheme. Even if you are in an employer's pension scheme, you can take out a *rebate-only personal plan* to contract out of the *State Earnings Related Pension Scheme* or *SERPS* (see Chapter 13), *unless* your employer's scheme itself is contracted out. And, if you are in an employer's scheme for your main employment, but have some freelance earnings, or a second job from which you will not benefit from a retirement pension, you can have a personal pension based on the earnings from these *non-pensionable* employments, while still remaining in your main employer's scheme.

If you have been in an employer's scheme in the past, you can transfer the money already built up in that scheme into a personal pension plan. (Alternatively, in some cases, you can set up a *Section 32* policy when you change jobs – see Chapter 14.) Be very wary of transferring out of a scheme that offers fully inflation-proofed pension rights – as is the case with many public-sector schemes – exceptionally good discretionary (i.e. not guaranteed) rights or post-April 1997 rights from a contracted-out scheme (in which case you might lose the right to an eventual lump sum at retirement – see page 203). It's unlikely that investing in a personal pension plan will produce benefits as good as those you're giving up. Similarly, if you have the option to join your current employer's scheme, think twice before taking out a personal plan instead. If you think you have been badly advised by a pensions salesman or independent adviser to transfer or opt out of an employer's scheme and into a personal pension plan, you should complain to the

How personal pension plans work

you pay premium contribution (say £5,000) to an insurance company or other pension provider. If you're an employee, you actually hand over only £3,850 in 1998–9 – because you can deduct basic-rate tax relief of £1,150. If you're self-employed, you hand over the full £5,000 and will get the tax relief through a lower tax bill

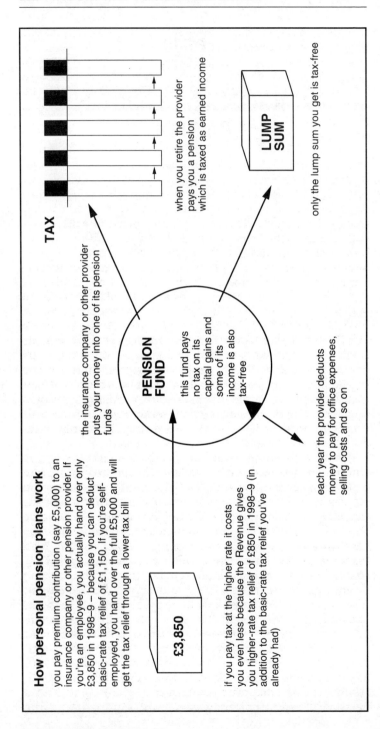

£3,850

if you pay tax at the higher rate it costs you even less because the Revenue gives you higher-rate tax relief of £850 in 1998–9 (in addition to the basic-rate tax relief you've already had)

PENSION FUND

this fund pays no tax on its capital gains and some of its income is also tax-free

each year the provider deducts money to pay for office expenses, selling costs and so on

TAX

the insurance company or other provider puts your money into one of its pension funds

when you retire the provider pays you a pension which is taxed as earned income

LUMP SUM

only the lump sum you get is tax-free

regulator – contact the Personal Investment Authority* or Financial Services Authority.*

You take out a personal pension plan by paying a premium, or agreeing to pay a series of premiums, to whichever pension provider you've chosen. They invest the money and, when you retire, the fund that has built up is used to pay you a pension for life, and usually a tax-free lump sum – see the diagram opposite.

For example, if you paid a lump sum of £5,000 into a scheme at age 39, you might build up a fund of, say, £38,600 by age 65. After taking a tax-free lump sum of £9,650, the remainder of the fund might buy a pension of £268 a month. As it stands, this projection takes no account of inflation. If prices rose even by a modest rate of, say 3 per cent a year between now and retirement, your £268 a month would buy only as much as £124 today. Clearly to build up an adequate retirement income, you will have to invest a sizeable sum year after year.

What are the advantages?

Pension schemes and plans get more generous tax treatment than any other investment. You get tax relief on your premiums, provided you keep within certain limits, at the highest rate of tax you pay. So if you paid tax at the basic rate of 23 per cent in 1998–9, each £1,000 you pay in premiums costs you only £770, or £600 if you paid tax at 40 per cent. If you're an employee, you hand over your contributions after deducting tax relief at the basic rate (see diagram opposite). For this purpose, the lower 20 per cent income tax rate is ignored, so you get relief at the full basic rate even if you pay only 20 per cent tax on some or all of your income. The provider does not pay tax on the gains from investing your money and part of the income is also tax-free. Up to 1 July 1997, all the income building up within a pension fund was tax-free but, from 2 July 1997 onwards, pension funds can no longer reclaim tax already deducted from income from shares, unit trusts and similar investments. At present tax on such income is paid at 20 per cent; from 1999–2000 the rate falls to 10 per cent. Pension funds still benefit from tax-free income from other investments, such as corporate bonds and British Government stocks. When you reach retirement, you can take part of the fund as a tax-free lump sum, although the pension itself is taxable. All in all, you are likely to get a higher income, after tax, from a pension scheme or plan than from a comparable investment in, say, investment-type life insurance.

Whether a pension scheme or plan is a good investment for *you* depends mainly on how long you live. If you live to a ripe old age you generally get much better value than if you die shortly after retiring. But what you're paying for is the certainty of having a regular income as long as you live.

What are the disadvantages?

These days, pension plans are usually very flexible about the age at which the pension can start, but you still cannot normally take anything out of the plan until you've reached at least 50. Even then, you can take only part as a lump sum; the bulk of the proceeds must be taken as a regular income. This means there is no scope for switching to some other form of investment that you think might give you a better return. However, many plans let you stop or vary your contributions without penalty, and you may be able to borrow money from the plan provider on the strength of the pension fund that you have already built up.

All this means is that a pension plan is not the place for money which you might possibly need back for some other purpose – e.g. for buying a home (but see 'Pension mortgages' on page 231) or paying school fees. On the other hand, you should not delay the start of your pension savings. It takes a long time to build up an adequate fund. For example, starting to save £1,000 a year at age 39 could provide a pension, in today's money, of £4,800 a year. But, on the same assumptions, if you delayed until age 55, your savings would produce just £1,500.

The example above is given in terms of today's money. It is crucial that you do strip out the effect of inflation. Most pension projections don't do this and paint a very rosy picture of your retirement income. But £10,000 a year in 25 years' time would be the equivalent of less than £3,000 today in terms of what it could buy, if inflation averaged 5 per cent a year. Even 2 per cent a year inflation would erode the value of the £10,000 to £6,100. And inflation does not stop once you retire. You need a large enough pension fund to protect you against inflation during your retirement years as well. We tell you later in this chapter how you can allow for inflation.

If you are a woman, you'll generally need to set aside more for your pension than a man. Women tend to live longer than men, so on average their pensions are paid for longer. With the exception of rebate-only plans, this is reflected in the rate (the *annuity rate*) at which you can convert your fund into pension. In other words, if a man and

What happened to the old system?

Up to 30 June 1988, self-employed people and those not in an employer's scheme could buy personal pensions in the form of policies called *retirement annuity contracts* (also known as *Section 620* or *Section 226* schemes). No more of these policies have been sold since 1 July 1988, but if you already have such a plan, you are allowed to keep it in force and increase your payments to it until you retire or decide you want to change it. You can take out a new personal pension plan as well, if you wish.

The old types of policy were less flexible than the newer personal pension plans; in particular, you could not normally have a retirement age of below 60. But on the other hand the lump sum available was generally larger than under the new arrangements. And, if your earnngs are exceptionally high, you can contribute more to an old-type plan than to a personal pension plan. If you already have one (or more) of these older policies, it may be worth maintaining it in its present form. But if you switch, even at retirement, to another plan provider, you'll automatically be covered by the rules for the newer personal pension plans.

a woman have the same size pension fund, the woman gets a smaller pension. This is particularly unfortunate, since women often have trouble building up a sufficient pension fund due to family responsibilities. With rebate-only plans, the annuity rate is the same for both men and women.

In the past, you were locked into whatever income your pension fund could buy at the time the pension started. If annuity rates were low at the time, you lost out permanently. Nowadays, you may be able to avoid this problem by deferring the time at which you switch to an annuity and, in the meantime, taking an income direct from the pension fund. But this option is not suitable for everyone.

When to start paying for a personal pension

The younger you are when you make contributions to a personal pension plan, the longer those contributions have to gather interest and dividends. If you paid the same amount in premiums each year, starting just one year earlier could easily increase your pension by over 10 per cent.

When can you start receiving the pension?

Generally speaking, at any time between the ages of 50 and 75. You may need to specify a 'retirement' age when you start the plan. More often, you can decide nearer the time. People in certain occupations can retire earlier, and you may also be able to do so if you become too ill to carry on working, though the pension payable will be at a very much reduced rate. If you have several plans, you can start receiving the benefits from each at different times. You don't have to stop working to do so. (We use *retire* in this chapter to mean *start receiving the benefits of the plan*, whether or not you actually stop work at the time.)

How your pension is worked out

Pension providers calculate benefits in different ways, depending on how your pension plan is worded.

A *deferred annuity* plan talks in terms of the pension you will get from a certain age. This will be based on the amount you've paid into the scheme. Taking the example from earlier in the chapter, if you pay in £1,000 for 26 years from age 39, the provider might quote a pension of £10,000 a year if you retire at 65.

A *cash-funded* plan (more common) talks in terms of the amount of money that accumulates to buy your pension with. For example, the plan may say that if you paid in the same amounts as in the example above, a cash fund of £94,000 would have accumulated by the age of 65.

When you retire, the fund is used to buy an *immediate annuity* that would pay you an income for life. The income you get will depend on the company's annuity rate for your age and gender when you retire and the type of annuity you choose. This will specify how much pension you get for each pound in your fund, usually in terms of pension per £10,000 in the fund. So, for example, your pension might be, say, £1,110 per £10,000 (11 per cent) for a 65-year-old man. Therefore, your pension might be 11 per cent of your cash fund of £94,000, which is about £10,300 (though you might swap part of this for tax-free cash). It all depends on the annuity rates at the time you retire.

This can cause problems. If annuity rates are low at the time you want to retire, you might face the stark choice of either locking into a low pension for life or putting off your retirement in the hope that annuity rates rise some time in the future. Since May 1995, there has been another option called *annuity deferral and income drawdown*. You put off buying an annuity up to the age of 75 and in the meantime take an income direct from the pension fund. You have the normal choice about whether to take a tax-free lump sum at the time you start to draw the income. The maximum income you can take is the amount which would have been provided by an annuity for a single person according to tables published by the government. The minimum is 35 per cent of that amount – for example, if the maximum is £10,000 a year, the minimum would be £3,500. The income is reviewed every three years to check that enough remains in your pension fund to provide an income throughout retirement. The pension fund remains invested until you switch to an annuity and you have the same investment choices as you did when building up your pension fund. To make this option worthwhile, you may need to choose investments which involve some risk to your capital, so annuity deferral and income drawdown are unlikely to be suitable for you if your pension plan is your only source of retirement income. There are also ongoing charges while your pension fund remains invested, making this option viable only if you have a reasonably large fund built up – say, £100,000 or more. You should take financial advice before going down this route.

Not all plan providers offer annuity deferral and income drawdown and it is not available with the older-style retirement annuity accounts. If you have one of these, you will need to transfer to a personal pension plan to have this option.

The types of plan

There are several hundred different personal pension plans. The main variations are in:
■ who is providing the scheme
■ how often you pay premiums
■ how your money is invested
■ the level of charges deducted from the plan.

Who is providing the scheme?

From July 1988, banks, building societies, unit trusts, insurance companies and friendly societies have all been able to offer personal pension plans. But, in practice, this has remained very much the province of the insurance companies and a few friendly societies. Many banks and building societies do offer pension plans but these are usually either the products of their own insurance subsidiaries or of another insurance company. Just a few unit trusts offer pension plans.

At retirement, only insurance companies and friendly societies are allowed to offer the pension itself, but you don't have to stay with the company that has been running your plan up to retirement. With most plans, you can shop around for the best pension (annuity) rates. This is called using your *open market option*. With a rebate-only plan, you must be given this option. You should always investigate using your open market option because some companies specialise in providing competitive annuities, while others do not.

How often you pay premiums

Traditionally, you have had the choice of either a single-premium plan, to which you pay a single lump sum, or a regular-premium plan, where you commit yourself to paying in contributions on a monthly, quarterly, half-yearly or yearly basis. But a growing number of companies now offer completely flexible plans which allow you to make contributions as and when you want on either a regular or an ad hoc basis. The pros and cons of each are:

■ **Discipline** A regular-premium plan commits you to saving steadily. Usually, there are penalties if you stop making the payments or reduce them, so you have a strong incentive to keep the plan going. This makes it more likely that you will achieve your target retirement income. If you opt for flexible or single-premium plans, you need a high level of self-discipline to make sure you keep on investing enough

■ **Adapting to changing circumstances** A flexible plan, or taking out single-premium plans as and when you can afford it, lets you tailor your retirement savings to your changing financial situation. This can be particularly useful if you are self-employed, with varying profits from year to year, if you are not in secure employment, or if you are a woman who plans to take career breaks or switch to part-time working while you bring up a family

■ **Coping with crisis** Similarly, a flexible or single-premium plan does not tie you into contributions you could no longer afford if you could not work because of illness or redundancy. But, with a regular-premium plan, you may be able to take out a waiver-of-premium option at the outset, which would let you stop your contributions without penalty in cases of illness or unemployment

■ **Charges** Charges for regular-premium plans are often higher than for other types of plan, particularly where the contributions are small and/or made very frequently (e.g.

monthly) because this involves a lot of administration relative to the amount being invested.

How your money is invested

Below, we give the details of four main types of plan. For which type to choose, see 'Planning your pension', on page 234.

With-profits

The premiums go into the provider's fund to be invested in, for example, shares, British Government stock and property. The plan guarantees from the outset the minimum pension it will pay you (if the policy is a deferred annuity one) or the minimum amount of money you'll have with which to buy an annuity (if it is cash-funded). These minimum amounts are low, but as the provider makes profits on its investments, it announces increases in the minimum you're guaranteed. These are called *reversionary bonuses*, and once they've been announced – usually every year – they cannot be taken away. A one-off *terminal bonus* is also added at the time you retire. You have no idea how much this will be until that time arrives.

Unit-linked and unit trust

Nearly all unit-linked policies are cash-funded. Your premiums buy units in one or more of a number of funds offered by the insurance or unit trust company. The most common types of fund are:

■ equity funds – invested in shares, directly or through unit trusts

■ fixed-interest funds – invested in British Government stocks, company loan stocks, and other investments which pay out a fixed income

■ property funds – invested in office blocks, factories, shops and so on

■ cash funds – invested in bank deposit accounts and other investments whose return varies along with interest rates in general

■ managed funds – invested in a range of the options listed above, in proportions decided by the investment managers.

Each fund is divided into a number of units. The price of each is, approximately, the value of the investments in the fund divided by the number of units that have been issued. So the unit price goes up and down as the value of the investments in the fund fluctuates. With most providers there's a choice of funds to invest in, and you can switch from one to another.

Unitised with-profits

This type is a cross between a unit-linked and a with-profits scheme. More and more providers are offering this type instead of traditional with-profits plans, either as a completely separate plan or as one of the range of funds available with a unit-linked plan (in which case it is usually called a 'with-profits fund'). They work in a similar way to a with-profits plan: your contributions are allocated to units in a fund, but the return comes as bonus units which are added and can't then be taken away. However, when your plan matures or you want to transfer it, the company does reserve the right in exceptional circumstances to revise the value of your units downwards if need be. This means that unitised with-profits plans are not as secure as the original with-profits version.

Deposit administration

This type of scheme is provided particularly by building societies, though other providers also offer it in some cases.

It works rather like a deposit account. Your premiums are put into an account with the provider, and interest is added from time to time. The interest rate will vary with the general level of interest rates, but there may be a guaranteed minimum amount, sometimes linked to the mortgage rate. The value of your fund, in pounds, can't go down. With some providers you can switch between deposit administration and unit-linked policies. It is often sensible to switch your pension savings into this type of fund (or to the cash fund in a unit-linked plan) as you near retirement, if you think that your unit-linked fund might go down in value.

All deposit administration schemes are cash-funded, and a few guarantee a minimum amount of cash fund you'll have at retirement. The amount of pension will depend on annuity rates at the time you retire, though many policies do guarantee a minimum annuity rate at retirement.

The level of charges

The plan provider deducts a variety of charges from your plan to cover the cost of administering it and investing your contributions. The overall impact of charges varies greatly from company to company, as the table opposite shows.

Impact of charges on the value of your fund

	5 years	10 years	15 years	20 years	25 years
			Reduction after:		
Regular premium of £200 a month					
Best plan	3.0%	5.3%	7.4%	8.9%	10.6%
Average plan	11.5%	13.4%	15.3%	17.5%	19.6%
Worst-charging plan	19.2%	22.0%	24.6%	28.2%	27.8%
Single premium of £10,000					
Best plan	3.9%	7.1%	9.2%	10.6%	10.4%
Average plan	10.1%	13.7%	16.7%	19.6%	22.5%
Worst-charging plan	17.4%	20.5%	27.0%	32.9%	38.2%

Source: *Money Management*, October 1997

A high-charging plan is not necessarily a bad plan, but clearly your investment is going to have to work a lot harder to overcome the high charges than it would if invested in a lower-charging plan.

Borrowing back from the provider

A few schemes include what's called a *loan-back facility*, so that you can borrow from the provider up to the amount you've got in the pension fund. There is a minimum amount, usually £5,000, and you need to be able to offer security such as your house, business premises or shares. You can repay the loan when you like, perhaps from selling your business when you retire, or out of the tax-free lump sum you get on retirement if this is large enough.

There may be little advantage in borrowing in this way rather than, say, getting a loan from a bank. The bank's interest rates may be more competitive than those charged by the provider. However, the facility could be useful if you wanted to borrow at a time when credit was difficult to obtain (though if you are turned down by a bank because you are not credit-worthy, you are also quite likely to be turned down by the pension provider).

Pension mortgages

It is also possible to arrange to link your pension and your mortgage. Legally, there is no link, because you are not allowed to *assign* your pension benefit, i.e. earmark it as security for a loan. Instead, what happens is that you take out an interest-only mortgage, and receive tax relief on the repayments as normal. You also pay your pension scheme contributions, receiving tax relief on them. At retirement date, you use your tax-free lump sum to pay off the capital on the mortgage. A legal link is unnecessary, as the bank or building society holding the mortgage can foreclose on your house if you do not pay them back.

Pension mortgages have some disadvantages. They can tie you to one provider, who may not offer the best rates or returns, and you may have to take the pension at a fixed date, which may be inconvenient for other reasons. You commit yourself many years ahead to a particular use for your tax-free lump sum, though there may be other things on which you would prefer to spend the money.

You may find that having a pension mortgage creates problems if later on you join an employer who has a good pension scheme. You will be able to join that only if you stop paying into the personal pension plan. It should usually be possible to make a new arrangement for paying off the mortgage, however, so you are not locked in to the personal pension altogether.

There will also be difficulties in keeping up payments to the pension scheme if you become unemployed, and so have no earnings from which to pay. You can buy insurance to cover the payments, but this won't help if you have no relevant earnings (see 'The tax rules', on page 244) and so are not entitled to make pension contributions. With a mortgage linked to the employer's pension scheme (which is also possible), there is the added problem of rearranging the scheme if you leave that employment, though again this will become easier if pension mortgages become more common.

Above all, taking a pension mortgage could reduce your income in retirement. If you're using part of your pension fund to repay a mortgage, there will be less available to provide a pension for you.

Although the tax advantages are considerable, they don't necessarily outweigh the disadvantages. Think carefully before deciding to take out a pension mortgage.

Rebate-only personal pensions

These policies let you contract out of SERPS. Only employees can take these out – the self-employed are not in SERPS.

You cannot have more than one rebate-only personal pension in any one tax year, but you can pay additional contributions to it and add as many ordinary personal pension plans on top as you like (if you are not in an employer's pension scheme). In practice, if your *only* pension provision was a rebate-only plan you would get a very poor and inflexible pension, so it is not recommended. You would also forgo the chance of a lump sum at retirement, or of retiring at any age earlier than state pension age.

The contributions to a rebate-only plan are made up of:

■ the National Insurance rebate. From April 1997, this comprises a flat-rate element equal to 3.4 per cent of your earnings between the lower and upper earnings limits plus an age-related element which ranges from nothing at the age of 16 through to 5.6 per cent of those earnings from the age of 46 onwards. The age-related element is being increased slightly from 1999–2000

■ tax relief on your rebate which comes to roughly another 0.48 per cent of your earnings in the 1998–9 tax year.

These contributions are paid over by the Department of Social Security (DSS) after the end of the tax year, when it has sorted out the paperwork. They are not counted by the Inland Revenue against their limits for tax relief, explained on page 244. For whether or not a rebate-only plan would be a sensible choice for you, see Chapter 12.

What contributions to a rebate-only personal plan will buy you

You can choose to contribute:
extra payments, up to 17.5% of earnings
(more if aged over 35)

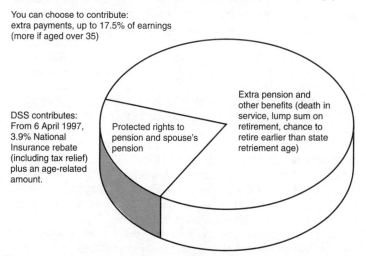

DSS contributes:
From 6 April 1997,
3.9% National
Insurance rebate
(including tax relief)
plus an age-related
amount.

Protected rights to
pension and spouse's
pension

Extra pension and
other benefits (death in
service, lump sum on
retirement, chance to
retire earlier than state
retirement age)

Planning your pension

Which type of policy?

Deposit administration policies and the cash funds of unit-linked policies are very dependent on levels of interest rates. So they look good when interest rates are high, but less good when the rates are lower. Because the value of your fund or the price of your units (in pounds) can't go down, these policies are useful for people nearing retirement who want to make sure they don't lose any money. If you have a unit-linked policy, switching into the cash fund or a deposit administration scheme can be useful if you're worried about units going down in value. But the pension will still be dependent on annuity rates when you retire.

For the longer term, the choice is between with-profits and unit-linked policies. With-profits schemes are the less risky. Although the guaranteed pension or cash fund is initially low, it is reasonably certain to be increased steadily over the period to retirement. However, many insurance companies have been piling a large proportion of the 'profits' into the terminal bonus, which is not guaranteed and can be held static or cut, and even future rates of reversionary bonus can be reduced if a company falls on hard times.

If you go for a deferred annuity scheme, your pension will not suffer if annuity rates are low at the time you retire (though some companies will increase your pension if annuity rates are high). With unit-linked policies (apart from the small number of index-linked ones available), the return is much more dependent on when you make your payments and when you start taking the benefits. Although you may do very well with a unit-linked policy, you could also do rather badly.

One good compromise would be to take out a regular-premium with-profits policy for an amount you can fairly easily afford, at as young an age as possible – say, 30. It is worth going for a policy that allows you to increase premiums on guaranteed terms in future years, if you can find one. But in years in which you can afford to pay a substantial extra amount, take out a single-premium policy, perhaps a unit-linked one. As time passes, in order to protect your pension from inflation you would need to take out further policies, which would help spread the risks, or to pay more into your existing policies.

This strategy should make sure that you have enough pension from with-profits policies whenever you want to retire. So you'll then be in a better position to choose a good time for taking the benefits of the unit-linked policies, when the prices of the units or annuity rates (or both) are high. Alternatively, in the few years before you intend to retire, switch into a cash fund or a deposit administration fund. You could do this when the price of the units reaches high levels or you think they are going to go down.

How much to pay in

With regular-premium policies, most companies set a minimum regular premium of, say, £250 a year or £25 a month. The minimum for a single-premium policy could be £500 or £1,000, but can be a good deal higher for a scheme specially tailored for senior people on high salaries.

The maximum you can pay is the maximum amount you can get tax relief on, explained on page 244.

Organisations selling pension plans give very accurate looking and impressive figures showing the pension you'd get from each pound you pay from a certain age. But these quotations are only estimates, based on set assumptions about future investment returns. For most plans, these assumptions are laid down under the Financial Services Act. Except with rebate-only plans, the estimates take no account of inflation, which can be devastating over long periods of time (though you get a separate, and rather confusing, statement about inflation).

For example, if you started paying £1,000 a year into a regular premium policy at age 35, you might imagine yourself living in comfort on the £14,800 a year the insurance company quotes you. But if inflation averaged 3 per cent over the rest of your working life, the buying power of this pension at 65 would be only £6,100 a year. Ten years after retirement it would be worth only about £4,500 a year, if inflation continued at 3 per cent.

This makes it extremely difficult to know how much you should be paying in to your pension. But you should consider the following points:
■ how much income you'll have after retirement from other sources, such as state retirement pension, from selling your business, or from part-time work
■ the age you intend to retire at – the older this is, the more pension you'll get for each pound you've paid in
■ inflation after retirement. At age 65, you can expect to live to 79, on average, if you're a man, 83 if you're a woman.

You'll still want your pension to have reasonable purchasing power in your old age, so your pension in the first year of retirement will need to be much higher in pounds than you'd think. Alternatively, you could give up some pension in the early years of retirement in order to have a pension which increases each year – see 'Level or increasing pension?', on page 243

■ inflation between now and retirement. Over such a long period of time, inflation can make mincemeat of your pension.

You can use the table below to work out what value of pension you'll need for various rates of inflation. For example, if you think you'll need a pension of £10,000 a year (in today's money) in 30 years' time, and you reckon inflation will average 4 per cent over that time, you'll need to get £10,000 × 3.2 = £32,000 a year from the scheme to achieve this.

To take account of inflation both before and after retirement, use the number of years up to your 70th or 75th birthday, say, even if you intend to retire younger.

You might find that you cannot possibly afford the contributions for a pension of the amount you've worked out. The best you can do for now is to save the highest amount you can and to set aside extra amounts in future if you have an opportunity to do so. Bear in mind that you cannot pay in more than the Inland Revenue limits allow. If you need to save above those limits, consider paying the maximum into your pension plan and topping up by saving through another investment, such as a Personal Equity Plan (PEP) up to 5 April 1999 and an Individual Savings Account (ISA) thereafter. If you are an employee, can you persuade your employer to contribute to your personal pension plan?

Yearly rate of inflation	Pounds you'd need in future to match the buying power of each pound today				
	in	in	in	in	in
	10yrs	20yrs	30yrs	40yrs	50yrs
2%	1.2	1.5	1.8	2.2	2.7
4%	1.5	2.2	3.2	4.8	7.1
6%	1.8	3.2	5.7	10.3	18.4
8%	2.2	4.7	10.1	21.7	46.9

When to start

If you are aiming to get a pension at age 65 of two-thirds of your final pay (which is the most that someone in an employer's scheme would be allowed to have) you'll need to pay the full percentage of earnings allowed by the Inland Revenue each year from about age 44 onwards. This *might* give you a fully index-linked two-thirds pension, plus a pension of two-thirds of that for your spouse if you died in retirement.

However, you'd be unwise to leave starting a scheme as late as this. There may be years when you can afford to pay only a small amount in premiums; you may decide to use some of the premiums qualifying for tax relief to get life insurance or a pension for your dependants; you may need to retire before 65, perhaps because of ill-health; and inflation may be very high in the first few years of your retirement. So, unless you are confident you would have substantial income from elsewhere, you should certainly start paying for your pension by your early 30s.

If you stop paying

You may need to stop paying into a regular-premium policy, perhaps because you have no qualifying earnings in a tax year, or find yourself short of cash. Most providers will let you miss one or two payments, but there is usually a limit at which the policy has to be made *paid-up*. This means that your money remains invested in the fund, and you'll get a pension when you retire, though it will be smaller than if you had kept paying. Check with the provider how it would work out the pension and watch out for charges that continue to be deducted from your plan even when it's paid up and reduce the amount available for your pension. If your plan has been running only a few years when you stop paying premiums, you may find it has a very low value or may be worth nothing at all.

You can often reinstate a policy within a year or so of its being made paid-up. With with-profits policies, you'll normally have to pay all the premiums you've missed and perhaps a fee as well. But this could be worth doing if the guarantees on your old policies are better than they would be on a new one, or if the old policy is a retirement annuity account with the higher level of lump sum available. Make sure you'll qualify for tax relief on the premiums.

If you expect your earnings to fluctuate from year to year, do not choose a regular premium plan. Instead go either for a series of single premium plans or a plan which is flexible and allows payments to be made on an ad hoc basis.

When you plan to retire

You must start to take the benefits from a personal pension plan some time between your 50th and 75th birthday, unless your job is recognised as having a lower retirement age. There are now only a few of these, such as various groups of sportsmen and athletes with retirement ages of 35 or 40. Under the older, retirement annuity accounts, the minimum retirement age was 60, so there was a far longer list of exceptions.

If you have a retirement annuity account and want to retire at an age between 50 and 60, it will be possible to switch into a personal pension plan, but you will lose the right to the greater lump sum if you do so.

There's no need to stop working in order to draw your pension and lump sum.

If you have become too ill to work before the lowest age at which you can retire, you can start taking the benefits then, but the amount will be much reduced. This is because you'll have been paying in for a shorter period and will expect to draw out for longer.

With some policies, you have to say at the outset when you intend to retire, though you can change your mind later. Other policies have a standard retirement age, but you can still retire when you like within the age range allowed. If you don't know when you'll want to retire, check that you won't lose out by retiring earlier or later than the date you name.

Phasing your retirement

You may not want to stop work suddenly but would rather slide out gradually over a period of years. If so, you may want to supplement your earnings over a number of years by drawing a small amount of pension, increasing year by year until you draw your full pension when you've stopped working altogether.

You could do this by having several policies and taking the benefits from each at a different time. Or you could invest with companies which design their policies as a series of separate units, each of which can start paying out at a different time. But check that this doesn't mean you are paying too much in administration charges. Since May 1995, annuity deferral and income drawdown has been available and this can also be used to provide a low or increasing income as you phase in your retirement.

If you die before retirement

With most policies, a lump sum will be paid to your heirs if you die before you have started taking the policy benefits.

This will usually be the value of your fund at the date of death or your contributions plus interest or bonuses.

If you want a higher level of cover, you can arrange extra life insurance separately (see box below), though you can get tax relief on life insurance premiums only if you use part of the overall contribution limit available for personal pension payments. To weigh up which is best for you, ask the insurance company (or other provider) to give you illustrations of the costs of both options.

A few providers will pay out a pension for a dependant instead of a lump sum, but the dependant might be able to get a better income by investing a lump sum.

See 'Your choices at retirement', on page 241 for how personal pensions can be used to provide for dependants if you die after retirement.

Additional life insurance

If you qualify for a personal pension plan, you'll be able to use part of your contributions – up to 5 per cent of your earnings – to buy life insurance. This is particularly valuable because you get tax relief at your top rate on the life insurance premiums.

You don't have to take out a pension plan as well – you can just have the life insurance – and you don't have to get the life insurance from the same provider whose personal pension plan you are paying into, although it may give you a discount. Shop around for a discount, or get a broker to do so for you.

For more on the important subject of life insurance for your family, see Chapter 21.

Choosing a policy

There are hundreds of different personal pension plans to choose from. Choosing among them isn't easy and, if this is going to be your main way of saving for retirement, it might be sensible to spread your investment over more than one plan, though each extra scheme you take out means an extra administration charge.

To find out for yourself which policies offer which features, get hold of the most recent edition of the *FT Personal Pensions* published by FT Financial Publishing.* This gives useful comparative details on most plans.

You'll want to find a company that will give a better-than-average return on your investment, but there's no sure way of knowing how each company will perform.

With *with-profits* policies you could check what you'd get from different companies if current bonus rates were maintained, and how they've done in the past. However, there's no guarantee that companies that have done well in the past will continue to do well in the future. A company with relatively high reserves may be better placed to maintain its bonus levels in the future.

With *unit-linked* and *deposit administration* schemes, the past is, again, little guide to the future, nor are current growth rates. However, it seems sensible to concentrate on those providers who have produced results which have been *consistently* above average. Plan providers issue illustrations giving an example of the benefits your plan might produce, but these should be used with care. The regulatory authorities lay down the assumptions about investment performance and all providers must base their illustrations on the same standardised growth rates. However, since January 1995, plan providers use their own charges, so comparing illustrations from different providers for the same contributions and benefits shows you how the costs compare. A high-charging provider is not necessarily a worse choice than a low-charging one, but the high charger will have to make the investments work harder to overcome the extra charges and you need to know why that provider's investments are expected to do so much better.

Gathering information about plans and making comparisons is time-consuming. You can save yourself a lot of work by going to an independent financial adviser – make sure you choose one who specialises in pensions business. A good independent adviser will have access to computer databases that make plan comparisons very quick and straightforward once you know the type of features you are looking for. Bear in mind that independent financial advice is not free.

The clearer your own ideas of what you want, before you visit an adviser, the more effectively you and the adviser will be able to decide on the most suitable course of action for you. You may also increase your chances of getting good advice if you go to more than one adviser. You can get a list of advisers in your area by contacting IFA Promotion* or the Money Management National Register of Independent Fee-Based Advisers*.

The security of your plan

Insurance companies are covered by the Policyholders' Protection Act. If the company fails, then the Policyholders' Protection Board, set up by the government to administer the Act, has to try to get another company to take on the policy. Provided you carry on paying the premiums due, the Act guarantees that you'll get at least 90 per cent of the amount guaranteed at the time the company went bust, unless the Board considers this to be excessive.

However, you get no guarantees of future bonuses from the new company that takes over your policy. So you could lose quite a lot if your company goes bust – it's prudent to stick with a large, well-established company.

Very few insurance companies do go bust. Sometimes they get taken over instead, and sometimes, if they get into financial trouble, they have to cut their bonus rates. In those cases, you won't lose the guarantees, but the rate of growth on the policies will be slower than you had expected.

Other pension providers are covered by compensation funds (though in some cases these cover smaller amounts than the Policyholders' Protection Act). Providers have to abide by rules laid down by the Financial Services Act or the laws for banks and building societies – see Chapter 5. In every case, therefore, at least part of your money is protected, but you could lose the rest.

Your choices at retirement

When to retire

Once you reach an age at which you can start taking the benefits under your plan (between 50 and 75 for a plan taken out on or after 1 July 1988, or between 60 and 75 for a retirement annuity account), you can write to the provider at any time saying you want to start taking the benefits of your policy. Before committing yourself, find out what sort of benefits you'll get, so that you can postpone your decision if necessary.

Shopping around for a higher pension

With all rebate-only personal pensions and nearly all other personal pension plans, you don't have to take your pension from the providers with which you have been saving. When you retire, you can shop around to see if you can get a better deal for the money that's built up for you. This is called the *open market option*.

If you want to do this, you first have to find out the value of your cash fund. If the policy is a deferred annuity, the provider will have to work out (using what is called its *commutation* rate) the number of pounds of fund you're allocated for the pension to which you're entitled. You then compare the benefits you would have got from this provider with the benefits you could get if you switched this amount to someone else. If, over the years, you've taken out a number of different plans, you could transfer them all at retirement to the insurance company offering the best package of benefits.

With some providers, the cash fund you can transfer is slightly lower than the one with which the original provider would have credited you.

To find the best company for you, contact one of the independent financial advisers that specialises in annuity business, such as the Annuity Bureau* or Annuity Direct.*

If annuity rates are low at the time you want to retire, you might consider a flexible annuity or annuity deferral. But these options won't suit everyone, so get advice before deciding on this route.

Lump sum

When you retire, you can normally choose to have a reduced pension, and a tax-free lump sum. You may be glad to have a lump sum to spend at the start of your retirement, or you could invest the money and draw on it later. Even if you used the money to buy an *immediate* annuity, you could end up with a higher after-tax income than the pension you've given up. For more on immediate annuities, see Chapter 23.

The Inland Revenue's rules on the size of the lump sum depend on whether you have a retirement annuity account (started before 1 July 1988) or a personal pension plan (started on or after 1 July 1988).

The retirement annuity account rules say that the maximum lump sum you can have is whatever amount would be three times the pension payable after the lump sum has been deducted from your fund. (There is a cash limit for policies taken out on or after 17 March 1987 though, in practice, the limit is easily avoided.) The personal pension rules, on the other hand, say that you can take a quarter of your fund (after some deductions) as a lump sum. If you have a rebate-only personal pension as part of the plan, you must not take any of that part as a lump sum – it must be paid as pension.

In many cases, the retirement annuity account rules give the larger lump sum but this depends on your age and annuity rates at the time you start to take your pension. At an annuity rate of around 11 per cent, the lump sums from a retirement annuity account and a personal plan are about the same. At higher annuity rates, the lump sum from the retirement annuity account is greater. If you have a retirement annuity account, using your open market option at retirement automatically switches you to a personal plan and you become caught by the limits of those plans. This means that you'll need to weigh up any loss of lump sum against the possible gain in pension by shopping around for the best annuity rates.

Level or increasing pension?

The buying power of a level pension will quickly be eaten away by inflation. You could instead choose a pension that increases each year. It will, though, be smaller to start off with. For example, a pension for a 65-year old man that increases by 5 per cent compound each year will start off at around two-thirds of the amount of a level pension. Although the increasing pension would catch the level pension up in about ten years, it would take about 18 years before you'd actually received the same *total* number of pounds in pension.

A few providers offer pensions which are linked to an index – often the Retail Prices Index (RPI). But a pension that is increased in line with such an index will start off much lower than a level pension. If it started off at half as much when you retired at 65, it would have to increase by an average of 20 per cent a year if you were to have received the same total buying power by the time you were 75, or 12.5 per cent a year if you were to have received the same total buying power by the time you were 80.

With many unit-linked policies, you can choose to have the pension unit-linked as well. This means it will go up and down in line with the price of units in the fund. This could be a good idea for part of your pension, but it would be unwise to link too much of your pension in this way, in case the fund hits bad times.

If you have a rebate-only personal pension as part of your policy, that must be increased by a certain amount. Contracted-out pensions built up from April 1997 onwards must be increased by inflation up to a maximum of 5 per cent each year. Contracted-out pensions built up before then must be increased by inflation up to 3 per cent a year, with some topping up by the DSS if inflation exceeds this.

A pension for a dependant after you die

There are two ways in which you can provide an income for your husband or wife (or other person you name) if you die after you start drawing the pension. The first is to choose to have a pension paid as long as you or someone else is alive (called a joint life, last survivor annuity). The pension may continue at the same level, or it can be higher while you are both alive. A joint-life pension (if the man is 65 and the woman 60 and the pension stays level) might be around 25 per cent lower than a pension payable on one life only for the man, 7 per cent lower than that for the woman.

Alternatively, you can choose to have the pension paid for a certain period (often five or ten years) whether you live that long or not. As this removes the risk of getting virtually nothing back if you die soon after retirement, the pension for a man aged 65 will be around 2.5 per cent less if it's guaranteed for five years (around 1 per cent less for a woman of the same age). If you died, your dependant would receive nothing at the end of the guaranteed period, so don't look on this as adequate protection.

With a rebate-only personal pension, the policy must provide for a pension of half of what you would get, for your widow or widower after your death (even if you are not married at the time when you retire).

If you opt for annuity deferral and income drawdown and you die before switching to an annuity, a surviving dependent has three choices: he or she can use the fund to buy an annuity; continue to draw an income direct from the fund until either he or she reaches the age of 75 or the date at which you would have been 75, whichever comes sooner; or take the fund as a lump sum after deduction of tax at a special rate of 35 per cent.

The tax rules

Following are the main rules about how much you can pay into personal pension plans each year.

If you pay in more than the maximum you are allowed in any one year to a personal pension plan, the excess must be returned to you – but you get no interest on it.

How much tax relief

You get tax relief at your highest rate of tax on premiums of up to a percentage of your *net relevant earnings* (see below) for that year. The maximum contribution depends on your age, although there is also a limit on the earnings that can be taken into account of £87,600 (in the 1998–9 tax year). This limit, which applies only to new-style plans and not the old retirement annuity accounts, is usually increased each year in line with price inflation. The percentage limits are:

Age	Limits
up to 35	17.5 per cent
36–45	20 per cent
46–50	25 per cent
51–55	30 per cent
56–60	35 per cent
61 to 74	40 per cent
75 and over	nil

Lower limits apply to retirement annuity accounts if you are aged 35 or more. If you have both a retirement annuity account and a new-style plan, your overall contributions to *both* must not exceed the limits for new-style plans.

Husband and wife each have their own limit worked out on their net relative earnings and ages.

If your own contributions are below these limits, your employer is allowed to make contributions up to the balance (though they don't normally do so).

If you are an employee, you make payments *net* of basic-rate tax: that is, you just pay the after-tax relief amount and the provider reclaims the tax from the Inland Revenue. So if you wanted to pay a total premium of £100, you would actually pay in £77 in the 1998–9 tax year, and the provider would reclaim £23 (with basic-rate tax at 23 per cent) from the Inland Revenue. If you're a higher-rate taxpayer, you have to reclaim the higher-rate relief through your tax office.

If you're self-employed, you make *gross* payments and claim back the tax relief through your tax return (i.e. if you want £100 to go into the plan, *you* pay in the full £100).

Your net relevant earnings

Net relevant earnings are your earned income for the tax year in which the contributions are paid (or treated as paid – see below). If you are an employee, they are the earnings from your job on which you pay tax under the PAYE.

If you are self-employed, net relevant earnings are the taxable profits which are being assessed during that tax year. For most businesses, in 1998–9, this will be the profits for the accounting period ending during the tax year. But, if you have newly started in business, a different basis may apply for the first two or three years. Your taxable profits are broadly your takings less the following deductions:

- allowable business expenses
- capital allowances for the cost of machinery and plant (including a car) used in your business
- losses made in the same business in earlier years which you have carried forward and set against profits for the current year.

Unused relief for the last six years

You can get tax relief on premiums you pay on top of the normal limit, and up to the whole of your net relevant earnings in that tax year, if you didn't pay the maximum premiums allowed in any of the previous six tax years (though you can't count earnings from which you made contributions to an employer's pension scheme, unless your contributions were refunded). You have to use up the earliest unused relief first. You receive the relief at your current tax rate. So a basic-rate taxpayer would get relief at only 23 per cent in 1998–9 even though the tax rate was higher in the earlier year.

If you contribute to both a retirement annuity account and a personal pension plan, there may be a restriction on the relief carried forward. The rules are complex, so get help from a financial adviser or your tax office.

Looking over your shoulder

You can ask in any tax year to have all or part of the premiums you pay in that year treated as if you'd paid them in the previous tax year, provided you have sufficient net relevant earnings for that year. If you didn't have *any* net relevant earnings in the previous tax year, you'll be able to get the premiums treated as if you'd paid them in the year before that. You get tax relief at the rate at which tax was payable in the earlier year rather than at the current rate. Using these rules means you usually get tax relief earlier and, if you're self-employed, lets you wait to see how your profits turn out before committing yourself to a pension contribution.

SECTION III

Other Ways of Investing

16

SHARES

The number of private shareholders declined steadily from the early 1960s until the early 1980s. Then came the government's programme of selling off government-owned industries like British Gas, British Telecom, the water companies and the electricity companies. Largely as a result of privatisation and building society conversions the number of private shareholders has grown dramatically. By 1979 only 3 million people had their own direct share holdings – now the figure is nearer 16 million.

Investing directly in shares is a risky business, as was demonstrated in the October 1987 stock market crash, when shares lost 20 per cent of their value in a few days. Although if you were prepared to invest for the long term, this loss was, on average, recovered within two years or so. To reduce risk, you need to be prepared to invest for a reasonable length of time, say five years or more, and to spread your money around a number of companies in different industries.

If you do not have enough money to be able to spread your investment, and are not attracted to the risks of direct investment in shares, there are various ways of investing indirectly in shares. By investing indirectly and pooling your money with that of other investors, you can spread your risk, because your money will be invested in a wide range of companies. One way of indirect share investment is to put your money in unit trusts or investment trusts, dealt with in Chapters 17 and 18. Other ways of investing in shares are detailed at the end of this chapter.

Investing directly in shares is a way of investing in the performance of a company. You can expect two sorts of return:

■ *income* – the company will pay out an income (called dividend) to its shareholders. The hope is that this income will increase over the years as company profits rise

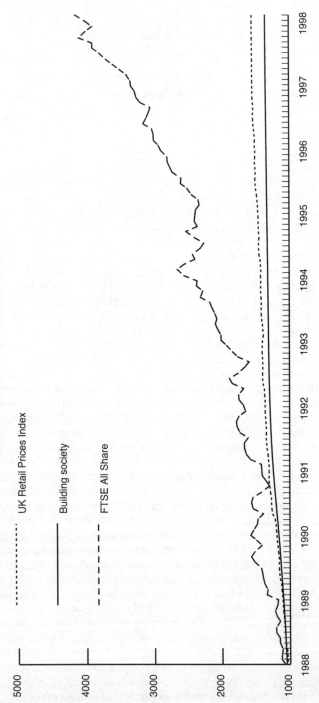

An investment in shares: 1988–98

UK Retail Prices Index

Building society

FTSE All Share

Source: Micropal

■ *capital gain* – the hope is that the share price of the company will rise over the years. This may happen if, for example, the company's prospects improve. But you should not expect the share price to rise steadily.

Looking at what's happened in the past gives some sort of idea of the ups and downs of investing in shares. The chart on page 251 shows how the value of the stock market has varied between 1988 and 1998. As you can see, it's been a bumpy ride. Within the market as a whole some shares will have produced a smoother performance while others will have been even more volatile. The success of your investment depends crucially on when you buy the shares and when you sell, and no one has a cast-iron method of forecasting the right moment to buy and sell.

Over the years, however, the return on shares has, on average, been higher than with safer investments, e.g. an investment in building societies. But because the past is not a guide to the future, the average investor should assume that investing in shares is a long-term business.

Spreading your investment

Three major factors influence the share price of any company. First, the profitability of that company and, probably more accurately, the expectations of its future profitability. Second, the industry the company works in. You may believe that BP, say, is the best performing oil company, but if the oil sector is depressed because of a glut in oil supply then you may do better investing in another area of the market. Third, the market itself may be performing badly because of economic factors or fears of recession. All these factors must be considered before investing in shares and reviewed regularly after you've bought shares. If you can choose the right company, in the right sector, at the right time you could do very well indeed, but you could also do very badly if you get it wrong.

If you buy shares in more than one company, then your chances of an extreme result become much smaller. And if you spread your money over the shares of as many as 12 or so companies, covering different sectors of the market, the chances of them all doing much worse than average are small. You should be able to reduce both the company risk and the sector risk. Unfortunately, the chance of a much above average return is also reduced. You can also go one step further by spreading your investments over different countries (see Chapter 25), so that the outcome of your investment doesn't depend entirely on the UK stock market.

But remember, share prices fluctuate both individually and on average. So, even if you invest in a wide spread of shares, you cannot be sure that the value of your share investment will not fall, particularly in the short or even medium term.

Because of buying and selling costs, it makes no sense to invest small amounts in shares – less than about £1,500 to £2,000 per company say. So to get a good spread – of shares in, say, five to ten companies – you'd need around, say, £15,000 or more for this type of investment.

Ways of choosing shares

If you've made the decision to buy shares, you are still faced with the problem of choosing which ones.

Often, the amateur investor won't do the choosing entirely on his or her own, but will get professional advice (see Chapter 6) from a stockbroker, for example, or from the business pages of a newspaper. However, in order to understand this advice, and to assess its worth, it would be helpful to know something about the different methods of choosing shares which may be used by advisers. There are four main ways of choosing shares:
- fundamental analysis
- technical analysis (chartism)
- quantitative analysis
- general observations and personal views.

For more detailed information on choosing shares see *The Which? Guide to Shares* by Jonquil Lowe, published by Which? Books.*

Fundamental analysis

The basic assumption here is that, at any given time, a company's shares have an intrinsic value. This value depends normally on the earning capacity of the company, which in turn depends on such things as the quality of management, and the outlook for the industry and for the economy as a whole. If the current market price of the shares is lower than what you suppose the intrinsic value to be, the share is one to consider buying because the assumption is that the share price will eventually reflect the underlying worth of the company.

Fundamental analysis will sometimes calculate a precise intrinsic value for a share, based on detailed estimates of the company's future earnings.

The analysis will use any information that can be obtained, e.g. by visiting companies, talking to the management and analysing the company report and accounts. Companies are obliged by law to publish the accounts of their business at least once a year, and to provide certain information. These accounts may reveal some important facts about the company's performance during the period covered by the accounts.

Specialist investment analysts study these accounts with the idea of discovering how well the company is really doing. By working out the relationships between various factors (the EPS – see box below, is probably the most commonly used – also see 'What the papers say', on page 262, for price/earnings ratio) they build up a picture of the company's financial position. This can be compared with other companies in the same industry to assess the performance of the company and its management. In addition, by studying the economic background, this method is used to make predictions about how well, or badly, particular industries (e.g. heavy engineering) or even whole countries are going to fare.

But there are problems. The information available is far from comprehensive and not sufficiently standardised, and information in accounts is out of date. For example, after the most skilful reading of a company's accounts, you may still not know whether one part of the company's business is making losses and is being subsidised by more profitable parts, although often these are the types of companies to avoid.

A few examples of common terms and ratios

Earnings per share (EPS)
EPS is the amount of profit per share from the *ordinary* activities of the company, after tax and all other charges. It does not include any profit (or loss) made outside the company's normal business, called extraordinary items, say the sale of land by a manufacturing company. The EPS is worked out by dividing the profits for ordinary shareholders by the total number of shares in the issue.

Profit margin
This is worked out by finding what the profit of the company is as a percentage of its sales.

Return on capital employed
This is worked out by finding what the profit of the company is as a percentage of its assets, i.e the sum of the value of its property, its stock, what it is owed by its customers and so on.

Technical analysis (*chartism*)

Technical analysis is concerned with the behaviour of the stock market, i.e. the rises and falls in share prices, rather than the details of a company's management, earnings and so on. The method normally includes the study of charts, hence *chartism*.

The assumption is that investors, collectively, have all the available facts about companies, and that movements of share prices accurately and quickly reflect this knowledge. But technical analysts believe that share prices may not move instantly to take account of the information, and so believe they can predict price movements.

The method involves studying charts or graphs showing the range of prices at which each company's shares are bought and sold. The share price record of a company can indicate periods when investors have displayed confidence (or lack of it) in the company, and have built up (or sold) large holdings of its shares. Chartists argue that their graphs can tell them when such periods are about to recur, and they look for *trendlines*, and for significant shapes like *head and shoulder* patterns. If the chart of the share price of a company has completed a head and shoulder (see chart below), a chartist would say it was time to sell that share.

A typical chart

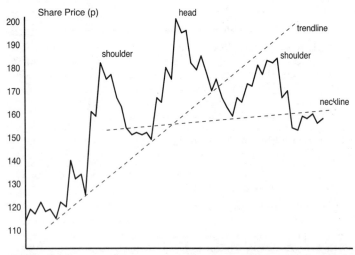

Quantitative analysis

This is a highly mathematical method of share analysis that concentrates on the riskiness of a share. It looks at the past performance of individual shares relative to the market as a whole. Those shares that perform better than the market do so because they are riskier investments than those which perform in line with the market. Beta analysis, which is the most commonly used part of quantitative analysis, is a means of measuring the risk.

A share which has moved exactly in line with the FT-Actuaries All-Share Index is said to have a beta of one. But some shares and unit trusts go up and down more than average. These are described as *aggressive* – i.e. when the index goes up, the share or unit trust goes up relatively more, and when the index goes down, it goes down relatively more. The value of beta for aggressive shares or unit trusts is more than one. Some shares and unit trusts are described as *defensive* – i.e. they go up and down less than the average (and the value of beta is less than one). Other shares and unit trusts fall somewhere between the extremes. The beta of a share is a measure of how much the rate of return on that share is likely to be affected by general stock market movements and it can change from week to week. It's normally worked out from the past performance of the share, which, of course, is not necessarily a good guide to the future.

Some people use this analysis so that, if they think the general level of prices in the stock market is going to rise, they can invest in shares with high betas, because their prices will (they hope) go up correspondingly more. And if they think share prices in general are going to fall, they will switch to shares with low betas, whose prices should fall less than average. Another way of using this analysis is to find the right mix of investments for people, taking into account the amount of risk they want to take.

General observations and personal views

Of course, you could choose your shares by your own observations. For example, you may see people spending more money in the high street and want to invest in the retail sector, or you may read about a company you think has a good product or the right approach. A gut feeling about a company or market is often dismissed in favour of more sophisticated methods, though it may be the correct conclusion and should not be ignored.

Some professional investors make a great deal of money by taking a contrary approach: when everyone else is buying, it's time to sell. For most individual investors it may not be possible to get the information to follow this approach for short-term trading, but by reading the financial press and following share price movements you may be able to spot when a share is becoming 'over-bought' or 'over-sold'.

Verdict

There is no effective, reliable, proven and generally usable method of picking out which shares are going to be winners. Apart from your general observations, all the methods described depend, to some extent at least, on looking at how shares have fared in the past. But past performance is not a reliable guide to the future. A share can perform well for many months, then fall in value unexpectedly overnight.

This does not mean, however, that you cannot make a sensible choice of shares. A collection of shares that a person holds is called a *portfolio*; and a portfolio chosen to match *your* objectives and circumstances and preferred level of risk should certainly give you better results than one that hasn't been chosen in this way. In broad outline, choose your shares as follows:

■ decide what your objectives are, because different shares are likely to suit different objectives. For example, you may (or may not) attach importance to drawing an income from your investment

■ decide on your time horizon for any given investment. Are you prepared to hold the share for say one or two years or longer, perhaps five years?

■ choose shares which carry the degree of risk you are willing to accept. If you want to speculate, you could invest in a collection of very risky shares. Alternatively, see the end of this chapter for other ways of investing in companies – *warrants*, *options* and *traded options*, in particular. On the other hand, if you are investing for the long term, divide your money among the shares of a fair number of companies and spread your investment over a number of carefully selected different industries

■ consider reducing the influence of the stock market on your investments by putting some of your money in other investments, which are less risky, e.g. building society accounts, British Government stock or corporate bonds (see Chapters 19 and 20). And look at the possibilities of investing

some of your money overseas and giving yourself a spread of geographical areas and currencies – see Chapter 25
■ in general, the best policy is likely to be *buy and hold*. Don't buy and sell shares too frequently. The costs of doing this will eat into any profits that you make.

Buying and selling shares

You can buy or sell shares by going to a stockbroker. A *Private Investors' Directory* is available from the Association of Private Client Investment Managers and Stockbrokers (APCIMS).* Alternatively, you could go to a bank or building society, many of whom own or have agreements with stockbroking firms. For more details, see Chapter 6. Whichever you choose, the procedure is more or less the same.

There are a number of market places for buying and selling shares. Novice investors should probably stick to shares that are quoted on the main market place, i.e. those with a full listing on the Stock Exchange.

However, the Stock Exchange also runs the Alternative Investment Market (AIM) which in effect replaced the old Unlisted Securities Market in 1995. AIM is for small companies which may not qualify for (or do not want) a full listing on the Stock Exchange. Companies in this market are likely to be relatively new and therefore may be a higher risk for investors than those quoted in the main market.

Buying shares

Suppose that you have found a broker to deal with you, and that you decide you would like to buy 600 Newco Electronics shares. You look at the share price lists in the morning paper and see that they are quoted at 300p.

There are two points that must be made at once about this price. First, it is normally the previous day's closing mid-market price – the price being quoted towards the close of Stock Exchange business. Second, the price quoted in most of the newspapers is normally a middle price. If the newspaper says that Newco Electronics PLC was 300p, it probably means that the *offer* price (the price at which you could have bought Newco) was 303p, while the *bid price* (the price at which you could have sold) was 297p. The difference between the two figures is called the *spread*.

You can give your order to your broker in one of two ways. One is simply to ring up and say, 'Buy me 600 Newco Electronics.' The broker will take this as an order to buy this number of shares at the best (i.e. cheapest) available price *now*. The other way is to give the broker a *limit*. Suppose you decide the shares would be a good buy at 295p but no more. You ring up your broker and say, 'Buy me 600 Newco, at not more than 295p.'

So you lose nothing by setting a limit, and you protect yourself from the risk of buying at a higher price than you expected. However, it is no use setting too low a limit: you won't get your shares, and will have wasted your time, and the broker's. You should also make sure your broker knows how long you want your limit to stand (they may hold your order as 'good-till-cancelled' or there may be a standard time limit, e.g. one month, or only for the day you place your order).

Once you've placed your order, it is too late to change your mind: you've made a verbal contract. For the most actively traded shares the broker will call up the Stock Exchange Electronic Trading Service (SETS). On 20 October 1997 this replaced SEAQ as the main way of trading in the shares of the UK's major companies. This system matches buyers and sellers electronically. If, however, your order is relatively small (fewer than 500 shares where they are priced £5 or more each, or fewer than 1,000 shares where they are priced at less than £5 each) or you want longer than five days (three days from 1998) in which to settle, your deal will be handled 'away from the order book'. Your broker will deal directly with a market-maker. Similarly if your order is for shares not yet traded through SETS, your broker will deal directly with the market-makers. The price the broker will quote to you will not include the commission or other dealing costs.

At the broker's office, a contract note will be made out for the shares you have bought. You should get this on the following day, or soon after and check it at once to see that the details of what you have bought are correct. Keep this contract note safe, as evidence of what you have paid for the shares. It will look something like the example overleaf.

Selling shares

As with buying shares, there are two kinds of order that you can give to your broker. You can simply ring up your broker and say, 'Sell 600 Newco Electronics', or you can set a limit, e.g. say, 'Sell 600 Newco Electronics if the price reaches 320p.'

ABC STOCKBROKERS AND COMPANY

A member firm of The London Stock Exchange
Regulated by The Securities and Futures Authority Limited

CONTRACT NOTE

UNIQUE CODE No.	DATE & TAX POINT	EXECUTED AT
6405/97Z	21 APRIL 1998	12.00

F MURRAY ESQ

WE HAVE <u>BOUGHT</u> ON YOUR BEHALF AS AGENTS,
FOR SETTLEMENT ON 28 APRIL 1998

600	NEWCO ELECTRONICS ORD £1	295P*	£1,770.00
600			£1,770.00
	TRANSFER STAMP	9.00 †	
	COMMISSION	29.21 ‡	
	TOTAL CHARGES		£38.21
	DUE TO US		£1,808.21

COMMISSION DETAILS
£1,770 AT 1.65%

signed by:

DIRECTOR
for and on behalf of ABC Stockbrokers and Company

UK RESIDENTS SHOULD RETAIN THIS CONTRACT NOTE AS
THEY MAY REQUIRE IT FOR CAPITAL GAINS TAX

BARGAIN No.	REFERENCE No.
0928	01435

Subject to the Rules and Regulations of The London Stock Exchange
including any temporary regulations made by or under the authority of
The London Stock Exchange – or The Securities and Futures Authority

* Consideration   The name sometimes given to the amount you pay for the shares (or get for them if you're selling) before the various deductions are made. In our example, the consideration is £1,770.

† Stamp duty   This is the main government duty on the deal. It is 0.5 per cent of what you pay for the shares (rounded up to the nearest £50). In our example, the stamp duty is 0.5 per cent of £1,800 (i.e. £1,770 rounded up to the nearest £50).

‡ Commission   The rate of commission varies depending on individual broker's charges and the size of the consideration (see note *).

PTM Levy   If the cost of shares is £10,000 or more, an additional charge of £2 is made – this is a levy for the Panel on Takeovers and Mergers. This levy applies on both sales and purchases.

The contract note for a sale looks much like the contract note for a purchase. Minimum commission rates used to be fixed, but now brokers can charge what they like, and rates and minimum charges vary widely. Charges usually range between 1 per cent and 1.9 per cent on a deal of up to, say, £7,000. A typical minimum commission can be £20 or £25, but with a sale there is no stamp duty. Some brokers may also charge a flat fee e.g. £2.50 or £10 – which they call a 'compliance levy'.

When the contract note for your sale has been made out, the broker will send it to you. If you still hold certificates for the shares you have sold you will be sent a transfer form for you to sign and return to the broker with the certificates. If, on the other hand, your shareholding is registered through CREST (see page 261) there will be no forms to sign.

Rolling settlement

In July 1994 the settlement system changed from an account settlement to a 'rolling settlement'. When rolling settlement was first introduced, the settlement date was ten working days after the transaction date (known as T+10). In June 1995 the settlement period was reduced to T+5, although many brokers will still deal T+10 for private investors. There are plans to reduce the settlement period further to T+3 or less; however, again it is likely that you can agree a longer settlement period with your broker if you need it. If you hold your shares in a nominee account (see below) you won't need the longer settlement time, but if you still hold certificates you probably will.

A shorter settlement period means you will need to act quickly after you sell shares to return the share certificate and signed transfer form to your broker. If there is a long delay after the settlement date, the market-maker has the right to go back into the market to buy the same amount of shares (at the prevailing market price) and he or she will charge you for any extra costs. This process, called 'buying-in' is not new, but may become more frequent as the settlement period becomes shorter.

Nominee accounts

You may want to consider a nominee account, to avoid being caught out with too little time to complete a sold transfer form and return your share certificate to your broker following the sale of your shares. Your stockbroker will have a nominee company with whom you can open an account. If you transfer your shares into the name of the nominee company they will be held on your behalf. Legally the shares are yours and you will still be liable for any capital gains tax liability when they are sold. The nominee company can collect the dividends from your shares on your behalf or you can arrange for them to be directly 'mandated' to your bank or savings account. However, when you decide to sell the shares you won't need to sign a sold transfer form – you will still get a contract note but you won't hold any share certificates – the settlement will be completed by your stockbroker and the nominee company. Check what charges are involved before setting up a nominee account; it may be cheaper to ask your broker to send the transfer form to be signed before you sell your shares, particularly if you buy and sell shares only occasionally.

CREST

CREST, a new computerised settlement system, was developed to replace the outdated paper-based Talisman system. CREST started in July 1996 and the transfer was completed in April 1997. Trading for about 90 per cent of all stocks is settled through CREST. Rather than holding a paper certificate, you have an electronic entry in a company's share register, in much the same way that your current account is logged at your bank. When you buy or sell shares the transfer happens electronically enabling settlement to take place very rapidly.

You can choose to keep your shareholdings in paper certificates but you will need to arrange delayed settlement with your broker in order to complete the paperwork – say T+10 or even T+25. There may be an additional charge to cover the extra administration involved.

Shares in detail

What is a share?

When you buy ordinary shares you are literally buying a share in the company, and a right to benefit from its earnings (if any). You can go to general meetings and vote on matters to do with the company.

Some companies issue ordinary shares only. The net (i.e. after-tax) profits of such a company all count as earnings available to the ordinary shareholders. This does not mean, however, that all such earnings will actually be paid to the ordinary shareholders – see 'Dividend yield', on page 263.

Companies may raise additional capital in other ways, e.g. occasionally by issuing *preference shares*, or more commonly by issuing *loan stock* or *debentures* (see 'Other ways of investing in companies' on page 268). The company's first commitment is to pay the fixed income to its lenders and preference shareholders, which is why all such payments are commonly called *prior charges*. With such companies, the earnings available to the ordinary shareholders are the profits after deducting the prior charges and tax.

What the papers say

The shares page of a daily newspaper can be puzzling, but it contains a lot of useful information.

Let's suppose you wanted to find out about Newco Electronics. The relevant section of the newspaper would look something like this:

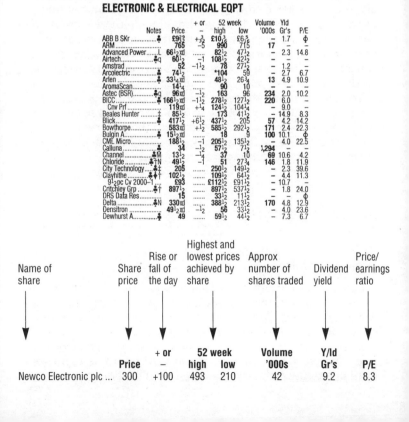

ELECTRONIC & ELECTRICAL EQPT

	Notes	Price	+ or –	52 week high	52 week low	Volume '000s	Yld Gr's	P/E
ABB B SKr	♣	£9 29/32	+3/32	£10 3/16	£6 5/16	–	1.7	Φ
ARM		765	–5	990	715	17	–	–
Advanced Power	L	66½xd	......	82½	47½	–	2.3	14.8
Airtech	♣q	60½	–1	108½	42½	–	–	–
Amstrad		52	–1½	78	27½	–	1.2	–
Arcolectric	♣	74½	......	*104	59	–	2.7	6.7
Arlen	♣	33¼xd	......	48½	26¾	13	4.9	10.9
AromaScan		14¼	......	90	10	–	–	–
Astec (BSR)	♣q	96xd	–½	163	96	234	2.0	10.2
BICC	♣	166½xd	–1½	278½	127½	220	6.0	–
Cnv Prf		119xd	+¼	124½	104¼	–	9.0	–
Beales Hunter	‡	85½	......	173	41½	–	14.9	8.3
Blick	♣	417½	+6½	437½	205	57	4.2	14.2
Bowthorpe		583xd	+½	585½	292½	171	2.4	22.3
Bulgin A	♣	15½xd	......	18	9	100	10.1	Φ
CML Micro		188½	–1	205½	135½	–	4.0	22.5
Calluna	♣	34	–½	57½	7½	1,294	–	–
Channel	♣M	13½	–¼	37	10	69	10.6	4.2
Chloride	♣†N	49½	–1	51	27¾	146	1.8	11.9
City Technology	♣‡	205	......	250½	149½	–	2.3	39.6
Clayhithe	♣♦†	102½	......	109½	64½	–	4.4	11.3
9½pc Cv 2000–1		£93	......	£112½	£91½	–	10.7	–
Critchley Grp	♣†	897½	......	897½	537½	–	1.8	24.0
DRS Data Res		15	......	33½	11½	–	–	Φ
Delta	♣N	330xd	......	388½	213½	170	4.8	12.9
Densitron		49½xd	–½	56	33½	–	4.0	23.6
Dewhurst A	♣	49	......	59½	44½	–	7.3	6.7

Name of share	Share price	Rise or fall of the day	Highest and lowest prices achieved by share		Approx number of shares traded	Dividend yield	Price/ earnings ratio
↓	↓	↓	↓		↓	↓	↓
	Price	**+ or –**	**52 week high**	**52 week low**	**Volume '000s**	**Y/ld Gr's**	**P/E**
Newco Electronic plc ...	300	+100	493	210	42	9.2	8.3

The share price
This is usually the previous day's closing mid-market price in pence (i.e. halfway between offer and bid price at the 4.30 pm close).

+ or –
The price change from the previous trading day.

Volume
This shows the number of shares to the nearest thousand traded through the Stock Exchange Electronic Trading Service (SETs), see page 258. On its own it does not give any indication of whether investors are selling or buying shares but the price movement will help you guess. But it does show whether any price movement has been as a result of a lot of activity in the market or whether it is just market-makers changing their prices.

Dividend yield
Shareholders receive their share of the company profits as dividends. Dividends will be sent to you at the address that your broker puts on the transfer form. Dividends come in the form of dividend warrants. These are in effect cheques, which can be paid into your bank account. Newco Electronics last year declared dividends of 22p per share. Twenty per cent tax had already been deducted (in other words, it is a *net dividend*), so it is equivalent to 27.5p per share before tax. For more details of how dividends are taxed, see 'Investment income paid with tax deducted', in Chapter 7.

The dividend of 27.5p is 9.2 per cent of the share price – 300p. Therefore the yield on your money would be 9.2 per cent a year (provided future dividends are the same as last year's). This yield is called the gross dividend yield.

Companies usually pay dividends twice a year (as long as they have earnings to distribute). About six to eight weeks before each dividend is paid, the company declares a dividend, i.e. announces what the next dividend will be. A week or two later, the company's shares go *ex-dividend* (the share price is marked 'xd') and the register of shareholders is temporarily closed. The coming dividend will be paid only to those people who are on the register of shareholders on the day it was closed. Anyone who buys shares in the company after they have gone ex-dividend will not get the coming dividend, and if you sell your shares before they have gone ex-dividend you will need to return the dividend to your broker.

A company normally keeps back part of its net profit (in our example on page 266, £1,800,000 – £1,050,000 = £750,000) to finance expansion of its business, or to build up cash balances, or both. Amounts kept back are called *retained profits* or *earnings*, or *retentions*.

Price/earnings ratio

A common way of looking at share prices is to say that in buying a share what you are really doing is buying a right to benefit from a corresponding share in the company's yearly stream of earnings. The price/earnings ratio (or PE ratio for short) is a way of saying at what expense (or how cheaply) you're buying that stream of earnings.

To work out a PE ratio, first work out how much earnings there are for each share, i.e. divide the total after-tax earnings of the company by the number of shares. The PE ratio is found by dividing the current market price by the earnings per share.

Take our Newco Electronics example (see box on page 266). Suppose the company's earnings in the last reported year were £1,800,000, which, since the company has five million ordinary shares, works out at 36p for each share. Each share actually costs 300p at current prices, so to buy earnings of 36p a year, you have to pay 300p. Newco Electronics would, therefore, be said to have a PE ratio of 300 divided by 36 = 8.3.

Dividend cover

Some newspapers also show the *dividend cover* – i.e. how many times the company could have paid its dividend out of the profit for that year.

New issues

If a company is not quoted on the Stock Exchange, it may be difficult to buy or sell its shares. You have to find an individual or an organisation who is prepared to deal with you. When the company decides it wants to make a better market in its shares, it may offer its shares to the public and become quoted on the Stock Exchange.

The most usual method for marketing a new issue is an *offer for sale* by an *issuing house*, often a merchant bank. The issuing house puts advertisements in newspapers giving details of the company and offering a stated number of shares at a stated price (the *prospectus*). The advertisement normally includes an application form. If you want to buy some of the shares, fill in the form saying how many you want, and send it with a cheque for the value of the shares.

If the terms on which a new issue is made look attractive to the investing public, the issue may be over-subscribed, i.e. more shares may be asked for than are on offer. In that case, the shares will be allocated by the issuing house (there are a variety of methods for doing this).

Scrip (or bonus) issue

As a company grows, its share price may increase so much that it becomes too unwieldy to trade easily. So the company may make an extra issue of free shares to its existing shareholders. This is called a scrip or bonus issue. If, for example, you have 500 shares in Newco Electronics and the share price is 300p each, your shareholding is worth £1,500. If the company makes a one-for-one scrip issue, you will get another 500 shares, making 1,000 in total. But the share price will instantly fall to around 150p each, so your shareholding is still worth £1,500. In practice the share price is unlikely to fall to exactly 150p. After a time, the share price will go ex-scrip, marked 'xc'. This works in much the same way as ex-dividend – see page 263.

Rights issue

Occasionally, a company may decide it needs to raise more money from its shareholders, perhaps to finance some new investment. It usually makes a rights issue to its existing shareholders. This means the company offers the right to invest more money in exchange for new shares.

You will know about this rights issue because the company will send you a document, telling you what it is raising money for and enclosing a form so that you can apply to take up some new shares. Do not ignore this document, it is valuable. If you don't understand what it is, ask a professional adviser.

As a shareholder you have four choices:
- you can do nothing
- you can pay up
- you can sell your rights to the new shares on the Stock Exchange
- you can sell part of your rights and take up part, so keeping your investment in the company at the same level.

What you do will depend on whether you have the cash available and whether you want to increase your investment in the company.

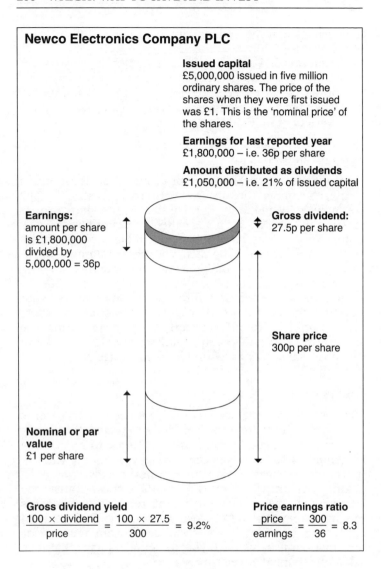

Newco Electronics Company PLC

Issued capital
£5,000,000 issued in five million ordinary shares. The price of the shares when they were first issued was £1. This is the 'nominal price' of the shares.

Earnings for last reported year
£1,800,000 – i.e. 36p per share

Amount distributed as dividends
£1,050,000 – i.e. 21% of issued capital

Earnings:
amount per share is £1,800,000 divided by 5,000,000 = 36p

Gross dividend:
27.5p per share

Share price
300p per share

Nominal or par value
£1 per share

Gross dividend yield
$$\frac{100 \times \text{dividend}}{\text{price}} = \frac{100 \times 27.5}{300} = 9.2\%$$

Price earnings ratio
$$\frac{\text{price}}{\text{earnings}} = \frac{300}{36} = 8.3$$

Suppose, for example, you have 500 shares in Hightech Power, the share price is 400p each and the company makes a one-for-one rights issue at 200p each. If the company has three million shares already issued, it is raising £6 million by the rights issue (issuing another three million shares for 200p each). The market value of the company before the rights issue is £12 million; afterwards it is £18 million. The share price after the rights issue will be:

$$£18 \text{ million} \div 6 \text{ million} = £3 \text{ each}$$

If you do nothing, your 500 shares are now worth only £1,500, so on the face of it you might have lost £500. However, all UK companies will sell rights that have not been taken up and send you the proceeds. If you take up your rights, your investment is now worth £3,000, but you've had to hand over another £1,000 to the company. Alternatively, you can sell your rights to the new shares on the Stock Exchange – in theory, for £500. This is worked out by taking the new share price from the old one, i.e. £4 – £3 = £1 per share.

Your fourth choice is to sell part of your rights and use the proceeds to buy the rest of the new shares.

After a while, the share price will go ex-rights (marked 'xr'). This works in much the same way as ex-dividend – see page 263.

Mergers, demergers and takeovers

One company may decide it would like to acquire another company and it therefore offers to buy the shares from the company's shareholders. For example, suppose Hightech Power decides to take over Newco Electronics. Hightech will send you a document offering to buy your shares. This document will contain a lot of information, including:
- what Hightech will pay for your shares. It may offer you cash, or some of its own shares in exchange, or a mixture of loan stock and shares and possibly cash
- why Hightech wants to buy Newco
- a profit forecast for Hightech
- the date on which its offer closes.

If Newco decides it doesn't want to be taken over, it will also send you a document telling you why you shouldn't accept Hightech's offer, probably giving a profit forecast for Newco, and so on.

Things can get very complicated after this, if, for example, a second company decides it would like to acquire Newco, or Hightech decides its first offer will not be accepted by the majority of shareholders and so increases its offer. You might end up with quite a few documents. Don't ignore them. You have to decide which is better – sticking with Newco or accepting one of the offers. In most cases you would be wise to seek the advice of a professional adviser before making your decision.

Although mergers still happen, the trend today is towards the demerger of the larger conglomerates. In this way, companies that may have a range of businesses split into their component parts. As a shareholder you do not have the same decisions to make because you will simply be given a basket of shares in the component companies in place of the shares in the bigger original company. If 'focusing', as it is called, works, the new shareholding should be ultimately more profitable. However, if you have a relatively small shareholding, you may be left with very small, and uneconomical, holdings in each component company.

Other ways of investing in companies

Companies can raise money by issuing *company loan stock* or *debentures*. They work like British Government stocks – they normally pay a fixed rate of interest and the loan will be repaid some time in the future. Because they are riskier than British Government stocks, you can expect the return to be higher. And if the company is in financial difficulties, the return – and the risk you have to take – may be very high indeed. For more details see Chapter 20.

A variation on this is a *convertible loan stock.* This starts out as a loan when the company first gets the money. But the person holding the loan stock has the right to convert it or part of it into an agreed number of shares on a fixed date (or between certain dates). If the share price of the company rises, this may make the price of a convertible loan stock rise substantially too. If the share price falls, then it may not be worth converting the loan.

Some companies have *preference* shareholders, though these are becoming less common. A fixed rate of dividend is usually paid on preference shares. There are different types of these shares, which include for example, cumulative preference or stepped preference. Each type of preference share has different terms, so check carefully before investing.

There are some very risky types of investments you can buy and sell on the stock market – *warrants, options* and *traded options*. A *warrant* is issued by the company, and is often tacked on to a loan stock – it can be detached and sold by the loan stockholder if he or she wants. A warrant gives you the right to buy shares in the company, usually during a fixed period and at a fixed price. If the shares of the company never reach that price, the warrant is worthless. However if the share price does rise, the price of a warrant will rise substantially.

An *option* is similar but is not issued by the company. Instead you pay a market-maker (share wholesaler) for the right to buy or sell shares in a company at a fixed price within a three-month period. Once you've got the option you can't sell it. You can buy and sell only the shares of the company.

A *traded option* is slightly different and can itself be bought and sold. There is an active traded options market where you can buy or sell options in many of the major UK shares. Each share has a number of different options. The exercise dates of different options are three months apart and as one series expires another one, for expiry nine months hence, is issued, so at any given time you can choose an option that has about three, six or nine months to run. There is also a choice of exercise prices.

You can use a traded option to buy shares at a predetermined price, or if you hold shares you can sell an option *against* your shares (where someone else buys the right from you to buy your shares at the predetermined price).

Other ways of investing in shares

Employee share schemes

Some employers encourage their employees to invest in the company that they work for through employee share schemes. There are three types:

■ **approved profit-sharing schemes** – open to all employees who have been with the company for a qualifying period set by the company but no longer than five years. The company sets aside some of its profits to buy ordinary shares which are then allocated to employees. All employees must participate on the same terms. The maximum one employee can get is shares with an initial value of £3,000 or 10 per cent of earnings if higher, with an overall limit of £8,000 worth of shares. There is no tax to pay when the shares are allocated. You have to keep the shares for two years. If you keep them for three years, there is no income tax to pay on the money you make from selling them. However, you will have to pay income tax on dividends and any profit you make on the sale could be liable to capital gains tax.

■ **Company Share Option Plans (CSOPs)** – These Plans replaced Executive Share Option Shares (ESOPs) on 17 July

1995, although they work in the same way. You are given a right (i.e. an option) to buy your company's shares at some future date(s) for some set price. If at that time the market value of the shares is greater than the price at which you can exercise the option, you make an immediate profit. Ordinarily you would pay tax on the profit (as the option would be counted as part of your income) unless you receive the option under an approved scheme. CSOPs are free of tax provided the exercise price is not lower than the share price at the time the option is granted (ESOPs could be granted at a discount to market value although the discount was taxable) and the maximum value of shares over which you have an option is £20,000 (£10,000 for ESOPs).

■ **SAYE share option schemes** – again, open to all employees who have been with the company five years or more. The employee agrees to pay a fixed monthly sum up to £250 (minimum £5) into a Save-As-You-Earn (SAYE) account, for five (or sometimes seven) years. At the end of the period there is a bonus. At the outset, you are given the option to buy shares in your company at a set price some years in the future.

Verdict
Share option schemes can be a good deal, but don't be tempted to buy shares in your company if, for example, it's in difficulties.

The Enterprise Investment Scheme

When you buy shares in a company that qualifies under the Enterprise Investment Scheme (EIS) rules, you get tax relief at 20 per cent on investments of up to £150,000 each tax year. For more details on how the scheme works, see page 125.

Verdict
Because EIS companies tend to be new and small, they're likely to be risky. You shouldn't invest in an EIS unless you're prepared for the chance that you might lose the lot.

Venture Capital Trusts

An investment in a Venture Capital Trust (VCT) gives you similar tax breaks as investing through the EIS but it is not quite as risky because a VCT is a fund which is set up to invest in a range of unquoted trading companies. The VCT itself is a quoted company and so selling your investment is likely to be a lot easier than if you had to sell the shares of the individual companies held by the VCT. For more details see page 126.

Verdict
Because you are investing in a collection of unquoted trading companies with the VCT fund, your investment is not as risky as a direct investment in individual unquoted companies. But do not let the tax advantages alone encourage you to make a riskier investment than you would otherwise make.

Investment clubs

The principle behind investment clubs is very simple: rather than attempting to develop your investment skills alone you club together with a group of like-minded people to create your own small-scale unit trust. In this way you can develop your interest in the stock market with others while investing only a small part of your disposable income. Clubs are a sociable way of learning more about shares and portfolio management. Investment clubs are not new (the first started in Texas in 1898) but in recent years they have become increasingly popular in the UK.

Each club decides its own rules and method of dealing but the general principle is:
■ each member starts by paying an initial lump sum into the club, thereafter an agreed monthly amount (typically about £25)
■ club members meet regularly, often at a pub or other social place, to discuss the affairs of the club and their views on the stock market
■ as the cash builds up, the members buy shares
■ gradually the club builds a fund portfolio of shares which are selected by the members (in an agreed and democratic way) and changes to the fund are made in the same way
■ each member of the club owns a proportion of the fund depending on how much they have paid into the club. Usually clubs use a form of unitisation to work this out, i.e. as members pay into the club they are allocated units depending on the value of the fund at the time (this is similar to the way unit trusts work).

You may be able to join an existing club, although for legal and practical reasons membership to each club is limited to a maximum of 20 people. In practice most people who develop an interest in investment clubs will start their own with friends and family.

ProShare Investment Clubs (PIC)* is a national association of investment clubs and has around 500 members. Your club does not need to be a member of PIC but its manual gives an easy-to-read and detailed guide to how investment clubs work, with a step-by-step guide to setting up and running a club, guidance on tax and tips for avoiding potential pitfalls. The manual draws on the experiences of many different investment clubs for its wide-ranging information. PIC also publishes a quarterly newsletter for its members and runs competitions to find the best-performing clubs.

Personal Equity Plans (PEPs)

From April 1999 no new investments can be made through a PEP. The new Individual Savings Account (ISA) will incorporate the tax-free benefits of PEPs. Anyone holding existing PEPs on that date will continue to receive the tax benefits while the shares are still held in PEPs. For more details on how PEPs work, see Chapter 8.

17

UNIT TRUSTS

Unit trusts have traditionally been a way of investing in shares. However, some unit trusts invest in British Government and other loan stock, and a few invest in other unit trusts. They can also be used to invest in deposits and short-term loan stock, property, futures, options and commodities or a mixture of all these investments.

For many investors, investing in a unit trust is less risky and more convenient than investing directly in shares, for example. If you invested directly, and put all your money in one company, say, you'd lose it all if that company went bust. But a unit trust invests in the shares of a lot of companies (around 60 or 70, say – though it varies widely), so if one company goes bust you lose only a bit of your money. Of course, you can invest directly in many companies' shares, but this involves more money and more work. For more details on different ways of investing in shares, see Chapter 16.

The return you get back from a unit trust comes in two parts:

■ **income** – this is made up of dividends and interest from the securities in which the unit trust invests and interest from cash on deposit. It can normally be paid out to you

■ **capital growth** – the aim is that the prices of shares which the unit trust has invested in will rise.

One benefit of using unit trusts is that the managers do not have to pay capital gains tax on any gains made within the trust – see 'Tax', on page 289.

This chapter looks at the points to consider before investing in unit trusts and the choices open to you if you decide to invest. Then it moves on to look at the nitty-gritty of unit trust investment, including how prices are calculated, how to buy and sell, and what charges you can expect to pay.

Timing your investment

Investing in unit trusts is riskier than many types of investment, e.g. building society accounts, because it is a stock market investment. But although there is a chance of you losing money with a unit trust, the hope is that you get a better return. You can see from the diagrams in this chapter that investors in unit trusts have had a bumpy ride over the years, doing very well in some periods, very badly in others. So the success of an investment depends very much on when you invest and when you cash in your investment. If you'd invested in a typical unit trust in February 1994 and cashed in around July the same year, you'd have lost about 10 per cent of your money, but if you had continued with your investment over a longer period you'd have done well. The chart on page 278 shows the average of all unit trusts compared with a building society savings account over the last ten years.

Sadly, there's no foolproof way of forecasting *when* share prices are going to rise or fall, or *which* unit trusts you should invest in.

For the long term or short term?

There are two schools of thought about how long you should invest in a unit trust. Either:
- you invest for a long time (at least five years) and stick pretty well to the same trust (or trusts);
  or
- you invest for a shorter time and move your money in and out of unit trusts or from trust to trust as the prospects alter.

For most small investors, the former is most probably the better strategy. Generally all equity investment, either direct or via a unit trust, should be considered on a long-term basis. Switching your money in, out or between trusts, could be expensive (see 'Charges', on page 287) and unless you're lucky or very knowledgeable you might time it badly. Unless you're prepared to do the work and take the chance of getting the timing wrong, you should think of unit trusts as a long-term investment.

Size of investment

The minimum you can invest varies, but with most unit trusts it's in the £250 to £1,500 range, or, for regular saving, from £10 to £100 a month. Regular saving means less worry about timing your investment – see 'Size of investment', on page 291.

Different types of unit trust

The diagram on page 279 shows how the outcome of an investment in unit trusts could have varied depending on the trust you'd chosen. It shows how a notional £1,000 invested in a specialist unit trust sector, such as Japan, would have performed very differently to the overall unit trust market. It also shows how volatile a specialist sector can be.

No magic formula exists to tell you which trust will do best – several popular systems are tested later on in this chapter. And you cannot automatically expect that an investment adviser or newspaper will pick a trust which is going to perform well. But the step-by-step guide below should help you narrow down the choices.

Different investment strategies

The Association of Unit Trusts and Investment Funds (AUTIF) categorises each unit trust into one of the 26 different types of fund listed below:

UK
- UK Income & Growth
- UK Equity Income
- UK Growth
- UK Smaller Companies
- UK Gilts
- Other UK Fixed Interest
- UK Equity & Bond Income
- UK Equity & Bond
- Managed

International
- Intl. Equity Income
- Intl. Growth
- Intl. Fixed Interest
- Intl. Equity & Bond

Specific region
- Japan
- Far East inc Japan
- Far East exc Japan
- North America
- Europe
- Global Emerging Markets

Specialist
- Commodity & Energy
- Financial & Property
- Investment Trust Funds
- Fund of Funds
- Money Market
- Index 'Bear' Funds
- Personal Pension Funds

These categories help to divide the thousand or so unit trusts into comparable groups. However, even within each of these categories different funds may have slightly different investment objectives. The name of the fund will help to identify some differences but you need to check the specific details of any unit trust investment policy before you buy. Some of the investment objectives are explained below.

Income and Growth funds

These are the most general types of unit trusts (often called 'general' funds). The objective is to provide a mixture of income and growth from an equity fund and so investment is in shares across the whole market. You should expect a yield of between 80 and 110 per cent of the FT-SE Actuaries All-Share Index for UK funds. Because these funds do not specialise in one area, they are unlikely ever to be among the top-performing funds, but by the same token they are unlikely ever to be among the worst-performing funds either.

Tracker funds

Within the income and growth sector, tracker funds deserve a specific mention. They are designed, as the name implies, to track the market index. Most tracker funds follow the UK market and are measured against either the FT-SE Actuaries All-Share Index or the FT-SE 100 Index, although there are others which track overseas markets. Trackers can never exactly track their chosen index because of management charges and dealing costs but they do offer a share-based fund without the fund managers' subjective investment view. Because they are not 'actively' managed (see page 277), the management charges tend to be slightly less than for other unit trusts.

Equity Income funds

These funds are often called *High Yield*, *Extra Income* and the like. The objective of the fund might be described by the company as:

> *Designed for investors whose primary requirement is an above-average and increasing income. The fund's objective is to provide a return about 110 per cent of the FT-SE Actuaries All-Share Index.*

Growth funds

The aim of these funds is to concentrate on getting increases in the unit price, rather than to pay out a high income. Many funds with names like *Capital Growth*, *Special Situations* or *Smaller Companies* come into this category. The aim of this type of fund might be described in company literature as:

The investment aim is maximum capital growth through the active management of a small portfolio of shares. Income is not usually a major investment consideration.

Some capital growth funds feature *active management*, meaning that the shares in the fund may be changed more frequently than with other types of funds, thereby incurring a higher level of costs, because of buying and selling shares.

Equity and Bond funds

As the name suggests, these funds invest in a mixture of shares and bonds, including British Government stocks, preference shares and loan stock. Since corporate bonds became qualified for PEPs, funds can invest in a high proportion of bonds and still be acceptable for PEPs. Because bonds tend to be a lower-risk investment than equities, these funds can be attractive to investors who are not prepared to invest in a pure equity product. Equity and bond funds will usually produce a higher income than an equity income and growth fund and some invest for high income.

International funds

Some general funds (often called *international funds*) invest in several different stock markets around the world, so the fortune of your investment is not so tightly tied to the UK stock market. This means the overall performance of the fund should be more stable than one investing only in the UK stock market. However, international funds are subject to an additional risk: currencies can fluctuate as well as share prices.

Specialist sector funds

These funds invest in particular industries, e.g. financial or energy. The aim of a specialist fund might be described as:

The fund's main objective is long-term capital growth, but there may be wider than average day-to-day price fluctuations.

In other words, the managers are warning you that you could be in for a bumpy ride, because if a unit trust invests its money in one UK industry and that industry does particularly badly or well the unit trust will perform likewise.

The average of all unit trusts compared with building society savings accounts

Unit trust ———

Building society - - - -

Source: Micropal   Figures for building society and unit trust include income reinvested net of tax.

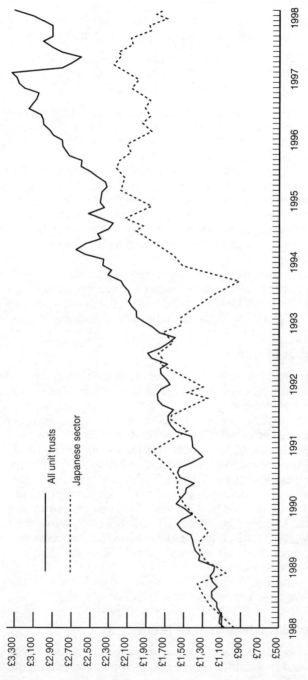

The average of all unit trusts compared with Japanese sector

All unit trusts

Japanese sector

£3,300
£3,100
£2,900
£2,700
£2,500
£2,300
£2,100
£1,900
£1,700
£1,500
£1,300
£1,100
£900
£700
£500

1988   1989   1990   1991   1992   1993   1994   1995   1996   1997   1998

Source: Micropal   Figures include income reinvested net of tax. Includes buying and selling costs.

Specialist regional funds

These unit trusts invest in certain overseas stock markets. A typical fund might have an objective such as:

> *This fund aims to achieve growth of capital through investment in the Far East in countries such as Japan, Hong Kong, Australia and Singapore.*

These funds concentrate mainly on getting increases in unit prices rather than income. Typically there are funds specialising in Europe, Japan, the USA, the Far East and Australia.

You should not expect specialist funds to move in line with the UK stock market. The Japanese and other Far Eastern economies, for example, have shown both excellent and disastrous performance over the last ten years. This is why specialist regional funds and commodity funds often appear at the top and the bottom of tables showing unit trust performance.

Note that funds that invest overseas are also affected by the caprices of the currency market – the unit price of an overseas trust will tend to rise if the exchange rate of the pound goes down, fall if the exchange rate of the pound goes up.

Funds of funds

The idea behind funds of funds is that one unit trust invests in other unit trusts, with the aim of providing a managed investment for more cautious investors. With over 1,000 unit trusts to choose from, there is a good argument for leaving the selection to a professional fund manager. There are rules about how such unit trusts can be invested. They cannot invest in another fund of funds and must invest in at least five unit trusts. There are no limits on what management charges can be made but charges in both tiers of the fund must be disclosed. These funds cannot make an initial charge, but you will still have to pay this when it invests in other unit trusts. However, the managers of funds of funds are allowed to make a yearly charge.

Because there are in effect two levels of charges, the returns are unlikely to be dramatic. However they are among the lowest risk unit trusts available.

Verdict: which type of fund?

To select the right type of fund for your needs you must consider whether you want income or capital gain, how much risk you are prepared to take and how long you want to invest for. If you want to invest for a short time (say, one to three years) or you don't want to take many risks, stick with a money market or bond fund. If you are investing for longer (at least three years) and are prepared to take some risks, consider a bond or balanced fund. If you are investing for at least five years look at the equity funds which offer you the right balance of income and capital gain for your needs. Only consider specialist funds if you have other investments and are prepared to take a higher risk with your money.

Best and worst performing unit trusts over five years

Best performers

Jupiter European	+227.22%	(£1,000 now £3,272)
Old Mutual European	+220.68%	(£1,000 now £3,207)
Gartmore European Select Opps	+211.75%	(£1,000 now £3,117)
INVESCO European Growth	+210.74%	(£1,000 now £3,107)
GA North American Growth	+209.97%	(£1,000 now £3,100)
Exeter Capital Growth	+201.67%	(£1,000 now £3,017)
Royal & SunAll North America	+196.71%	(£1,000 now £2,967)
Baring Europe Select	+195.84%	(£1,000 now £2,958)
S&P Financial Securities	+194.01%	(£1,000 now £2,940)
Jupiter Income	+192.18%	(£1,000 now £2,922)

Worst performers

Edinburgh Japan Smaller Cos	−37.73%	(£1,000 now £623)
S&P Japan Smaller Companies	−38.31%	(£1,000 now £617)
Baring Japan Sunrise	−39.61%	(£1,000 now £604)
Fidelity Japan Smaller Cos	−39.88%	(£1,000 now £601)
Henderson Japan Smaller Cos	−42.08%	(£1,000 now £579)
Baring Korea Trust	−43.85%	(£1,000 now £561)
Old Mutual Thailand	−44.06%	(£1,000 now £559)
Govett UK Bear	−44.07%	(£1,000 now £559)
Govett US Bear	−56.72%	(£1,000 now £433)
S&P Korea	−73.79%	(£1,000 now £262)

Average for all unit trusts — **+72.77%** — **(£1,000 now £1,728)**

Note: from 1 March 1993 to 1 March 1998; includes net income; valued on an offer to bid basis
Source: *Micropal*

How to choose a unit trust

There is no magic recipe for choosing a unit trust. Here, some well-known systems for picking a winner are put to the test. The verdicts given on these theories are general: there are always exceptions to a rule.

None of the systems below would prove to be an ideal strategy to pick winners. There may be slight evidence to support one or other of the theories, but any advantage is for a limited period, and any short-term gain could be cancelled out by buying and selling costs if you switch your investments too frequently.

'Small funds do best'

It's argued that the managers of small funds can buy and sell investments more easily and so get the best return.

We looked at how all UK trusts had performed over four-year and nine-year periods. The results showed that you could rely on neither large funds nor small funds to be consistently good performers; but small funds tended to move more in line with UK stock markets than larger funds.
Verdict: Size is not a particularly useful criterion for picking a unit trust.

'Go for last year's winners'

This theory claims that trusts that have done well in the past will do well in the future.

We looked at the performance of all UK trusts over five 12-month periods and found no evidence that the trusts would do well in the future just because they had done well in the past. The table of the best and worst performing trusts over a five-year period illustrates at least one reason why this should be the case even over this longer time-frame – the best performance should come from the highest risk funds (as should the worst) i.e. the specialist funds.
Verdict: Past performance will never point you to the next year's winners, rather you should use past performance only to find those trusts that have above-average performance in the long term.

'Go for last year's losers'

Is it true that last year's winners are likely to be this year's losers, and *vice versa*? That if things are bad they can only get better?

When we tested the theory, consistently investing in previous years' losers (over five years) looked to be a good way of losing money. The test was more promising when we invested in the bottom five and held them for five years.

But again by concentrating on those trusts with extreme performance (in this case extremely bad performance) you will end up with specialist trusts.

Verdict: Unless you are prepared to take the risk, avoid the trusts that produce extreme performance (good or bad).

'New is best'

Because the managers will be giving a new unit trust a lot of expert attention, it's claimed they'll do better than with old unit trusts.

We looked at new trusts launched each year over a five-year period in each unit trust sector and compared them with other trusts in the particular sector. There was an initial benefit, but it didn't last for very long.

Verdict: A newly launched trust may have some initial benefit compared with others in its sector, but it's not guaranteed (and it may not compare well with unit trusts in other sectors).

'Pick a management company'

It's claimed that some management companies do better than others.

We looked at trusts managed by companies with at least five trusts, and measured their performance over one, five and seventeen years. We couldn't find any evidence that good performance in one period would mean good performance in the next.

Verdict: There was little evidence that choosing by management company was a reliable way to pick a unit trust, though, of course, a unit trust performance could have changed because the individual manager of the fund was replaced. But if you do believe in going for the 'best' managers, you'll have to keep a very close eye on developments.

'Look for investments in small companies'

There is a theory that the shares of small companies are likely to produce better results than those of larger companies. Some evidence from studying the UK and US stock markets supports this view. However, we looked at trusts whose names suggested that they specialised in this sort of investment. Only over the longest period at which we looked (17 years) was there the possibility that investing in smaller companies improved the performance of these trusts compared with all other trusts investing in similar (though not necessarily small) companies.

Verdict: There's just a little evidence to back up this theory, but only over the very long term.

A step-by-step guide to choosing a unit trust

Although there's no certain way of choosing the unit trust that will perform best, you can narrow down your choice among the bewildering number available by following the steps below. But be warned – it's a long job. You could ask advisers to do it for you – see opposite.

Step 1 Make sure a unit trust really is a suitable investment for you – see Chapters 1 and 2. Don't feel that you have to invest *now* just because you've got the cash available; bear in mind that the success of your investment will depend very much on when you buy and when you sell.

Step 2 Work out how much risk you are prepared to take with your investment. You may decide to invest in more than one trust, in which case decide on what level of risk you want to take for each amount.

Step 3 Decide which types of fund to go for. You may want to consider a fund that holds cash, a tracker fund or bonds, particularly as corporate bonds are allowable for PEPs and from 1999 Individual Savings Accounts (ISAs) – see 'Equity and Bond funds', on page 277.

Step 4 Do you want to invest a lump sum or a regular amount each month? If you want to save a certain amount each month, look for a unit trust that offers a savings plan. You could consider investing via a life insurance policy instead – see Chapter 22.

Step 5 Find out when you can deal. With a few unit trusts you can't deal daily, and this may be inconvenient.

Step 6 Still left with lots of unit trusts to choose from? Look at the different management and fund performance figures, and compare charges. You shouldn't base your decision on only one of these factors, but taking them together, some funds will come out better than others.

Step 7 If you are still undecided, look at the investments the funds hold. Ask the company to send you the manager's report and the scheme particulars.

Getting information

From the company

If you want information about a unit trust, ask to see the latest *manager's report* and the *scheme particulars*. What goes in each of these documents is laid down by the Financial Services Authority (FSA)* – see Chapter 5. The scheme particulars have to be revised once a year, or more frequently if a major change occurs in the unit trust. The managers of the unit trust have to produce a report every six months. From these two documents you should be able to find out most of what you want to know about the unit trust.

The manager's report should, among other things, tell you what the objectives of the fund are, how the fund has done over the last six months, how much income will be paid out, what changes have occurred in the investments and information about the highest buying and lowest selling prices for the last ten years (or since the fund began, if less).

The scheme particulars will give the name and address of the manager, the trustee, the investment adviser for the fund (if there is one), the auditor and the registrar (if there is one). There must be a statement saying what the investment policy of the fund will be, what, if any, the borrowing powers of the fund are, and giving details about its valuation, the charges and expenses of the fund.

From newspapers and magazines
Daily prices of most unit trusts are listed in several newspapers. An entry might look like this:

Westover income 494.8 523.2 0.3 3.83.

This tells you the name of the unit trust and (in the order above) the price you could sell your units for yesterday (494.8), the price at which you could buy them yesterday (523.2), how much the price has changed since the previous day (0.3), and the yield (3.83) – see 'Size of income', on page 291. Once a week the initial charge will be shown as a percentage of the price.

Magazines, such as *Money Management*,* *What Investment** and *Moneywise** give other details, e.g. what £1,000 invested five years ago would be worth now.

You can get an information pack from the Unit Trust Information Service, which is run by the Association of Unit Trusts and Investment Funds (AUTIF).*

From investment advisers
In Chapter 6 we looked at the various sources of professional advice, many of which will help in choosing unit trusts. But remember that it's up to you to evaluate their advice.

Both independent advisers and unit trust company representatives can sell you unit trusts, and will generally get a commission on the value of unit trusts they buy for you.

If you buy from one of these groups as a result of a recommendation you will have the right to cancel the investment within 14 days of receiving a notice of your rights. This is discussed in more detail in Chapter 5. What you will get back will be the price you would have paid if you had bought on the day you decided to cancel, plus the initial charge.

Investing in unit trusts

Units

When you invest in a unit trust you buy units directly from the management company. When you cash your investments, you sell units back to the management company (it *has* to buy them from you). The management company puts the cash you pay for units into the fund and it is used to buy investments, such as shares.

Prices

A unit trust has two prices. These prices are based on the value of the investments in the trust fund. The higher price (the *offer* or buying price) is what you pay to buy units. The lower price (the *bid* or selling price) is what you get if you sell units. You usually buy or sell at the price worked out when the fund is next valued (called the *forward* price), which means that, as with shares, you will not know the exact price until the deal is done. But some funds deal at the price that was worked out when the fund was last valued (the *historic* price) and others may use a mixture of forward and historic pricing. If the latter method is used then, for example, the valuation is done at noon, dealing in the afternoon may use that price, and deals from the morning will also use that price, i.e. a forward price. Generally speaking, the fund is valued once a day, but a few are valued less frequently.

The prices are worked out using a method set out in the FSA's rules. To arrive at the offer price, the company finds out the best available price it would have to pay to buy the investments currently in the unit trust fund. It then adds the costs of dealing in the shares, the income accrued less charges and management expenses. The value it has after doing this sum is divided by the number of units the trust has issued, and this gives the maximum offer price the company can charge you to buy units.

The lowest bid price, i.e. the price the company has to pay you for your units, is worked out in a similar way. Again, the company must use the best available price it could get if it sold the investments currently in the unit trust fund.

The difference between these two prices is called the *spread*. The average spread quoted in the newspapers is around 6 per cent, which includes the initial charges. If you want to sell a large number of units (£15,000 plus), the management company does not necessarily have to buy at the bid price it is quoting other sellers of units. Instead, it could offer to buy your units at a price nearer or equal to the minimum bid price, i.e. the lowest price permitted under the FSA regulations.

In fact, it's possible for the unit price for any size of purchase to rise or fall without the share prices of the investments in the unit trust rising or falling. This is because the management company is permitted to move the price within a range laid down by the FSA. So, for example, if many unit-holders are selling, the management company can shift the unit prices downwards to discourage selling and attract buyers. However, if it wants to alter the pricing basis within the permitted range, the company cannot do so mid-way through the dealing period.

Buying and selling

You can buy or sell in several ways, e.g. over the telephone, by letter or through a company representative or independent adviser. Note that an order over the telephone is just as binding as one made in writing. If the fund is dealing only at the prices worked out at the next valuation, you can, of course, set a limit on the price you're prepared to pay for units or accept if you sell them, e.g. only sell at £2 or more. In this way, you should get no surprises.

Once the unit trust manager has received your unit trust certificate or other relevant documentary evidence, if you are selling, you will get the money in five days.

Charges

There are three different sorts of charges. These are:

■ **initial charge** – often 5 per cent and included in the spread between the bid and offer prices, although some companies have now cut their initial charge to as little as 1 per cent, others have dropped initial charges in favour of exit charges

■ **annual management charge** – often in the range 1 per cent to 1.5 per cent a year, but can be higher, especially if the initial charge is low. This charge is usually taken from the income of the fund. The trust deeds allow some funds to raise charges to 2 per cent or 2.5 per cent after giving the required notice.

■ **exit charges** – often 4 per cent if selling within the first year, reducing to 0 per cent if you hold the units for three or four years. It is possible for a combination of initial and exit charges to be made.

Management of the unit trust

There may be three groups of people involved. First, a management company, which does the administration and advertising. Second, an investment adviser, usually from the same company as the management company, although some have advisers such as stockbrokers deciding how the fund should be invested. Third is the trustee (see below).

Under the Financial Services Act (see Chapter 5), there is a procedure for handling complaints about unit trusts. Contact the unit trust company first, and it will advise you who to contact in the event that you're not satisfied with the company's resolution of your complaint. The manager will refer you either to the Investment Ombudsman* Bureau* or the Personal Investment Authority (PIA) Ombudsman* depending on the nature of your complaint.

Trustees

The benefit to investors of trustees is that they are independent of the management and hold the assets of the fund in trust for the unit holders. This means the assets of the fund are safeguarded if anything happens to the management company. Over a dozen companies, mainly banks, act as trustees to hundreds of different unit trusts. Trustees have several jobs. First, the trustee keeps all the cash and investments of the fund in its name.

Secondly, the trustee makes sure that the managers stick to the terms of the trust deed and the scheme particulars – see above. The trust deed will have the following information among other things:

- name of the fund and its investment aim
- the currency of the fund
- when income of the fund will be paid out.

Thirdly, the trustee checks that the unit price calculation has been done correctly and cancels and creates units.

Finally, the trustee checks that the management company is generally operating in accordance with the regulations.

Income

The investments that are held in the unit trust fund get income in the form of share dividends, interest from British Government stocks and so on. The management company takes its regular charge from the income and will usually pay out what's left to unit-holders in the form of *distributions*. If it is not paid out it is reinvested through the fund for the benefit of the unit-holders. There are usually two distributions a year, but some trusts, which concentrate on producing income, pay out distributions quarterly or monthly.

As the income comes into the fund, the unit price rises to take account of this, until it finally includes the whole of the distribution. On a certain day, the price will be marked *xd* (i.e *ex distribution*) and will fall by the amount of the distribution. After that time, if you buy units, you will not get the next distribution to be paid; if you sell units, you still get the next distribution. Accumulation trusts that pay no dividends will not have ex-distribution dates.

There are two different types of units a trust can issue:
- accumulation units
- distribution or income units.

With accumulation units, the income of the unit trust fund is not paid to you in pounds. Instead, the unit price is simply increased to reflect the amount of income retained.

With many unit trusts, you can buy either accumulation units (where the income of the fund is used to increase the unit price) or distribution units (where the income of the fund is paid out to you).

With the rest of the funds, you can choose to have the income automatically reinvested (rather than paid out). This means the income is used to buy more units – you may have to pay an initial charge on these.

Tax

Dividend distributions from a unit trust come with a *tax credit*. The effect of this is that if you're a lower-rate or basic-rate taxpayer there's no income tax to pay on the distribution. If you pay tax at the higher rate, you'll have to pay more tax. If you're a non-taxpayer you'll be able to claim tax back.

The normal capital gains tax rules apply to unit trust investments. Although there is no capital gains tax liability when managers sell shares *within* the funds. See Chapter 7 for details.

Size of income

If you are buying a unit trust as a way of getting an income, look at the *yield* of the fund. The higher the yield, the higher the income is compared to the money you invest.

To get the yield, the amount of the distribution per unit is divided by the unit price. This is then multiplied by 100 to give a percentage. For example, if the distribution per unit is 3p and the unit price is 60p, the yield is $3 \div 60 \times 100 = 5$ per cent.

Of course, if you were to buy units when the price was lower, say 50p, the yield on your investment would be $3 \div 50 \times 100 = 6$ per cent.

Note that the yield usually quoted is the gross yield, i.e. based on the distribution *plus* tax credit.

Another way of getting an income from unit trusts

The disadvantage of using the distribution from a unit trust to provide you with an income, if you need a steady income, is that it can go up and down, because the dividends paid by shares held by the unit trust fund can also go up and down. It alters also because managers of the fund will buy and sell the investments of the fund. Some unit trust companies have *withdrawal schemes* that allow you to have as your income either:

■ a percentage, say 5 per cent, of the original amount you invest, so you can be certain you get the same income each year, or

■ a percentage, say 5 per cent, of the current value of your investment. In this case, the income would still go up and down each year.

If the distributions of the unit trust are not high enough to meet this amount of income, then some of your units are sold. But more units will have to be sold to make up your income when unit prices are low than when they are high – the opposite of what you want. And selling units can lead to you using up your capital increasingly quickly – the more units you sell, the lower your income from distributions in the future, so that more units will have to be sold in the future.

If you decide a withdrawal scheme could be useful, you'll need to check the minimum investment the company will take; it varies, but can be as high as £15,000.

Some unit trust groups organise regular income schemes, where you invest in three or more unit trusts, each with a different month for paying income. In this way, you can get a regular, if varying, monthly income.

Size of investment

For lump sum investments, all unit trusts ask for a minimum investment when you first invest, e.g. £250 or £1,500. If you want to increase your investment you can usually do so by smaller amounts.

Some unit trust companies will let you invest a regular amount, e.g. £25 a month. This is known as a *savings plan*. For an explanation of how this can be linked to a life insurance policy, see Chapter 22.

One advantage of a savings plan is that you don't have to worry as much about when you should invest as you would with a lump sum. *Pound-cost averaging* is sometimes cited as being one advantage of a regular savings plan. What this seems to show is that you can get a bargain by investing regularly. This is because, if the unit price goes up and down, the average cost of your units will be less than the average of unit prices – when the unit price is low your fixed sum of money buys more units than when it is high. But there's nothing magic about this, it just shows the advantage of not having to worry about timing your investment correctly. Don't let this sort of advertising for savings plans persuade you that you are getting a bargain. You still have to worry about when you should cash in your investment.

If you already hold shares, you could swap these for units, through a *share exchange scheme*. The unit trust company will usually do one of two things with your shares:

■ put them in one of its funds, if the fund already holds that company's shares. In this case, in exchange for the shares, the company will often give you units equal in value to the price that it would have to pay to buy them through the Stock Exchange. As this is more than you could get by selling the shares yourself through the Stock Exchange, this seems to be a good saving

■ sell them for you if the company does not want to put

them in a fund. In this case, the company often pays the selling costs, e.g. stockbroker's commission.

Most unit trust companies have a share exchange scheme. The details about minimum value of shares, number of shares and so on vary from company to company. But don't let quite small savings push you into poor investment decisions.

Cost of switching

With the growth of more and more specialist funds and specialist advisers, there has been an increase in the number of companies which will let you switch your investment from one of their unit trusts to another for a lower-than-normal initial charge. Most unit trust companies will normally give you a discount of between 1 per cent and 4 per cent off the price of units in the trust to which you are switching.

Open-Ended Investment Company (OEIC)

From January 1997 investment managers have been able to sell a new type of collective investment scheme called an OEIC (pronounced 'oik'). These funds are neither unit trusts nor investment trusts but are very similar to both of them. An OEIC is a company rather than a trust, like an investment trust, but it can issue (or cancel) new shares like a unit trust.

Most of the differences between an OEIC and the other types of trusts are fairly technical and make little difference to investors. Also an OEIC is regulated in the same way as a unit trust to ensure the equivalent level of investor protection. This new vehicle was considered necessary for UK fund managers to sell their funds on the same terms as other continental or US-managed funds and open up their international markets.

Pricing

One area where OEICs differ from both unit trusts and investment trusts is in the way they are priced. Like other continental investment funds they are traded on a single price. There is one price for both buyers and sellers, and any managers' charges or dealing commissions are shown separately. With traditional unit trusts there are two prices: an 'offer' price which includes any initial managers' charges and a 'bid' price. Both include adviser commissions. Similarly, with an investment trust there is a bid and offer price; the difference, the 'spread', is the market-makers' margin, although broker commissions and charges are paid separately.

The single price is based on the valuation of the fund like a unit trust (but without any price leeway for the bid/offer spread). This is unlike an investment trust where the price is dictated by supply and demand for the shares rather than just the underlying value of the fund. The single price is both simpler to understand and the charges are more transparent to investors.

Which type of fund?

Once you have decided to invest in a collective fund, your decision should still be dictated, to a major extent, by the underlying investments rather than the fund structure. Use the step-by-step guide in this chapter to help you. Only once you know what type of investment you want should you consider which kind of fund you should buy. Your choice may be limited to whatever is available.

Conversion from other trusts

There are now half a dozen or so OEICs in the UK and you may find that existing unit trusts or investment trusts elect to convert to OEICs in the future. If you are an existing investor you will be asked for your opinion or permission to change. There is unlikely to be any major change if this happens. But check the information you receive from the fund carefully before making your decision, particularly if the conversion includes a change in the investment aims and objectives.

Where can you buy them?

Like unit trusts, you will be able to buy OEICs directly from the fund manager but if the manager elects to list the company on the Stock Exchange you will also be able to buy them there. If you have any doubts about whether OEICs are suitable for you or concerns about buying them, consult an independent financial adviser before you invest.

18

INVESTMENT TRUSTS

Investment trusts, like unit trusts, are a way of investing in shares, Government stock and property throughout the world. An investment trust can hold a number of different types of investment, in a range of different industries and countries. The funds are managed by professional investment managers. However, unlike a unit trust, you cannot put money into the fund, nor can you take money out again. Instead, you can buy shares in the company that manages the fund.

Investment trusts are limited companies floated on the Stock Exchange. When an investment trust is created, its shares are sold on the stock market, just like any other company, but the money raised is then reinvested in shares, loans and property. The Memorandum and Articles and the prospectus – the documents that set up the company – will specify what investments the trust can invest in and what sort of return the trust aims to make.

You can invest in investment trusts either for income, capital growth or both. Holders of the investment trust shares receive dividends from their shares, and as the value of the fund rises, the value of the shares should also rise. Some types of share (i.e. Far East companies) pay very small dividends and so not all types of trusts are suitable for investors looking for an income.

Investment trusts are like unit trusts or shares in that the value of your investment can fall as well as rise. If you buy shares in an investment trust, you cannot be sure of getting back the amount you invested at any particular time; and the income you receive from the fund can fluctuate. So do not invest money in an investment trust unless you are certain you will not need it in the near future.

Investment trusts versus unit trusts

When it comes to choosing between unit trusts (see Chapter 17) and investment trusts there are a number of differences to consider. Investment trusts are *closed end* funds. This means that once an investment trust is created, the number of shares is fixed and cannot be altered (except in the case of a rights or scrip issue – see Chapter 16). The money raised forms the trust's capital, and investors cannot add to or take money from the trust's capital. Shares in the trust cease to be under the control of the managers of the trust after it is launched and are traded on the Stock Exchange.

This is very different from a unit trust, whose managers create units when you want to buy them and buy units back from you when you want to sell them.

Pricing

The difference between unit trusts and investment trusts has important consequences for the way the trusts are priced. Unit trusts are priced according to the value of the assets they hold. The managers create as many units as people want to buy at that price. The price of investment trust shares is determined by supply and demand for them on the stock market. If nobody wants to buy shares in a particular investment trust, their price will be low, regardless of how valuable the assets held by the trust are.

Occasionally, the shares of very popular investment trusts sell for more than the value of the assets held by the trust (or the *net asset value*, as it is called). This price is *at a premium*. But most investment trust shares tend to sell at a price below the net asset value of the trust. This is known as *discount to net asset value*. The discount for most investment trusts has risen in recent years from an average of about 7 per cent to as much as 20 per cent of the net asset value.

A high discount can be bad news for the managers of trusts since it encourages large institutions to buy up investment trusts and then sell off their assets at a profit. But for the investor it is good news, you will benefit from the income and capital appreciation produced by a correspondingly larger investment.

Discounts are not as good for the investor if the discount rises or increases during the time you hold the shares. If, for example, you buy shares in an investment trust at the launch (when there will be no discount) you may find, when you come to sell your shares, that they are trading at a discount, thus preventing you from realising the full capital gain of the underlying assets. However, over the long term the movement in discounts has a smaller effect compared to the change in the underlying price of the trust.

The Association of Investment Trust Companies (AITC)* publishes information about the net asset value and discounts of most investment trusts.

Selling assets

Another important difference between unit trusts and investment trusts may be seen when stock market values are falling rapidly. If unit trust investors rush to cash in their investments, the managers have to sell off assets to pay back the investors. Unfortunately, if the stock market is spiralling downwards, managers may have to sell the best shares first, since no one wants the worst shares. As a result, the value of units can accelerate downwards as unit trusts sell off their best holdings.

Investment trust managers, in the same circumstances, are under less pressure to sell their investments and can take a more strategic view of the falling markets.

Borrowing money

Because investment trusts are companies, they can borrow money on behalf of their investors. Unit trusts are not allowed to do this. When an investment trust borrows money and invests it, the result is known as *gearing*. Gearing increases the volatility of the share price. When the market is rising, gearing will make the shareholders' funds rise even quicker than the market; but when the market is falling, the shareholders' fund of a geared investment trust will fall in value that much quicker than the market.

Gearing is a double-edged sword. If the investments bought with the borrowed money produce a greater return than the interest payments, the additional return will make the shareholders' funds rise more quickly than they would otherwise. However, if the interest on the loan comes to more than the return on the investment, then the funds will be worth less than they would be otherwise. If share prices generally start falling, a heavily geared trust, i.e. one which has borrowed large amounts of money, can fall in value very quickly.

Most investment trusts involve some degree of gearing. The amount an investment trust has borrowed can be seen in the trust's annual report. The Association of Investment Trust Companies publishes information on the level of gearing for most investment trusts.

Costs

The costs of investing in a unit trust are fixed by the trust managers and usually consist of an initial charge of, say, 5 per cent plus an annual charge of between 1 and 1.5 per cent. The costs of investing in an investment trust vary according to how you buy. First, there will be the cost of commission to whichever stockbroker or savings scheme you buy from – see 'Buying investment trust shares', on page 301. This cost alone will almost certainly be less than the charges made by a unit trust unless you buy very small amounts where the broker will charge a minimum commission.

However, to make a fair comparison you also need to take into account the cost of the *spread* between *bid* and *offer* prices quoted by dealers in the shares. Share dealers make their money by buying at one price (bid) and selling at another higher price (offer). The spread between them represents a cost to the person investing in the shares. The spread between bid and offer prices can change from day to day, but generally it is related to the size of the trust, the liquidity of shares (which can be a problem with many small investment trust shares) or even popularity – regularly traded shares tend to have smaller spreads.

This means that it is hard to say whether investment trusts are cheaper or more expensive than unit trusts to buy. If you bought a popular investment trust, i.e. one which is traded often, the spread would probably be less than 1 per cent, and it would almost certainly be cheaper than a unit trust. But for investment trust shares which are less often traded, the bid/offer spread can be nearer 10 per cent.

Reinvesting income

Unit trusts usually have a facility to allow you to reinvest your income from your investment directly back into the unit trust. This is very useful if you are investing solely for capital growth. Investment trusts do not have this facility, unless you buy shares through a saving scheme or Personal Equity Plan (PEP) where some managers allow you to do this.

Specialisation

Unit trusts can be set up at little cost, and they are also allowed to advertise themselves much more easily than investment trusts. As a result there are hundreds of small specialised unit trusts, set up to take advantage of particular opportunities, which invest in specific markets, e.g. Japanese Warrant Funds or American Smaller Companies.

Investment trusts are more difficult to establish, requiring a full stock market flotation. As a result there are fewer of them.

Different types of investment trusts

Investment trusts, like unit trusts, break down into about 20 different categories, for example:

- **international** with less than 80 per cent of assets in any one geographical area. International trusts break down into three varieties: *general*, which aims to produce balanced income and growth; *income growth*, which aims to maximise the level of income produced; and *capital growth* which concentrates on increasing capital

- **UK** with at least 80 per cent of assets in the UK. Like the international trusts they are divided into *general, income growth* and *capital growth*

- **Far East (excluding Japan)** with 80 per cent of assets in the Far East and no Japanese assets

- **commodity and energy** with at least 80 per cent of assets in commodities and energy

- **venture and development capital** concentrating on small and growing companies. As well as investing in shares, they will provide capital for buy-outs and new companies, which unit trusts are not allowed to do. The risks of such investments are greater, but so are the possible rewards.

Split-capital investment trusts

Split-capital investment trusts are not new but became more popular in the 1980s. They had been heralded as the way forward for investment trusts, offering a range of different ways of investing in a single fund. However, despite dominating the new issues market for a few years, they have all but disappeared from that market recently. Split-capital trusts currently make up only 10 per cent of all investment trusts. Throughout the last few years the vast majority of new funds launched were single-share investment trusts in the specialist sectors such as emerging markets or smaller companies. These funds are high-risk investments in themselves and so the managers did not need to offer split-capital shares to attract investors. In fact some of the larger split-capital funds, on maturing, are being replaced by traditional single-share trusts.

In a split-capital investment trust there are different classes of shares which give different kinds of returns. In the simplest form the trust is divided between *income shares* and *capital shares*. People with income shares will receive all the income from the fund and people with capital shares will receive all the capital growth from the fund. Both will receive more income or capital growth than they would have received otherwise, since the income or capital growth that would normally have been distributed among all shares will go only to those shares designated income or capital.

So that investors in the capital shares can be certain of realising the full value of their investment, split-capital trusts are given a fixed life and are wound up at the end of that time; otherwise the price of capital shares might be constantly at a discount preventing investors from getting back their return.

Income shares will produce a higher income than other shares. And if the fund grows, the income produced will also grow. This may also result in the price of the shares rising, giving investors some capital growth. However, at the end of the term the trust will pay back only a predetermined sum – often the original amount invested. Some income shares pay back a proportion of capital growth, although others may pay back a token penny at the end of the trust's life. Even this may not be guaranteed but may depend on how well the fund has performed.

Capital shares will behave very much like heavily geared investments. When the market is rising they will rise much quicker than other investments. However, when the market is falling they will fall much quicker. This makes them a risky investment over the short term. But if you are investing for the longer term and you want to invest for capital growth, capital shares in an investment trust are worth considering.

Other types of split-capital shares include the following:
■ *Preference shares* These give you a fixed income and you get paid before ordinary or capital shareholders if the company is wound up.

■ *Stepped preference shares* Like normal preference shares but the income increases each year and sometimes so does the final lump sum.
■ *Zero dividend preference shares* (often just called 'zeros') don't provide any income, but you get a fixed capital amount on winding up. These are less risky than other shares and may be suitable for, say, school fees planning.

Warrants

Many new investment trusts' shares are issued with warrants attached, and many existing investment trusts have issued warrants in recent years. When you buy a warrant you have the *right*, but not the *obligation*, to buy shares at a fixed price, the exercise price, at some time in the future. Because you have bought the right to buy shares rather than the shares themselves, the cost is much less but the risks are much higher. Warrants usually pay no dividends and if you don't exercise them (agree to buy the shares) before the final exercise date they become worthless. Warrants are more risky than shares because they are geared. Most warrants tend to be sold at a premium (not to be confused with the premium or discount to net asset value discussed earlier in this chapter), that is, the cost of buying a warrant and exercising it immediately is more than the cost of buying the shares directly.

Who should invest in investment trusts?

Whether they are the right investment for you depends on how much you have to invest, over what time period you are investing, what kind of return you hope to get from your investment, and how much risk you are prepared to tolerate. Ultimately, your choice of investment will also depend on how you think different investments and markets are going to perform in the future.

How long are you investing the money for?

Investment trusts are medium- to long-term investments. Because investment trust companies invest in a number of different shares, the share price is less likely to make sharp short-term moves up or down than the shares of individual companies.

What are your investment objectives?

If you are looking solely for *capital growth*, over the medium- to long-term an investment trust or a unit trust would be a suitable investment. If you are looking for capital growth over a period of five years or more, then investment in a capital growth fund or capital shares from a split-capital investment trust could be worth considering.

If you are looking for a *moderate income* (say a yield of 4 to 6 per cent) and want some capital growth, e.g. to compensate for inflation, then an investment in a general investment trust might be the answer.

If you are looking to *maximise income*, investment trusts are not the obvious choice of investment. However, if you are prepared to risk your capital and feel that shares are likely to perform very well in the future, you might consider investing in an income growth fund or the income shares of a split-capital investment trust.

How much risk are you prepared to accept?

If you need to be certain of being able to draw out your capital at any moment, then investment trusts are not for you. However, if you are prepared to see the value of your investments rise and fall, investment trusts could be a suitable long-term investment. Some investment trusts are riskier than others. Emerging markets and venture capital trusts are relatively high risk. They can perform spectacularly well but they can also perform extremely badly. The more general a trust, the less risk involved. A general international trust, which spreads your investments worldwide, will be less risky than a trust that invests in only a few countries.

Buying investment trust shares

There are two ways to buy investment trust shares. You can buy them through a stockbroker or other intermediary, like any other share, or you can buy shares in many investment trusts from the management company through an investment trust savings scheme.

Stockbroker

The cost of buying and selling shares from a stockbroker means that it is impractical to buy shares worth less than say, £1,500 to £2,000. Most stockbrokers will charge commission and have a minimum charge – see Chapter 16.

Savings schemes

Many investment trust managers run savings schemes for their investment trusts, set up to encourage private investors to invest in them. Companies are not allowed to advertise their own shares but investment trusts can advertise their savings schemes. An advantage for private investors is that the brokerage costs are normally far lower than using a stockbroker. The cost of buying investment trust shares through a savings scheme is much less than buying from a stockbroker. Most savings schemes charge less than 1 per cent of your investment in commission and some charge no commission at all, just stamp duty. Investment trust savings schemes have minimum investment levels which vary, but most are either £25 per month or £250 as a lump sum.

Information about savings schemes is available from the AITC. Many of them are advertised in the national weekend newspapers.

Tax

The shares of investment trusts are taxed in the same way as other shares. The dividends are subject to income tax and any growth in the value of the shares could lead to a capital gains tax bill (see Chapter 7).

19

BRITISH GOVERNMENT STOCKS

The government issues British Government stocks as a way of borrowing money. There is a very large market in them and Government stocks can prove to be good investments; but they can also turn out to be poor investments, e.g. when interest rates and inflation rise.

British Government stocks could suit four quite different categories of people:
■ those who want a regular (normally fixed) income and who are confident that they won't want their money back in a hurry
■ those who want to invest for a specific time period and want a fixed return over that period, and may not be too bothered how much of that return comes as income or how much as capital gain, but don't want to risk losing money
■ those who want to gamble that interest rates, in general, will fall (stock prices are then likely to rise, leading to a capital gain)
■ those who want to protect some of their money against inflation – they could choose index-linked British Government stocks.

First we describe how *conventional* stocks work, then we take a look at *index-linked* stocks and their pros and cons.

Conventional stocks

How they work

Most British Government stocks (commonly called *gilt-edged securities* or just *gilts*) pay a fixed amount of income each year (though there have also been a few issues of stocks whose income could vary).

With stocks that are *dated*, the government also promises to pay the holder of the stock a fixed number of pounds in a lump sum at the time the stock comes to an end. With a few stocks you can choose to convert them into another specified one offering a different *coupon* (see page 306) and redemption date; these are called *convertible* stocks. Normally you can choose to convert your stock on one particular date each year. However, once you have converted you cannot change your holding back to the original stock. It's worth consulting a financial adviser before buying a convertible stock and checking each year whether you should convert. With *undated* stocks, no final date is specified, so the government need never pay off its debt.

Like shares, stocks are bought and sold on the Stock Exchange. And, as with shares, the prices of stocks fluctuate, so once you've bought some stock, the value of your investment can vary widely but not usually as widely as shares.

The diagram overleaf shows what has happened to the price of an undated stock since 1979. You can see, for example, that if you'd bought in August 1979 and sold two years later you'd have done badly. You'd have got a before-tax income of 10.5 per cent a year on your original investment, but when you sold you would have got back only three-quarters of the money you originally invested – an overall loss of around 4.5 per cent a year for a basic-rate taxpayer.

If, on the other hand, you'd been lucky (or shrewd) enough to invest in October 1981 and sell four and a half years after that, you'd have done very much better. You'd have got a before-tax income of 14.2 per cent a year on your original investment and your investment would have increased in value by 66 per cent by the time you sold – an overall return to a basic-rate taxpayer of around 19.7 per cent a year.

So when you buy and when you sell is crucial to the success or failure of your investment. Of course, if you buy a dated stock and hold it until it comes to an end, you'll know from the outset what you'll get, both in income and capital gain (or loss).

Getting to know the different stocks

Nominal value
British Government stocks are bought and sold in amounts which have a nominal value (or *face* value) of so many pounds and pence. For each £100 nominal of stock you hold, the government promises to pay you £100 in cash at an agreed time in the future – see 'Redemption date', below.

How the price of undated stock [1] has changed

£ for each nominal
£100 of stock

Tory Government elected

August 1979 Before-tax income yield 10.5%

Unemployment exceeds 2 million

MLR hits new record 17%. Inflation 17.4% and rising

October 1981 Before-tax income yield 14.2%

Inflation rate falls to 4.9%

£ weak. Bank base rates rise to 12%

May 1986 Before-tax income yield 8.6%

Bank base rates down to 10% – lowest since January 1985

£ strong. Base rates falling. Tories expected to win June election

Equity market crash

Basic rate of tax reduced to 25%

Start of economic recession

Tories win 4th election

UK leaves ERM

Major takes over from Thatcher

UK joins ERM

Unemployment figures peak (end of recession!)

Base rates fall to 5.25% – lowest since October 1977

Labour Government elected 1 May 1997

[1] Average monthly price of Consols 2½%
Source: Datastream International

But you don't have to buy stocks in multiples of £100 nominal. You could, for example, invest £260 in a stock costing £80 for each £100 nominal. You would then get: £100 × 260 ÷ 80 = £325 nominal of stock.

Name
Each stock has a name, like Exchequer, Treasury or War Loan. This is of no particular significance to investors but helps to distinguish one stock from another.

Coupon
The percentage immediately after the name of each stock, e.g. 8½ per cent, in Treasury 8½ per cent 2007, is called the *coupon*. It tells you the before-tax income the stock pays out each year, expressed as a percentage of the nominal value; in the case of Treasury 8½ per cent 2007, the stock pays out £8.50 for every £100 nominal. Interest on nearly all stocks is paid twice yearly in two equal instalments. And from 6 April 1998 the income from all gilts is normally paid gross, that is without any deduction of tax.

Redemption date
Following the name and the coupon is a year – 2007 in the example above. The date on which the government has promised to redeem the stock, i.e. to pay out the nominal value of the stock, falls in this year.

The date may be a range of years, e.g. Treasury 8 per cent 2002/06. In this case, the government (but not the investor) can choose in which year out of this range to redeem the stock. The government is unlikely to redeem a stock before the last redemption date if the general level of interest rates remains higher than the coupon. In the case of convertible stocks you may be able to convert your stock into another with a later redemption date (see above).

With a few stocks, the coupon is followed by a year and the words *or after*, e.g. 1923 *or after*. This means that the government can choose 1923 or any later year which suits it in which to redeem the stock. These, and a few other stocks which have no year quoted, are called *undated* and need never be redeemed, e.g. War Loan 3½ per cent or Consols 2½ per cent. Again it is unlikely that the government will ever redeem these stocks unless interest rates in general fall below the level of the coupon.

The life of a stock
Stocks are generally split into four groups according to the length of their remaining life, i.e. the time left until

redemption. The precise splits vary somewhat depending on their use, but these are what the groups are called:
- **short-dated** if the stocks must be redeemed in the next five (or sometimes seven) years
- **medium-dated** if their latest redemption date is more than five (or seven), but not more than fifteen, years away
- **long-dated** if over fifteen years
- **undated** if no latest redemption date is given.

What makes stock prices change?

In general, it is changes in interest rates, inflation, or the expectation of changes in the economy as a whole. If interest rates are expected to rise, the price of stocks is likely to fall. If interest rates are expected to fall, stock prices are likely to rise. Why is this?

Suppose you invest £100 in an undated British Government stock which pays out an income of £10 a year at a time when interest rates are 10 per cent (these figures are used for simplicity as interest rates are nearer 6 per cent at the time of going to press). The yearly return is then roughly 10 per cent. But suppose interest rates in the economy as a whole were expected to rise. New investors could then get a higher return on their money by investing elsewhere, so they'll hold off buying British Government stock. This means that the price of Government stock is likely to fall until the yearly return it offers is comparable to the return investors could get elsewhere. For example, if interest rates double, the price of the undated stock that pays out £10 a year may have to halve to £50, so that the yearly return it then offers is roughly 20 per cent.

Similarly, if interest rates as a whole fall, the price of British Government stock is likely to rise.

Dated stocks, however, pose more problems because there are other factors at work, the most important of which are:
- **how long there is to go until the stock comes to an end**
In general, the shorter the period left to run, the smaller the fluctuations in price and the more emphasis there is on interest rate changes rather than inflation rates. Take the example above of an undated stock paying interest of £10 a year and halving in price from £100 to £50. Suppose this stock was due to end in a year's time when the government would pay the holder £100. If the price was £50, someone buying it now would get back £100 in a year's time plus £10 in income in the meantime, which gives a return of around 120 per cent a year. The price needs to fall

from £100 to only £90 or so to give a total return of around 20 per cent.

■ **the stock's coupon** (see page 306). In general, the higher the coupon, the smaller the fluctuations in price. Take a stock with a coupon of 10 per cent, for example, and five years to go before it comes to an end. If it is currently selling for its nominal value of £100, the yearly return will be 10 per cent. For the return (taking account of both income and capital growth over the next five years) to rise to 20 per cent, the price of the stock would have to fall by about 28 per cent to £72. But if the coupon was only 2 per cent, the stock would have to be selling for around £71 to give a yearly return of 10 per cent. For this return to rise to 20 per cent the price would have to fall by around 32 per cent to £48 or so.

What makes interest rates change?
There's a whole host of reasons. For example, the government may increase interest rates to discourage people from borrowing, or to attract investors' money from abroad. Alternatively the government may cut interest rates to stimulate the economy. An important influence will be the gap, if any, between the government's income and its spending, which will determine how much the government needs to borrow (by issuing Government stocks and by other methods).

The price you pay

The price of British Government stocks is quoted as the price for each £100 nominal of stock. Prices are normally quoted in pounds and fractions of a pound, and shown to the nearest £1/32 (just over 3p) for short-dated stocks, and to the nearest £1/16 (just over 6p) for others.

Buyers pay more than the quoted price, sellers get less. For example, buyers might pay £1/8 more and sellers get £1/8 less. The difference between these two prices – the *spread* – will vary according to the size of your transaction and how actively the particular stock is traded. Spreads will tend to be larger with inactive stocks and small deals.

The price at which you buy or sell will be adjusted for something called *accrued interest* (see opposite).

Cum-dividend and ex-dividend
Most of the time, when you buy a stock, you buy it *cum-dividend*. This means that you are entitled to a full half-year's interest when it next becomes due, even if you have not held the stock for that long. The price will be shown as,

say, £98⅛ + 23 days accrued interest; this means you have paid for 23 days of interest which will be included in the next dividend.

However, some five weeks before the interest is due to be paid, the stock is declared *ex-dividend*. If you buy a stock ex-dividend, you are not entitled to the next interest payment and therefore have a longer-than-normal wait for your first interest payment. The quoted price for an ex-dividend stock has *xd* written after it.

For stocks with more than five years to go before redemption, except War Loan 3½ per cent, there's an additional period of three weeks before the stock is declared ex-dividend, during which you can choose to buy or sell the stock either cum-dividend or ex-dividend; during this time, the ex-dividend version is called *special ex-dividend*. Because the cum-dividend version of the stock entitles you to the next interest payment, it costs more than the ex-dividend version. You'll find only the cum-dividend price quoted in the newspapers during this three-week period.

Accrued interest
This is the interest that a cum-dividend buyer gets for the period when he or she didn't own the stock, or which an ex-dividend buyer forfeits by getting his or her first interest payment late. From 6 April 1998 accrued interest will be charged at 20 per cent if you sell with accrued interest, and relief given at 20 per cent if you buy with accrued interest attached to your gilt (or other bond).

The quoted prices for all stocks do not include the accrued interest. This means that you have to pay more than the quoted price when you buy cum-dividend, less when you buy ex-dividend. Similarly, when you sell you'll receive more or less than the quoted price.

This extra amount can be almost as much as half the coupon if you deal just before the stock goes ex-dividend. It is particularly important that you are aware of the dividend payment dates when buying or selling high-coupon stocks.

Working out accrued interest
Since the quoted price of a stock does not include the accrued interest, you'll need to work out the amount of interest accrued so far in order to find out the total price you'll have to pay.

Accrued interest should be worked out in a way that takes each day's interest into account. But you won't go far wrong if you do the sums in terms of weeks.

Accrued interest

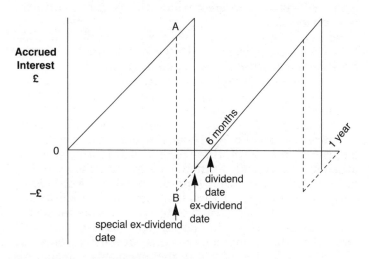

When the stock is special ex-dividend you can choose to buy or sell the stock cum-dividend (A) or special ex-dividend (B)

For a cum-dividend stock, count the number of weeks between the last date interest was paid and the date for which you want the accrued interest. For an ex-dividend stock, count the number of weeks still to go before the next interest date. Ignore odd days. The approximate accrued interest in pence is then:

coupon × weeks just counted × 2.

For a cum-dividend stock, you need to *add* the answer you get to the quoted price to give you the total price you'll pay. For an ex-dividend stock, you need to *subtract* the answer from the quoted price to get the total price you'll pay.

The return you get

In income

A stock's coupon tells you the before-tax income paid on each £100 nominal of stock. But it won't tell you how much income you'll get as a percentage of the amount invested, because you are unlikely to pay £100 for each £100 nominal of stock. To work out the percentage income you'll get, do this sum:

coupon × 100 ÷ quoted price for each £100 nominal of stock.

This is known as the income yield (or running yield).

Capital gain (or loss)
If you hold the stock until it comes to an end, you know you'll be paid its nominal value, so you can work out the capital gain (or loss) you'll make. But with undated stocks or stocks sold before they come to an end, you don't know in advance what price you'll get, so you can't be sure of what capital gain (or loss) you'll make.

The total return
With a dated stock, you can get some idea of the average yearly return on the stock if you hold it until it is redeemed by looking at what's known as the redemption yield. This takes account of both income paid out and the capital gain (or loss) you make in redemption. However, it doesn't normally take account of buying and selling costs, and it assumes that the income paid out is reinvested at a rate of return equal to the redemption yield (for higher coupon stocks this overstates the return you're likely to get in practice). Before-tax redemption yields are printed daily in the *Financial Times* and *The Times*.

Working out the after-tax redemption yields for any stock is not easy. It depends not only on whether you pay tax at 20 per cent or 40 per cent, but also on how much of the return comes as taxable income and how much as tax-free capital gain.

In general:
■ stocks vary widely in redemption yields
■ for stocks with about the same period of time left to run, people who pay the higher rate of tax tend to get the best after-tax redemption yields from relatively low coupon stocks. By contrast, people who pay no tax tend to get the best redemption yields from high coupon stocks
■ when it is possible to buy the same stock in the special ex-dividend period, taxpayers normally get better redemption yields if they buy ex-dividend.

Gilt Strips

In late 1997 Gilt Strips were introduced with a view to modernising the gilts market. A single gilt produces a stream of income payments and the capital payment at redemption. Some stocks can now be split up ('stripped') into components. This allows investors to buy the different components individually. Those who want a fixed sum of money after a fixed period of time buy the principal part of the gilt, while those who want income can buy one or more of the interest payments. Gilt strips provide a very flexible form of investment and can be used, for example, to design an income flow tailored to your needs.

Index-linked stocks

How they work

When the life of an index-linked stock comes to an end, the person then owning it will be paid the nominal value of the stock increased in line with inflation over the lifetime of the stock. So, for example, someone owning £1,000 nominal of 1999 stock, issued in 1983, would get however many pounds are needed in 1999 in order to have the same buying power as £1,000 back in 1983. This might be £2,000, £3,000, or more, depending on the rate of inflation between 1983 and 1999.

All the stocks also pay out a small income; their coupon is usually 2 per cent or 2½ per cent depending on the stock, although a few now offer coupons over 4 per cent. The income is guaranteed to increase each year in line with inflation.

For technical reasons, inflation is measured by the twelve-month change in the Retail Prices Index (RPI) recorded eight months before the dividend dates.

What happens to the buying and selling prices of the stocks?

Over the long term, the prices of the stocks will tend to rise roughly in line with inflation. If the price is £100 and the RPI goes up by 5 per cent a year, the price after a year might well be £105. But the price will also be affected by people's views on the future rate of inflation and interest rates, and by the return they can get on other investments.

The price of stocks with a longer life may well fluctuate more than the price of those with a short life.

Will your investment keep pace with inflation?

This depends entirely on the price at which you buy (or sell) the stock and whether or not you hold the stock until redemption. If you bought £100 nominal value of stock for £100 when the stock was issued, and if you then kept it throughout the lifetime of the stock, the increase in capital would exactly match the increase in inflation.

But suppose you had bought your £100 nominal value of stock for £90. As it's the £100 nominal value which is index-linked, your capital gain at the end of the stock's lifetime would be more than the rate of inflation. If you'd bought at £110, your capital gain would be less.

If you want to buy stocks some time after they are first issued, you should compare the current market price with the nominal value adjusted for the increase in the RPI between the issue date and the time at which you want to buy. If the RPI has increased by 10 per cent, say, you should compare the market price with £110. If the price is higher, then your capital gain if you hold the stock to redemption will be less than inflation; if the price is lower, your capital gain will be more than inflation.

If you can't hold on to the stock until redemption, your gain will depend on the price at which you can sell.

How do they compare with other British Government stocks?

■ **pro:** If you buy at the right price (see above) and hold them until redemption, you're guaranteed that the money you invest will at least keep pace with inflation.

■ **con:** The coupon for all index-linked stocks is low, and it could be costly to sell small amounts of stock to boost the income. So if you're after income, a high coupon stock may suit you better.

Are they worth buying?

If you're a higher-rate taxpayer not looking for a large increase in income, you should consider putting some of your money into these stocks. For anyone who wants to keep a nest-egg on ice for a fairly long time they are worth considering.

If you need to sell stocks, the price should roughly match inflation over the time you've owned it, though fluctuations in price may work against you.

New issues of stocks

In the more distant past, stocks were usually issued for sale at a fixed price, but this method was replaced with issues *by tender*. With a tender issue, it's usual for only a minimum price to be quoted. You can offer to buy stock at whatever price you like at or above the minimum.

If the whole issue (of, say, £800 million) is able to be sold at or above the minimum price, the issue is closed. But you don't need to worry about bidding too high, as everyone who bids pays the price paid by the lowest successful bidder, rather than the price they themselves bid. And issues don't normally sell out on the first day, so everyone who applies usually gets stock at the minimum price. After the initial offer, the stock that's left over is sold on the Stock Exchange by the Gilt-Edged Division of the Bank of England over a period of time, and not necessarily at the issue price.

During this period, the stock is commonly called a tap stock (because the supply of the stock is turned on and off like a tap, depending on the demand for it). When all this extra stock is sold, the tap is said to be exhausted. New short-dated stocks are called short taps; new medium-dated stocks, medium taps; and so on.

More recently, another method has become the preferred way of issuing stocks – the *bid price auction*. In an auction, you also choose the price at which you bid for stock. The main difference between a tender and an auction is that at auction all the stock is usually sold and the bidders pay the price they bid – so bidding too high could turn out to be costly. However, 'small' investors do not have to join the main auction. They can put in non-competitive bids, in which case they will be sure of getting stock at the *average* price of the issue.

Buying stock direct from the Bank of England when first issued has the advantage that you don't have to pay any stockbroker's commission (and there's no price spread). Most newly issued stocks can eventually be registered on the National Savings Stock Register (see below), which may keep your eventual selling costs down too.

New issues of stock may be partly paid. This means that you don't have to pay the full cost of the stock when you first buy it, e.g. you may have to pay 15 per cent with your application and the remainder a month later.

How stocks are taxed

Government stocks are completely free of capital gains tax. You have to pay income tax on the income you get from the stocks at your highest rate of tax.

From 6 April 1998 the income from all gilts is normally paid without the deduction of tax. Prior to this date it was just the gilts on the National Savings Stock Register (bought through the Post Office) and War Loan 3½ per cent that paid interest gross to UK residents. This change is especially convenient for non-taxpayers but because the interest is taxable all taxpayers will still need to pay the tax. Any gilts already held on 6 April 1998 will continue to pay interest net of tax at 20 per cent unless you specifically request to switch to gross payments.

The price you pay for, or get from, stocks equals the quoted price with accrued interest either added or deducted. The amount of this accrued interest used to be treated as part of your capital gains or loss and was subject to the capital gains tax rules, which often meant no tax to pay at all. But since 28 February 1986, accrued interest has been treated as income and is subject to income tax rules. There are a few exceptions: the main one for private investors is that, if the total nominal value of *all* the stocks you hold is no more than £5,000, the accrued income scheme does not apply; in this case, there is no income tax on accrued interest. But you'll get taxed on all the interest you receive and you won't be able to deduct the interest that accrued on the stock before you bought it.

The contract note you get when you buy or sell stock will show how much accrued interest is involved in the deal. How it is treated for income tax depends on whether you are a buyer or a seller:
- if you sell cum-dividend, you are taxed at 20 per cent on the accrued interest included in the price you get
- if you sell ex-dividend, you get tax relief at 20 per cent on the accrued interest that has been deducted from the quoted price, which can be offset against the tax on the dividend you receive
- if you buy cum-dividend, you get tax relief at 20 per cent on the accrued interest included in the price you pay
- if you buy ex-dividend, you are taxed at 20 per cent on the accrued interest which has been deducted from the quoted price.

For more details about how accrued interest is taxed, see Inland Revenue leaflet *IR68* (available from tax offices and Tax Enquiry Centres).

Choosing a stock

Which stock to choose depends on what you want from your investment.

A high fixed income?
Go for a high coupon stock; but if you want a higher income than the current interest rate you will sacrifice some of your capital to produce this income. Beware of choosing a stock that has a long time to go before it has to be redeemed. If you're forced to sell before then, you may lose heavily if the price of the stock has fallen in the meantime.

A known total return over a fixed period?
Go for a stock that lasts for the period you're interested in. If there's a choice, choose one that gives the best after-tax redemption yield for someone in your tax position. In general, a higher-rate taxpayer should go for a low coupon stock, a non-taxpayer for a high coupon stock.

Want to gamble on interest rates falling?
Go for a stock with a long time to run, or for an undated stock, and choose one with a low coupon. But bear in mind that if interest rates rise, you may end up losing heavily.

Protection against inflation?
Index-linked stocks might suit you. But bear in mind that you have to buy stock at the right price and hold it until redemption to be sure that the full index-linking will apply; the extent to which your investment will be protected against inflation will depend on the price at which you buy.

Where to get information and advice

Several newspapers give information each day about British Government stock prices; the most comprehensive information is given in the *Financial Times* and *The Times*.

To find the after-tax redemption yield for someone paying tax at the rate you pay it, and to get advice on which stock would best suit your needs, contact a stockbroker, bank or one of the increasing number of other organisations offering a similar service.

How to buy and sell

You can buy and sell British Government stocks through a stockbroker, high-street bank (many have their own stockbroking arm rather than simply acting as agents for other stockbrokers), or through some building societies and solicitors or accountants, say, who act as agents for stockbrokers. Most financial advisers will buy or sell stock for you on the Bank of England Register unless you specifically ask otherwise. Around two-thirds of the stocks are also listed on the National Savings Stock Register (you get forms for buying and selling these at post offices). There are important differences between buying and selling on the Bank of England Register and via the National Savings Stock Register. In particular, buying through the National Savings Stock Register is much cheaper, except for large amounts of stock. If you own stock on the National Savings Register you cannot sell it in the stock market and *vice versa*, so it's important if you decide to sell your stock to be clear about where the stock is registered.

Investing via a unit trust

A wide range of unit trusts now specialise in British Government stocks and other fixed income investments.

Investing via a unit trust is generally more expensive than investing in stocks direct. The difference between the buying and selling prices of units can be as high as 5 per cent, and there's a yearly charge (although most unit trusts charge a lot less than this). For this extra cost you get professional management of a large portfolio of stocks, and the manager may be able to switch between stock more actively than you could afford to do as a single investor.

From the income tax point of view, there's not a lot of difference between investing in a unit trust or investing direct. There is a difference with capital gains tax. British Government stocks are not liable for capital gains tax, but gains on trusts are, though the first £6,800 of gains made by selling assets (in the 1998–9 tax year) is exempt. Nor can you get an *indexation allowance* to reduce your capital gain – see Chapter 7.

Another problem with unit trust investment is that you have to accept the spread of stocks in which the trust chooses to invest. By investing directly, you can choose the particular stock that is best for your particular tax rate and investment needs.

20

CORPORATE BONDS, PREFERENCE SHARES AND CONVERTIBLES

Since 1995, certain corporate bonds, convertibles and preference shares have been permitted to be included in general Personal Equity Plans (PEPs). Since then, many of the corporate bond PEPs that have become available are through existing gilt and fixed-income unit trusts. Furthermore, when the new Individual Savings Accounts (ISAs) are introduced on 6 April 1999 corporate bonds will be eligible for inclusion. A corporate bond fund offers a higher income yield than most equity-based funds (yields of 8 per cent or more have been offered), and because bonds tend to be less volatile than shares, the risk of losing a large part of your capital is less. But a fund of bonds cannot offer the same certainty of return as a single bond. If you buy a bond and hold it until maturity you will know exactly how much income and capital return you will receive, just as you do with conventional gilts (see Chapter 19). A bond fund will not mature at a fixed price and as the fund manager buys and sells bonds within the fund both the income and the capital value of your units will vary. This chapter explains the different types of bonds available and how they work.

Corporate bonds

Companies generally raise money in two ways: either they can issue more share capital – by offering shareholders a rights issue, see Chapter 16 – or they can decide to borrow money by issuing **corporate bonds**. Because bonds, or loan stocks, are simply borrowed money, the bond holders have no voting rights in the company, except in special circumstances, such as default. Some corporate bonds are secured by specific assets in the company, for example property, but most are unsecured. Corporate loan stocks tend to offer higher rates of interest than gilts or other Government stocks; this is because there is a higher risk that the company will default on the loan. A higher risk deserves a higher reward, in this case higher yields.

How they work
Corporate bonds work in the same way as gilts: they have a 'face' or 'nominal' value, a coupon (or interest rate) and a maturity date. Rather than buying a number of shares or units you buy pounds nominal. The company agrees to pay to the bond holder interest at the coupon rate every year until maturity. For example, Newco Electronics 9 per cent 2002 will pay the bond holder £9 a year for every £100 nominal until 2002. As with gilts, interest is usually paid in two equal payments a year.

Debentures

Debentures work in exactly the same way as corporate bonds but they are always secured on specific assets of the company and so are safer than other corporate bonds. Even if the company goes into liquidation, you should expect to get your capital back. Because the risks of losing money are lower with debentures, the yield is normally lower than from an unsecured loan.

How they work
Debentures behave in exactly the same way as other corporate loan stocks.

Preference Shares

Preference shares are not loans to a company but like ordinary shares give you a stake in the ownership of a company. They act like corporate bonds or debentures because they usually offer a fixed income, which is paid before any dividends to ordinary shareholders (hence, 'preference' shares). If the company goes into liquidation the preference shareholder will get paid before ordinary shareholders but after all loans have been repaid.

How they work
Preference shares behave in exactly the same way as corporate loan stocks. Some preference shares have a redemption date, others are irredeemable.

Convertibles

A convertible loan stock is a fixed-interest bond that carries with it the right to convert into ordinary shares on the terms and conditions set out when the convertible is first issued.

How they work

The right, but not obligation, to convert a bond into shares is offered on a specific date (or within specific time periods) and at a specific share price. If the conversion rights are not exercised by the expiry date, the bond will then revert to a conventional dated corporate bond (see page 318).

There are two basic types of convertibles – **convertible loan stocks** and **convertible preference shares**. Convertible loan stocks are redeemed like other loan stocks, unless the holder has decided to convert the bond to shares before the redemption date. The same applies to most convertible preference shares, though some do have other arrangements. One point about convertible preference shares, which often causes confusion, is that their coupon is quoted *net* of basic-rate tax, while redemption yields are always quoted *gross*. So the yield on the convertible preference shares always seems impossibly high, simply because the yield and the coupon are stated on different tax bases.

Because a convertible bond can either become shares (if you choose) or stay as a bond, it is harder to work out whether or not they are better value than simple bonds or ordinary shares. For example, Newco Electronics 6.3 per cent convertible preference shares have a nominal value of £1 each. The terms of conversion are that as holder of convertible preference shares, you may exchange your holding for ordinary shares at any time between 1989 and 2015 at a rate of 14½ ordinary shares for every 100 preference shares held. If you don't exercise your conversion rights by 2015, your convertible preference shares will be redeemed at par (i.e. at the nominal value).

If the convertible preference share price is 109p, and the ordinary share price is 695p, to work out whether you should convert to ordinary shares, the calculation would be as follows:

100 nominal of preference shares costs £109
14½ ordinary shares cost £100.775 (if bought in the market, excluding costs)

Therefore, the premium you would pay if you bought the convertible preference shares and converted them would be:

$$\left(\frac{109}{100.775} - 1\right) \times 100 = 8.2\%$$

So, at the moment it would be better to buy the shares directly if you wanted a share holding in Newco Electronics and to buy the convertible preference shares if you wanted a fixed-income bond. If the share price in Newco rose, the conversion premium would get smaller, and you might do better to convert to the shares. However, before you decide to convert a convertible bond into shares you need to remember that you will lose the fixed income that the convertible bond pays and will get share dividends instead, which are likely to vary and may be much smaller.

Bulldog bonds and Eurosterling bonds

Bulldog bonds are loan stocks that are issued in sterling by foreign borrowers and traded on the UK Stock Exchange. Eurosterling bonds are issued in sterling by both UK and foreign organisations. Both are large-denomination bonds and are mainly used by professional investors. As with Eurobonds denominated in other currencies, Eurosterling bonds are traded offshore. The interest is paid gross but is liable for UK income tax and any gains are liable for capital gains tax.

Buying and selling bonds

You can buy or sell corporate bonds, debentures, convertibles and other bonds through a stockbroker or financial adviser as with shares, gilts and other stock market investments.

21

WITH-PROFITS LIFE INSURANCE

A with-profits policy is basically a long-term investment with life insurance tacked on; it can also be the basis for a pension plan. It's a way of investing in a mixture of shares, British Government stocks, company loans, property and so on, but you invest via a life insurance company. 'With-profits' refers to the way in which investment returns are added to your policy. The policy holders get a share of the excess profits the insurance company makes from its business, in the form of bonuses. Because there is usually some form of smoothing applied to avoid sharp variations in bonuses from year to year, with-profits policies tend to give you steady growth.

Friendly societies

You can buy savings-type life insurance from friendly societies as well as insurance companies. Friendly societies were originally self-help organisations, providing financial protection such as sickness benefits for their members, but nowadays the larger societies also offer with-profits endowment policies and unit-linked savings plans which operate in the same way as insurance company policies.

As well as conventional savings policies, friendly societies can, unlike insurance companies, offer 'tax-exempt savings plans' where your premiums are invested in a tax-free fund and the maturity value is free of tax. (They will also receive a 10 per cent tax credit on the interest from 5 April 1999 to 5 April 2004 in line with the Individual Savings Accounts (ISAs)). However, there are strict limits on the amount you can invest, with a maximum premium of £270 a year (£25 a month). Partly because of the cost of administering lots of small policies, friendly societies' expenses have tended to be high. A society's investment performance has to be particularly good to make up for this.

How an endowment policy works

You agree to save for a certain period, which must normally be for ten years or more. With a *with-profits endowment policy* you are guaranteed at the outset that if you save until the end of the period you will get a guaranteed lump sum in return; but you hope that you will get much more than the guaranteed sum when your policy comes to an end.

What happens is that the guaranteed sum grows over the years as the life insurance company adds *bonuses* to it – see below. If you had started saving ten years ago in a ten-year with-profits endowment policy you would find that when the policy pays out you would be getting an average annual return of around 10 per cent. The average return for a ten-year policy maturing in 1998 was just under 10 per cent, say; for a 25-year policy the return is a bit more, around 13 per cent (the latter figure ignores the tax relief that you could have got at that time).

Bonuses

There are two sorts of bonuses:
- *regular*, and
- *terminal*.

Regular bonuses (usually called *annual* or *reversionary* bonuses by the insurance companies) are added to your with-profits policy. Once a reversionary bonus has been added to your policy, this new figure becomes your new guaranteed sum; it cannot be taken away once it has been added. See below for how bonuses are decided.

If the company announces a compound bonus of 3 per cent, say, it works out what this would be on the guaranteed sum. If, for example, your original guaranteed sum is £6,000, the amount of the bonus at the end of the first year would be £180, and the new guaranteed sum would be £6,180. At the end of the second year, the bonus would be 3 per cent of £6,180, which is £185, and the new guaranteed sum would become £6,365.

Some companies add different rates to the original guaranteed sum and to the reversionary bonuses already added to the policy. For example, a bonus of 3 per cent might be added to the original guaranteed sum and a bonus of 5 per cent to the reversionary bonuses already announced.

It's important to realise that there's no guarantee a bonus will be added each year. In the past, it was rare for a company to reduce its rate of bonus, let alone not pay one. But since 1990 reversionary bonus rates have generally fallen.

Life insurance companies usually also pay a *terminal* bonus as well as reversionary bonuses. This is a one-off bonus added at the end of the policy, either the end of the savings period or on earlier death. If you cash in your policy early (see page 326), you normally get no share of the terminal bonus.

These terminal bonuses can vary widely from one company to another and from year to year, depending on the current market value of the insurance company's investments, e.g. the shares it owns, and on the insurance company's policy: for example, on 25-year policies as much as 60 per cent of some top performing companies' payouts may be made up of terminal bonuses. However, a much smaller percentage of the total payout from shorter-term policies tends to come from terminal bonuses: for example, around 20 to 30 per cent on ten-year policies from top-performing companies; and in 1993 and 1994 one company paid no terminal bonus at all – the first time this has happened since 1977. However, bonuses have improved since 1994.

Comparing bonus rates with other rates of return

You can't compare them directly. First, you have to work out what a given bonus rate means in terms of the cash you get back at the end of the policy. Then you have to take a view on what the terminal bonus might be. Finally, you have to work out what rate of return this represents on the amount you save each month. Only then can you compare the rate of return you might get on a with-profits endowment policy with the rate currently offered by, say, a building society, and as you can see you have to make a number of assumptions to arrive at a rate of return, so your actual return may be very different.

Life insurance or investment?

A with-profits endowment policy is a regular savings life policy with a high investment element. If what you want is life cover to protect your family from financial hardship in the event of your early death, you should take out *term insurance*. With this sort of insurance, you insure for an agreed period. If you die within that period, the insurance pays out. If you survive, the policy pays nothing.

For a given amount of cover, term insurance is usually much cheaper than other types of life insurance. You can also take out term insurance policies that pay out a tax-free income (instead of a lump sum) if you die within the term. These are known as *family income benefit policies. Whole-life insurance* is also worth considering in some circumstances – see 'Other types of policy', on page 329.

What sort of return do you get?

The returns you get depend on your age, your gender and your health. A younger person, therefore, would get a slightly better return than an older person, a woman a slightly better return than a man, and a healthy person a better return than someone in poor health. This is because life insurance is tacked on to the investment and the life insurance company deducts some money from the premium you invest to pay for the life insurance.

The returns you could have got in the past vary widely from company to company. For example, during 1998 the best-performing company could be paying out nearly half as much again as the worst-performing company for the same amount of savings. Sadly, you can't be sure in advance which is going to be the best-performing policy.

How endowment policies are taxed

There's normally no tax to pay on the money you get back from an endowment policy provided you don't cash it in (or make it *paid-up* – see overleaf) within its first ten years or within the first three-quarters of the period you insured for, if this is shorter. But if you do cash it in before this time, and you pay tax at the higher rate or would do if the gain on your policy is added to your income, there may be some tax to pay. The amount of the gain is normally the amount you get less the total of the premiums paid. There is no basic-rate tax to pay on the gain, because the life insurance fund has already paid tax.

Any gain on cashing in a policy counts as part of your 'total income', which is used to work out the age-related allowances you can get. So, if you are 65 or over during the tax year, be careful about cashing in an endowment policy before the end of the agreed saving period. It may mean a reduction in your allowances and more tax to pay.

Before 14 March 1984, when you took out an endowment policy you also got tax relief (really a premium subsidy) on what you paid for the policy. You can carry on getting the premium subsidy on a policy that you took out before that date, as long as you have not changed the policy to give you more benefits, e.g. by extending its term or increasing its cover. The amount of the subsidy is currently 12.5 per cent.

Ending a policy early

To get the best return on a with-profits endowment policy, you have to keep it going for the period you originally agreed, often 10, 15 or 25 years. But your financial life could be drastically altered during this time (through marriage, divorce, having children, moving home, being made redundant or starting your own business, for example). So you may find yourself wanting to end the policy early.

There's no doubt that a substantial number of endowment policies are cashed in early (or simply allowed to lapse). In 1995 alone, nearly 300,000 endowment policies worth £5.7 billion were cashed in early. (For more details on early encashment see, *The Which? Guide to Insurance.* *) If you need your savings back early, or can no longer afford the premiums, what are the alternatives?

Cashing in your policy

The cash-in value (also called the *surrender value*) of an endowment policy is usually decided entirely at the discretion of the insurance company.

Cashing in a policy early can reduce considerably the return on your investment. With a few companies you get nothing back if you cash in your policy within its first two years, and even after five years you will be lucky to get back as much as you have paid in. And on a 25-year policy you are unlikely to break even within ten years.

Making the policy paid-up

You stop paying the premiums and the insurance company reduces the guaranteed sum for which you are insured. This new guaranteed sum, called the *paid-up value*, is paid out at the end of the period you originally insured for (or when you die, if this is earlier). Most insurance companies that offer this option continue to add bonuses to the paid-up value of a with-profits policy. However, not all companies will make a policy paid-up because of the tax implications (a qualifying policy may become non-qualifying if the premiums are not maintained). You won't get any cash now with this option but at least you pay no more into the policy either.

Getting a loan on it

Many insurance companies will consider lending you money, using your policy as security for the loan. Generally, the maximum loan is between 75 per cent and 90 per cent of the cash-in value. Some companies will not make a loan of less than a certain amount, say £100 to £250. If you are considering a loan, check the current rate of interest and compare it with what's available from other sources.

Selling your policy

You may be able to sell your with-profits policy on the traded endowment policy market. Usually, policies must have a surrender value of at least £1,500 and have been running for seven or more years to be eligible. When you sell, the buyer takes over payment of the premiums and gets the benefits on maturity (or when you die).

There are three ways to sell your policy: at auction, to a market-maker or via an intermediary. Selling to a market-maker or through an intermediary may be the easiest option but you might get a better price at auction. If you decide to auction your policy, it's worth getting quotes from a market-maker first to work out a realistic reserve price.

One firm that auctions policies is H. E. Foster & Cranfield.* If the policy is sold, it currently charges a fee of £50 plus a commission of one-third of the difference between what the policy sells for and its cash-in value. (You don't have to sell the policy if the highest bid is below the cash-in value or whatever you set as a reserve price.)

You can contact the Association of Policy Market Makers (APMM)* or the Association of Policy Traders (APT)* for information.

What should you do?

If you need the cash, you'll have to choose between cashing in your policy, getting a loan on it or selling it. If you don't need the cash, but can no longer afford the premiums, you could also consider making your policy paid-up.

The best choice for you will depend on your particular circumstances. The first thing to do is to ask the insurance company for:

- the policy's cash-in value
- details of any loan you can use your policy to get (e.g. rate of interest charged and how much you can borrow)
- the current sum guaranteed by the policy
- the current rate of bonus and, if you don't need the cash,
- the paid-up value and whether bonuses will continue to be added to this value.

Then you'll have to work out for yourself what the best course of action is. The example below will give you an idea of how to do this.

Example: deciding what to do

Simon Smart has a 25-year with-profits endowment policy, for which he has been paying premiums of £30 a month for the last 15 years. (He actually pays less than this because he is getting the premium subsidy not now available for new policies, see page 325). In November 1997 he finds he cannot afford to carry on paying his premiums. He writes to his insurance company and finds:

- the cash-in value is £13,765
- he can borrow up to £12,388 on his policy. The rate of interest would be 9 per cent at present, but could vary
- the current sum guaranteed by the policy is £15,741 (the original £8,685 plus £7,056 in bonuses)
- the current rate of bonus is 3.5 per cent compound plus 2.25 per cent extra on the bonuses.

Cashing in
Simon doesn't need the cash. So if he cashed his policy in, he'd invest the £13,765. He finds that if he invested the money in a ten-year British Government stock, for example, he might get a return of around 5.7 per cent a year after tax. He'd get a total of around £23,950 in ten years' time (assuming he could reinvest the interest at 5.7 per cent too, which, of course, may not be possible).

Getting a loan
Though Simon doesn't need the cash at the moment, it might still make sense for him to get a loan on his policy and use this to help pay his premiums.

The amount his policy is likely to pay out if he continues to pay the premiums is £30,800 based on a future rate of return of 5 per cent. As he took out the policy before 14 March 1984, Simon gets the premium subsidy of 12.5 per cent and his £30 a month premium actually costs him £26.25. So he'd need to borrow around £3,150 over the ten years.

When his policy came to an end and based on a 10 per cent rate of return he could expect to get back £39,200 less the £3,150 loan, i.e. £36,050.

Of course, he'd also have to pay interest on the loan. This could be kept to a minimum if he borrowed the money in instalments, rather than borrowing the full £3,150 straight away. In this case, the interest might work out at about £2,930 over the ten years.

Deducting £2,930 interest from the £36,050 he'd get back from the policy leaves a net amount of £33,120.

What Simon decides to do

Simon sees that, in his particular case, the best thing to do would be to get a loan from the company to pay his premiums. If he can, he'll get a loan each year; if not, he'll get a loan now to pay all the premiums, and invest the money in a building society until it's needed.

The worst thing he could do at the moment is to cash in the policy. He realises, however, that he can only make an estimate of the outcome. Things could alter in the next ten years – interest rates could go up and bonus rates could go down, for example. Before he makes his decision he decides to contact some of the companies mentioned above to see how much he might get from selling his policy.

Other types of policy

There are a number of variations and similar policies. These are:

■ **non-profit** endowment policies. These were common 15 or 20 years ago, but are rare today. With a non-profit policy you agree to save for a certain period, which must be ten years or more. The policy gives a poor, but guaranteed, return. You get the amount guaranteed if you save to the end of the agreed period; your heirs get the same amount if you die within the period. You get no bonuses on the guaranteed amount

■ **low-cost** endowment policies. These are sold linked to mortgages for the purpose of buying a home, and are a special type of insurance package. The package is a combination of a with-profits endowment policy (which has bonuses added on over the years) and term insurance: the guaranteed sum assured is for less than the mortgage to keep premiums affordable. Whether or not there will be enough to pay off the mortgage will depend on how well the policy does. It looks increasingly likely that some people who took out policies in the late 1980s will have to increase their premiums to make sure they do

■ **unitised with-profits** endowment policies. These policies are increasingly available, either as stand-alone policies or as an investment option on a unit-linked policy (see Chapter 22). Your contributions buy units in a with-profits fund. At regular intervals, either the value of your units is increased or bonus units are added (the equivalent of traditional reversionary bonuses). When the policy matures or on death, a terminal bonus may be added. The bonuses reflect the investment experience of the insurance fund, but instead of expenses entering into the bonus calculation, distinct charges are set against the plan. Although more secure for investors than unit-linked policies, unitised with-profits plans are not as secure as traditional with-profits plans, because the insurance company retains the right to revalue the cash-in value of units – downwards as well as upwards – if investment experience suggests this is warranted

■ **with-profits bonds.** You pay a single premium, which is invested in a unitised with-profits fund. The policy terms vary considerably from company to company, and there may be hefty penalties if you cash them in or take early withdrawals: tread carefully

■ **whole-life policies.** With these, you agree to pay premiums for the rest of your life or up to a certain age, often 85. Premiums could rise after ten years, and at set intervals after that. The policy pays out only when you die, not at the end of the premium-paying period. The insurance company agrees to pay out a fixed sum (plus bonuses if the policy is a with-profits one). You can cash in your policy at any time, but even after a very long time, the cash-in value is likely to be fairly low.

In general, if you want protection for your dependants, it would be better to go for *term insurance*, which is cheaper, unless you are getting on in years. If you're looking for an investment, you may get a better return elsewhere, without being tied to such a long savings period.

But a whole-life policy may be useful if you're sure you want lifelong protection, for example to pay an inheritance tax bill on your death – see Chapter 7. The policy should be made out so that the proceeds go to your heirs, not to you (otherwise the proceeds could form part of your estate and become liable for inheritance tax). You can do this by having the policy 'written in trust': the insurance company can arrange this for you. If you go for a whole-life policy, don't take out a non-profit one (see page 329), which will give a poor return.

Is a with-profits policy suitable for you?

With-profits policies with their wide mix of investments (shares, property and fixed-interest investments), provide a safer home for your money than, say, unit trusts alone. The way that policies work means that the ups and downs in performance, which can be experienced from year to year, are smoothed out by the actuary, and so there will not be a huge difference between the payment for a policy maturing in one year and the payment for another policy maturing in the next year. In return for this lower risk, you have to expect that you may experience a lower return than you would from some other investments.

Of course, it is possible for you to spread your own savings among a number of different types of investments and to avoid cashing your investments all at the same time. If you do it yourself, you do not incur the expenses of the life insurance company, which are mainly its costs of marketing and selling policies. However, you may not want to undertake it yourself, prefer saving regularly or simply not have enough money to get a reasonable spread of investments. If so, you could consider a with-profits policy as a relatively safe home for part of your savings.

You should, however, think carefully before committing yourself to such a long-term savings plan, as cashing in a policy before the agreed saving period is up usually means a poor return, and, in the first five years or so, not even getting your money back.

Buying a policy

If anyone tries to sell you a with-profits policy, whether from a life insurance company or friendly society, they must work within the investor protection rules (see Chapter 5). In particular, they should either be a company representative or an independent financial adviser. They are normally paid by commission on the policies they sell. The amount should be shown in the *'key features'* document.

The 'key features' document must include:

- the nature of the policy or plan, including its aims, what commitment is required from you (i.e. regular savings for a minimum time period) and the risks inherent in the policy
- an illustration of the return you could expect based on growth rates laid down by the PIA. The illustration needs to include the company's charges and your relevant details: age, sex, amount of cover you want, etc.
- statements clearly showing that the illustration is simply an example and is not guaranteed, and a warning that inflation will erode the values (or buying power) given in the illustration
- a description of the main terms of the policy or plan, set out in a question-and-answer format
- tables showing the amount you could get back if you stopped the plan early, showing what would happen in the first five years and the last five years (to show the importance of the initial charges and the terminal bonus)
- a statement that over the lifetime of the policy the effect of charges is to reduce the rate of growth of your investment
- a warning that if you cash in your policy you may get back less than you have paid into it in premiums
- the amount of commission which will be paid to an adviser if you use one.

Guaranteed income and growth bonds

These are investments issued by insurance companies, which are suitable for lump sums. You have to invest your money for a fixed period (often four or five years, but it can vary between one and ten years). In return, you normally get a fixed rate of return for that period. Do not confuse them with National Savings Pensioners Guaranteed Income Bonds, see Chapter 12. Although these are also fixed-term, fixed-rate bonds, they work (and are taxed) very differently.

With an *income bond*, the return is paid out as a regular income (usually yearly, but some companies will pay monthly). Some bonds may eat into your capital to provide the income, if investment performance is weak. With a *growth bond*, it is left to accumulate, and paid out when the bond comes to an end.

If you die before the bond comes to an end, the insurance company normally pays out the amount you originally invested plus, with some growth bonds, the return accumulated to date.

There's normally no basic-rate tax to pay on the return from an income or growth bond (because the insurance fund has already paid tax). If you pay tax at no more than the basic rate (even after adding what you make on the bond to the rest of your income) you should get the return quoted in the advertisements. But if you or your husband or wife are 65 or over (or approaching 65), and you receive age-related allowances, the return from the bond may increase your income to the point that you lose your allowance.

Remember, if you choose an income bond that pays out a regular income, inflation will reduce the value of the fixed return. Alternatives to consider include National Savings Certificates, the various National Savings Bonds, bank and building society fixed interest accounts and guaranteed equity bonds (explained on page 335).

Don't invest in a bond if you may need to cash it in early. Some insurance companies don't allow you to do this, while others may give you back less than you originally invested.

How bonds work

Bonds are normally available for only limited periods of time, and the mechanics of newly issued bonds change from time to time. These days, virtually all bonds are based on single-premium endowment policies and this chapter describes how such bonds work. But in the past, some bonds were based on annuities (see Chapter 23) which are taxed quite differently. Before buying, check with the company how any bond is taxed.

Single-premium endowment bonds
Your investment buys a single-premium endowment policy with guaranteed bonuses. You can choose whether to have bonuses paid out as income or reinvested for growth (or you may be able to have part paid out, part reinvested). At the end of the term, you get back your original investment plus bonuses that you haven't cashed in.

Series of single-premium endowment bonds
Your bond is divided up into a series of single-premium policies, one to provide an income for each year of the term and one to return the original lump sum at the end of the investment term.

Tax

There is no tax to pay on either the income or the final payout for basic-rate taxpayers, because this has already been paid by the insurance company. Non-taxpayers and lower-rate taxpayers cannot claim this tax back, though.

With a single endowment bond, you can take income of up to 5 per cent of the investment each year until the end of the bond's term without paying any tax. If income of more than 5 per cent is taken, a higher-rate taxpayer may have to pay some tax.

With a series of endowments, an endowment policy is cashed in every year to provide the income. This income is effectively tax-free (although the company may have paid some tax).

At the end of the term the proceeds from an endowment bond are free of tax unless you are a higher-rate taxpayer, but you may get *top-slicing relief* – see Chapter 7 for details.

Note that the taxation of all single-premium bonds is being reviewed, and in November 1996 the government issued a consultative document containing proposals for reform of these special tax rules for discussion within the insurance industry and with other interested parties (including Consumers' Association). The government announced in the March 1998 Budget that it is giving further consideration to those proposals aimed at closing the main tax-avoidance loopholes, but as we went to press no changes have been made.

How to choose a bond

For a list of which companies issue which types of bond, get a copy of the most recent issue of *Money Management** magazine. But because bonds may be available for a short period only, the returns listed in such a magazine may soon be out of date.

Telephone the companies offering the best returns on suitable bonds and ask for details of their latest bonds. The interest rates companies quote are usually those which a basic-rate taxpayer would get. If you're not a basic-rate taxpayer, ask them what someone in your tax position would get from their bond (after tax). Then choose the bond that gives the best return for the period for which you want to invest. You could ask a couple of independent financial advisers to do this for you.

In general:
■ if you don't pay tax or you are a lower-rate taxpayer, a guaranteed income or growth bond is unlikely to be suitable for you – see Chapter 2 for alternatives
■ if you pay tax at the higher rate, a series of single-premium endowments may well give you the best returns

or, if you can arrange for the bond to end in a year when you pay only basic-rate tax (after you've retired, perhaps), one single-premium endowment bond.

Warning: if you cash in all (or part) of a bond based on an endowment policy, your 'total income' (see Chapter 7) is increased. For most people, this has no significance at all. But if you get age-related tax allowances, for people who are 65 or over during the tax year, you could find that your tax bill rises – see Chapter 3 for details.

Guaranteed equity bonds

These are a relatively new form of investment that provide a guaranteed return linked in some way to the growth in share prices. So, for example, you might be offered 133 per cent of the growth in the FTSE-100 share index, or 100 per cent of your initial investment. Beyond this common purpose, they come in a myriad different forms, which makes it particularly difficult to compare them. Broadly, however, they fall into three categories:

■ **bonds based on building society accounts** These are effectively just high-interest building society accounts, with a fixed term and fixed interest rate (expressed as a percentage of the growth in share prices)
■ **single-premium insurance bonds** If based on endowment policies, these usually have a fixed term of around five years, while those based on whole-life policies may have no fixed term
■ **unit trusts with a guarantee attached**.

It follows, therefore, that their tax treatment will depend on the underlying investments. See Chapter 22 for the comparative merits of insurance bonds and unit trusts, and Chapter 11 for the taxation of building society accounts.

When guaranteed equity bonds first appeared, some were advertised and sold in a particularly misleading way: for example, the guaranteed return related purely to the growth in share prices, the income that shares also provide being conveniently forgotten. The industry regulators expressed their disapproval, and practices should have improved, but even so it is worth proceeding with caution. In particular, check the following:

■ what exactly is guaranteed? Remember that the better the guarantee, the more the cost of providing it – particularly if interest rates are low. So, very broadly, if you go for a lower guarantee, the bond is more likely to beat it than if you go for a higher guarantee

- how much would you get if you cashed in early? Some bonds guarantee the amount, others just pay the 'market value' of the bond
- do you have to take your money out at the end of the investment period? If you don't, you have more flexibility in case share prices are low at the end of the normal term
- what charges will you pay? This will depend on the underlying investment, so, for example, building society bond charges are rolled into their rate of return, while insurance bonds usually have an initial charge of around 5 per cent and an annual charge of, say, 1 per cent.

Company safety

At the moment insurance companies are closely supervised by the Department of Trade and Industry (DTI), which can intervene in the affairs of an insurance company if it's getting into difficulties, e.g. by preventing it taking on any new business. Friendly societies are supervised in much the same way, but by the Friendly Societies Commission* (a different government department). As a result of the changes to the financial regulatory system (see Chapter 5), the Financial Services Authority (FSA)* will take over the powers and responsibilities of both the Insurance Directorate of the DTI* and the Friendly Societies Commission from 1999.

22

UNIT-LINKED LIFE INSURANCE

In the past, unit-linked insurance was attractive mainly because of the favourable tax rules – in particular, tax relief on the premiums you paid. Over the years, the tax rules have become less favourable, and alternatives such as Personal Equity Plans (PEPs) or the new Individual Savings Accounts (ISAs) may be more attractive to some investors – see Chapter 8.

If you want to invest in shares (direct or via unit trusts), whether regularly month by month or in a lump sum, a PEP or an ISA have clear advantages over unit-linked insurance, since the return from the money you invest is totally free of tax, and charges can be lower. But if you want to invest more than the upper limits for a PEP (in the 1998–9 tax year, £6,000 in a general PEP plus £3,000 in a 'single-company' PEP), or from April 1999, £5,000 in an ISA (of which £1,000 may go into life insurance), unit-linked insurance could still be worth considering. Unit-linked insurance bonds could also be worth considering if you want to draw an income.

To invest, you buy either a single-premium bond, e.g. an equity, property or managed bond, or a unit-linked regular premium plan. Both are technically life insurance policies, though the amount of life cover you get may be small.

In general, when you invest, your money buys you units in a fund of investments run by an insurance company or friendly society, less a deduction for charges. The unit price goes up and down as the value of the investment in the fund, e.g. property, shares and so on, fluctuates.

When you sell your units, what you get back depends on the price of the units at the time. If the fund has been performing badly, you could make a loss. On the other hand, you stand the chance of making a profit if the fund is doing well when you sell.

The first part of this chapter deals with things that apply in general, whether you've got a lump sum to invest or want to save something each month. The second part of the chapter looks at particular types of policy.

How unit-linking works

Where your money is invested

Your money goes into a fund of investments, usually run by the insurance company or friendly society. Most companies run a number of funds. The main types are: equity funds investing in the UK, or other countries such as North American funds, European funds or Far Eastern funds; fixed-interest funds or cash funds – so investing in short-term loans, bank deposit accounts, or other money market investments; property funds investing directly into properties (usually commercial); or managed funds which invest in a mixture of all the different types of investments.

A number of equity funds are invested through a unit trust, and managed funds may be invested in a selection of unit trusts. In the next section we help you decide whether unit trusts or unit-linked insurance funds are the best type of investment for you.

What should you expect if you invest?

Funds investing in property and shares all aim at long-term growth.

Investing on a regular basis, instead of putting a lump sum into a bond, removes the danger of investing all your money at the wrong time. On the other hand, it also removes the chance of doing extremely well by investing all your money when unit prices are low; and the success of your investment, whichever way you choose, will still depend very much on the price of your units at the time you cash them in.

Reducing the risks

Unit values can go down as well as up and the unit values of funds in different geographical or industrial sectors can rise and fall at different times. In general, the more specialised a fund is, the more you should avoid putting all or most of your money into it.

A fund specialising in Japanese stocks, for example, at one time showed spectacular returns (throughout the 1980s) but this type of fund has performed very badly since, particularly when compared to other countries' stocks. To minimise the risk of having your money in the wrong sector at the wrong time and to maximise your chances of being ready to take advantage of a rising sector, you should spread your money across different types of investment.

The easiest way to do this is by investing in a managed fund. Alternatively, try to invest in two or more different types of fund, if you have a large sum to invest.

Keeping track of your investment

You can follow the fortunes of your investment by looking up the unit price in a newspaper (the *Financial Times* lists most companies' unit prices – look under the section headed *Insurances* in the FT *Managed Funds Service* section).

Buying and selling

Buying and selling units in a unit-linked insurance fund is the same as buying and selling units in a unit trust, and you can switch your money between the company's funds fairly easily. However, there may be heavy penalties if you cash in your policy early.

Each unit normally has two prices. What you pay for the units (the *offer* price) is usually between 5 and 6 per cent more than what you can sell your units for (the *bid* price). Details of buying and selling units are given in Chapter 17.

Switching

The majority of insurance companies allow you to switch your money from one fund to another, e.g. from the equity fund to the property fund, without paying their initial charge again. This could prove to be a useful facility for investors who want to move their money around between different types of investment from time to time in the hope of keeping it in the type of investment that will increase in value quickest.

Most companies make some charge when you switch, typically £15 each time you move. But most companies allow you one free switch a year. There may be a minimum amount you can switch, usually £250, £500 or £1,000.

Policy wording

The policy document is the contract between you and the insurance company, so it makes sense to see a copy before you invest. Check that most of the following points are spelled out:

■ how the fund is valued. For example, it might show that stocks and shares are valued at the market prices quoted on the Stock Exchange

■ that property in the fund is valued by an independent valuer, such as a surveyor

■ the maximum period between valuations

■ how unit prices are worked out

■ the charges the company makes, and the other costs it can deduct from the fund

■ that you won't be double-charged if your fund invests in other funds run by the company

■ what happens to the fund's income.

Single-premium bonds

With these policies, you hand over a lump sum to the insurance company. The company takes part of the money to cover its expenses and to provide you with a little life insurance. The rest of the money buys units in whichever fund you choose.

Who should consider investing in these bonds?

The current tax rules give them some advantage for higher-rate taxpayers who've used up their capital gains tax allowance, though a PEP or ISA, where the return is totally free of tax, would be a better choice. Single-premium bonds can also be useful for higher-rate taxpayers who want to draw an income from the bond. However, the taxation of these is being reviewed.

In theory, bonds are also suitable for people who will want to switch from one type of fund to another from time to time, in the hope of putting their money where it will increase in value quickest, though the chances of doing this successfully are not great.

If you are not in one of these groups, but still want an investment where you lock a lump sum away for several years in the hope that it will increase in value in the long term, a unit trust is an alternative worth considering.

Bonds or unit trusts?

Investing in a single-premium bond is very similar to investing a lump sum in a unit trust. The advantages or disadvantages of either investment depend largely on taxation and how the charges compare.

Life insurance companies and unit trust companies pay income tax on the dividends they receive on shares in their portfolios. If you are a non-taxpayer, you can reclaim this tax from the Inland Revenue for a unit trust investment, but not for an insurance-based investment.

When shares in an insurance fund are sold at a profit, insurance funds have to pay capital gains tax. Insurance companies set aside an amount to meet this tax which is passed on to the policyholder indirectly, through lower unit values.

Unit trust investors pay capital gains tax according to their own personal liability when they cash in their units. Since you are allowed to make a certain amount of gains (£6,800 in the 1998–9 tax year) before having to pay capital gains tax, you should invest in a unit trust if you are not likely to use up this allowance.

If you want to withdraw money from a unit trust to provide an income, you could face a capital gains tax bill. But special rules let you take some income from a bond without paying tax at the time. See 'Taking an income', below, for details. When the bond is finally cashed in, at present only higher-rate taxpayers have to pay income tax on the gains they have made and only at the higher rate. They may have to pay a slightly higher rate of extra tax on unit trust income. This is explained in greater detail in Chapter 7.

Single-premium bonds are more suitable for investors who want a spread of investments and like to change from fund to fund. You pay higher charges for taking your money out of one unit trust and putting it into another and you will either use up some of your capital gains tax allowance or face a capital gains tax liability every time you do this. See 'Switching',on page 339.

Taking an income

With most insurance company funds, the income earned by the fund's investments is generally put back into the fund to buy more shares, property or whatever.

You can normally arrange to cash in part of your investment from time to time, on either a regular basis (under a withdrawal scheme) or an irregular basis. If you're a higher-rate taxpayer, cashing in part of your bond could possibly lead to a bill for income tax (see Chapter 7), but under the current rules paying tax on the gain you make at the time can generally be avoided if you withdraw no more than 5 per cent (or one-twentieth) of your original investment in any one year.

To make getting an income easier, bonds are often sold as a cluster or series of identical mini-policies so that you can cash in a whole policy, or several policies at a time, according to your needs. The tax rules are simpler, too, if you cash in a whole policy rather than part of one. Of course, cashing units to get an income will start eating into the value of your investment if the unit price is increasing at a lower rate than the rate at which you are cashing units.

Charges

The insurance companies normally make:
- an initial charge of around 5 per cent of the amount you invest. This is usually included in the spread between the buying and selling prices
- a regular charge. The insurance company deducts a charge from the fund at regular intervals to cover the costs of managing the fund. This charge might add up to between 0.5 and 1.5 per cent of the value of the fund each year. Brokers charge between 0.75 per cent and 1 per cent on top of these charges for investment in a broker-managed fund.

However, check if (and by how much) charges can change once you've invested.

Tax

When you cash your bond, the gain you make is added to your investment income for the tax year. The gain is the amount you get (including any amounts you got earlier on which you weren't taxed at the time) less the amount you paid for the bond in the first place. You don't pay basic-rate tax on the gain (the insurance company has already paid tax on the income and capital gains of the fund), but you do have to pay any higher-rate tax that is due, though your tax bill may be reduced by *top-slicing relief*. The tax rules are complicated (especially if you cash in only part of your bond), but can be used to your advantage, if you are careful over when you cash your units in – see Chapter 7.

Switching your investment between funds does not count as cashing in your bond for tax purposes, so does not affect your tax position at all.

Warning
The tax rules are being reviewed and are likely to change in the future. It might be sensible to wait until detailed rules are available before committing yourself.

How to invest in single-premium bonds

Minimum investment
All the companies set a minimum amount you can invest, usually £1,000. Note that if you invest a substantial amount in one go, over £25,000, say, or invest in a newly launched fund, some companies give you extra units, e.g. 1 per cent more.

Age limits
Many insurance companies set minimum age limits for bondholders, 18, say. And a few set maximum age limits for new bondholders, 80, say.

Adding to your investment
As the term implies, a single-premium bond is bought with one lump sum payment. With an *additional premium facility* you have the option of buying more units at any one time by paying an additional premium. (This is subject to a minimum amount, which varies from £250 to £1,000 depending on the company.) These units are added to the original policy you took out. The advantage in doing this is that if you are liable to tax on the gain when you cash the policy in, top-slicing relief relating to the additional premium can be spread over all the years since you originally invested, and not only from the date you paid the additional premium. This could reduce your tax bill.

Cashing in part of your investment
Most companies allow you to cash, i.e. sell, part of your bond, but you often have to cash a minimum amount, and

---

Life insurance

Single-premium bonds normally pay out only slightly more than the value of the investment if the investor dies, say 101 per cent of the value of the units. For a young man under 30, however, the death benefit could be 2½ times the value of the bond. The death benefits are limited to reduce the costs. A large amount of life cover would be expensive for an older person. If what you want is greater protection for your dependants, see page 324.

leave a minimum amount. The minimum amount you can cash is usually £50 or £100, and the minimum amount you must leave varies between £100 and £1,000. There may be a maximum on the amount you can cash in – say 10 per cent of the value of your investment.

If you already have shares

Most companies are prepared to give you units in their funds in exchange for your holdings of stocks and shares through their *share exchange schemes*, though different companies have different rules about the size of the holdings they'll accept and the value they'll place on them.

Usually, if the company is happy to put your shares into one of its funds, it will value them at the price it would have to pay to buy them on the open market. This benefits you because if you sold them, you'd normally get a somewhat lower price and would have to pay commission to a stockbroker.

Note that exchanging your shareholding counts as a disposal for capital gains tax purposes, i.e. you may have to pay capital gains tax on any gain you've made. However, there are ways in which the tax can be kept to a minimum, so get professional advice, particularly if you are exchanging substantial shareholdings.

Where to buy bonds

Bonds are sold in a variety of ways: through newspaper advertisements, by independent financial advisers, by company salespeople, and by agents such as accountants and solicitors. Advisers, agents and so on normally get commission from the insurance company for selling bonds; the rate varies between 3 and 6 per cent or so of what you pay for the bond. The amount must be shown in the *key features document* you get before you buy the policy see pages 331–2.

Some independent advisers offer their own *broker-managed bonds*. An insurance company provides the life cover while the adviser chooses from that company's range of funds to make up what he or she thinks is the best mix in his or her own fund. Many such funds are listed in the *Financial Times* under the insurance company's funds.

Unit-linked regular premium plans

With a unit-linked regular premium plan you agree to pay premiums at regular intervals. In return, the insurance company uses some of your money to pay for life cover and expenses. The rest is invested in the funds of your choice.

You can select a plan that lasts for between ten years and the rest of your life (a few plans last for fewer than ten years, but they're not common). You can choose, within certain limits, the amount you think your dependants would need were you to die before the end of the policy.

Types of plan

Unit-linked plans fall into three main categories:
- maximum investment plans – for minimum life cover and high investment
- endowment plans – for higher life cover and longer-term investment
- flexible cover plans – the percentage of your premium that provides investment, and that provides protection, can be varied throughout your life.

If you die

If you die during the period of your plan, the life insurance company guarantees to pay out a set amount of life cover or death benefit. However, your dependants would receive the full value of your units if this is more than the death benefit.

The amount of death benefit payable under your policy depends on the length of your plan and the premiums you pay as well as your age and state of health when you take out your plan.

The end of your plan

When your plan comes to an end you should be entitled to a lump sum on which you do not have to pay tax. This is because most unit-linked policies are set up as *qualifying policies* under the Inland Revenue rules – see Chapter 7. However, although the lump sum is tax-free in your hands, the insurance company will already have paid tax on the money in its funds. With some plans, a *capital gains tax deduction* is shown on the statement you get when the plan matures. This is tax on the company's gains, not yours; you cannot claim it back, even if it is below your annual capital gains tax-free slice.

Insurance companies will give you an illustration of what a plan will provide, based on a standard growth rate laid down by industry regulators, but using the company's own charges. Remember, though, that the final payout is not guaranteed and neither are these growth rates. Only the death benefit is guaranteed.

At the end of some plans you may have the option of continuing your plan, normally with a higher proportion of future premiums being invested for you.

How the plans work

Maximum investment plans

These plans may also be known as capital accumulation plans. They usually last for ten years but on maturity some plans give you the option to carry on the policy while drawing an income, providing you keep paying premiums of at least half the largest annual premium paid during the initial ten-year term. The minimum premium can be as little as £10 per month or as much as £100 per month, and there is no maximum investment.

These plans usually provide the minimum life cover under the 'qualifying' rules. A low level of life cover means that the maximum amount of your premiums can be invested.

Unit-linked endowment plans

Endowment plans, often called savings plans, can last for up to 25, or even 30 years, and provide a higher level of life cover. Minimum premiums for these policies vary from £10 per month to £50 per month.

These plans have become accepted by many lenders as a way of repaying a mortgage, although in recent years there have been more attractive types of mortgage schemes than an endowment mortgage.

Flexible cover plans

Sometimes called flexible whole life plans, these plans last throughout your life, though you may have to pay premiums only until a given age, 85, say. Given the size of the premium and your age and state of health at the start of the plan, you can choose the amount of cover you want.

You can alter the level of cover and premiums to suit your needs during the various stages of your life. Some plans include a variety of benefits and insurance you can add on to the plan as and when you need them.

Monitoring your investment

With longer-term policies and whole life policies, life insurance companies keep an eye on your investment to make sure its value will be sufficient to provide the expected payouts. This is done by reviewing your policy, usually after ten years and then every five years.

During the last few years your policy may be reviewed once a year. Some companies suggest you invest in a cash fund during the last five years so as not to lose any of the money you have made if share prices fall suddenly near the end of your plan.

If the growth of your investments has fallen below the expected rate, you will probably have to pay higher premiums (at the rate applying to your age at the time) or accept reduced benefits.

On the other hand, if the growth of your investment is greater than the expected rate, you may be able to reduce your premiums or build up a larger sum. If you have an endowment mortgage, you may be able to repay your mortgage early (with the lender's agreement). However, it is looking more likely that some borrowers who took out policies in the late 1980s will have to increase premiums.

If you stop your plan early

You should look on most unit-linked life insurance plans as a long-term commitment. The way that most companies arrange their charges means that their expenses, such as administration and commission to brokers or salespeople as well as life cover, are deducted from the premiums in the first few years.

If you cashed in your policy (often called *surrendering* it) in the first two years, say, you may not get anything back and you would be most unlikely to get back as much as you had paid in. The amount you would get varies from company to company, depending on how they calculate the cash-in value.

If you don't need to cash in your plan but want to stop investing, you could make your plan *paid up*. This means you stop paying your premiums but the money you've already paid in is invested in the fund. Even so, you may be allocated only the number of units that you could buy with the money you'd get if you actually cashed in your plan.

Alternatively, go for a plan that is broken up into a series of mini-policies. Then, if your circumstances change later, you have the option of cashing just some of your units, keeping your plan going and paying a reduced premium.

Provided you've kept the policy going for ten years, or three-quarters of the premium-paying term if less, you shouldn't have to pay tax on any gains from cashing in your policy.

You may also be able to get cash from your policy by taking out a *policy loan*, which you could then use to pay the premiums. Normally you can borrow up to 90 per cent of the cash-in value of your plan, and the interest rate will often be lower than that for other forms of borrowing. The loan repayments and interest payments are usually paid annually in addition to your normal premiums. See Chapter 21 for guidance on working out the best way of stopping your plan early, but note that it is not generally possible to sell a unit-linked policy.

Charges

As we've already said, the costs of administration and life insurance are met by deductions from your premiums in the first few years.

For example, with an endowment plan you might get a unit allocation of 55 per cent in the first year. In other words, just under half of your premiums are going towards administration costs and life cover in the first year. Your unit allocations depend on the length of your plan, the amount of life cover and the premiums you pay.

Don't forget that there is also a difference between the price at which you buy and the price at which you sell units, usually 5 to 6 per cent. Also, a management fee is deducted from the fund, usually between 0.5 and 1.5 per cent a year. Companies now have to tell you how their current charges reduce the value of your policy, assuming you keep it for the whole term. You get this information built into the *key features document* the company must provide before you buy. It is shown as the 'Reduction in Yield' (RIY). The smaller the RIY the better, but charges can go up or down during the life of the plan, and are much higher if you cash in early.

Should you invest?

Keeping insurance and investment separate

Unit-linked life insurance policies can lock away your money for a long time. It is best to keep your insurance and your investment separate – you might want your money back early but still need protection for your dependants.

If all you want is life cover to protect your dependants from financial hardship, term insurance is the cheapest way to buy life cover – see Chapter 21. It may be possible to convert it into an investment-type policy during its term without having to give proof of continued good health.

If you are considering a unit-linked insurance plan, compare the costs and the benefits with a separate term insurance policy and a savings plan suited to your tax position, e.g. a unit trust savings plan. Higher-rate taxpayers in particular should consider a PEP, or from 6 April 1999 an ISA, which produces income and capital gains totally free of tax. Chapter 9 gives a bird's-eye view of the main investments available.

Provided none of the points above applies to you, a unit-linked regular premium plan may be suitable if you are a higher-rate taxpayer and already have the maximum PEP allowed (£6,000 a year, plus a further £3,000 a year in a single-company PEP in the 1998–9 tax year).

If you want to invest in a fund, the main differences between the taxation of unit trust savings plans and unit-linked insurance plans are set out in the table below.

Life insurance or unit trusts?

	Unit-linked regular premium plan	Unit trust savings plan
Income tax	Paid by the life insurance company and *cannot* be claimed back by non-taxpayers: no further tax payable by higher-rate taxpayers	Tax credit of 20 per cent deducted by the unit trust company and *can* be claimed back by non-taxpayers: no further tax payable by basic-rate taxpayers, but higher-rate taxpayers pay an extra 20 per cent
Capital gains tax	Paid by the insurance company and reflected in lower unit values	Not paid by the unit trust company
At the end of a plan	No tax is payable on qualifying policies (tax has already been paid within the funds)	Capital gains tax is charged according to personal liability – you get a tax-free allowance (£6,800 in the 1998–9 tax year)
Cashing in a plan early	If policy has been going less than 10 years or ¾ of the policy term, whichever is less, higher-rate taxpayers may pay the difference between the higher and lower rate of income tax on any gains	

Special features to look out for

Endowment plans and flexible cover plans may offer some of these features:

- **waiver of premium option** – you stop paying premiums if you become ill or disabled over a long period (more than six months, say) and can't continue with your normal job. Some companies will continue the plan for you if you have a joint policy and either partner is ill or disabled
- **total disability cover** – some companies will pay out the death benefit if an accident or illness leaves you unable to work again
- **accidental death benefit** – if you die as the result of an accident, the plan pays out an extra lump sum
- **inflation linking** – you can increase your cover (or premium) in line with changes in the RPI
- **special event cover** – a further plan can be taken out, or your cover can be increased, on marriage or the birth (or adoption) of a child without your having to prove you are still in good health
- **family income benefit** – if you die, the plan pays out a regular tax-free income for a given number of years rather than a lump sum
- **low-start option** – for the first year of your plan, premiums are reduced to, say, half the normal amount. Then they will increase by, say, 20 per cent a year for 5 years or 10 per cent a year for 10 years, and be level for the rest of your plan. This option usually costs more in the long run
- **stop-start option** – if you are made redundant or suffer financial hardship, you may be allowed to stop paying premiums for a limited period (up to two years, say) and keep your policy going. You will have to make up for these missed premiums at a later date, though
- **increasing or extending options** – you may be able to increase your cover or extend the term of the policy without having to prove that you are still in good health
- **term insurance** – if you die within a given period, the plan pays out an extra lump sum. Check, though, that it isn't cheaper to take a separate term insurance policy.

Increasingly, whole-life plans are giving you the option of building in permanent health insurance (which pays out if you are off work through illness) or cover against critical or terminal illness or major medical expenses. This may be convenient, but if you need this cover you could get it more cheaply by buying a separate policy from another company. Watch out, too, for any differences in the tax treatment of such plans: they may be 'non-qualifying' in tax terms (see

Chapter 7), which means that higher-rate taxpayers may have a tax bill when the policy pays out. Non-qualifying whole-life plans are often called 'universal life' plans.

If you already have a unit-linked policy

Over the years, unit-linked policies have changed a great deal. If you already have a unit-linked policy, you may find it is different from the types of policies now available and described in this chapter. It would be unwise to cash in an old-style policy in favour of a new one without considering the surrender value and the cost of setting up a new policy. What is more, your life cover will be more expensive now that you are older than when you took out your policy.

The government still subsidises the premiums on policies taken out before the Budget in March 1984 – see page 325.

Choosing a company

Sadly, there is no foolproof way of picking a company whose policies are going to perform better than those of other companies. In particular, just because a company's funds have done well in the past it does not mean that they will do as well in the future. But, when choosing a company, there are a number of things to watch out for most, if not all of which should be indicated in the *key features document* (see pages 331–2 for more details).

If things go wrong

It's important to realise that although the performance of your bond or policy depends upon the performance of a fund of investments, investors do not own the investments. However, insurance companies, but not friendly societies (to which different legislation applies), are covered by the Policyholders' Protection Act. See Chapter 21 for details.

The selling and marketing of these plans are also covered by the Financial Services Act allowing you to take up complaints with the relevant *Self-Regulating Organisation*. See Chapter 5 for details of these and other useful organisations.

23

ANNUITIES

You may come across annuities either in connection with pensions, or as a form of investment you buy yourself. In this chapter, we concentrate on annuities you buy yourself, separately from a pension: for more on annuities tied to pensions, see Chapter 15.

An annuity you buy yourself is probably worth considering only if you've reached your 70s. You hand over a lump sum to an insurance company in return for a guaranteed income for the rest of your life. The older you are when the annuity begins, the larger the income it gives you. For example, in return for £10,000, a 72-year-old man who paid basic-rate tax could (in March 1998) have got an after-tax income of around £1,050 for life.

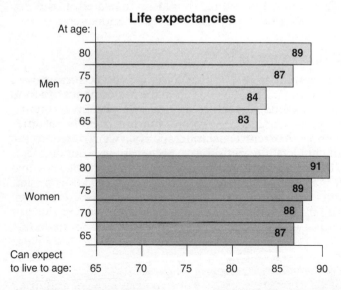

Life expectancies

At age:

Men
- 80: 89
- 75: 87
- 70: 84
- 65: 83

Women
- 80: 91
- 75: 89
- 70: 88
- 65: 87

Can expect to live to age: 65 70 75 80 85 90

Source: Equitable Life

The insurance company will make a large loss on people who live for years and years, but will make a handsome profit on those who die early, because with most types of annuity, however soon you die after buying it, you get none of your lump sum back. The diagram opposite shows what age you can expect to live to, if you're 65, 70, 75 or 80. You'll see that someone who has already reached 80 can be expected to live to a greater age than a 70-year-old.

People who buy annuities tend to be healthier than those who don't, and the insurance companies allow for this in the income they offer. In this chapter we look at the various different types of annuity that are available, and assess their pros and cons. Then you'll find details of home income schemes – where you borrow money to buy an annuity and use your home as security.

Types of annuity

This chapter deals with *immediate* annuities. With these, the company starts paying you the income 'immediately'. There are also *deferred* annuities, where you pay a lump sum now and arrange for the income to start in the future (in five years' time, say). Deferred annuities form the basis of many personal pension plans.

The most common type of immediate annuity is a *level* annuity, where the income is the same each year. For a given outlay, this type will probably give you the largest income to start with, though, of course, inflation will erode its buying-power over the years. Another type is an *increasing* annuity, where the income increases at regular intervals by an amount you decide on when buying the annuity. *Unit-linked* annuities are offered by a few companies. With these, your income is linked to the performance of the fund (e.g. of property) and so goes up and down in amount. *With-profits* annuities were offered by only three of the largest companies as we went to press. The initial income is comparable to other types of annuities and each year extra bonuses are added depending on the profitability of the company. Their attraction lies in the prospects of high bonuses, although they are not guaranteed. *Inflation-linked* annuities (also offered by a few companies) give an income that is linked to the Retail Prices Index; but this type usually provides the lowest starting income.

The basic type of annuity stops when the person buying it dies: a *single life* annuity. But you can also get annuities that carry on until both the person buying the annuity and someone else, usually a wife or husband, are dead. These are called *joint life, last survivor* annuities.

Variations

Companies normally quote their annuity rates on the basis that the income will be paid to you half-yearly, starting six months after you buy the annuity. These terms may not suit you, e.g. you might want to be paid monthly; you can usually get any of the variations listed below, although some are fairly costly in terms of a reduced yearly income.

■ Payments to be made more frequently than half-yearly, i.e. quarterly or monthly. The same outlay gives a smaller yearly income than an annuity paid half-yearly – the more frequent the payments, the smaller the income.

■ First payment to be made at the time you buy the annuity. The same outlay gives rather less income than an annuity paid half-yearly, starting six months after you buy it.

■ First payment to be made a year after you buy the annuity, then at yearly intervals. The same outlay gives a higher yearly income than an annuity paid half-yearly.

■ An extra, proportionate, payment (made after you die) for the period between the date you receive the last half-yearly payment and the date you die. This will give less income than the normal version.

■ Some of the payments to be *guaranteed*, i.e. paid out by the company for a minimum number of years even if you die early. The same outlay gives you less income than the normal version – how much less depends on your age and the length of the guaranteed period (usually, five or ten years).

■ A payment (made after you die) of the difference between your outlay and the income paid out so far by the company. You get less income than with the normal version.

■ With a joint life, last survivor annuity, less income to be paid after the first person dies, often half or two-thirds of the amount paid while both are alive. The starting income will be higher than normal.

The income you get

This depends on a number of factors, in particular your age when you buy the annuity, the type of annuity you go for and the level of interest rates in general at the time you take the annuity out. A woman gets a lower income than a man of the same age (women, on average, live longer than men).

Joint life, last survivor annuities pay lower amounts overall.

Insurance companies tend to vary their annuity rates frequently and at short notice, but what you get stays at the rate that applied when you bought the annuity.

Tax at 20 per cent will normally have been deducted from the annuity income before you get it and basic-rate taxpayers will not need to pay any more tax, although higher-rate taxpayers will need to pay an additional 20 per cent on the income element. The income you get from an annuity consists partly of interest and partly of a return of the capital you invested, and each part is treated differently for tax purposes – see page 357.

Inflation

When deciding whether to buy an annuity you should consider the effect that rising prices will have on the buying power of your income. For example, a woman of 70 who buys an annuity could expect to live for about another 18 years. If prices rise at about 3 per cent a year, each £100 of income she gets at the start will be worth only £60 or so in 18 years' time. Of course, no one knows what inflation will be over the next 18 years: it could be more than 3 per cent a year; 6 per cent inflation a year would make it worth only £35 after the same time. To see how rising prices might reduce the buying power of an annuity, look at the diagram overleaf.

To protect the buying power of your capital you could consider investing in index-linked National Savings Certificates (see Chapter 12) – cashing them in if you need income – or index-linked British Government stocks (see Chapter 19).

An annuity would then be worth considering for part of your remaining money if you're over 70 or so.

Why an annuity is a gamble

Whether or not an annuity proves to be a good buy in the long run depends on:

■ *how long you live*. Obviously an annuity will be a better buy if you live for years and years after buying it, than if you die soon after investing your money. If you are in poor health, you'd be wise to steer clear of annuities, and invest your money elsewhere

■ *what happens to interest rates after you have bought your annuity*. The annuity income offered by an insurance company is related to the general level of interest rates *at*

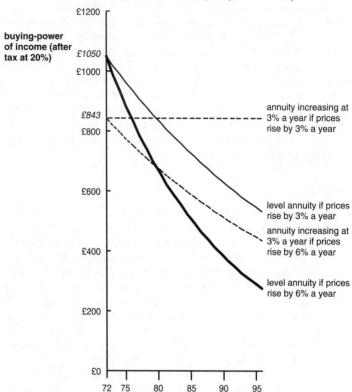

Fall in buying power of income from an annuity
(annuity bought for £10,000 by 72-year-old man)

buying-power of income (after tax at 20%)

annuity increasing at 3% a year if prices rise by 3% a year

level annuity if prices rise by 3% a year

annuity increasing at 3% a year if prices rise by 6% a year

level annuity if prices rise by 6% a year

the time you buy. If, later on, interest rates go up, companies are likely to offer better annuities, but you'll be stuck with your relatively poor-value-for-money annuity. On the other hand, if interest rates go down, companies will offer poorer annuities, and you'll be sitting pretty
■ *the extent to which inflation will erode the buying power of your income.*

However, you have no idea how long you're going to live, nor what's going to happen to interest rates or to inflation, so you cannot know if an annuity will turn out to be a good buy or not.

Should you buy an annuity?

Once you have bought an annuity and handed over your money, you can't go back on the arrangement, so you shouldn't buy one without pausing for thought. You should first make sure your dependants would have enough to live on when you die. Then consider how much you want to leave your family (or favourite charity), how much you want to put by for a rainy day, and how much you want to leave available for holidays, replacing your car, television and so on. You could consider spending part of what is left on an annuity – *provided* the extra income you get, compared with what you'd get from another type of investment, is large enough to compensate you for handing over part of your savings for good.

Which type?

A unit-linked annuity, where your income is linked to investment performance, is unlikely to suit most people. The income will vary from year to year, and might be very low in some years.

Your choice, therefore, lies among the remaining types. A level annuity pays the highest starting income, but gives you no protection against inflation. An increasing annuity, where, for example, each year's income is 3 per cent higher than the year before, gives protection against lowish rates of inflation. A with-profits annuity combines the advantage of an increasing income with the benefits of possible bonuses. While the initial income may be high, the bonuses are not guaranteed so you can't depend on them and in extreme circumstances they may go down. An inflation-linked (index-linked) annuity is the type that provides the best protection against inflation, but pays the lowest starting income. The tax-free part of the income (see below) is fixed with level and inflation-linked annuities, but rises with increasing annuities (in step with the increases in the annuity). This treats index-linked annuities unfairly, because the whole of any increases are fully taxed: so even this type cannot protect you fully against inflation. Increasing and inflation-linked annuities, which start at a relatively low level, work out best if you live a long time.

All in all, unless you sincerely believe that inflation will stay at a low level, an increasing or inflation-linked annuity is probably the most sensible choice.

Tax treatment

Part of the income is treated as your initial outlay being returned to you, and is tax-free. The remainder counts as interest, and is added to your income.

The amount of the tax-free part is worked out according to Inland Revenue rules. It is fixed as an amount of money, not as a proportion of the income from the annuity. For each type of annuity the tax-free amount is based on your age when you buy the annuity, the amount you pay for it, and how often the income is paid. The older you are when you take out the annuity, the higher the capital part of the income you get, and the higher the total amount of income. This is because the older you are, the shorter the period for which the insurance company expects to have to pay the income.

With increasing annuities, the tax-free amount normally increases at the same rate as the income from the annuity increases. With unit-linked and inflation-linked annuities the tax-free amount stays fixed.

An annuity is treated in this special way only if you buy it voluntarily with your own money, e.g. if you use a lump sum from your employer's pension scheme.

The insurance company normally deducts tax at 20 per cent from the taxable part of your annuity income before paying you. If you are a basic-rate taxpayer you will not need to pay anything more. If you are a non-taxpayer, you can claim tax back from your tax office. If you pay tax at the higher rate, you'll have to pay the extra 20 per cent tax.

If your income from all sources, including the taxable part of the annuity, is below certain limits, you can apply through the insurance company to have your annuity income paid without deduction of tax.

From which company?

Companies can change their annuity rates frequently. To choose a company yourself, get an up-to-date copy of *Money Management** magazine, which regularly compares companies' immediate annuity rates.

Company safety

At present the Policyholders' Protection Act gives you partial protection should your insurance company go bust. As a result of the changes to the financial regulatory system (see Chapter 5) the Financial Services Authority (FSA)* will take over the powers and responsibilities from 1999. However, you'd still be faced with a lot of anxiety while it was happening. To avoid this, you may do as well to avoid very new or very small insurance companies. Get an independent insurance adviser to check for you.

Get quotations from companies that do well for your age (or one close to it). The rates, however, may well have changed since the magazine went to press, so it might be as well to consult an independent insurance adviser. Some advisers subscribe to computer systems that list annuity income from different companies.

Home income schemes

If you're elderly and own your home outright, you may be able to boost your income with a home income scheme.

How the schemes work

You get a loan based on the security of your home. The loan is used to buy an annuity from an insurance company. While you live, you get the income from the annuity from which tax at 20 per cent and interest on the loan have been deducted. When you die, the loan is repaid out of your estate (possibly by the sale of the home) before inheritance tax is worked out. (Note that with some schemes, called *reversions*, you sell all or part of your house to the company. Any increase in the value of the part you have sold then goes to the company, not to you.)

Everyone aged over 65, taxpayer and non-taxpayer, gets tax relief at 23 per cent on the full amount of the loan interest (provided the loan is not more than £30,000). This means their interest payments are reduced by 23p in each pound (in the 1998–9 tax year).

The nuts and bolts

The schemes are available for freehold houses, and for leasehold property with a substantial part of the lease still to run (75 to 80 years, depending on the company). When you apply for a scheme, your home will be valued by an independent valuer – you pay the fee, but it will usually be refunded if you take out the scheme. The most you can usually borrow is a percentage (usually 70 per cent) of the market value of your home up to £30,000.

You may be able to take part of the loan in cash, although at least 90 per cent of the loan must be used to buy an annuity in order to qualify for tax relief. There's often a minimum loan, usually £15,000 or so.

If the house is occupied by two people (husband and wife, or brother and sister, say) the annuity is arranged so that it continues for as long as either person is alive. You generally have to be at least 70 to be eligible for a home income plan (somewhat older if you're a couple applying).

The interest rate is normally fixed at the time you take the loan, and so is the income from the annuity. This means that the income you get from the scheme won't change as time passes. However, there are schemes where the interest rate varies – we don't recommend them, because if interest rates rise, your income would drop. You should also be wary of rolled-up interest schemes, where the payments on the loan are 'rolled-up' and added to the amount you owe; the size of your loan will increase at an alarming rate. With this type, you may have to pay interest (or even sell your home) if the total you owe gets close to the home's value. Fortunately, variable interest rate schemes or roll-up interest schemes are offered by very few lenders.

Pros and cons

If the value of your home goes up after you've taken out the loan, you may be able to use the increase in value to get a further loan and buy another annuity. In this way you might be able to increase your income to keep up with inflation.

Also, while inflation still reduces the buying power of your fixed income, it correspondingly reduces the value of your debt to the insurance company. So rising prices do not wholly work against you.

On the other hand, you'd be almost certain to get a better after-tax increase in your income by paying cash for an annuity (if you could do so) rather than mortgaging your home, and if it's likely you'll have to sell your home in the near future (to move in with relatives or into an old people's home, say) think twice before going for a home income plan. If you do move out altogether later on, you'll have to repay the loan, and may get left with a rather low fixed-income annuity. If you simply move to another house, you can transfer the loan (as with other types of mortgages).

If you get state benefits, such as income support or housing benefit, a home income plan could mean that you'll lose some or all of that benefit; so get advice from an independent adviser before going ahead.

24

COMMODITIES

You might think that investing in commodities is a way of investing your long-term savings so that they stand a chance of keeping pace with inflation. Investing in commodities can, however, give you a very bumpy ride. Chapter 26 tells you about investing in things like stamps, antiques and wine. Here we deal with a different group of commodities: raw materials that are bought and sold in large quantities on organised markets based in the City of London or Chicago. The main raw materials which come into this category fall into the following groups: *metals*, such as copper, lead, gold, silver and zinc; *soft* commodities such as cocoa, coffee, potatoes, wool, nuts and rubber; *energy*, such as crude oil, heating oil and gas; and *grains*, such as maize and soyabeans.

Investment in commodities is high risk, which means that while you might make large gains, you might instead make large losses. So it's suitable only for investors who understand what they are doing, and who have the resources to withstand the possible losses. Indeed, under the *know your customer* provisions of the Financial Services Act (see Chapter 5), commodity brokers are required to be careful about whom they accept as a private investor.

How commodity markets work

Commodities are bought and sold in two main ways:
- for delivery straight away, but in the main, it's end-users of the commodity who buy in this way
- for delivery at an agreed date in the future. This is the market in which investors (often called speculators) are more likely to be interested.

For delivery straight away

You can buy or sell copper, for example, which has already been mined, and is being stored in a warehouse. In the trade, this is known as buying or selling *physicals* or *actuals*; and the price you pay is known as a *spot price*. You have to pay (in full) for the commodity at the time you buy it; and you have to buy at least a minimum amount, e.g. 25 metric tonnes of copper.

The commodity will be kept in a warehouse, and you'll have to pay charges for storing and insuring it.

If you buy a commodity for delivery straight away as an investment, you are hoping that the price of the commodity will go up and you'll eventually be able to sell it at a profit (after taking account of buying and selling costs, and storage and insurance charges).

For delivery on an agreed date in the future

This is the usual way in which investors buy and sell commodities. You agree *now* to buy or sell a fixed amount of, for example, copper at a fixed price for delivery on some agreed date in the future. In the trade, this is known as dealing in *futures* and your agreement is known as a *futures contract*. There are rules about how far in advance you can arrange to buy or sell each commodity. The normal forward period is three months but in some markets you can arrange to buy up to three or more years ahead. If you agree to buy or sell cocoa in December 1998, say, you are said to be dealing in *December 1998 cocoa*.

If you buy a commodity for delivery in the future, you are hoping that its price will rise above the price you've agreed to buy it at, and that you'll be able to sell it at a profit before it is due to be delivered.

However, you can also make a profit if you expect the price of a commodity to fall. You can agree to *sell*, rather than buy, December 1998 cocoa, for example, at a fixed price. You then have to buy, before December 1998 arrives, the cocoa you've agreed to sell. If the price of December 1998 cocoa does indeed fall below the price you've agreed to sell at, you will be able to make a profit on the deal. But if it goes up in price, you'll end up having to buy your cocoa at a higher price than the one you've agreed to sell at, and so make a loss on the deal.

You don't have to pay out the full cost of the futures contract you are dealing in, only a deposit called the *initial margin* (of perhaps 10 per cent of its value). But this doesn't mean that it's only your deposit you can lose. You'll indeed lose a 10 per cent deposit if the value of a futures contract you've bought goes down by 10 per cent by the time you sell it. But if the price goes down by 50 per cent before you sell, you'll lose five times that amount. In practice, if the price falls, your broker (see pages 369–70) will ask you for more money (this is known as a *variation margin call*). If you don't hand over this extra money, the broker is likely to insist that you close down your futures contract straight away and accept the loss you've already made.

Trading in futures is not a long-term investment

If you're an investor (or speculator) who deals in commodity futures, you are not making a long-term investment. You are gambling on what will happen to the price of a commodity over a relatively short period. If you buy December 1998 cocoa, for example, it's what happens to cocoa prices before December 1998 that decides whether you profit or lose on your trade.

You may believe – quite correctly, perhaps – that cocoa prices will double over the next five years, but you can't buy a futures contract which lasts that long. Buying December 1998 cocoa doesn't make sense unless you believe that cocoa prices are going to go up more than expected over the period before then.

Commodity options

A commodity *option* gives you the right to buy or sell a commodity futures contract at a fixed price at any time up to an agreed date. The amount you have to pay to buy an option varies widely, depending on what is expected to happen to the price of the particular futures contract in which you are interested.

The advantage of taking out an option to buy a futures contract is that it gives you the chance of making a profit if the price of the commodity goes up, while at the same time limiting the amount of money you can lose if the price of the commodity falls, to the amount you paid for the option. The main disadvantage is that the price of the futures contract has to go up by at least the amount you paid for the option before you start making a profit, unless the price fluctuations in the commodity make the probable price in the future uncertain. Then your option will go up because you have fixed your purchase price.

Why futures markets exist

Futures markets enable people who trade in commodities, e.g. raw material producers (such as mine-owners and farmers), manufacturers or end-users (such as chocolate firms) and wholesalers, to reduce the risk they face of losing money because of changes in the prices of commodities. Futures markets allow the raw material producers to get a guaranteed price for raw materials they haven't yet produced; and they allow manufacturers to know exactly how much they'll have to pay for their raw materials some months hence. This, in effect, spreads the risk of an unknown sale price of a commodity and tends to have the side effect of lowering the average price of the end products to the consumer.

The investor, who has no intention of producing or using commodities, is one of the people who take on the risk that the producers and manufacturers want to avoid. You, the investor, are the person who loses if, say, you have bought December 1998 cocoa and the price falls before you can sell it. However, you are the person who gains if the price goes up before you sell it.

How commodity prices vary

Commodity prices in general

The chart overleaf shows how the Commodity Research Bureau (CRB) commodity futures index has changed between 1974, when the index started, and the end of 1997. The index is quoted in US dollars, but includes the range of metals, grains and soft commodities and energy that can be traded in London as well as Chicago. The CRB index is one of the most popular indices used to monitor the changes in the commodity futures market.

Twenty years before the start of this chart, commodities were trading at very high prices, due mainly to shortages caused by the Korean War. In the intervening period prices fell fairly steadily until the early 1970s when they shot up again. This chart starts just after the world oil crisis and shows how prices in recent years tend to go up and down fairly quickly. A change of 5 per cent in a month is quite common.

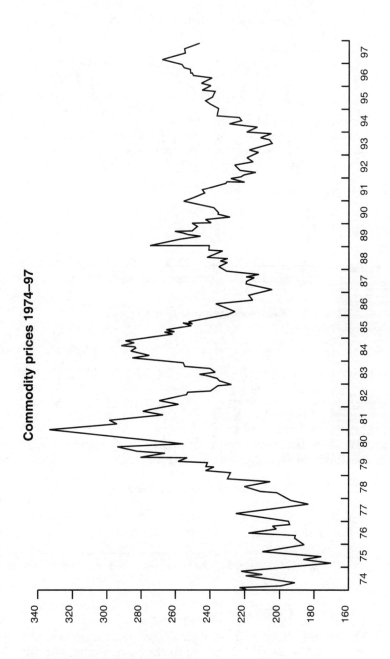

Commodity prices 1974–97

CRB Index of commodity prices (US$)

Source: Datastream/ICV

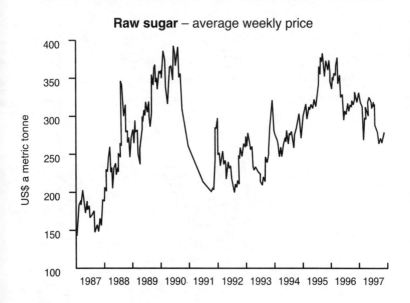

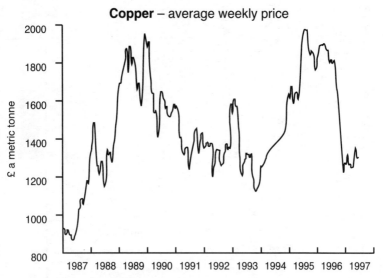

Source: Datastream/ICV

Prices of individual commodities

The charts above and overleaf show the average weekly prices (not adjusted for the fall in the buying power of the pound) of three commodities – sugar, copper and cocoa – from 1987 to 1997. You can see that all three commodities fluctuated in price during this period.

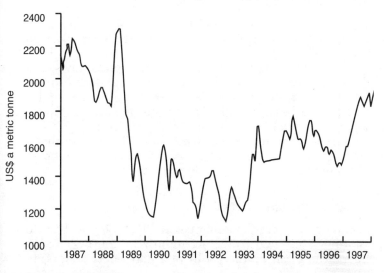

Cocoa – average weekly price

Source: Datastream/ICV

Looking at past performance, commodities would seem to offer the investor a rough passage: their price may well double or halve in a year or two, as illustrated by the movement of copper over the last few years. You can, of course, make a profit on commodities even when their price is falling, if you are successful in your use of futures or options contracts, but you should never underestimate your possible losses.

What commodity prices depend on

The prices of most commodities depend on supply and demand. In the end, the demand for a commodity comes from us, the consumers. To make the things that we want to buy, firms have to buy raw materials, e.g. copper for making electrical wire and copper pipes, cocoa for making chocolate.

If firms want to buy more of a commodity than is available, its price will rise. This may persuade producers that it will be profitable to produce more, e.g. start another copper mine, or plant more cocoa trees. But it may take some years before any more copper or cocoa is actually produced. The production of some other commodities, e.g. sugar, can be increased within a year or so of producers deciding to produce more (weather permitting).

Prices in the long term

There's no way of predicting what will happen to commodity prices over the long term, the next 20 or 50 years, say.

You might think that if the world economy grows, and the total amount of goods and services produced in the world goes up, the price of raw materials would tend to rise in response to increased demand. But if new and better ways of producing raw materials are found, if new producers come into the market, or if cheaper synthetic alternatives to some raw materials are developed, commodity prices *may* go down over the long term.

Prices in the short term

Commodity prices have fluctuated a lot from one year to another, and even from one month to another. These fluctuations can be the result of a number of factors, in particular:

■ **natural disasters** Droughts, floods, hurricanes, disease, and so on, may damage crops, and so lead to higher prices for commodities such as sugar, coffee and cocoa. Conversely, good harvests may lead to lower prices. Natural disasters can also damage mining areas, causing reduced production and high prices for a commodity such as copper

■ **booms and recessions** In the past, most economies have had periods of boom (with low unemployment and a high rate of growth of the amount of goods and services produced) followed by periods of recession (high unemployment and little, if any, growth in the amount of goods and services produced). In a boom, firms need to buy more raw materials in order to increase the amounts they produce, so raw material prices tend to rise. In a recession, demand for products is reduced so firms cut back on production and so raw material prices tend to fall. In the early 1990s, much of the developed world was in recession but by the mid- to late-1990s most economies, with the notable exception of the Far Eastern economies, returned to growth.

■ **wars** If a war breaks out, or a political revolution takes place, in an area of the world where a large proportion of the world's supply of a particular commodity is produced, the price of that commodity is likely to rise because of fears that supplies of the commodity will be reduced. For example, the invasion of Kuwait by Iraq in the summer of 1990 led to dramatic increases in the price of oil

■ **the exchange rate of the pound** Most of the world supply of commodities is bought by foreign firms who naturally work out their cost in foreign currencies, such as US dollars and German marks. If they continue to pay the same price for their commodities, and if the exchange rate of the pound (i.e. the number of US dollars, German marks, and so on, you can get for a pound) goes down, the price of commodities in terms of pounds will go up. Conversely, if the exchange rate of the pound goes up, the price of commodities in terms of pounds will go down. If however, the commodity is traded in pounds, then the foreign firms will have to account for the changes in currency separately.

Commodity price agreements

With some commodities, the main producing and consuming countries have got together in cartels to try to reduce price fluctuations. Most of these efforts have not been very successful as there has always been the chance that some country will break an agreement by exporting more of a commodity than it is supposed to. And not all producing countries may join an agreement in the first place.

The best known commodity price agreement is probably the one for oil, run by OPEC (the Organisation of Petroleum Exporting Countries), but this depends on the co-operation of producing countries only. The UK is not a member of OPEC.

In October 1985, The International Tin Council, which controlled the price and supply of 52 per cent of tin production, defaulted on huge debts. The London Metal Exchange suspended tin trading and the price of tin collapsed from around £9,000 per tonne to around £3,500 per tonne. It was not until June 1989 that tin trading was restarted.

How you can invest in commodities

You can invest directly in commodities in two ways:
■ by buying and selling commodities through a commodity broker
■ by putting money into a fund which has been set up specially to invest in commodities.

Buying and selling through a broker

Investing in physical commodities isn't a practical idea for most people. The minimum quantities you can buy are very large, and so is the corresponding cost of the investment; and with many commodities, such as cocoa and coffee, you run the risk of your commodity deteriorating in quality before you sell it.

If you deal in futures, you don't have to pay out such large sums of money, and you don't have to worry about the quality of your commodity. You have to put down only a deposit, perhaps 10 per cent of the value of what you're buying or selling; but the risk of losing a large sum of money is still there. Suppose, for example, you bought the minimum possible quantity of cocoa for delivery in a year's time. You might have to put down a £900 deposit at the time you arranged the deal. But then, if the price of cocoa fell, you'd have to hand over more money to the broker; and if the price fell by 50 per cent before you decided it was time to get rid of your cocoa, you would have lost around £4,500 (half of the £9,000 the cocoa was worth when you arranged the deal).

You may be able to join a syndicate of people who pool their money and invest in commodities. Some commodity brokers run such syndicates; and, in some cases, there's a guarantee that you can't lose more than the amount of your original investment. But you might face problems about getting your money out when you want to, and there's still a fairly high chance of losing a lot of money.

Offshore commodity funds

Putting money into a fund that has been set up specially to invest in commodities has three main advantages. First, it allows you to invest in commodities even if you can afford to lose only a more modest amount (£3,000 perhaps, though £5,000 or £10,000 may be a more common minimum investment). Secondly, you can choose a fund that guarantees you won't lose more than the amount you put into the fund. Thirdly, most of the funds invest your money in a lot of different commodities, something you couldn't do yourself without investing a good deal of money. This means that if one commodity does very badly, it won't have a disastrous effect on the value of your investment.

For legal and tax reasons, the commodity funds currently available to the public are based outside the UK, often in the Isle of Man or the Channel Islands. This means that investors do not have the protection provided by the Financial Services Act, although most offshore financial centres have their own regulations and compensation schemes – but you have to check carefully before you start. Offshore investments such as these are not allowed to send their booklets, prospectuses and so on, direct to members of the public. So if you want these, you'll have to ask for them to be sent via a professional adviser, such as a bank manager or stockbroker.

How the funds work

Commodity funds work in much the same way as unit trusts. The fund is divided into a number of units, and your stake in the fund is represented by the number of units you own. The value of a unit is roughly the value of the fund divided by the total number of units.

Most of the commodity funds can invest in both commodity futures and physical commodities, but a few invest only in physical stocks of just one commodity, e.g. copper or silver.

The performance of the funds that deal in one single commodity depends, on the whole, on what happens to the price of that commodity. But how your investment fares if you invest in a fund which deals in futures depends, to a large extent, on the skill of the fund managers. Since these funds started there have been some vast differences in performance. For example, assuming all income had been reinvested in the fund, if you'd invested £1,000 in 1983, it would have been worth over £2,837 five years later if you'd chosen the best performing fund. If you'd chosen the worst, £1,000 would have dwindled to £908 or so (worth only around £711 in terms of buying power).

All the funds have minimum investments – £5,000 perhaps; and all make charges – perhaps an initial charge of 5 per cent of the amount you invest, a yearly charge of 2 per cent of the value of the fund and, in some cases, a 'performance' fee of, say, 10 per cent of any increase in the price of units. Some of the funds pay out an income, but some don't. And the funds vary in how often the unit price is calculated and, therefore, how long you may have to wait to buy or sell units; with some this happens daily, with others you may have to wait a week or possibly even longer. Some of the funds, but not all, have independent trustees or custodians who look after the fund's cash and the documents that say what assets the fund owns.

Futures and Options Funds (FOFs)

Futures and options can be used either to increase the risk (and, it is hoped, the reward) of an investment or reduce the risk by setting a limit on the amount you can lose. Some unit trust tracker funds (see page 276) use options or futures to track the index at low risk, while FOFs use them to increase the risk. Geared Futures and Option Funds (GFOFs) can also borrow money to do this, which makes them even riskier.) The first fund of this type was launched in 1995 but so far there are very few funds to choose from. They are only suitable for highly sophisticated investors, such as institutions.

Is commodity investment for you?

Buying physical commodities and storing them in the hope that their value will rise is not a practical idea for most people; and with commodities such as cocoa and coffee you run the risk of the stocks deteriorating in quality before you sell them. Also, there's no guarantee that commodity prices will, in the long run, rise as quickly as prices in general.

Buying and selling commodity futures is a way of gambling on what's going to happen to the price of a commodity over a relatively short period – two years at the most. It could be a way of making, or losing, a lot of money in a short period. One large firm of commodity brokers estimated that 95 per cent of commodity speculators who take their own investment decisions lose money.

If you decide that, despite the drawbacks, you do want to invest in commodities, putting your money in a commodity fund has advantages.

Tax

How any profits you make from investing in commodities will be taxed is far from certain.

Profits from buying and selling physical commodities are likely to be treated as trading profits, and so taxed as earned income. A loss might count as a trading loss and you could set it off against the total of your income from all sources, but not normally against capital gains.

Just one isolated venture into the commodity futures market is likely to be treated as giving rise to a capital gain (or loss). But if you make a profit from a series of transactions, or invest as a member of a syndicate run by brokers or by a professional manager, this is likely to be treated as investment income. In this case, a loss could be set off only against profits of the same kind, or against certain other income. For more on tax, see Chapter 7.

25

INVESTING ABROAD

If you have several thousand pounds to invest, investing some of it abroad is worth considering. Although you cannot rely on getting a better return than in the UK, spreading your money among different countries could cut down the risk of your investments, as a whole, doing badly. Bear in mind that the outcome of your investment depends not just on how well it does in terms of local currency, but also on what happens to exchange rates. And because exchange rates are influenced by relative inflation rates and political and economic developments, future changes can be very hard to anticipate.

Investing abroad involves more risk than investing in the UK, as more uncertainties are involved. There are many different levels of investment, from the occasional few pounds in overseas-based unit trusts or investment trusts through to perhaps the purchase of a holiday property or even daily participation in the foreign exchange or foreign stock markets, although a good deal of time, resources and skill would be needed to succeed at this most serious level.

You may decide to invest abroad for two main reasons:
■ you believe that you'll get a better return on your money than with UK investments
■ you want to spread your money across different countries in the hope of cutting down the risk of your investments, as a whole, doing very badly.

Overleaf we look in more detail at these reasons. Bear in mind that investing overseas should form only part of your overall investment strategy. The first two chapters of this book give general advice on how to plan your investments, and can also to overseas investments.

Better return abroad?

Just as you might compare different investments in the UK to check which would give you the best return, so you should consider overseas investments as an alternative to UK ones. For example, you may have decided that a British Government stock paying a high income meets your investment needs. It could be worth checking whether a similar foreign investment might offer the prospect of a better return. The same goes, if, for example, you are looking for a capital gain from unit trusts, or want to put money in a bank savings account.

When comparing the returns, do not look only at the return in local currency (e.g. the rate of interest you'd get on your deposit account). You need to be aware that ups and downs in the exchange rate can affect your total return. Suppose, for example, you invest £100 in the US, at an exchange rate of US$1.70 to the pound, i.e. you invest US$170. If you get interest of 7 per cent, at the end of the year you'll have US$182 (ignoring, for the sake of simplicity, tax and the cost of buying and selling the investment). You discover that the pound has gone down a lot over the year compared with the dollar and that the exchange rate is now US$1.50 to the pound. In this case, you'd get back £121 (i.e. $182 ÷ 1.5), giving you a total rate of return of 21 per cent – three times the 7 per cent you get in local currency.

Of course, things may not work out in your favour. For example, you may find at the end of the year that the pound has gone up in value and that the exchange rate is now US$1.90 to the pound. In this case, you'd get back about £96 (i.e. $182 ÷ 1.90), which is less than the £100 you originally invested, despite the 7 per cent your money has been earning.

In short, it's good for your overseas investment if the exchange rate of the pound goes down against the currency concerned. It's bad if the exchange rate of the pound goes up. But beware: a country offering high interest rates is very likely to have a currency which is falling against the pound unless there are special circumstances.

Beware, also, of hidden costs. At each stage of foreign transactions there will be fees: for exchanging your pounds for foreign currency and back again, and for briefing UK or foreign agents to act on your behalf in whatever capacity and for holding securities for you abroad.

Check up as well on the tax situation and make sure you understand the range of local and other taxes to which your investment may be subject.

Spreading the risk

It's all very well to go for the best return on the money you invest, but few people are willing to face the risk of losing a lot of it in the process. One way of cutting down this risk is to spread your money around different types of investments. The chance of *all* these different investments doing extremely badly is lower than the chance of just one of them turning out to be a dud. Of course, reducing your risk of loss in this way also reduces your chance of winning the jackpot.

Spreading your investments across different countries is a way of cutting down another type of risk, e.g. the possibility of an economic setback in your home country. Although the economies of (and the health of investments in) some countries may, at times, move up and down more or less together, this is not true of all countries. For example, the problems faced by Japan are different from those faced by Germany, and different again from those faced by the USA.

So, by choosing investments in a cross-section of countries you reduce the risk of all of them doing badly at once. However, it also exposes you to new risks, such as currency movements, unforeseen political developments and foreign regulations or costs.

A way of reducing the effect of short-term fluctuations in exchange rates is to take out a *forward-exchange contract*. This is a way of buying or selling foreign currency for delivery at a date in the future. There is a cost attached, but you may decide it is worth it for the certainty of a fixed exchange rate. Your bank or stockbroker should be able to give you more information.

Investing directly in foreign shares or Government stocks is a particularly risky route to take, exposing you directly to the problems of obtaining up-to-date and accurate information on the economy, taxes, legal system and political developments in your chosen area, and to the full range of administrative problems and costs. You can find special feature articles on different countries published in the financial press from time to time.

For most people, the best way of spreading the risk is to invest in a UK-based unit trust or investment trust, and take advantage of the expertise of the investment managers in their specialist areas. In addition, there are usually no currency transactions, and costs and information are available from the fund management group.

Where to invest

Overseas, as in the UK, there is a wide range of possible investments (for a summary of the main types, see pages

381–91) and since 23 October 1979, when UK exchange control restrictions were removed, you have been free to invest world-wide.

Exchange rate of the pound

Changes in exchange rates can have a significant effect on your investment returns. Diagram 1 shows how the exchange rate of the pound has changed against six other currencies since 1981, while Diagram 2 shows how the effect of exchange rates alone could have led to a gain or loss over the last ten years if you had bought £100 worth of each of the currencies in Diagram 1 in April 1988, and changed it back into pounds in April 1998. And Diagram 3 shows the maximum gain that could have been made within the same ten years.

In practice, currency speculation is an extremely risky form of investment requiring large resources and a strong nerve. You could make a lot of money, but you could lose even more – see 'Warning'; and, of course, small gains could be turned into losses by the costs of buying and selling.

The changes in exchange rates shown in Diagram 1 reflect the changing economic and political situations in the UK and in the other countries shown. However, from the start of 1999, 11 European countries will enter a single currency. This will force the constituent countries to maintain the same interest and inflation rates. If, for example, German interest rates were 4 per cent and Italian rates were 6 per cent, speculators would borrow money in Germany and lend it in Italy. They would make a profit because there would be no currency transaction. (Many economists question whether a single currency will survive in the long term because countries within the European Monetary Union (EMU) will be unable to compete by lowering their interest rates.)

While the UK remains outside the EMU the pound will fluctuate against the ecu (European Currency Unit) as it does against the US dollar or the Japanese yen. The benefit to investors will be to simplify investments within the EMU – i.e. an investment in a German company can be compared directly to a French or Italian one as they will all trade in the same currency.

Warning

Just because you could have made large gains over the period shown, it doesn't mean the same will apply in the future. A major problem in choosing where to invest is

Diagram 1: Annual average exchange rate of the £

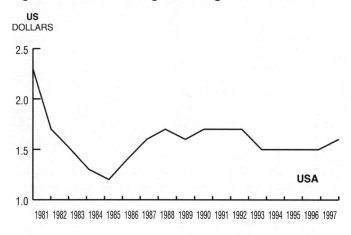

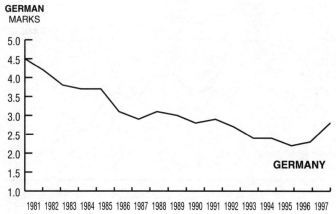

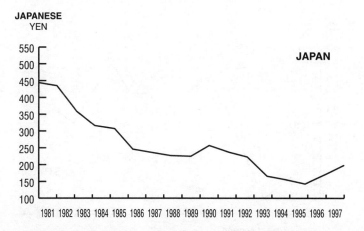

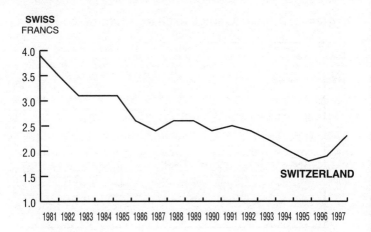

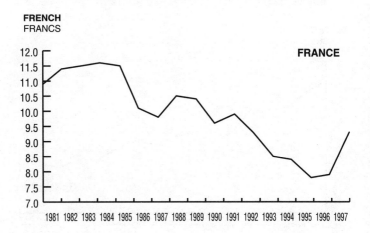

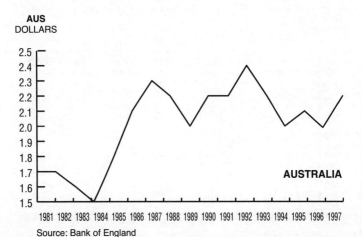

Source: Bank of England

trying to predict what will happen to exchange rates. The pound could rise against other currencies, and your gains could be wiped out. It's important to be aware of significant economic events and trends in your chosen areas that can bring about changes in the exchange rate.

Interest rates and inflation

In the long term, a key factor affecting exchange rates is interest rates, which, in turn, reflects the rate of inflation; if the interest rate in one country is considerably higher than in another, the first country's exchange rate is likely to fall relative to the second. You can see from Diagram 4 on page 382 that during the period when the exchange rate of the pound tended to be falling, the inflation rate in the UK was generally higher than in the other countries at which we looked.

Diagram 2: Gains made on foreign currency
April 1988–April 1998 (ignoring buying and selling costs)

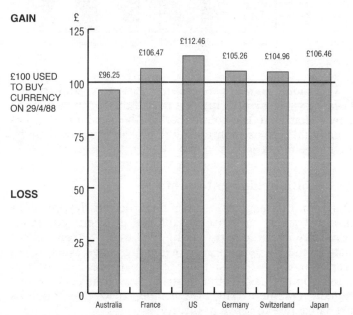

All these gains (and losses) may seem quite small if you spread them over the ten years involved. However, the picture looks very different if you imagine the gains you could have made if you bought the currency at the highest and sold at the lowest rates over the same period – see Diagram 3.

Source: Datastream/ICV

Diagram 3: Maximum gain on foreign currency
Jan 1987–Jan 1997 (ignoring buying and selling costs)

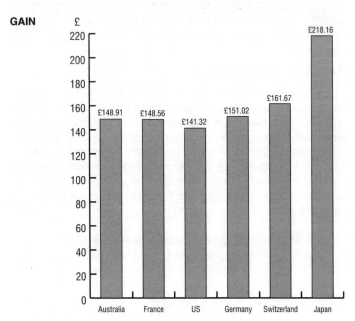

Source: Datastream/ICV

The moral is, *don't* invest in a particular country just because you get a high interest rate. If the currency is going down relative to the pound (perhaps because inflation has been high) your extra interest will probably be wiped out by exchange rate losses.

The return in different countries

Diagram 5 on page 383 shows how the returns on stocks issued by the governments of the different countries compared over the period from 1988 to 1998. You can see that in the UK returns were generally above average, but were outstripped consistently by Australia. The interest rate a country has to offer to attract foreign investors must reflect, to some extent, how people expect that country's exchange rate to move in future.

Diagram 6 on page 383 shows how share prices have changed since 1988. You can see how Japan has continued to underperform the Western markets throughout the 1990s and by contrast how Switzerland, Germany and the USA have seen spectacular growth over the last year.

Cost of buying and selling foreign currency

Unless you're investing in UK-based foreign investments (e.g. a unit trust), you're likely to have to exchange the cash for foreign currency; and when you cash your investment, you may have to turn your foreign currency back into pounds again. In both cases, you'll be charged for the transaction (the charge may be hidden in that different exchange rates will be used depending on whether you're buying or selling foreign currency). If you're changing a lot of money – several thousand pounds, say – you should get a better deal than with smaller amounts. And if you're dealing through a stockbroker or other agent you may be able to benefit from the favourable exchange rates and lower charges he or she can get.

Administrative problems

If you have foreign investments, you have to make arrangements in the foreign country for the share certificate (or whatever) to be held by an agent, e.g. a bank or stockbroker, and passed on to the new owner when you sell, and for dividends, interest, and so on, to be collected and sent on to you. Ask a UK agent, such as a stockbroker, to make these arrangements for you, but there'll be a fee to pay and it could be high.

Ways of investing abroad

Foreign currency bank accounts

It is possible to make money simply by buying and selling currencies on the foreign exchange markets and taking advantage of differences in interest rates.

High-street banks will open foreign currency accounts for UK residents. These can be either current accounts (i.e. you can draw cheques on them), or deposit accounts (where interest is paid). Some accounts may offer current account facilities and pay interest if a certain balance is maintained. You may, however, have to pay charges. You don't need to have a UK account with a bank to open a foreign account.

Interest rates vary substantially between currencies and can change from day to day. In general, the more you invest the higher the rate of interest you can get. If you have to

Diagram 4: Inflation rates

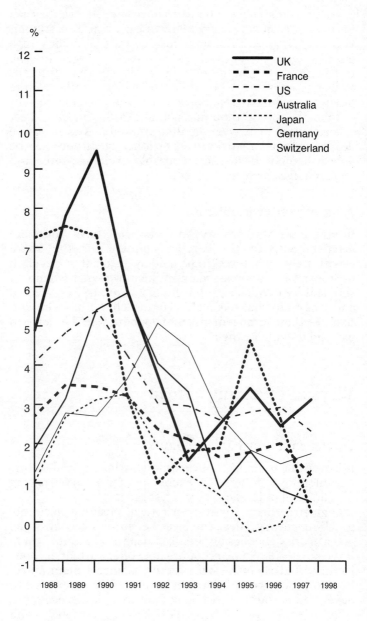

Source: Datastream/ICV

Diagram 5: Return on government stocks [1]

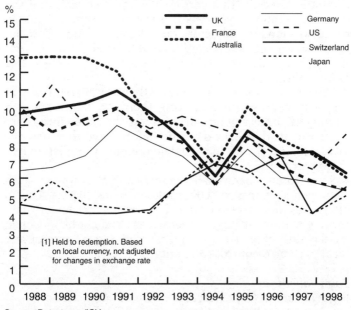

Source: Datastream/ICV

Diagram 6: How share prices have done [1]

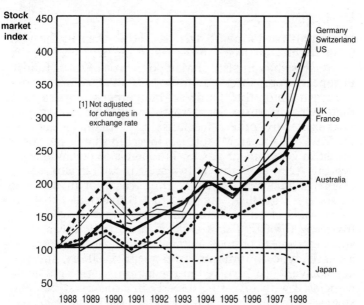

Source: Datastream/ICV

give notice to withdraw your money, the rate of interest is normally fixed for this period. The interest rates and the minimum amount you have to invest vary from bank to bank, so shop around before opening an account. You can now also get accounts denominated in ecus.

Points to watch
■ Current accounts do not normally pay interest, and you may pay charges for operating them. So it's not worth having one unless you plan to invest the funds into other securities in that country and need to have the currency available, travel a lot in a particular country, or plan to live there part of the time.
■ Some foreign banks with branches in this country will also open accounts for UK residents. These banks tend to offer rates of interest similar to (or somewhat lower than) those given by UK high-street banks. You could also open an account direct with a bank abroad, but beware of any local exchange-control restrictions.

Points about tax
Interest on UK-based accounts is paid after deduction of tax. Interest will be paid gross generally only if the account is held *offshore* – in the Channel Islands, say.

Unit trusts

Many unit trusts invest overseas rather than in the UK. Some of these are based in the UK, some in places like the Channel Islands and Isle of Man (known as *offshore* funds). European companies can now sell unit trusts across European Union (EU) borders. Many other countries have their own unit trusts. Some trusts spread their investments internationally, others specialise in particular areas, e.g. the USA or Far East. Most trusts invest in shares, but some invest in government stocks, Eurobonds or put money on deposit. A few specialise in investing in foreign currencies.

For the majority of people, unit trusts (or investment trusts – see overleaf) are the most convenient and least risky ways of enjoying benefits from investing abroad. Investing through a unit trust means that you can get a stake in a spread of investments in an overseas country for a relatively low minimum investment, £500 say, and you don't have to get involved in the administrative problems associated with investing directly in overseas stocks and shares – see page 387. For more details see Chapter 17.

Points to watch
■ Unit trusts are not a home for money you might need at short notice. They should be considered mainly as a long-term investment, though they can also be used for short-term speculation if you're prepared to take a higher risk.
■ If you invest via UK-based unit trusts (but not offshore funds), you get the protection of the Financial Services Act – see Chapter 5.

Points about tax
Distributions from UK-based unit trusts are paid with only UK tax deducted, while distributions from most offshore funds are paid with little or no tax deducted, so there are no problems with reclaiming tax held back by foreign governments. With foreign-based unit trusts, distributions are normally paid with some tax withheld by the foreign government. You'll have to arrange to get a credit for any tax deducted – see page 391.

Investment trusts

Investment trusts are companies which, in turn, invest in the shares of other companies – see Chapter 18 for more details. Many UK investment trusts hold overseas shares (perhaps specialising in particular areas of the world, such as the USA, Far East and Australia). UK investment trust shares can be bought and sold on the UK Stock Exchange. Details of UK investment trusts, some of which specialise in particular parts of the world, are published annually in a directory available from the Association of Investment Trust Companies (AITC).*
    Investment trusts also exist in other countries; a few major foreign trusts are quoted on the UK Stock Exchange.

Points to watch
The same points apply as for unit trusts.

Points about tax
The same points apply as for unit trusts.

Foreign currency funds

These offer a means of investing in a range of currencies without opening individual bank accounts. You buy units in a fund (rather like buying unit trusts). The investment managers then shift the money in the fund around, among a range of currencies, in the hope of taking advantage both of high interest rates and favourable exchange rate movements. So, in effect, you are staking your money on the skill and luck of the managers. Some of the funds are based in the Channel Islands (*offshore* funds), and operate like unit trusts. Others are linked to life insurance.

Points to watch
■ These funds give the opportunity of investing in currencies for a relatively low outlay – the minimum investment ranges from £1,000 to £10,000. But the funds all charge an annual management fee, often around 1 per cent.
■ Currency funds are *not* recommended as a home for money you cannot afford to lose. You are taking on substantial currency risks.

Points about tax
UK-based funds pay interest after deduction of tax at 20 per cent, so higher-rate taxpayers may have to pay more tax. Offshore funds have the choice of taking either *accumulator* or *distributor* status. Funds with distributor status have to distribute at least 85 per cent of their income, and you are taxed on this at your top rate of income tax. When you sell units, you pay capital gains tax on any increase in their value, but you qualify for the annual tax-free slice – see Chapter 7. Accumulator funds accumulate income in the price of the unit, but any profits made are taxed at your top rate of income tax when you sell the units. So which type of fund is better for you will depend on your tax position.

Government stocks and company stocks

Just as the UK Government raises money through issuing British Government stocks, so there is a wide range of fixed-interest stocks issued by foreign governments, and the return may be better than that available in the UK, even after allowing for currency differences. These are bought and sold on foreign stock exchanges and some are also traded on the UK Stock Exchange.

Many foreign companies issue fixed-interest securities which work in a similar way to government stocks, but they normally pay higher interest, reflecting the higher risk.

Points to watch
■ As with shares, extra costs and a certain amount of administrative hassle are involved in dealing in foreign

stocks on foreign stock exchanges – see below. It may be simpler to invest through a unit trust that specialises in foreign fixed-interest stocks.

■ Remember that some governments may be offering high interest rates to offset a falling exchange rate.

Points about tax

Gains on foreign stocks are liable to capital gains tax, unlike gains on British Government stocks, which are tax-free. Interest payments are generally made after deduction of some foreign tax, so you may have to arrange to get a credit for the tax deducted – see page 391.

Shares

Direct investment in shares on foreign markets isn't a straightforward process. You may find it difficult to get information on specific foreign companies or up-to-the-minute information on prices on the foreign stock exchange even though the financial press is becoming increasingly international. There are also practical problems in finding an agent to deal for you and get the currency with which to deal. You run the risk that, by the time you've set up the contacts and the currency for a particular deal, exchange rates or prices could have changed, and not in your favour. Your stockbroker may be happy to deal in overseas markets on your behalf and arrange all the details for you, but you may find the additional costs involved are high unless you are dealing in substantial sums of money. So, at present, direct investment abroad is not generally recommended for non-professionals, although the increasingly international nature of securities trading and the effort to create a single European market-place mean that this may well change over the next few years.

A less problematic way to deal in foreign shares might be through the UK Stock Exchange. Many major international companies are already quoted there; there are no currency deals to arrange and you face fewer administrative problems. Alternatively, stick to investing via unit trusts or, possibly, investment trusts.

Points to watch

■ To spread the risks adequately across countries and industrial sectors, substantial sums of money are required for direct investment in overseas stocks and shares – say at least £10,000 to £20,000.

■ Shares are not a home for money you might need at short notice. They should be considered, in the main, as a long-term investment, though they can also be used for short-term speculation.

■ Some countries' protection for shareholders is less extensive than is the case in the UK. It may be advisable, therefore, to stick to large, well-established stock markets, such as the US or Japan.

■ It is likely to be difficult for you (or your adviser) to have detailed knowledge about a lot of foreign companies, and the economic environment in which they function. Even if you have some knowledge of the country it is often difficult to be as up to date as those living in the country itself. So a broker who seeks advice for you from a local broking company may be the best solution.

■ If you hold foreign investments abroad, you may have to make arrangements for the share certificate, or bond, to be held by an agent, e.g. a bank or stockbroker, and passed on to the new owner when you sell. In the same way, dividends and interest have to be collected and sent on to you. You could make these arrangements yourself or ask a UK agent, such as a stockbroker, to make them for you. Either way, there'll be a fee to pay, and it could be high in relation to the value of the investment.

Points about tax
Dividends and stock interest are often paid with some tax withheld by the foreign government, so you may have to arrange to get a credit for the tax deducted.

Eurobonds

Eurobonds are a way in which international borrowers, e.g. governments, large companies and international institutions like the World Bank, raise money. The bonds, which pay interest, are generally issued in a particular currency, e.g. US dollars or German marks, and are quoted on various stock exchanges. Eurobonds issued by companies (rather than governments, say) normally pay a slightly higher rate of interest, reflecting their slightly lower credit rating with the markets. A credit rating is a measurement of the risk of offering credit to a company or government (see Chapter 20 for Eurosterling bonds).

Points to watch
■ Eurobonds come in fairly large units, e.g. US$1,000. The minimum investment is around US$50,000, and

many dealers will not deal with members of the public. You may do better to go for a unit trust specialising in Eurobonds.

■ The interest rate may be fixed, or may be changed at set intervals.

■ Interest rates on Eurobonds generally reflect interest rates in the country of the currency in which they are issued.

Points about tax

As with capital gains on foreign stocks, capital gains on Eurobonds are liable to capital gains tax. Interest is paid without any foreign tax being deducted, but is liable for UK tax, and you must declare it on your tax return.

Property

Buying property abroad is full of pitfalls for the unwary. For example, the costs of buying and selling are usually considerably greater abroad than they are in the UK: perhaps 10 per cent on both buying and selling. If you need to borrow money to buy the property, you may find it difficult to get a loan from a UK institution. There may be severe restrictions on taking your money out of the foreign country again if you decide to sell; and there's always the chance that, at some time in the future, the political climate in the country might change and foreigners won't be welcome. You should certainly get professional advice before contemplating an investment in property abroad.

If you haven't the money to buy a property outright, you could buy a timeshare. This will give you a set number of weeks in your holiday home every year. The time share business has had very bad press over the years with reports of high-pressure selling and problems with selling your timeshare if needed. Increasingly timeshares today are sold more on the membership to organisations that give you the ability to swap your holiday with other timeshare resorts than on the benefits of holidaying in the same place year after year. Therefore, rather than viewing a timeshare as an investment in property, it would probably be more accurate to view it as an investment in holidays.

Points to watch

■ Always visit a home before buying – don't rely on glossy brochures. Try to spend time in the area and see the house at different times of the day, and even in different seasons.

■ Check carefully on factors such as the reliability of local water, electricity supplies, sewerage, and on the structure and surroundings of the house you have in mind.

■ Planning permission for new buildings is easier to get in many countries abroad than in the UK: your idyllic country retreat may become the centre of a concrete jungle.

■ If you are planning to retire abroad, be particularly cautious, and check on medical facilities.

Points about tax

Gains you make on selling property abroad are liable to capital gains tax in the UK. Income you get from letting property is taxed as investment income, and you must declare it on your tax return. You can deduct any expenses incurred abroad in managing and collecting the income, e.g. paying an agent. If some foreign tax has been deducted, you'll have to arrange to get a tax credit.

Unit-linked life insurance

Many life insurance companies run funds that invest abroad. These work a bit like unit trusts. For more details, see Chapter 22.

Tax on overseas investments

The tax treatment of investments held abroad (as opposed to UK-based foreign investments) can be extremely complicated. But even if you plan to hand over your tax affairs to advisers, a bit of background knowledge will help you to understand what they're up to.

Income tax

In general, if you're a UK resident all your income is liable to UK tax, whether or not it is brought into this country. So if, say, you have a bank deposit account in Switzerland, you have to declare the interest you get from it on your tax return, even if you kept the interest (or spent it) abroad. When converting foreign income into pounds, use the exchange rate applying at the time it was due to be paid to you (not when you actually changed it into pounds).

Income from overseas investments is often taxed in the country in which it originates; so two lots of tax could be charged on one lot of income. The UK government has made agreements with a wide range of countries to limit the extent to which income may be taxed twice. Under one of these *double taxation agreements* the amount of tax which a foreign government deducts from income before it reaches you is reduced, and the tax actually deducted is allowed a tax credit against the UK tax charged on the same income.

Suppose, for example, that you're entitled to £1,000 in dividends from the USA. Tax at 30 per cent would normally be deducted in the USA before paying over the dividends to non-US residents.

However, because of our double taxation agreement with the USA, only 15 per cent is withheld, i.e. you get £850. If, say, you're liable for tax in the UK at 40 per cent on your £1,000 gross dividends, there'd be £400 tax to pay. But the £150 you've paid in tax to the USA would be allowed as a credit against the £400 of UK tax you're liable for, so you'd have a UK tax bill of £250, not £400.

If you are liable for no UK tax (or less than has been deducted under a double taxation agreement), there'll be no further UK tax to pay, but you can't claim back the extra foreign tax you've paid.

In general, double taxation agreements mean that tax on dividends is withheld at a rate of 15 per cent. With interest payments, the rate at which tax is withheld varies more between countries. For details of double taxation agreements, see the free Inland Revenue leaflet *IR6*.

How to get your relief

If your foreign income is paid to you through an agent, e.g. a bank in the UK, which passes it on to you after deducting tax at 20 per cent, the agent should allow for any double taxation agreement when doing the sums.

But if the income is paid direct to you from abroad, you have to apply for double taxation relief yourself – and until you do so, you may find the income arrives with substantial amounts of foreign tax withheld, and no credit against UK tax allowed for it. To get the foreign tax reduced, get an application form from the Financial Intermediaries and Claims Office International.* To get the withheld foreign tax allowed as a credit against your UK tax bill, apply to your tax inspector.

When UK tax is due

From 6 April 1996, all foreign income you get is taxed on a current-year basis. This means you need to include in your 1998–9 tax return all foreign income earned between 6

April 1998 and 5 April 1999. (Prior to 1996, foreign income, along with some other forms of income, was taxed on a preceding year's basis, i.e. tax paid in the 1995–6 tax bill was based on income earned in the 1994–5 tax year.) Any additional tax to pay on foreign income earned in the 1998–9 tax year will be payable on 31 January 2000.

Other tax deducted
In certain countries, foreign dividends are paid after deducting tax other than personal income tax, and non-residents may not be able to reclaim this tax. So before investing in a particular country, check that the return you hope to get allows for *all* the tax deducted.

Capital gains tax

Gains you make on overseas investments are liable for UK capital gains tax in the normal way – see Chapter 7. In general, you'll be taxed on gains whether or not you bring the sale proceeds into the UK. Your capital gain will be the difference between the value of the asset in sterling when you acquired it, and its value in sterling when you disposed of it, using the exchange rates that applied at the relevant times. Note that gains you make on foreign currency are liable for capital gains tax in the normal way (unless you use the currency for holidays or living expenses abroad).

There's normally no foreign capital gains tax to pay if you're a UK resident. However, gains on selling a foreign home may be taxed in the country where the home is situated; and if you have a permanent home in one of certain foreign countries, e.g. a ranch in California, USA or spend substantial parts of the year there, you may find that you're treated as a resident of the country and are liable for local capital gains tax. Any foreign tax you pay is allowed as a credit against your UK capital gains tax.

Inheritance tax

UK inheritance tax is charged on foreign assets in the normal way – see Chapter 7. A similar tax is likely to be charged by the country in which the assets are situated. The foreign inheritance tax (or its equivalent) is normally allowed as a credit against UK inheritance tax.

Note that there are likely to be delays (perhaps lengthy ones) and complications in obtaining probate for assets held abroad in your name, on your death. It may be better to have them held in the name of a UK agent, such as a bank.

26

ALTERNATIVE INVESTMENTS

If you are worried about inflation starting to rise again, you may want to look for less conventional investments.

The table on page 18 shows how gold bullion and antique furniture have performed over four different periods since 1977 compared with investing in shares, buying a home and so on. You can see from the table that antique furniture has performed reasonably well over 20 years, although over shorter periods it has proved to be a poor investment only just matching inflation over five years and not even keeping up over 10 years. However, in earlier editions of this book when earlier years were compared the results looked very different with furniture outperforming everything but shares. These figures are for average performance and so you may do well by buying a very good piece of furniture cheaply or do badly by buying the wrong piece.

Which alternative investment to go for

Limited supply plus growing demand is what to look for in an alternative investment. Things like old stamps, Georgian silver and Roman coins are available in limited quantities; there is no way that more can be produced (forgeries apart). So if more people want to own them, or the existing number of collectors can afford to pay more (because of inflation, say), prices will increase.

But limited supply, on its own, is not sufficient to make a good investment. For example, limited editions (see page 398) are produced in quantities of a few hundred or a few thousand, but they are unlikely to prove good investments unless people will want to buy them in the future.

Nor is a high level of demand enough to make a good investment. For example, many collectors will snap up new issues of British stamps (the Diana commemorative issue is expected to be widely bought when it is issued later in

1998, for example). But if several million are issued, it's unlikely they will become valuable. For the investor, only stamps in fairly short supply and popular with collectors are likely to gain significantly in value.

Should you put your money in alternative investments?

You should consider investing only part of your savings in this way – no more than 10 per cent, say – and certainly not your emergency fund or money you can't afford to lose. Bear in mind that:

- because of the expenses of buying and selling, such as an auctioneer's commission or dealer's mark-up, you may not make a profit unless you keep your money invested for a fairly long time – say, five years or more
- money invested in this way won't give you a regular income, and you may have to pay for storage and insurance
- fashions in collecting change; what may have been an appreciating asset ten years ago may no longer be today. You may even make a loss when you come to sell
- you may find it hard to decide on what price to ask when you sell, and, unless you sell at an auction, some haggling with buyers is likely to be involved. Going for a quick sale could mean you get a poor price.

Alternative investments have one advantage that most other types of investment lack: you can get pleasure out of finding and owning things in which you invest. Indeed, you're more likely to invest successfully if you do take an interest in them. Also, if your investments turn out to be unsuccessful, you at least have the consolation of owning a stamp collection, a rock legend's guitar or whatever.

In this chapter we look at a few of the wide range of alternative investments available. Bear in mind that these are included as examples only – we are not suggesting that these investments in particular are ones you should choose; but you should get hints on what to watch out for even if you decide to specialise in an area we haven't mentioned.

How should you invest?

- Do your homework before you invest. Read up on the subject, join societies for collectors of the things you are interested in, visit exhibitions, study auctioneers' catalogues and dealers' price lists, and talk to experts.
- Start small. Buy a few items. Develop your knowledge before spending more, and then stick to a narrow field.

■ Aim for items in very good condition. You might have to settle for a poor-quality item – to complete a set, say. But, in general, two or three items in top condition are likely to do better than several tatty ones.

■ Shop around. Prices are likely to vary considerably between dealers, so don't be afraid to haggle.

■ Be sceptical of 'guarantees' (to buy back the things you invest in at double what you paid for them after five years, say). These 'guarantees' are only as good as the dealer who gives them and are of no value at all if he or she goes bust.

■ Invest in things that are collected worldwide, so that the price you get when you sell will not necessarily be reduced if UK demand slumps.

Ahead of the crowd?

You can make more money if you invest in things that other investors haven't woken up to and which subsequently become popular with collectors. You can't expect to be right every time (or even most of the time) with this sort of speculation. If you're only in it for the money, and other speculators do catch on, you may need to be quick at spotting when a craze is reaching its height so that you sell before prices start tumbling.

Storage and insurance

Careful storage may be important with things like stamps, wine or paintings. Damp, sudden changes in temperature, sunlight, insects and so on could reduce (or even wipe out) the value of the items you collect.

You'll also need to insure your valuables against events like theft or fire. Typically, this might cost around £4.50 to £15 a year for each £1,000 of cover as part of a normal house contents policy (more if you live in a high-risk area). Many house contents policies also offer cover against accidental damage as an optional extra.

Before you decide on a policy, check its terms carefully. There may be an unwelcome restriction, such as a low limit on the amount of cover for individual items. You might prefer to buy a special insurance policy for your collection. Consult the *Insurance Buyer's Guide 1998.* *

If your collection is worth a lot of money (more than a few thousand pounds, say), the insurer is likely to insist on a safe, special locks and burglar alarms. It is also likely to ask for proof of your collection's value, so it's sensible to keep photographs of it, as well as a regularly updated professional valuation. A professional valuer (or a dealer) may charge perhaps 1.5 per cent of the valuation figure given for your collection. Remember to review the level of your insurance regularly.

Alternatively, you could store your collection in a bank's strongroom; insurance may be less if you do this. The bank makes a charge for storage – from £6 to £23.50 a year for an envelope, say, up to £50 a year or more for a bulky item. You may also have to pay an inspection charge of around £5 each time you need to remove your collection. Some dealers will also store and insure the things you buy from them; this may seem the simplest solution, but remember that you could have problems if the dealer you store with goes bust.

What about tax?

Because there's usually no income from investing in physical items, there's usually no income tax to pay (unless the Revenue decides you are carrying on a trade or business and taxes your profits as income).

You might be liable for capital gains tax if you make a gain when you sell or give away things in which you have invested. But the first £6,800 a year of gains are normally tax-free (in the 1998–9 tax year). You may benefit after April 1998 from the newly introduced tapered reduction of chargeable gains if you hold the asset for a number of years. Gains on chattels such as individual antiques, items of jewellery and other tangible moveable objects which you sell for a value of £6,000 or less, unless the items are part of a set with an overall value above £6,000, are also tax free.

You may have to pay VAT if you buy from dealers.

Some alternative investments

Wine

Laying down vintage wines and ports has been, in the past, a highly profitable investment. The return is free of tax unless the Inland Revenue believes you have gone into the wine trade and taxes the gain as your business profits. Note that private individuals without a licence are not allowed to advertise or sell any alcohol except via an auctioneer or wine merchant.

Vintage wines must be stored in carefully regulated conditions to maintain their quality and value. So unless you are in the enviable position of having your own suitable cellar, you will have to pay yearly storage and insurance costs to a wine merchant. For storage you can currently expect to pay from £4.50 to £6.50 per case per year, and this will normally include insurance cover at either the original purchase price or, now more commonly, the current value.

Not all wine bought for investment can be expected to produce a high return. The advice from *The Which? Wine Guide 1998** is to avoid the smaller wine sellers offering great investment opportunities (particularly in champagne) ahead of the Millennium. Some have already declared bankruptcy, leaving investors seriously out of pocket. Look for long-established merchants who predominantly sell wines for drinking. Having said that, the Guide also acknowledges that certain fine and rare wines have produced exceptional investment performance over the last year or so and currently recommends:

- 1988 and 1989 Bordeaux and Burgundy reds and whites
- 1994 Rhône reds
- vintage ports from 1983 and 1985
- classic New World wine from merchants who do not have a reputation as New World specialists.

Stamps

Apart from what they cost to use for postage, stamps are intrinsically worthless bits of paper. But they are avidly collected by many people all over the world, some of whom are prepared to pay very large sums of money for stamps that are extremely rare, or of historical interest.

Some stamps have increased in value much more than others. For instance, in 1994 Far Eastern stamps, particularly those from Hong Kong, leapt in value as Hong Kong investors sought to put their money in tangibles before the return to Chinese rule. Values can fall as well as rise.

Stamps which, in the past, have shown some of the largest increases in value have included examples (in fine condition) of rare nineteenth-century issues, sometimes called *classics*.

If you want to invest seriously in stamps, you will have to approach this as a hobby first, and get to know a lot about them, through studying catalogues and auction results, visiting dealers, joining a philatelic society and so on. Small variations in printing and watermarks, and even the sheet from which the stamp has been torn, can affect the price drastically. The condition of the stamp is also very important. Stamps with printing errors and, occasionally, forgeries can be worth much more than ordinary stamps.

Buying special issues of modern commemorative stamps is unlikely to be a good investment because they are generally issued in very large quantities. Don't take catalogue prices as fixed values of stamps, or proof of increases in value. Catalogues show the prices at which a dealer would hope to sell stamps in first-class condition. A dealer would normally pay much less to buy the stamps. The prices fetched at auctions are a more reliable guide.

Limited editions

Many items are sold as limited editions, e.g. plates, porcelain figures and prints. There are basically two ways to produce a limited edition:
■ the number to be sold is specified at the outset – 50 or 500 or 5,000, say.
■ the number sold is the number ordered or bought by a certain date, e.g. 50 if only 50 are sold by that date, 50,000 if that is the number sold. With this method the total number to be sold (important in evaluating scarcity) is normally known only after you've agreed to buy.

There are variations on these themes. For example, with some limited editions, the limit mentioned in the advertisement may apply only to the UK, and more of the item may be sold in other countries.

Of course, the investment potential of limited editions depends not only on the number produced, but also on the demand for them from collectors. And with many editions, there's little hope of a big demand, even if only a few dozen were issued.

With some limited editions you may find that it's not the limited nature of the item that makes it profitable but the intrinsic value of the material from which it's made. A set of commemorative silver ingots, say, may be worth more for their silver content as scrap, so they could make you money in times when silver prices are high.

Memorabilia

An interest in collecting memorabilia can produce a healthy investment return if you tune into the right fashion at the right time. Items which may have cost you little or nothing, such as autographs, programmes and posters, can be worth large sums of money if the celebrity they're tied to becomes famous. However, fame is notoriously fickle, and there's no guarantee that your prized set of 'Spice Girls' autographs will be worth anything in the future.

There's a market for all sorts of memorabilia, with sporting, film and music items being among the most popular. Memorabilia need not necessarily be old to be worth something – items of Madonna's clothing have changed hands at extraordinary prices in recent years – what's more important is that it can be verified that the item is associated with the star, sporting team or movie with which it's alleged to have a connection.

In the pop world, the 1950s and 1960s still provide the most collectable items, with, rather macabrely, pieces closely linked with dead stars such as John Lennon, Jim Morrison, Buddy Holly and Elvis Presley being especially valuable. A velvet stage shirt worn by Elvis Presley in 1956 recently sold for £10,000, while any of John Lennon's drawings found in your attic are likely to weigh in at high four figure sums. If you're beginning a collection now, items belonging to the late Freddie Mercury may appreciate.

The magic of the cinema has made items associated with it very collectable. Again, if an actor or film-maker dies, the value of associated items tends to increase. Autographed pictures can gain in value – but only if the signature is authentic (in 1997 autographed letters from Oscar Wilde fetched a record £23,000 at auction) – while props or costumes from hit movies command big prices due to being essentially one-offs. In 1996 a Paramount US one-sheet poster for *Breakfast at Tiffany's* sold for a record £8,625 and a three-sheet poster for *Casablanca* sold for £23,000.

Sporting items are becoming increasingly attractive investments. Pre-nineteenth-century golf equipment, for instance, is very rare, and an eighteenth-century golf club recently raised more than £90,000 at auction. Bats, balls and other sporting equipment with a history attached can also prove valuable, particularly if tied to a popular competitor from a popular sport. Another recent example in 1993 was the sale of the former England football international Ray Kennedy's personal memorabilia collection, which raised a world record sum in excess of £80,000. Teddy bears have not lost their appeal: in 1996, 'Teddy Edward' – the star bear from BBC's *Watch with Mother* – sold for £34,500 and a fine Steiff teddy bear from circa 1905 sold in 1997 for £23,000.

As with almost any alternative investment, an interest in, and knowledge of what you are buying will stand you in good stead, and, no matter how popular or unpopular your 'stars' are, you will always retain a stake in their history.

Forestry

Clearing land and planting trees for the production of timber is one way you can watch your investment grow physically, as well as in terms of its value. But investing in forestry, or commercial woodlands should be seen as a strictly long-term process unless you buy an existing woodland. Timber from new plantings takes, on average, about 25 years to produce any income, so it may be more likely that your children will get the benefit of the investment rather than you (since 1992–3, they have also benefited from some relief from inheritance tax on your death). The benefits of investing in timber last however, as timber is felled and sold over a long period.

The government offers incentives to investors, in the form of grants to plant trees, while the proceeds from the sale of timber are now tax-free.

Direct investment in forestry is pricey, and your minimum outlay would have to be at least £20,000. If you don't want to tie up so much for so long, you can invest a much lower figure in joint ownership of a forest, available from forestry management companies. Share schemes cover portfolios of both bare land to be planted or young plantations and productive woodland. The minimum investment in these schemes is around £10,000.

Demand for timber is still high, so the long-term prospects look good. But, you have to be prepared to tie up quite a lot of money for a very long time, so someone looking for a quick return should look elsewhere. However, there may be other benefits to be had, such as sporting rights, which can add to the attraction as can the sheer pleasure of owning a piece of the countryside.

Diamonds

Diamonds have always held a fascination for investors, but they are not a 'commodity' investment like gold or other precious metals. The price of rough and polished diamonds has kept up with inflation since the mid-1950s but has not made any significant gain in real terms. The main reason for this is that the market is dominated by De Beers (it sells about 80 per cent of the world's uncut diamonds). The main interest of De Beers is to release new diamonds on to the market without lowering the price.

There used to be three ways of investing in diamonds: buying them over the counter, buying from a diamond investment company, or putting money into a scheme which in turn invested on the diamond market. But with the losses made by investors in the 1980s, the second option has all but disappeared.

Buying diamonds over the counter

You can buy diamonds from a jeweller or a diamond merchant, or at an auction; they may be loose or mounted in jewellery. When you want to sell, you can hawk the stones around dealers, or put them in an auction.

Buying and selling loose diamonds over the counter seems to be a mug's game. Even if you get good value when you buy (and you've no way of being certain about that), the dealer's mark-up, which can be as high as several hundred per cent, is likely to make diamonds a poor investment, even over a ten-year period; and particularly if you're looking for a sale on the spot, offers from jewellers are likely to be on the low side. Diamonds are valued on the 'four Cs' – cut, colour, carat and clarity – and there are thousands of different categories of quality. Most jewellers can't accurately establish the value of a diamond on the spot, though having certificates from a specialist diamond-grading laboratory should help.

As for diamonds mounted in jewellery, you're unlikely to show a profit on *new* jewellery for a very long time. The investment market for *antique* jewellery is more like that for antique furniture or porcelain, say, than for loose diamonds. Putting antique diamond jewellery into an auction may be the best way to sell.

Buying shares in a diamond company

Most diamond exploration companies are listed abroad, particularly on the various Canadian exchanges, but a few companies are listed in the UK, including De Beers, RioTinto, Reunion Mining, Petra Diamonds and Cambridge Mineral Resources. Buying shares may be an easier option than buying diamonds, however, it is still a specialist area of the market and so to get advice you may have to find a specialist broker.

Gold

For thousands of years, gold has been looked on as a store of wealth, and many people the world over believe that gold is a good asset to hold in times of political, financial or currency upheavals; but if you are tempted to invest in gold, be prepared for a bumpy ride. Even daily fluctuations can be alarming, so gold is not suitable for the faint-hearted.

For an indication of how gold has performed over longer periods, see the table on page 18. Nowadays, you can buy and sell gold in any form. Here we look at buying gold coins (not to be confused with the rare coins that collectors go for) and gold bars. Other ways of investing include buying gold shares (e.g. the shares of companies that mine gold), buying units in a unit trust that specialises in gold shares and dealing in gold futures.

The main ways of buying and selling coins and bullion are through banks, coin-dealers, jewellers and stockbrokers; you may pay VAT on your purchase unless your purchases come under the Global Scheme. Some banks offer to buy, hold and sell your gold through an offshore subsidiary, say in the Channel Islands; VAT is not payable providing it stays offshore. The bullion-dealing companies that make up the London Bullion Market Association will not normally deal with transactions for small amounts and may not deal with the general public. It's probably advisable to steer clear of jewellers because they tend to have high mark-ups on their prices. Note that if you invest via intermediaries such as stockbrokers, you will have to pay commission on buying and selling.

Bear in mind that the price at which a coin or bar is offered for sale will be higher than the current value of the gold in it. On top of the value of the gold content you'll have to pay a *premium* for the cost of manufacture and distribution of the coins a 3.5 per cent premium is usual for a 1oz coin, and a new half sovereign has a 16 per cent premium. Premiums for particular coins fluctuate according to supply and demand. Note that bullion and foreign coins (but not post-1837 sovereigns and Britannias, the latest British gold coins) are liable for capital gains tax.

Most of us could not possibly afford to invest in gold bars in the standard sizes in which they are traded (400 troy ounces, around 12.5kg), though it is possible to obtain much smaller sizes, from 1kg (costing around £6,000 in March 1998) down to a 5g 'wafer' (£35 in March 1998). But the very small bars are not usually a sensible investment as the smaller the bar, the higher the premium.

A few sources of information

Books
Miller's Antiques Price Guide 1998 (Miller's Publications Ltd, £22.50)

*The Which? Wine Guide 1998**

The Antique Collectors' Club* publishes specialist books on art and antiques.

Standard catalogues
The Simplified Catalogue of Stamps of the World 1998 (Stanley Gibbons Publications, 3 volumes, £75.00)

1998: The Coins of England and the United Kingdom (Spink and Son, £15.00)

Societies
There are many societies, local and national. For societies near you, see the *Directory of British Associations* (ask at your local library).

Magazines and journals
There are too many to name. Look in large newsagents or see *Willings Press Guide* or *Benn's Media Directory* at your local library.

Antique and collectors' fairs
These are listed under 'Collecting' in the 'Leisure' section of *Exchange & Mart* (available at newsagents) and are often advertised in local newspapers. Advice on alternative investments is also given in the personal finance columns of several national newspapers.

ADDRESSES

The Antique Collectors' Club
5 Church Street
Woodbridge
Suffolk IP12 1DS
Tel: (01394) 385501
Fax: (01394) 384434
Email: accvs@aol.com

**Association of Chartered
Certified Accountants (ACCA)**
29 Lincoln's Inn Fields
London WC2A 3EE
Tel: 0171–242 6855 (general enquiries)
    0171–396 5900 (members)
Fax: 0171–831 8054 (general enquiries)
    0171–396 5959 (members)
Email: services.enquiries@acca.
co.uk
Web site: www.acca.co.uk

**Association of Investment Trust
Companies (AITC)**
Durrant House
8–13 Chiswell Street
London EC1Y 4YY
Tel: 0171–588 5347
Fax: 0171–282 5556
Email: info@aitc.co.uk
Web site: www.iii.co.uk/aitc

**Association of Policy Market
Makers (APMM)**
Holywell Centre
1 Phipp Street
London EC2A 4PS
Tel: 0171–739 3949
Fax: 0171–613 2990
Email: apmm@dircon.co.uk
Web site:
www.moneyworld.co.uk/apmm

**Association of Policy Traders
(APT)**
Skipton Chambers
12 Market Street
Bury BL9 0AJ
Tel: (0345) 191919 (local rates)
Other tel no: 0161–763 1919
Fax: 0161–797 1919
Email: polreg@cix.co.uk

**Association of Private Client
Investment Managers and
Stockbrokers (APCIMS)**
112 Middlesex Street
London E1 7HY
Email: www.apcims.org
Written enquiries only; APCIMS
produces a directory of its
members and the services they
offer

Association of Unit Trusts and Investment Funds (AUTIF)
65 Kingsway
London WC2B 6TD
Tel: 0171–831 0898
Fax: 0171–831 9975
Unit Trust Information Service
(8am–11pm daily)
Tel: 0181–207 1361

Bank of England
Threadneedle Street
London EC2R 8AH
Tel: 0171–601 4878 (public enquiries)
Fax: 0171–601 5771
Web site:
www.bankofengland.co.uk

For prospectuses for new issues of British Government stocks:
Bank of England
Registrar's Department
Southgate House
Southgate Street
Gloucester GL1 1WW
Tel: (01452) 398000
Fax: (01452) 398020

Building Societies Commission
Victory House, 30–34 Kingsway
London WC2B 6ES
Tel: 0171–663 5000
Fax: 0171–663 5060

Building Societies Ombudsman
Millbank Tower
Millbank
London SW1P 4XS
Tel: 0171–931 0044
Fax: 0171–931 8485

CRESTCo Ltd
9 Thomas More Street
Trinity Tower
London E1 9YN
Tel: 0171–459 3000
Fax: 0171–459 3130

Ethical Investment Research Service (EIRIS)
504 Bondway Business Centre
71 Bondway
London SW8 1SQ
Tel: 0171–735 1351
Fax: 0171–735 5323
Email: ethics@eiris.win-uk.net

Financial Intermediaries and Claims Office International
Fitzroy House
PO Box 46
Nottingham NG2 1BD
Tel: (0115) 974 2000
Fax: (0115) 974 1919

Financial Services Authority (FSA)
25 The North Colonnade
London E14 5HS
Tel: (0845) 6061234 (Enquiries Unit)
Fax: 0171–676 1099
Web site: www.fsa.gov.uk

Friendly Societies Commission
Victory House
30–34 Kingsway
London WC2B 6ES
Tel: 0171–663 5000
Fax: 0171–663 5060

H. E. Foster & Cranfield
20 Britton Street
London EC1M 5NQ
Tel: 0171–608 1941

IFA Promotion
17–19 Emery Road
Brislington
Bristol BS4 5PF
For a list of independent financial advisers in your area
Tel: 0117–971 1177
Fax: 0117–972 4509

Independent Schools Information Service (ISIS)
56 Buckingham Gate
London SW1E 6AG
Tel: 0171–630 8793
Fax: 0171–630 5013
Email: national@isis.org.uk
Web site: www.isis.org.uk

Institute of Actuaries
Staple Inn Hall
High Holborn
London WC1V 7QJ
Tel: 0171–632 2100
Fax: 0171–632 2111
Email: institute@actuaries.org.uk
Web site: ww.actuaries.org.uk

**Institute of Chartered
Accountants in England and
Wales**
PO Box 433
Chartered Accountants' Hall
Moorgate Place
London EC2P 2BJ
Tel: 0171–920 8100
Fax: 0171–920 0547
Web site: www.icaew.co.uk

**Institute of Chartered
Accountants in Ireland**
Chartered Accountants' House
87–9 Pembroke Road
Dublin 4
Tel: (00 53) 1 668 0400
Web site: www.icae.ie

**Institute of Chartered
Accountants of Scotland**
27 Queen Street
Edinburgh EH2 1LA
Tel: 0131–225 5673
Fax: 0131–225 3813
Web site: www.icas.org.uk

**Insurance Brokers Registration
Council (IBRC)**
63 St Mary Axe
London EC3A 8NB
Tel: 0171–621 1061
Fax: 0171–621 0840

**Insurance Directorate of the
Department of Trade and
Industry**
1 Victoria Street
London SW1H 0ET
Tel: 0171–215 0136

Insurance Ombudsman Bureau
City Gate One
135 Park Street
London SE1 9EA
Tel: 0171–902 8100
Fax: 0171–902 8197
Web site: www.theiob.org.uk

**Investment Managers Regulatory
Organisation (IMRO)**
5th Floor
Lloyd's Chambers
1 Portsoken Street
London E1 8BT
Tel: 0171–390 5000
Fax: 0171–680 0550
Web site: www.imro.co.uk

**Investors Compensation Scheme
(ICS)**
Gavrelle House
2–14 Bunhill Row
London EC1Y 8RA
Tel: 0171–628 8820
Fax: 0171–477 1814

**Law Society of England and
Wales**
113 Chancery Lane
London WC2A 1PL
Tel: 0171–242 1222
Call for relevant fax number
Web site: www.lawsociety.org.uk

Law Society of Northern Ireland
Law Society House
98 Victoria Street
Belfast BT1 3JZ
Tel: (01232) 231614
Fax: (01232) 232606

Law Society of Scotland
26 Drumsheugh Gardens
Edinburgh EH3 7YR
Tel: 0131–226 7411
Fax: 0131–225 2934
Email: lawscot@lawscot.org.uk

Micropal
Web site: www.micropal.com

Money Management National Register of Independent Fee-based Advisers
c/o Matrix Data Ltd
FREEPOST 22 (SW1565)
London W1E 7EZ
Tel: 0117–976 9444

National Savings
Sales Information Unit
FREEPOST BJ881
Lytham St Anne's
Lancashire FT0 1BR
Tel: (0645) 645000 (calls charged at local rates)

Occupational Pensions Advisory Service (OPAS)
11 Belgrave Road
London SW1V 1RB
Tel: 0171–233 8080
Fax: 0171–233 8016
Email: opas@iclweb.com
Web site: www.opas.org.uk

Occupational Pensions Regulatory Authority (OPRA)
Invicta House
Trafalgar Place
Brighton
East Sussex BN1 4DW
Tel: (01273) 627600
Fax: (01273) 627 688
Email: helpdesk@opra.gov.uk
Web site: www.opra.gov.uk

Office of the Banking Ombudsman
70 Gray's Inn Road
London WC1X 8NB
Tel: (0345) 660902
Fax: 0171–405 5052
Web site: www.intervid.co.uk/obo

Office of the Investment Ombudsman
6 Frederick's Place
London EC2R 8BT
Tel: 0171–796 3065
Fax: 0171–726 0574

Pensions Ombudsman
11 Belgrave Road
London SW1V 1RB
Tel: 0171–834 9144
Fax: 0171–821 0065

Personal Investment Authority (PIA)
7th Floor
1 Canada Square
Canary Wharf
London E14 5AZ
Tel: 0171–538 8860
Fax: 0171–418 9300

Personal Investment Authority (PIA) Ombudsman
Hertsmere House
Hertsmere Road
London E14 4AB
Tel: 0171–216 0016
Fax: 0171–712 8742

ProShare Investment Clubs (PIC)
Library Chambers
13–14 Basinghall Street
London EC2V 5BQ
Information line: 0171–394 5200
Web site: www.proshare.org.uk

Securities and Futures Authority (SFA)
Cottons Centre
Cottons Lane
London SE1 2QB
Tel: 0171–378 9000
Fax: 0171–403 7569
Web site: www.sfa.org.uk

PUBLICATIONS
Inclusion in this list of publications in no way constitutes an endorsement by Consumers' Association or Which?, except in relation to its own publications

Chase de Vere PEP Guide
Chase de Vere Investments plc
FREEPOST
Bristol BS38 7JX
Tel: (0800) 526092

Croner Publications Ltd
Croner House
London Road
Kingston-upon-Thames
Surrey KT2 6SR
Tel: 0181–547 3333
Fax: 0181–547 2637
Web site: www.croner.co.uk

FT Financial Publishing
Maple House
149 Tottenham Court Road
London W1P 9LL
Tel: 0171–896 2525

Investors Chronicle
Money Management
Pensions Management
Subscriptions/back issues
FT Finance
PO Box 387
Haywards Heath
West Sussex RH16 3GS
Tel: (01444) 445520
Fax: (01444) 445599

Moneyfacts
Moneyfacts House
66–70 Thorpe Road
Norwich
Norfolk NR1 1BJ
Tel: (01603) 476476
Fax: (01603) 476477

Money Observer
Subscription enquiries:
Tel: 0181–289 7960

Moneywise
Subscriptions
Towerhouse Publishing
Sovereign Park
Market Harborough LE16 9EF
Tel: (01858) 435366 (subscriptions)
Fax: (01858) 432164
Web site: www.Moneywise.co.uk

Planned Savings
33–39 Bowling Green Lane
London EC1R 0DA
Tel: 0171–505 8000
Fax: 0171–505 8186

What Investment
Charterhouse Communications
Group Ltd
3rd Floor
4–8 Tabernacle Street
London EC2A 4LU
Tel: 0171–638 1916
Fax: 0171–638 3128
Email: chartcom@dircon.co.uk

Which? and Which? Books
FREEPOST
PO Box 44
Hertford X, SG14 1YB
Tel: (0800) 252100
Fax: (0800) 533053
Web site: www.which.net/

INDEX